Bion and group psychotherapy

The International Library of Group Psychotherapy
and Group Process

General Editors

Dr Malcolm Pines
Tavistock Clinic, London

Dr Earl Hopper
Institute of Group Analysis

The International Library of Group Psychotherapy and Group Process is
published in association with the Institute of Group Analysis (London)
and is devoted to the systematic study and exploration of group psychotherapy

Bion and group psychotherapy

Edited by
Malcolm Pines
Institute of Group Analysis (London)
and the Tavistock Clinic, London

Routledge & Kegan Paul

London, Boston, Melbourne and Henley

First published in 1985
by Routledge & Kegan Paul plc

14 Leicester Square, London WC2H 7PH, England

9 Park Street, Boston, Mass. 02108, USA

464 St Kilda Road, Melbourne,
Victoria 3004, Australia and

Broadway House, Newtown Road,
Henley-on-Thames, Oxon RG9 1EN, England

Set in Times Press Roman 10/12pt
by Hope Services, Abingdon, Oxon
and printed in Great Britain
by Redwood Burn Ltd, Trowbridge, Wiltshire

Library of Congress Cataloguing in Publication Data

Bion and Group Psychotherapy.
(The International Library of Group Psychotherapy and
Group Process)
Bibliography; p.
Includes index.
1. Group psychotherapy—addresses, essays, lectures.
2. Bion, Wilfred R. (Wilfred Ruprecht), 1897–1979—
addresses, essays, lectures.   I. Pines, Malcolm.
II. Series.
RC488.B48 1985   616.89'152   84-9813

British Library CIP data also available

ISBN 0-7100-9949-5

Contents

Notes on contributors

Earl Hopper, PhD, (Member of the British Psychoanalytical Society and of the Institute of Group Analysis) is a psychoanalyst and group analyst in private practice in London. He is especially interested in the application of these disciplines to the study of social phenomenon and social issues. Drawing upon his previous experience as a Lecturer in Sociology at the London School of Economics, he also consults with organizations of various kinds. He has published numerous books and articles and most recently consulted on the script and its production of the film *Greystoke, The Legend of Tarzan, Lord of the Apes.*

Dennis Brown, MD, FRCP (Edin.) FRC Psych., DPM. Member, Institute of Group Analysis, Associate Member British Psychoanalytical Society. Consultant Psychotherapist, St Mary's Hospital, London.

Lowell Cooper, PhD, Yale 1966; Associate Professor, California School of Professional Psychology (Berkeley); Private Practice of Psychotherapy, Berkeley, California.

James Paul Gustafson, MD., Harvard 1967; Professor of Psychiatry, University of Wisconsin, in charge of Brief Psychotherapy Clinic, Group Training and Brief Family Therapy Team, Department of Psychiatry, University of Wisconsin Medical School.

Patrick de Maré, MD, was born in London in 1916, of Swedish parentage. He was educated at Wellington, Cambridge and St George's Hospital. He qualified as a doctor in 1941, and enlisted in the RAMC in 1942, where he was trained at Northfield Hospital by Rickman and Bion for Army psychiatry. He ran an Exhaustion Centre throughout the European campaign, at the end of which he returned to Northfield where he joined Foulkes and Main in the Northfield experiment.

After the War he became a Consultant Psychotherapist at St George's Hospital, and started off the Group Analytic Society with Foulkes in 1952, and later participated in setting up the Institute of Group Analysis and the Group Analytic Practice.

In 1972 he published *Perspectives in Group Psychotherapy* (Allen & Unwin) and in 1974 Lionel Kreeger and he published *Introduction to Group Treatments in Psychiatry* (Butterworth).

Prof. Dr med. Karl König, Director, Department of Clinical Psychotherapy, Georg-August-Universitat Gottingen, Humboldtallee 3, D-3400 Gottingen.

W. Gordon Lawrence, MA, Organization Consultant, Shell International Petroleum Company, London, UK Counsellor, Societé Internationale des Conseillers de Syntuese, Paris, France.

Olya Khaleelee, BSc, MA, Associate Member of Institute of Personnel Management. Director, OPUS; psychotherapist in private practice.

Eric Miller, MA, PhD, Fellow of Royal Anthropological Institute. Consultant, and Director of Group Relations Training Programme, Tavistock Institute of Human Relations. Policy Adviser, OPUS.

Barry Palmer is an independent consultant and trainer in group relations and organizational behaviour. He was a member of the staff of the Grubb Institute of Behavioural Studies and its parent body from 1962–82, and is a graduate in chemistry and theology.

Victor L. Schermer, MA, is a psychologist in private practice in Philadelphia, Pennsylvania. His current areas of theoretical interests include object relation theory, group psychology, and psychoanalysis as a system of thought. Mailing address is 330, Bainbridge Street, Apt. 38, Philadelphia, PA 19147.

John D. Sutherland, CBE, PhD, FRCPI, FRC Psych., formerly Medical Director Tavistock Clinic, London.

Herbert Thelen, MS, PhD, is a pioneer researcher in group dynamics who worked at the National Training Laboratory at Bethel, Maine. He is the co-author with Dorothy Stock of *Emotional Dynamics and Group Culture* (New York University Press, 1958). His other books include *Classroom Grouping for Teachability* (Wiley & Son, 1963) and *The Classroom Society: The Construction of Educational Experience* (Croom Helm, 1981)

León Grinberg, MD, is a Member and Training Analyst of the Madrid Psychoanalytical Association, and of the Buenos Aires Psychoanalytic Association; Founder and Member of the Argentine Association of Group Psychology and Psychotherapy; past Vice-President of the International Psychoanalytical Association. Author of several books on psychoanalysis and group psychotherapy (some translated into various languages) and many articles published in different journals.

Malcolm Pines, FRCP, FRC Psych., DPM, is a Consultant Psychotherapist at the Tavistock Clinic. He is a Member of the British Psychoanalytical Society and a Founder Member of the Institute of Group Analysis. He is a past President of the International Association of Group Psychotherapy. He is co-editor of this series and Editor of 'The Evolution of Group Analysis' devoted to the work of S. H. Foulkes.

Eric Trist, OBE, PhD, LL D (Hon.), was a founder member of the Tavistock Institute and is Professor Emeritus of Organizational Behavior and Social Ecology at the Wharton School, University of Pennsylvania.

Harold Bridger, TD, BSc, DipEd, trained in mathematics before his war-time involvement in human relations. He is a member of the British Psychoanalytical Society, a Council member of the Tavistock Institute for Medical Psychology, of the Scottish Institute for Human Relations, and of the M.T.L. Institute, Washington, USA.

He is a Fellow of the British Institute of Management and President of the Institute for Human Relations, Zurich. Author of many publications in the field of organizational relations, and management training.

Salomon Resnik, MD, is a full member of the International Psychoanalytic Association. He trained in Argentina and London, before moving to Paris where he now lives. He is Ancien Maître de Conférences, Faculté de Médecine, Université de Lyons. He is a member of the Group Analytic Society (London), and of the International Association of Group Psychotherapy.

Bernardo Blay-Neto, MD, is Professor of Psychoanalysis and Group Psychotherapy in the Department of Psychology, Catholic University, São Paolo, Brazil. He is a full member of the Brazilian Psychoanalytical Association, President of the Latin American Federation of Analytic Group Psychotherapy, and a corresponding editor of the *International Journal of Group Psychotherapy*.

K. and B.-Å. Armelius are both PhD's in psychology, Lecturers and Research Fellows in the Department of Applied Psychology, University of Umea, Sweden.

Introduction

Understanding the writings of W. R. Bion is a formidable intellectual task whether they be on group dynamics or on psychoanalysis. The reader is immediately struck by the qualities of his mind; the striking originality, the complexity of thought and density of context, the calm assumption that his own responses to the situation he describes are simultaneously noteworthy yet trivial.

Experiences in Groups is probably the shortest and most influential text in psychoanalytic group psychotherapy. Whether you agree or disagree with Bion, ignore him you cannot for he looms up at you from the darkness of the deepest areas of human experience, illuminating it with his 'beams of darkness'.

Bion did not write comprehensively on group psychotherapy as such and there is relatively little in his papers to guide the student, in contrast to his contemporary S. H. Foulkes. But his ideas were immediately and vigorously taken up and applied by a generation of psychoanalysts and social scientists at the Tavistock Clinic and the Tavistock Institute of Human Relations here in Britain and across the Atlantic by what became the A. K. Rice Institute. His ideas have attracted both devotees and disbelievers; only thoughtless imitation of his style and thought can spare one the effort of working out one's own attitude to him.

My own attitudes were formed in the early 1950s when I was a student, and later a colleague, of S. H. Foulkes and therefore found myself 'naturally' (only later did I see how far from the case this was) in some sort of opposition to Bion's ideas. He seemed to me to pay no attention to important 'group-specific factors' as described by Foulkes, to be unconcerned with the therapist's role as the 'dynamic administrator' and even by his interpretations to oppose the group members' efforts to use the therapeutic context in understanding and working through their neurotic problems. Though I have not changed my mind substantially on these matters, I have come to see from *Experiences in Groups* and from what I have been able to learn from the more accessible of his later writings that we all have a great deal to learn from Bion. He strikes at the heart of things, he seeks out danger, plunges as deeply as he can into the depths of the mind. Truth and falsehood, sanity and madness are the matters that concern him and which will not let him go and few who have read him will be free of his concerns thereafter.

The relationship of the man to his work, his personality to his ideas, is a matter we often need not concern ourselves about, as there are very few ideas of the first rank of originality to be found. However, we cannot set aside the personality of a Freud, a Jung and certainly not a Bion. My personal contact with him as a psychoanalytic seminar leader in London and later as President of the British Psychoanalytical Society impressed me with his unusual personality, by the density of his silences in seminars and the difficulty that I had in following his thoughts as he described his sessions with psychotic patients. My puzzlement grew greater as I struggled with his autobiographical novel *A Memoir of the Future*[1] but just recently, by reading his compelling account of his childhood and youth in his autobiography *The Long Weekend*,[2] so much more became clear for me. I can only advise all the readers of this volume to read this book. There they will meet the child trying to understand himself and to be understood by his awesome engineer father and see his very early awareness of the tragic consequences of not being understood; he writes of the warmth of his early years in Edwardian India of the Raj, the cold loneliness of boarding-school in England at the age of eight, where he puzzled through on his own his problems with sexuality and violence, which were problems indeed. The old man looking back on his childhood sees the great struggle that he endured to gain and to retain his capacity for love, work, friendship and sanity. Then at nineteen he was plunged into the grotesque and bloody muddle of the First World War, a young officer in the Royal Tank Corps where only he and two of his companions survived from the entire regiment. The reader of his narrative is seared by his rage at the stupidity and arrogance of the officer class and at the dreadful conditions which the soldiers had to endure. Reading this narrative with its barely suppressed ground-base of rage and despair, I could see how Bion became a man concerned primarily for the basic things of life and how this connected with his elucidation of the basic issues of group life and to his search for the truth that somewhere must be found in the bewildering tissue of falsehoods. Indeed, he emerges in Sutherland's phrase as the '*preux chevalier*'.

The distinguished contributors to this volume are all persons who have either been closely and personally associated with Bion in his group work (Sutherland, Trist, Bridger, Miller), or have been stimulated to research by his ideas (Thelen, Kerste & Bengt-Åke Armelius), or who have thoroughly studied and come to grips with thorny intellectual issues that he raises (Brown, Gustafson & Cooper, König, Schermer). Grinberg and Resnik write of Bion's later work with psychotic patients and Resnik shows how Bion's ideas can be put to creative and imaginative use. Bley-Nato and De Maré bring Bion's personality to gentle life in their memoirs and show how widely the cultural defusion of his ideas has been. Bion's seminal contributions to the Tavistock-style conference are described and expanded by Lawrence, Palmer, Kahleelee & Miller and these show how the seed has germinated, fertilized the ideas of a generation of creative workers.

The arrangement of the chapters will, I hope, take the reader from the war years and from the post-war flowering of the Tavistock Clinic to the context of the 1940s, so well described by Eric Trist, and then to a general overview of Bion's contribution by his long-standing colleague Sutherland, with a wealth of new and important historical material. The first Northfield experiment is described by his colleagues Bridger and De Maré, both bringing vividly to life that unique crucible of group psychotherapy. Thelen's account is of the historical context to research in group dynamics in the USA during the 1950s and 1960s and shows how this brilliant group of Chicago researchers were able creatively to use Bion's illuminations. Chapter 13 shows how tough-minded researchers still grapple with Bion's ideas.

The four papers which review basic assumption theory (Brown, Gustafson & Cooper, König and Schermer) show how important this great contribution is to a deep grasp of group dynamics and how grappling with Bion's theories can lead to innovation. Bion, whose concern was always with the areas of ignorance rather than those of certainty, would, I believe, have welcomed these signs of intellectual freedom.

Grinberg and Resnik range widely over Bion's early and later work and give the reader the opportunity to see the outreach of the mind and how the 'beams of darkness' can illuminate dark areas of group and individual life both in health and in psychosis.

The last section deals with context, the application and recent development of the Tavistock-style conferences. Palmer and Lawrence struggle with the paradoxes and limits of the conference framework, and Kahleelee and Miller take us into a fascinating view of the dynamics of society in its vastness. Hopper considers societal context as a determinant in the therapy group. Again I am certain that Bion would have been intrigued and stimulated by these developments of his work.

All the contributors were invited to write about the influence of Bion's personality and ideas on their own work and to reappraise these ideas critically from their present standpoints. I am more than gratified by their splendid responses, which to me clearly indicates the affection and esteem with which Bion inspired all those who had contact with him personally or intellectually.

Malcolm Pines

Notes and references

1 W. R. Bion, *A Memoir of the Future*, Book I: *The Dream*, Rio de Janeiro, Imago Editora, 1975; Book II: *The Past Presented*, Rio de Janeiro, Imago Editora, 1977; Book III: *The Dawn of Oblivion*, Perthshire, Clunie Press, 1979; *A Key to 'Memoir of the Future'*, compiled by W. R. & F. Bion, Clunie Press, 1981.
2 W. R. Bion, *The Long Week-end, 1897–1919: Part of a Life*, Abingdon, Fleetwood Press, 1982.

Chapter 1
Working with Bion in the 1940s: the group decade

Eric Trist

Introduction

During the decade of the 1940s, when World War II and its aftermath in the period of peace and reconstruction were the preoccupation of us all, Wilfrid Bion came forward with a number of ideas which changed the face of social psychiatry. Since that time they have exercised increasing influence on many areas in social psychology and sociology, for there was nothing inherently medical in them. To Bion himself, a hitherto unknown individual, they brought world-wide recognition. Yet at the end of the decade he left the study of groups as abruptly as he had entered it to devote himself exclusively to psychoanalysis. He now made a new series of contributions that established him in the front rank of this world.

In psychoanalysis he had a framework to build on. In the study of groups he had none. He had to build his own as he went along. In so doing he was at pains to elaborate it independently of psychoanalytic concepts so that the group could be investigated *sui generis*.

In his last paper on groups, 'Group dynamics: a review' (1952), he took the step of relating his novel and seminal ideas to psychoanalytic concepts, in particular to Melanie Klein's (1948, 1952) theories of the paranoid-schizoid and depressive positions, emphasizing the role of part-object relations and the importance of projective identification. He postulated that the group phenomena he had conceptualized as 'basic assumptions' were based on these mechanisms which established themselves in earliest infancy at the psychotic, rather than the neurotic, level of the human personality. He had reached the conclusion that he could not take his ideas about groups further until understanding of these very primitive mechanisms was itself increased.

Yet before leaving London he said it was his intention to return to

1

the field of the group. He said so again in Los Angeles. One memorable occasion was in 1968 when he addressed the Behavioral Science Group in the School of Management at UCLA on 'Group and Societal Phenomena'. Another was in his interview with Banet for *Group and Organization Studies* (Banet 1976). But he never did return to empirical work in the social field, though, as Isabel Menzies (1981) has pointed out, his later writing abounds in social reference, especially in *Attention and Interpretation* (Bion 1970).

Our regret that he did not return must be profound, for his ideas as he left them in *Experiences in Groups* (1961) were no more than the first etchings for a theory. In the Introduction he noted:

> I am impressed, as a practising psycho-analyst, by the fact that the psycho-analytic approach, through the individual, and the approach these papers describe, through the group, are dealing with different facets of the same phenomena. The two methods provide the practitioner with a rudimentary binocular vision. The observations tend to fall into two categories, whose affinity is shown by phenomena which, when examined by one method, centre on the Oedipal situation, related to the pairing group, and, when examined by the other, centre on the sphinx, related to problems of knowledge and scientific method.

Though Gustavson and Cooper (1979) have recently offered another framework for group interpretation based on a theory of unconscious planning developed by Weiss (1971), no one has so far appeared to continue the work of decoding the sphinx. Our understanding of the sphinx remains in much the same state as Bion left it in 1952. Most people have either repeated parrot-like what he did (ba D) or ignored it (ba F).[1]

What above all was needed were thoroughgoing empirical studies of groups taken by Bion himself or at least regularly monitored by him. Though several of his colleagues knew at first hand what he did during World War II, very few of us sat with him in the therapy groups he subsequently took at the Tavistock Clinic. We needed his involvement in the Institute's organizational and community projects; if not his direct participation in field-work, at least his being 'there' as someone with whom we could discuss findings, particularly the use we were making of his own theories. As none of this came to be, what Bion did in small groups and even in larger organizational settings has remained something of a mystery.

I had the good fortune to work closely with him throughout the ten years he was concerned with groups. My purpose in presenting this paper is to trace the evolution of his ideas from project to project and to show how these projects, several of which constituted breakthroughs, were 'directively correlated'[2] with the phases both of the war effort and of social transformation in early post-war Britain.

The major steps he took were not only intellectual steps but action steps. They involved him in taking very considerable personal risks as regards his professional reputation, in incurring undeflectable public exposure (this on the part of the most private of men), and in having to endure on more than one occasion surprise attacks from colleagues he had considered friends. In 1949, during a conference the Tavistock Institute held at Gerrards Cross with the Research Center for Group Dynamics (University of Michigan) which represented the Lewinian tradition, he remarked to me while we were out swimming at a place called Black Lake, 'Why does it always have to be me who has to bear the brunt? I feel as though I have been in the front line unrelieved for ten years. I do not want to stay there another ten years.' Were feelings of this kind the reason why he left the field of groups? In part I believe they were. He certainly needed a long respite.

There were other factors. Professionally he was a late developer. On returning from World War I he had read history at Oxford and then gone on to medical school in London. From this he entered psychiatry and, becoming interested in the new 'dynamic psychologies', associated himself with the Tavistock Clinic in its eclectic pre-war days. There he spent seven years in psychotherapeutic training with Hatfield,[3] who did not believe in the transference – causing A. T. M. Wilson[4] among others to wonder what happened, if anything, during all that time and to ask what Bion was trying to tell us by keeping on with it. Nevertheless, he was the first of the psychiatrists who entered the army from the Tavistock in World War II to find his way to psychoanalysis by undertaking a training analysis (with John Rickman[5]) in 1938. In conjunction with this he got out of his doldrums, entering on a late first marriage, publishing a late first paper (on psychological 'asepsis') and beginning for the first time to reveal some of his immense powers of insight and intellect. Past the age of forty, he was beginning to find himself.

His first analysis had to be broken off when, after Dunkirk, he joined the RAMC with other members of the 'Tavistock Group'. Now his military experience from World War I became of critical relevance and, linked to his growing psychoanalytic insight, enabled him to produce his social psychiatric innovations. His second training analysis (with

Melanie Klein) could begin only after the war had ended. It would then take him some time not only to qualify but to accumulate enough experience to become a major innovator within psychoanalysis itself. He could not have concentrated intensively on analysis and at the same time have actively maintained the scientific and public lead he had taken in work with groups, especially as he had come to believe that progress in the latter depended on progress in the former. This need not, however, have prevented him from returning to groups at a later date.

A still further factor was that Bion as an individual had, to use his own terms, unusually high valency for ba F. This shows in his remarkable career as a soldier in World War I and was called forth again in World War II, if on another front than the battlefield itself. After World War II Britain remained on something of a war footing throughout the period of the first Labour Government. The peace had to be won as well as the war itself. By the end of that period, however, the framework of a post-war international order had been established, and inside Britain the legislation was in place which sought to make reparation for pre-war ills and wartime privations. At the Tavistock, both Institute and Clinic, a redefinition of mission had been agreed on and the new post-war organization shaped — a process in which Bion had taken a major part. Indeed, without his participation it is doubtful if the attendant conflicts would have been resolved.

The 1950s opened a new decade in which the underlying relationship in society between the sophisticated group and the basic assumption group was changing. The Work Group was no longer constructively suffused by ba F. Many people with high valency for ba F went off stage or, like Bion, changed course.

In his case the change was total. It was the period of his second marriage. The death of his first wife in 1943, three days after the birth of their daughter when he had been told all was well, had been a bitter blow. It took five days to locate him with 21 Army Group in France to break the news. When he recovered from his very severe grief (fateful events of one kind or another haunted him during these years) he longed for a home, for marital happiness and to complete his family. All this was to happen, but as it came to him he withdrew not only from any work with groups but from all association with the Tavistock and the colleagues with whom he had gone through the war and founded the post-war Institute. He seemed to want to put behind him everything to do with what for him had been a painful and stressful decade despite his achievements. Supported by his new serenity he posted himself at the frontiers of psychoanalytic theory and proceeded to make many of the advances he thought necessary in order to further the study of groups. What turned out to be the next major phase of his professional life, his second more inward psychological journey as contrasted with his first more outward social journey, was coincidental with his completing his second analysis.

The Wharncliffe Memorandum

My first encounter with him, as an influence, was in 1940, when I was a clinical psychologist at the Institute of Psychiatry, which had then been split into two parts and evacuated to the outskirts of south-west and north-west London. I was at the north-west portion, housed in the premises of Mill Hill School as a neurosis centre in the Emergency Medical Service. After having set up a psychological testing procedure and started experimental work on the psychological effects of closed head injuries (which on the model of World War I were expected in large numbers), I felt very dissatisfied and undertook an anthropological survey of all the activities in the hospital in the hope of finding something that would give me a clue as to how the wider social environment might be used therapeutically. The last straw was meeting on my way to the occupational therapy workshops a large punch-drunk ex-boxer, now in the Guards, forlornly carrying an absurd peacock painted on glass. There had to be a better way.

I took some papers of Kurt Lewin to Sir Aubrey Lewis, who was then clinical director, and discussed with him the potential usefulness of considering the wider hospital environment as a therapeutically active social field. At this time Maxwell Jones (1952) was beginning to hold explanatory group discussions with his effort syndrome patients and was taking tentative steps towards the use of psychodrama; but he was still a long way from formulating the idea of a democratic therapeutic community which he later so richly developed and dedicated his life to fostering (Jones 1968, 1976). Lewis said that there was something going on at the Wharncliffe in Sheffield (a hospital similar to Mill Hill), started by a Dr John Rickman, that was in the direction of my interests. Accordingly, I went to Sheffield to find out what it was that Rickman was doing, or, as it turned out to be, not doing. Some time previously a former analytic trainee of his now in the army, a certain Wilfred Bion, had spent some time with him and prepared the document which became known as the Wharncliffe Memorandum. This document contained a prospectus for a therapeutic community. In the sense of making systematic use of the happenings and relationships in a hospital, it was the first time the concept had been formulated.[6]

This was what I was looking for, but Rickman cooled my enthusiasm by saying that any attempt on his part to put such ideas into practice had met with opposition from medical and non-medical staff alike. He said he thought this would be so anywhere as it meant going against the medical model. He did not know beyond a modest point how to proceed. Developments would have to wait on Bion.[7]

Not long after that I met Bion in the War Office. There were several officers in the room who looked exactly what they were – psychiatrists in uniform. Bion looked more like a general. The importance of this I was to realize later after I had become his military colleague. I asked about the Wharncliffe. 'There are other priorities just now', he said, 'but later in the war there may come a time when something along these lines can be tried.'

Leaderless Groups

Some months after this, in early 1942, I was asked to become the psychologist to the experimental unit of the War Office Selection Boards (WOSBs) that had been established in Edinburgh. Here I found Bion as senior psychiatrist with John Sutherland[8] (who had prepared a battery of projective tests for group administration) under pressure to develop an acceptable and effective operational procedure.

After the fall of France a large land army had to be raised and officered by individuals drawn largely from outside the customary officer class. Many of these fought shy of putting themselves forward as candidates for officer training as they feared class prejudice on the part of the colonels who would interview them and who felt less secure themselves in making judgments outside their own social bounds. They were overlooking good candidates and sending forward too many poor ones. The failure rate at Officer Cadet Training Units (OCTUs) had become alarming and had induced a morale crisis.[9]

The WOSB was being developed as a special purpose military institution to remedy this situation by improving the quality of trainee intake at OCTUs. Candidates would come into residence for two and a half days, thirty-two at a time. In four groups of eight they would go through a series of individual military exercises, of the type common in officer training, with a Military Testing Officer (MTO). The Commanding Officer

(Col.) and his Deputy (Lt-Col.) would each interview half of the candidates. The psychiatrists also each interviewed half while the psychologist gave a battery of tests. The former were thought of as screening out those likely to prove too unstable to lead troops, and the latter as screening out those likely to prove too stupid. Though all these officers met as a group to decide under the CO who was to pass and who fail, they had no common experience of the candidates. There was much disagreement and rising tension between the military and technical sides.

This was the point at which Bion proposed the method of Leaderless Groups. In this, each MTO would take his candidates through a series of group situations, beginning with the least structured and proceeding to more structured events. Formal leadership was removed and leadership patterns were left to emerge. The series began with *mutual introductions* in which each candidate had to affirm his personal and social identity in an order determined by himself. Next there would be a *free group discussion* on a subject chosen by the group, which would now proceed outdoors where they would be presented with several military problems in quick succession, the MTO using the immediate surroundings as material. This procedure was called *spontaneous situations*, after which came the *group task* where the candidates had to solve a practical problem and themselves sort out how they did it. Finally, one group would compete with another in the *inter-group game*.

All Board personnel, who had to learn not to interfere, observed these tests which took some two and a half hours. A common experience of the candidates was provided which laid the foundation for a constructive dialogue between the military and technical members. It also gave the candidates a common experience of each other. At one time we asked them to rate each other (though these ratings were not used in assessment). The ratings proved sufficiently similar to the Board's to encourage us to think that the latter's decisions would be perceived as just, a matter of major importance in gaining acceptability of the Boards among candidates.

As usual with Bion, the action step also contained a conceptual breakthrough, in which he offered a new theory of the relation of the real life situation to the ostensible situation in assessment procedures. The following account is quoted in full from his paper in the *Bulletin of the Menninger Clinic* (1946). This is his only public statement about Leaderless Groups.[10]

The essence of the technique which was evolved, and which has since become the basis of selection techniques in many different fields, was to provide a framework in which selecting officers, including a psychiatrist, could observe a man's capacity for maintaining personal relationships in a situation of strain that tempted him to disregard the interests of his fellows for the sake of his own. The situation had to be a real life situation. The situation of strain, and the temptation to give full rein to his personal ambitions was already there; the candidate arrived prepared to do his best and get himself a commission and, naturally, he feared the possibility of failure. Furthermore this was a real life situation. The problem was to make capital of this existing emotional field in order to test the quality of the man's relationships with his fellows.

This was done by a method so simple and so obvious, when it has been propounded, that its revolutionary nature can easily be lost sight of. A man found he was not entered in a free-for-all competition with other candidates. Instead he found himself a member of a group and, apparently, all the tests were tests, not of himself, but of the group. In concrete terms, a group of eight or nine candidates, an 'eye-full' from the testing officer's point of view, was told to build, say, a bridge. No lead was given about organization or leadership; these were left to emerge and it was the duty of the observing officers to watch how any given man was reconciling his personal ambitions, hopes and fears with the requirements exacted by the group for its success. That, in brief outline, is the basic principle of all the Leaderless Group Tests.

A little consideration will show that the situation thus created is very closely parallel with countless other emotional situations in an officer's life, not even excluding action. For though the emotional tensions in this situation are low compared with those in battle they are nevertheless sufficiently powerful to make all candidates feel that their time at a War Office Selection Board has been a heavy strain despite the interest of the experience and the apparent easy program. It was found that if the testing officers watch what they are meant to watch they have no difficulty in matching what they have found out about a man's personality with what they know will be the sort of job with which he will have to cope as an officer.

It is safe to say that nearly all mistakes arise through failure to keep the selecting officers mindful, throughout all the tests, of the very simple basic principles mentioned above. Either officers tend to interfere, and so distort the field, or else they watch how well the group does any given task. It is important to insist that the actual task of the test is merely a cloak of invisibility intended to explain, and therefore to explain away, the presence of the testing officers. It is not the artificial test, but the real life situation that has to be watched, — that is, the way in which a man's capacity for personal relationships stands up under the strain of his own and other men's fear of failure and desires for personal success.

As the crucial difference was grasped between the Board's procedures as a projective screen and the underlying real-life situation which generated the relevant tensions, the Leaderless Group method changed the entire character of the WOSB. The Board became a learning community which improved its collective capacity through the sharing of common 'here and now' experiences of the candidates instead of conducting acrimonious and unresolvable debates on independently based judgments. Pre-conferences were held after the Leaderless Group sequence, where decisions would be taken on how best to follow up particular candidates with individual procedures. The interviews took on a therapeutic colouring so that many candidates felt they had learnt something about themselves, whether they passed or failed. Each Board member had a common and a specialist role which were complementary. The final conferences where the accumulated learnings were shared impressed Commanding Officers who in the first few months of the experimental unit came to see the procedure from all over Scottish Command.

Their views were decisive in securing military acceptance of the Boards. The unification of the procedure through the Leaderless Group method convinced them that the decisions were being made by the army and not by 'shrinks' over-influencing bewildered Board Presidents. The Leaderless Group method had re-empowered the military side. The soliders were able to make better decisions. Because of their increased confidence they were prepared to accept greater technical assistance. This process, in which Bion was mentor to people such as myself, used to be called handing back control from the technical to the military side. It became a central component in the strategy of action research that emerged from World War II.

Bion would neither have been so perceptive nor so influential had it not been for his immense military experience and reputation which derived from his record in World War I.[11] Putting on his age he had joined the Royal Tank Regiment at seventeen, becoming a Brigade Major at nineteen. The following story became legendary. He was attending a Divisional Commander's Conference where it was proposed by the G(I)[12] to attack at 10.00 a.m., a plan which the Divisional Commander accepted. Bion, who was becoming increasingly agitated, intervened: 'If I attack at 10 o'clock I shall be wiped out. If the tanks are wiped out the whole operation will fail. Let me attack either at dawn or dusk with the cover of some mist.' This was at a time when higher commands knew little about the handling of tanks. The Divisional Commander replied, 'Wilfred, you may be one of my best officers but you are a boy. You may know more about these new machines than I do but you know less about battles. We will attack at 10 o'clock.' Bion rose again and said, 'Sir, as I am a soldier I obey orders and will attack at 10 o'clock, but as a staff officer I have the right to have my technical advice recorded in writing in the minutes of this meeting. You neglect it at your peril.' The tanks were wiped out. Only Bion came back. The plans not only of the Division but of an Army Corps were disrupted. The findings of an investigation went to Foch. As a result, tactics for tanks in World War I were changed. This story became a role model for many of us as regards technical relations with the military.

Major Bion, having on this occasion (as on others) performed acts of outstanding valour, was recommended for the Victoria Cross. When he was going over the citation with the Military Secretary in London, the latter showed too little understanding of what was going on at the front for him to stomach. In World War I, much more than in World War II, there was bitter antagonism between front-line soldiers and those in the War Office. Bion lost his temper (in the common rendering of the episode he performed the feat of letting off all known four-letter words at once and there was much speculation as to what this noise must have sounded like). At any rate his decoration was reduced to a DSO.[13] This story again was widely known, endearing him to many senior officers who remembered their troubles during World War I.

His military acceptability was reinforced by his record in sports. He had captained Oxford at swimming and played rugby for the university, though he had missed the Varsity Match through being down with 'flu. As a medical student he had played for the Corinthians and there had been the question of an international cap. An ex-Blue with a first-class military record would get a hearing when others could not. He was used by the Directorate of Army Psychiatry to give an opinion on a number of critical issues otherwise inaccessible to their influence. A form of battle training had been developed in which men went over an obstacle course under simulated battle conditions — an enormous din of artillery and machine-gun fire was made and the ground was covered with animal blood and guts. By way of psychiatric advice, Bion took the rifle from a man emerging from the course and displayed the muzzle which was choked with mud. 'A soldier's first job', he said, 'is to look after his weapons so that he can use them against the enemy. This form of training has failed to teach him that.' On another occasion he dissuaded the commanding general from recruiting to the Parachute Regiment over-adventurous types likely to develop their own (fanciful) objectives when once behind enemy lines. Suitable recruits would be better found among stolid citizens who, having no ideas of their own, could be relied on to abide by their orders when released from higher authority.

As the WOSB organization expanded it was decided toward the end of that summer (1942) to set up a headquarters, called the Research and Training Centre (RTC) near the War Office. John Pierpont Morgan's country house, Wall Hall (near Watford), had been offered. After discussions with Hargreaves,[14] an Establishment was created so that the senior psychiatrist would become a Lieutenant-Colonel and so that the Deputy President of the RTC Board, a Lieutenant-Colonel, might be a psychiatrist. Bion was promoted. We assumed that the two jobs were one. I had had to stay in Edinburgh for ten days to superintend a rather ridiculous 'mass testing' exercise insisted on by the then CO, and arrived late at Wall Hall expecting to find Bion already at work on new projects. To my astonishment I found him (and Sutherland) in gloom and anger. Out of the blue, T. Ferguson Rodger (later to become Professor of Psychiatry at Glasgow) had arrived, appointed by the Directorate of Army Psychiatry as Senior Psychiatrist (WOSBs). Bion was restricted to being Deputy President of RTC. It was then discovered that as an RAMC officer he could not pass candidates into officer training; only a regimental officer could do this. He could not, as he had wanted, have a Board under his own control to train incoming WOSB personnel in the Leaderless Group method for which there was an urgent need, considering the controversy it had aroused, or to develop pilot projects as new problems arose. He was trapped and had been made a fool of by his psychiatric colleagues in the War Office.

Just as no forewarning had been given, no official explanation was ever offered. At that time his first wife, who was a distinguished actress, was between plays and they were living in a cottage near Wall Hall. My bedroom faced the courtyard and every morning I would see him advancing up to it, his moustache grown long (fiercely so), a look of frozen defiance on his countenance, without a briefcase but with a knapsack slung over his shoulder, and in his right hand a long staff with a crook which he carried like an Old Testament prophet. He asked for a transfer and joined Rickman (now also in the army) at Northfield Military Hospital, to take up the trail of the Wharncliffe Memorandum.

Regimental Nomination

Before I go into this momentous episode, another project that Bion initiated in WOSBs must be described. Despite the growing acceptance of the Boards, there was a dearth of candidates. I had had made an analysis of candidate supply in Scottish Command.[15] The distribution was J-shaped: a few units were sending several candidates during an experimental quarter; many one or two; most none. The nearer a unit came to a theatre of war, the less likely it was to send a candidate. Bion was disquieted. In World War I he had seen the best officer-material slaughtered in the earlier battles and had experienced the fall-off in quality of officer reinforcements in the later campaigns. He knew about in-group mentality.

At a conference presided over by the Adjutant-General (the late Sir Ronald Adam), who more than anyone else had furthered the schemes put forward by the Directorates of Psychiatry and of Selection of Personnel, improving candidate supply was identified as the next priority. Bion proposed that, in addition to the usual nominees sent forward by the CO, a regiment that had shown itself to be a good unit should be given the privilege of sending to a Board candidates voted on by every soldier in the name of the regiment. The AG said he liked the idea, and the Army Commander (Scottish Command) who was present offered his assistance in identifying units which might like to take part in any experiments that would put the idea to the test. This was the beginning of what came to be known as the Regimental Nomination experiment.

It fell to me, in liaison with Bion, to work out a suitable procedure, based on sociometric concepts. In a selected unit – the first was a troop-carrying company of the RASC attached to the First Army – an explanation was made by their own CO of the army's need for officers and their own obligation to give up some of their best men. The CO then asked for the help of everyone in identifying these men; he needed their knowledge of them as well as his own. Each man entered on a secret ballot the names of those he considered should go forward to a WOSB. The votes were assessed on six criteria: the in-platoon vote; the out-platoon vote (other platoons in his company); the votes of privates, junior NCOs, senior NCOs and officers. Any soldier who showed up well on three or more of these criteria could go to a Board if he wished. Four units underwent this procedure. The pass-rate of the nominated candidates (whom the Boards saw blind) was the same as that of ordinary candidates (60 per cent). While quality was maintained, the supply rate increased 1,500 per cent. Bion's suggestion had led to the discovery of a method of overcoming the in-group mentality and of inducing co-operation in the larger enterprise of the army.

In the ensuing excitement a runaway process got under way. The whole of the 52 Highland Division asked for Regimental Nomination as did the whole of the Ordnance Corps. At RTC, inquirers were told that the work was experimental and would be discussed by the War Office when the results were to hand. Bion's view was that the runaway process would create a crisis that would wreck the scheme unless an operational plan were prepared to show how it could be safely implemented, selectively, in a low profile way. Criteria had to be worked out beyond those used in the experiment to enable suitable units to be identified, and special care needed to be taken with regard to the protocol of permission.

When the AG came down to see the detailed results, Bion had already departed for Northfield. Sir Ronald seemed immensely relieved at the indications of an untapped reserve of officer-material. He said he had tried using a wide range of supplementary opinions with some success in a project at the Staff College. He did not seem to be anticipating any grave difficulties in taking further steps. The rest of us (principally myself), being to some extent in collusion with the runaway process, did not present Bion's view as forcibly as he would have done himself, nor did we carry his authority. In consequence the AG, who was taken with the idea that the army might get one up on the authoritarian enemy by making judicious use of the democratic traditions of British society, allowed a premature reference to the scheme to appear in his fortnightly letter to Major Generals (Administration) in Home Commands. This was drawn to the attention of the Commander-in-Chief, who had not been specifically consulted and who did not always see eye-to-eye with the AG. (There had been a previous incident of mischief-making with him by one of his staff officers over WOSBs, which should have alerted us.)

The suggestion was made that the AG had exceeded his authority, though the C-in-C had some time back given general permission for experimental work in connection with WOSBs to proceed in Scottish Command with the agreement of the Army Commander, who had specifically approved Regimental Nomination. In the ensuing row a full meeting of the Army Council was called. The crisis was created that Bion had feared. The politicians and civil servants voted against the scheme as possibly subversive. The soldiers voted for it as in the best interests of the army. They were in the minority of four to six.[16] No one, however, expressed again the fear that the army would be unable to officer itself.

Northfield

Northfield was a large military psychiatric hospital which functioned as a clearing house. According to a man's condition, he would be discharged from the army, returned to his unit or found alternative military employment. The need for manpower was at its height. Any method was welcome which would encourage a body of disaffected men displaying a bewildering variety of symptoms in different degrees of acuteness, to re-engage with the role of being a soldier in an army at war. Methods so far tried had yielded poor results.

Bion took charge of the Military Training and Rehabilitation Wing where there would be some 200 patients at any one time sent on from the wards where Rickman was posted. As it turned out, their joint attempt at transforming a conventional hospital into an entirely new type of organization – a therapeutic community with a capability for continuous learning about the common group problem of neurotic disability, its consequences for themselves, their relations with others and their ability to function in a wartime society – was granted a life of no more than six weeks. Yet in that time a radical innovation was made.

An account of what took place was published at the time in the *Lancet* (Bion and Rickman 1943) and this account, since it has been included in *Experiences in Groups*, has become well known. The following extract is taken from Bion's (1946) paper in the *Bulletin of the Menninger Clinic* which gives an additional perspective:

> . . . briefly, it was essential first to find out what was the ailment afflicting the community, as opposed to the individuals composing it, and next to give the community a common aim. In general all psychiatric hospitals have the same ailment and the same common aim – to escape from the batterings of neurotic disorder. Unfortunately the attempt to get this relief is nearly always by futile means – retreat. Without realizing it doctors and patients alike are running away from the complaint.
>
> The first thing then was to teach the community (in this case the Military Training Wing) to seek a different method of release. The flight from a neurotic disorder had to be stopped; as in a regiment, morale had to be raised to the point where the real enemy could be faced. The establishment of morale is of course hardly a pre-requisite of treatment; it is treatment, or a part of it. The first thing was for the officer in charge not to be afraid of making a stand himself; the next to rally about him those patients who are not already too far

gone to be steadied. To this end discussions were carried out with small groups. In these the same freedom was allowed as is permitted in any form of free association; it was not abused. These small groups were similar in organization and appearance to the Leaderless Group Tests, known as group discussions, which had already been used, though for a different purpose, in the W.O.S.B.

As soon as a sufficient number of patients had in this way been persuaded to face their enemy instead of running away from it, a daily meeting of half an hour was arranged for the whole training wing, consisting of between 100 and 200 men. These meetings were ostensibly concerned only with the organization of the activities of the wing. The wing by now had been split up into a series of voluntary groups whose objects varied from learning dancing to studying the regulations governing army pay. In fact the problems of organization, of course, hinged on the problems of personal relationships . . . As a result almost immediately these big meetings as well as the small ones, spontaneously became a study of the intra-group tensions and this study was established as the main task of the whole group and all smaller groups within it.

. . . It was as a result of this therapeutic activity that the group began to think, and a deputation voiced the thought, that 80 per cent of the members of the training wing were 'skrim-shankers,' 'work-shys,' malingerers and the rest, and ought to be punished. A month before the training wing had complained indignantly that inmates of a psychiatric hospital were regarded by the rest of the community as being just these things. It was disconcerting, but a revelation of what psychiatry could mean, when the psychiatrist refused to accept this wholesale diagnosis, and simple proposal of punishment as the appropriate form of therapy, as a sound solution of a problem which has troubled society since its commencement. The therapeutic occupation had to be hard thinking and not the abreaction of moral indignation. Within a month of the start of this metier these patients began to bear at least a recognizable resemblance to soldiers.

Throughout the whole experiment certain basic principles, believed to be absolutely essential, were observed. In order of their importance they are set down here even though it involves repetition.
1. The objective of the wing was the study of its own internal tensions, in a real life situation, with a view to laying bare the influence of neurotic behaviour in producing frustration, waste of energy, and unhappiness in a group.
2. No problem was tackled until its nature and extent had become clear at least to the greater part of the group.

3. The remedy for any problem thus classified was only applied when the remedy itself had been scrutinized and understood by the group.
4. Study of the problem of intra-group tensions never ceased – the day consisted of 24 hours.
5. It was more important that the method should be grasped, and its rationale, than that some solution of a problem of the Wing should be achieved for all time. It was *not* our object to produce an ideal training wing. It *was* our object to send men out with at least some understanding of the nature of intra-group tensions and, if possible, with some idea of how to set about harmonizing them.
6. As in all group activities the study had to commend itself to the majority of the group as worth while and for this reason it had to be the study of a real life situation.

. . . Any psychiatrist who attempts to make groups study their own tensions, as a therapeutic occupation, is in today's conditions stopping a retreat and may as a result be shot at. But he will lose some of his feeling of guilt.

In conclusion it must be remembered that the study of intra-group tensions is a group job. Therefore, so long as the group survives, the psychiatrist must be prepared to take his own disappearance from the scene in not too tragic a sense. Once the rout is stopped even quite timid people can perform prodigies of valour so that there should be plenty of people to take his place.

Bion and Rickman were responsible for only part of the hospital. What they were doing profoundly disturbed the rest of the organization. It queried the medical model. The opposition which Rickman had feared in 1940 began to gather, but not so much in an overt as in a covert form, and erupted in the symptom of an absurd incident. Bion, as messing officer, came to know that there was something wrong with the accounts. It was his duty to find a way of dealing with it. A person of rather high rank seemed to be implicated. Any public disclosure would have created a scandal that could have reacted badly against army psychiatry just as it was establishing itself. In the War Office, Brigadier Rees[17] took no chances. He did not trust Bion, who was rather strict about regimental conduct, to handle the matter with the discretion he thought necessary. On his order Bion and Rickman were summarily posted back to WOSBs and arrived at Wall Hall late at night in a dazed state. The matter of the accounts was smoothed over at the cost of stopping the Northfield experiment.

The violence of this action left his colleagues at RTC even more shaken than by the duplicity over the Establishment. In our anguish and perplexity we found singular pertinence in a metaphor of Fairbairn's (1952) that Sutherland had made an 'idea in good currency' (Schon 1971) in our thinking about unconscious processes at that time — the notion of the 'internal saboteur'. This saboteur seemed to have the knack of appearing in oneself, in one's friends or in one's group, just when success seemed at hand for innovations of unusual relevance. Every step forward seemed to be accompanied by some further activation of destructive forces in the shadow of what Bion later called the 'group mentality'. In the space of three months we had had the ambiguous Establishment about the Senior Psychiatrist and the Deputy President, the premature reference to Regimental Nomination in the AG's letter, and now the destructive intrusion into the centre of the Northfield experiment of a trivial and seemingly irrelevant matter concerning mess accounts. There seemed to be another psychopathology of everyday life than that about which Freud had written, one more allied to Thanatos than to Eros. In our particular world at this time the main target was Bion — the main innovator. In the passage quoted from the *Menninger Bulletin* article he notes that the psychiatrist who takes a stand against the neurotic attack is the one most likely to be shot at. During this brief period he had been shot at three times and the wound caused by the last missile was the most serious. In wartime one has more scope than in peacetime for projecting the bastard in oneself on to the external enemy, but one does not get off scot-free for that reason. We hoped we were wiser, we were certainly sadder men as the result of these experiences.

Bion was posted to a Board in Winchester where the other senior officers had been through World War I and held him in esteem and affection. After a few days I went down to see the procedure and stay over with him. In the evening we strolled out by the rivers and creeks of the city, our sombre thoughts clouding a blaze of moonlight. His anger was still huge but he was recovering his detachment. He had been giving serious thought to making what had happened at Northfield public, facing the consequences for himself and everyone else. Rees and his War Office associates did not understand what he and Rickman had been attempting at Northfield. Did they want to? It represented too great a threat to them. They were developing army psychiatry on the wrong lines, despite their apparent success. They were creating medical dependencies and these would create vicious circles that would bottle up too many psychiatrists in repeat operations. Too few would then be available for new tasks. This was already happening in WOSBs. If the Leaderless Group method were followed in the way he had wanted to develop it and schemes such as Regimental Nomination prepared in a militarily acceptable way, the army would become capable of doing more for itself in these areas. A light technical rearguard could be left behind and most of the available psychiatrists and psychologists moved forward to the next round of tasks. He had wanted to finish Northfield; to demonstrate once and for all that the conventional concept of a military psychiatric centre with all its medical paraphernalia was obsolete; and that there was an alternative. If the community itself could learn to take a stand against the 'neurotic attack' it would free up a good many people, including psychiatrists, for dealing with the problems of the campaigns ahead. We had now reached that phase of the war. We needed first to develop new understanding, then spread it widely in a form other people could use; and then advance ourselves in a new mode, not stay behind and expand a technical empire based on what had already been accomplished.

If the Northfield affair were made public a constructive outcome would follow, it seemed to me, only if the strategy proposed by Bion were adopted. In due course this might happen (and in the end did happen) with Rees and his War Office colleagues still in power. To make it happen now, an alternative leadership would have to take over. Was one available? I could not see one, unless Bion himself. He would have had a good deal of military support had he thrown down the gauntlet, but very little professional support. He was still unknown in professional circles. He was also too far in advance of many even of his progressive colleagues. I asked him if he would take on a policy job in the War Office. He said that policies of that sort were not his metier. They were Hargreaves's metier. Had he been a political individual, either he would have avoided being victimized or he would have engaged in well-calculated moves to gain control (possibly through a nominee bound to himself). Then he would not have been Bion. Ironically, it was because they knew he was not a political individual that some of his colleagues, who were, did not trust him. They did not understand his innovations all that well and they did not think he understood all that well their consequences for various interest groups. By the end of our walk I knew he had decided not to make an issue of the Northfield catastrophe.

Sequelae to Northfield

I have found in several studies of substantial, as distinct from marginal, innovation (Chevalier and Burns 1979) that the first entry of the new model is arrested but that the learning acquired permits an extensive development when, after a delay, the environmental situation has become favourable towards a second entry. The seed planted at Northfield did not fall by the wayside. In another two years it flowered in several forms in relation to the concluding phases of the war. As Bion observed in 'Psychiatry in a time of crisis' (1948b), a chain reaction had been started.

Before this came about his military qualities found him once again called on to lead a special mission intended to open up new territory — to relate army psychiatry more directly to the battle front. He had been concerned at Winchester lest too few psychiatrists be available when other theatres of war opened up after the Middle East, where T.F.Main had pioneered a new role.

With the formation of 21 Army Group the question arose of finding a psychiatrist acceptable to Montgomery. Bion was the obvious choice. Accordingly he went over to Normandy with a WOSB whose mission (according to Exercise By-Pass) was to increase the supply of experienced candidates from Divisions resting after battle. Other tasks were expected to emerge. In North Africa it had been found that patients deteriorated once removed from the battle zone, arriving in base hospital in schizophrenic-like states. The need was to keep them as close to their units as possible. The scope for group methods which transcended the boundaries of the medical arm was enormous, but before Bion could get going on them the unexpected death of his first wife forced his recall. He did not return to 21 Army Group. For the record it may be noted that once again he had been selected 'to bear the brunt' of being the pathfinder in a new task.

He was posted to a Board at Sanderstead in Surrey. Those who visited him found a stoical widower, but few suspected the resilience that would push him once again into the vanguard of social psychiatric innovation. The war had reached a phase where the reclassification and redeployment of officers and their attendant rehabilitation had become more important than their selection. Under Bion's guidance the Board was turned into a special form of therapeutic community which provided the model for the transformation of other Boards. It became my task to make a study of his methods for this purpose. Officers were referred from France, Italy, the Middle East, India or Home Forces. They came voluntarily to sort out their problems and redefine their roles and careers as temporary or regular soldiers. There was a lot of depression about becoming surplus, reduced in rank, having become a misfit; confusion and anxiety about the future; ignorance of opportunities and loss of confidence in abilities. Bion treated all this in the broad context of what has come to be called life planning. He may have been the first to practise this approach. Transition-points created tensions and stresses that could be used to enhance personal growth and social learning through exploratory search.

A great step forward in his eyes was represented in the fact that these reclassification and rehabilitation units were under regimental rather than medical control. Without a medical frame of reference there was no division of intake into patients and non-patients. No one had to be labelled neurotic or normal or think of himself as suffering from a 'disease'. One did not have to be classified as belonging to a special category of persons in order to come to the unit. This minimized false problems.

He next instituted two simple but fundamental principles. There was no fixed length of stay; anyone could come back on request. The role of the unit was to be a 'depot ship'. He wanted it perceived as a persisting, reliable and accessible 'good project'. The degree to which one made use of its resources was determined by oneself.

As time went on, the bulk of the officers who came to his unit were returned prisoners of war — those who were staying on in the army as distinct from those returning to civil life. His work with the former greatly added to the understanding required to deal with the larger problem of the latter. His views on POWs and their problems were published in an unsigned editorial in the *British Medical Journal* on psychological survival under conditions in which one is met with total indifference in the field of one's object relations.

While at Sanderstead he experienced far-reaching influence on two schemes that were founded on his earlier Northfield work. One of these was in fact called the Second Northfield Experiment. The other was the scheme of the Civil Resettlement Units (CRUs) for repatriated prisoners of war returning to civilian life.

Northfield II, like Sanderstead, was concerned with reclassification, redevelopment and rehabilitation, but for those returning to civilian life as well as for those continuing in the Army and for other ranks rather than officers. Like Northfield I, it was a neurosis centre under medical control. One might have expected that Bion would have sought to return to it, but in advising on the scheme he was insistent that the equivalent of the Training Wing he headed should be in charge of a regimental officer and outside direct medical control. The person chosen for this role was Harold Bridger (RA),[18] an outstanding MTO from WOSBs not only well versed in the Leaderless Group method but with a background in education in which he had developed a special interest in the project method as originated by John Dewey. His meetings with Bion resulted in his developing the idea that each patient should have a 'selected activity' arrived at collaboratively between him and his psychiatrist. The extraordinary variety of activities which ensued, extending beyond the bounds of the hospital and involving industrial firms and many kinds of civil organization, is described by him in his article in the issue of the *Bulletin of the Menninger Clinic* devoted to Northfield (Bridger 1946). Bridger developed a social therapy staff and a social therapy programme complementary to the psychiatric staff and the psycho-therapy programme. The links between the two are described in S. H. Foulkes's (1946) article in the same issue, with special reference to the greater variety and amount of 'here and now' material made available for therapeutic purposes. This is an independent account of the way one can reinforce the other as Bion and Rickman had intended.

The concept of managing a whole hospital as a therapeutic community is given in T. F. Main's (1946) paper. Attention needs to be drawn to his remarks on the changed role of the psychiatrist:

> These are not small requirements and they have demanded a review of our attitudes as psychiatrists towards our own status and respon-sibilities. The anarchical rights of the doctor in the traditional hospital society have to be exchanged for the more sincere role of member in a real community, responsible not only to himself and his superiors, but to the community as a whole, privileged and restricted only insofar as the community allows or demands. He no longer owns 'his' patients. They are given up to the community which is to treat them, and which owns them and him. Patients are no longer his captive children, obedient in nursery-like activities, but have sincere adult roles to play, and are free to reach for responsibilities and opinions concerning the community of which they are a part. They, as well as he, must be free to discuss a rationale of daily hospital life, to identify and analyze the problems, formulate the conditions and forge the enthusiasms of group life.
>
> . . . he does not seek *ex cathedra* status. Indeed he must refuse any platform offered to him, and abrogate his usual right to pass judgment on inter-group claims or problems. The psychiatrist has to

tolerate disorder and tension up to the point when it is plain that the community itself must tackle these as problems of group life.

. . . It must be pointed out that the medical man, educated to play a grandiose role among the sick, finds it difficult to renounce his power and shoulder social responsibilities in a hospital and to grant sincerely to his patients independence and adulthood. But it is no easier for the rest of the staff. It is difficult to live in a field undergoing internal stress without wanting to trade upon authority and crush the spontaneity which gives rise to the stress, to demand dependence and to impose law and order from above. Such measures, however, do not solve the problem of neurosis in social life, but are a means of evading the issue.

The question of the renunciation of power and the sharing of responsibility with an interdisciplinary team on an equalitarian basis had been at the bottom of the trouble stirred up by Northfield I. This issue is still relevant, as Maxwell Jones's persistent struggles over it for thirty-five years have demonstrated.

Social innovations often have to start in special parts of an organization, as the Bion–Rickman project did in Northfield I, but, as had been learnt from subsequent studies, they will not survive unless the whole system changes in the direction of the innovation. By the time of Northfield II there were enough psychiatrists and other professionals who espoused the new approach and enough understanding in the wider environment to permit a whole psychiatric institution, for the first time, to be transformed into a therapeutic community.

While Northfield II was at its height, a large-scale project got under way concerned with repatriated prisoners of war returning to civilian life. The disturbed state of their forerunners in World War I had caused a lot of trouble after the 1918 peace, including difficulties with the law. Many of these men never fully recovered from the psychological effects of prolonged separation and incarceration in enemy hands. A number of distinguished soldiers wrote to the War Office to this effect recalling their own experiences as POWs. In 1943 A. T. M. Wilson had interviewed and conducted group sessions with escapers and medical repatriates and convinced the authorities that widespread trouble was likely again unless special measures were taken. He had carried out morale surveys of troops in the Middle East and found that after a period of about eighteen months something adverse seemed to happen to the images of an individual's 'good objects'. A large number of people could not hold their previous key relationships in good shape; their levels of paranoia and depression increased, while they became more rebellious against authority and prone to psychosomatic illness. POWs represented an exceptionally severe case of this syndrome with additional factors such as the anger and guilt associated with capture, the tendency to equate all authority with 'bad' enemy authority and to experience extreme 'dis-ease' with women.

A close colleague of Bion in the pre-war Tavistock, Tommy Wilson had followed Northfield I with intense interest, as he had the method of Leaderless Groups. He convinced the War Office (the eventual decision was taken at Cabinet level) that any therapeutic organization developed to cope with the problems of repatriated POWs could not be medically based. It had to be regimental. The army had been responsible for getting them into 'the bag'; it had now to accept responsibility for getting them out of it in as good shape as when they went in. Most POWs had been elite troops.

The main source of non-medical professionals was the WOSB organization. Wilson asked me to join him in planning the scheme and developing the pilot unit. I brought the Sanderstead model to this task. The first person I asked for was Harold Bridger, who brought the model of Northfield II. We then secured the services of Col. R. M. Rendel, one of the most insighted of the WOSB Presidents, as Commanding Officer, and two former MTOs, Ian Dawson, who had special gifts as a policy-planner, and Dick Braund, a regular soldier who was a natural clinician. All these people were linked in one way or another to Bion. They had espoused Leaderless Groups and Regimental Nomination, had been outraged over what had happened to Northfield I and were now engaged in Sanderstead type of work. These connections are mentioned to show how the main projects with which Bion was associated brought into being a set of people who, whatever the contributions of their own creativeness, and these were considerable, regarded themselves as based on him. They constituted a network that was mobilized in its most extensive form to provide the key staff for the Civil Resettlement Units. These units represented the final project of army psychiatry and the most advanced embodiment of the idea of a therapeutic community originally propounded by Bion in the Wharncliffe Memorandum.

CRUs were a large organization comprising twenty units positioned near the conurbations which represented the largest population centres, to be in reach of relatives. Some 400 repatriates were in residence in each at any one time. The mean stay was a month. Apart from A. T. M. Wilson at HQ, there were only two psychiatrists in the entire organization. Regimental officers were trained to handle group discussions, and each unit had a Ministry of Labour official to advise on vocational problems and a social worker to advise on family problems. A large proportion of the other-rank staff were ATS who, by the friendly and non-threatening way they interacted with the repatriates in carrying out their ordinary duties, were the main factor in undoing their fears about women. Bion's concept that the psychiatrist's job was to create conditions which would enable him largely to leave the scene and allow the ordinary resources of the society to do their work was closely approximated.

A continuous training activity had to be maintained by the HQ staff as the army was by this time demobilizing. Apart from this and engaging the co-operation of many kinds of civilian organizations (including industrial firms in large numbers), the main job of the HQ staff was protecting the units by warding off external attacks. The biggest of these came as a consequence of the atomic bomb, which brought a return of the men from the Japanese camps earlier than had been expected. There were (so it seemed) neither enough premises nor enough personnel to cope with them while intake from German camps was at its height. The War Office issued orders (not however through the Directorate of Psychiatry) to put back and even cancel the rights of the latter to give priority to the former. Such a betrayal was not acceptable to the group at HQ (CRUs). We had learnt a lot from the debacles of 1942 and managed to turn our orders inside out and expand the organization so that everyone was coped with. Nevertheless, ways were found of removing the original leaders (Wilson and Rendel). The saboteur was muted but not silenced.

A follow-up scheme was designed and carried out (Curle and Trist 1947) which showed that repatriates who attended CRUs made a better adjustment than those who did not, when their level of functioning was estimated in fifteen major life roles. The difference was large and significant at the 0.001 level. A further finding showed that a number of the CRU cases made what was called 'supra-norm' adjustment; there were few of these in the non-CRU sample, showing that maturation under adverse conditions can take place spontaneously, as the common wisdom has always maintained; but the CRU cases were more numerous, the difference again being statistically significant, as it was also between CRU cases and a civilian control group. Participation in a therapeutic community could be life-enhancing and contribute to personal growth. The mutual reinforcement of sociotherapeutic and psychotherapeutic procedures, together with the mobilization of the extended social field of the wider society, could produce humans capable of functioning at a higher level than their accustomed norm. Bion had expressed this hope to me in 1942 in our talks at Winchester when all seemed lost in North-field I. Now the first hard evidence was in.

Multiple group projects at the Tavistock

The belief is widely held that at the Tavistock Bion confined himself to group therapy with small patient groups. Indeed the *Human Relations* papers give this impression. In fact he inaugurated a broad programme with many different kinds of groups. He also took a major part in for-mulating the philosophy, planning the strategy and designing the shape of an organization that became radically different from the pre-war Clinic.

The Council of the Tavistock Institute of Medical Psychology, the governing body of the pre-war Clinic, had conducted a postal ballot at the height of World War II of all staff members to elect a Planning Com-mittee to make recommendations on the direction the organization should take in the post-war period and who should be in it. Those elected comprised the group of psychiatrists who had gone into the army. They could co-opt two members from outside and chose Suther-land and myself. This group met twice a week during the autumn of 1945, with J. R. Rees in the chair. The report was due by the end of the year, and a memorandum had been requested for the Rockefeller Foundation by the Director of the Medical Division (Alan Gregg). He had been impressed by the activities undertaken during the war and had been assured that the group intended to develop a programme that would seek to relate psychiatry to the wider society under conditions of peace. As the due date came nearer and a number of major issues still required resolution, by common consent, Bion was asked to take the chair and use his unique sociotherapeutic capabilities to take the group through the ordeal of agreeing on a final document. His first role there-fore was as the 'conductor' of a group whose task was what would now be called normative planning.[19] He was both the most trusted and the most competent individual amongst us to undertake this task which involved enormous skills in conflict resolution so that shared appreci-ations could arise.

The report of the Committee having been accepted by the Council, and a grant having been received from the Rockefeller Foundation, the new organization, which contained the newly founded Institute as well as the Clinic, commenced operations in February 1946. Bion was now asked to become Chairman of the working staff, a position he retained throughout most of that year.[20] His second role, therefore, was as an executive 'steersman'. He never sought such roles; they were thrust upon him then just as they were later in psychoanalytic circles. Bion served part-time, as he wished to retain a private psychoanalytic practice in Harley Street. He directed a programme of multiple group projects which included a student group and an industrial group as well as patient groups.

The members of the student group were non-medical interns interested in developing competence in taking groups in non-medical settings. They met with Bion every week in a regular group session; each prepared an account of what he thought had happened; the accounts were then compared at a subsequent session. Unfortunately, no arrangement was made to ensure that a copy of these accounts was deposited in a common file, with the result that this material has been lost to subsequent analysis. In due course most of these students began to take groups of their own, when they would meet Bion for group tutorials. Unfortunately, again, no record of these meetings was kept.

The industrial group was composed of senior managers from different organizations interested in group dynamics and participative management. A high fee was charged, which caused consternation in the early sessions and raised the issue of what was valued. Several members of this group undertook personal analysis and drifted away. If this was their hidden agenda, Bion's purpose was to obtain comparative data from groups in different settings, including organizational contexts and individuals occupying positions of power. Rickman and Sutherland attended sessions of the industrial group. Bion seemed intent on building a cadre of experienced analysts to open up group work in the industrial field.

In the immediate post-war years – up to 1948 – he was preoccupied by the role of psychiatry in the wider society and drew on the historian in himself. This is apparent in his presidential address to the Medical Section of the British Psychological Society – 'Psychiatry in a time of crisis' (Bion 1948b). Read now, it seems a rather rambling presentation; heard then, it felt more like a call to arms. Psychoanalysis and related disciplines, including work with groups, had brought a new type of knowledge to humankind. If used, it could be the means through which western societies could learn how to surmount their manifold crises and develop to a further stage. But would the leadership come forward to enable them to do so? Would the hatred of learning from experience be too great? He left the question open so far as the profession of psychiatry (or indeed any other group) was concerned. His manner on the platform, however, left one in no doubt that he himself was taking a stand – as he had at Northfield – and would welcome those who would join him.

Shortly after this address, which was given in January 1947, I received a message from him to come to a private meeting in his consulting room — a special group was to start. 'This', he said, 'is serious.' At the meeting were several analysts with a record of work with groups and one or two people, such as myself, in personal analysis if not in psychoanalytic training. Bion was sitting in a middle chair in the circle with Rickman beside him. He was subdued; Rickman was embarrassed; no one else knew what to say. There was some discussion about Bion taking a group of patients in analysis to get the binocular vision which interested him. But clearly this was not the point of the meeting. Those present were all people he trusted. He seemed to be asking something of us. He was subdued because he did not want to 'take' us as a group. He wanted to be with us in a group. To use terms that Rickman had used in a presentation to the London Psycho-analytical Society on the Creative Process, he wanted a 'pentecostal group' in which everyone could speak with tongues and would be accepted as on an equal level with everyone else. Such a group would be neither a therapy group nor a seminar but would represent a new mode — a mutually supporting nexus of 'selectively interdependent'[21] individuals — a network committed to taking up the challenge he had issued in his Medical Section address. Such a group would need to make what Sir Geoffrey Vickers (1965) has called 'new shared appreciations' and to engage in the process the Emerys (1979) have called 'searching'. It seemed important to Bion that the setting of such a group should be outside any particular organizational space. I would say now that he understood, however vaguely, that the members had to be directly related as persons to the problematic of the domain and not be lumbered by their organizational baggage. At that time, however, we did not have concepts of domain (Trist 1977), of selective interdependence, of appreciation or of searching; neither had we recognized the special role of social networks (Bott 1957), as distinct from holistic organizations, in fostering innovation. The consulting-room meetings petered out, partly for lack of conceptual clarity, partly because the unification of the social and psychological fields which had characterized the war period was beginning to break up and the society was moving away from a persisting ba F towards ba D. The Medical Section address was the last memorable statement I can remember of a modality in which Bion and his colleagues had lived for the better part of a decade and in terms of which our values and theories had evolved.

I think he felt left in the lurch and that this disappointment contributed to the feelings of depressive isolation he expressed at Black Lake. Remembering the consulting-room meetings, I tried myself in the mid-1960s to bring a group something like this into being among those concerned with the British Social Psychiatry Workshop. This group generated some important activities as well as giving personal satisfaction and emotional support to its members. I tried this model again in the 1970s with those concerned with group work at the University of Pennsylvania, where it showed every sign of persisting.

Therapeutic groups

The International Congress on Mental Health held in London in 1948 was the first international gathering at which group methods were systematically explored in a wide professional public. For Bion, it was his international debut. His conference paper – his first public statement on therapy groups (Bion 1948a) – created a considerable stir. It became evident that he was doing something different from what others were doing. He was neither applying psychoanalysis to groups nor was he just giving ego support. He was searching for the equivalent of the psychoanalytic method in the group situation and for concepts that would enable him to understand the material that emerged in it. This entailed a major change in frame of reference, which he was to spell out in *Experiences in Groups.*

Though this constituted a conceptual and methodological breakthrough, characteristically with Bion it also constituted an action step. At this time the joint Tavistock organization was preparing the Clinic to enter the National Health Service. It would not be permitted simply to give long-term, or even short-term, individual treatment to a few patients. It would have to meet criteria of patient load and economy in the use of scarce professional resources acceptable to a Regional Board. The mission of the Clinic was to pioneer a form of psychotherapeutically oriented out-patient psychiatry appropriate to and acceptable in a National Health Service. It was not just that the queueing problem of patients on the waiting-list had to be solved; unless a higher load could be carried with results that could be demonstrated as positive in some degree, the Clinic would not be allowed to continue on its chosen course. The cause of psychotherapeutically oriented psychiatry in the National Health Service would be set back.

No one knew what the demand was likely to be for out-patient psychological treatment. The Tavistock was the only institution entering the Health Service offering it in the adult field. The situation as regards children was a little but not much better, and one of the main child facilities (under Bowlby) was also at the Tavistock. Psychiatry by and large existed to deal with the psychotic patient in the mental hospital. Between this system and an out-patient clinic such as the Tavistock there were only two residential centres that were psychotherapeutically oriented — the Cassel Hospital for severe neurotics and borderline psychotics needing some in-patient care, where T. F. Main had become Director, and Maxwell Jones's new unit at Belmont Hospital, where a therapeutic community for psychopathic individuals was under development. It was of exceeding importance that the Tavistock as a pioneer should be seen to be reasonably successful in its out-patient mission.

In the Adult Department the development of some form of group treatment seemed the best prospect. Once more Bion was called upon to become the pioneer, though this time many were soon to join him. I remember him putting up a notice: 'You can have group treatment now or you can wait a year (or more) and have individual treatment.' There were no criteria available for selecting the kinds of patient most likely to benefit from treatment in a group. From the earliest applicants, he started the first group of eight patients who met twice a week for sessions of 90 minutes.

Any attempt to carry out group treatment in a civilian clinic destined for the National Health Service in the context of post-war Britain faced very different conditions from those faced in a military environment during World War II. In the latter, patients (all men) were referred because they could not perform the military duties required in their units; they were in transitional situations; there were broad classes of common problem; treatment was short-term but intensive in residential centres; many co-operative resources were available in the environment; disposals consisted of sending a man back to his unit, to alternative military employment or returning him to civil life. By contrast, patients (women as well as men) were referred to the Tavistock for all sorts of reasons from many sources (though a large number came through general practitioners). They were in chronic rather than transitional situations; it was difficult to distinguish common problems; treatment was for an indefinite period but spaced out on an out-patient basis; few external co-operative resources were available; disposal meant a termination decision — either the patient could now cope reasonably well by himself or, even if he could not, he was judged unlikely to benefit from further treatment; the criteria for outcome decisions of this kind were vague.

Bion began work with his twice-a-week group knowing that the conditions expressed a discontinuity with what he had been doing during the war. Neither he nor anyone else knew quite what to expect. He wanted someone to talk to about the group. It was better that someone was present in the group with him. He invited me to join him for this purpose. I was the obvious choice as, not being a psychiatrist, I would not, like most of my colleagues, be taking a patient group of my own yet needed experience of one for my work in non-medical settings. He and I had worked well together during the war and the level of trust between us was high. He warned me the group would not allow me to be silent all the time, so that I should be prepared to comment. At my second session the women brought along their knitting and one or two of the men fiddled with pipes and keys. When there was a lot of glancing at me I said I felt like Dr Bion's knitting. Apparently this remark admitted me to the fellowship of the group, for at subsequent sessions no knitting, pipes or keys were in evidence.

The group was composed of some very disturbed individuals. One frequently and another occasionally exhibited bizarre behaviour that was unmistakably psychotic and at times one or other would be absent in mental hospital; one man was what would conventionally be called an aggressive psychopath who at times was intensely hostile to various group members and to Bion; the others were complex character cases exhibiting mixes of depressive and obsessional symptoms along with episodes of acute anxiety. As I realized the magnitude of their difficulties I became increasingly depressed. I mentioned this to Bion, who said, 'What does it make you want to do?' I said, 'Give up.' He said, 'That is what the group with the part of themselves that has no intention of changing wants you to do. If you go along with them on this you will not help them. Always pay attention to what the group makes you feel.' This was my first lesson; the memory of it is as vivid today as at the time.

Several features characterized Bion's group 'style'. He was detached yet warm, utterly imperturbable and inexhaustibly patient. He gave rise to feelings of immense security – his Rock of Gibraltar quality. But the Rock of Gibraltar is also powerful and he exuded power (he was also a very large man). This did not make the patients afraid of him; rather it endowed him with a special kind of authority which gained him added attention. The patients became aware that they had secured a very exceptional person as their therapist. It represented an X factor, the effects of which I could not fathom.

His interventions were on the sparse side and tended to be terse. They could be kept so because he always waited until the evidence for what he would say was abundant. He then expressed himself in direct, concise language that everyone could understand. If a patient made an intervention before he did, so much the better; there was no need for him to make it. He seemed to want to make the group as self-interpretative as possible and to facilitate its learning to become so.

Through the personal qualities mentioned, as well as his method of centring his interpretations on the relation between the group and himself, he made it safe for the group to dramatize its unconscious situation. Episodes would occur within sessions and sometimes across sessions in which huge dramas would be played through, replete with rich symbolic material. Everyone participated in these episodes at many levels (including myself as participant observer and, in some way, himself). Experience of these episodes led me to think of group therapy as a theatre, or as peaking in theatre, for there were periods in between where everything stayed in the doldrums or swirled round in confusion. He accepted these troughs and whirlpools as requiring his attention as much as the peaks. One reason why the group felt free to dramatize its deeper phantasies was because he never forced it to. Some of these episodes were massive and have remained in my mind for years. One of them, which continued over several sessions, centred on primal scene material of great complexity and violence, some of it bizarre (he may have been referring to this sequence in his statement about such material in 'Group dynamics: a review', p. 164).

I came to think of these participant dramas as expressing the essence of what was therapeutic in the group process. Verbal and non-verbal inputs combined to produce experiences that heightened one's sense of existence and illuminated its meaning, however painful the material being worked through.

For weeks on end I remained completely at sea about what he was doing though I knew well enough his distinction between group and individual interpretations, his principle of keeping to the former and of concentrating on the group's attitude to himself, etc. In terms of cricket he was letting go by balls I would have expected him to hit and hitting balls I would have expected him to let go by. He was following a pattern unintelligible to me and using a map I did not know. We made a custom of repairing for a brief discussion of the session to a pub round the corner from Beaumont Street (where the Clinic was then situated). On these occasions I would go ahead to find if the coast was clear; if it was he would come along. He did not want the patients to have any knowledge of him outside the sessions, far less to see him going into a pub.

At one of these pub discussions he began to talk of a new concept he was developing, tentatively called 'the group mentality'. Disowned and disavowed responses of the patients which were hostile to the purposes

of treatment were split off from what they would consciously acknowledge in the group and collected anonymously into a pool which constituted a negative unacknowledged system — the group mentality. He did
not like the term, but could not find a better one, though he was quite
taken with the vernacular connotation of the word 'mentality'.

Once he had identified this concept, he was in possession of a referent
for the group setting analogous to the unconscious in the individual
setting. This enabled him to produce the conceptual frame he outlined
in the early *Human Relations* papers and to see the group process as an
interplay between the group mentality, group culture and the individual
who needed yet was frustrated by the group.

Now that I had the cognitive map from which he was working, I
began to follow more clearly the logic of his interventions. As the result
of this I pestered him less about the meaning of particular incidents in
the group and our pub conversations centred more on the development
of his ideas. It seemed to me that the group mentality was the emergent
and innovative concept; the others one had heard before. I pressed him
to develop it.

The next step, however, took quite a long time to come. One evening
there was a quiet excitement in him and he came out with the notions
of basic assumption groups, the work group and the three forms that
basic assumptions could take. These provided him with the clue he was
looking for to the structure of the group mentality.

As well as being elated, he was anxious. He felt obliged to introduce
new and abstract terms in order to keep clear of psychoanalytic implications that only future work could establish — and maybe there were
non-analytic interpretations. Yet he was getting very far out on a limb.
A matter which particularly bothered him was his hypothesis about the
alternation of the basic assumptions. He enjoined me to observe the
group repeatedly to check his own observations. As far as I could tell,
his alternation hypothesis was upheld in the behaviour of the therapy
group. On the other hand there were many times when none of the ba's
were in evidence and when yet there was little evidence of a work group
orientation. It did not seem to me that the group mentality could be
reduced to the ba's. He said he had never intended that it should,
though the later *Human Relations* papers make it appear so.

He now asked himself what happened to the ba's which were latent
at any one time. Eventually he came up with his idea of the proto-mental
level. The speculative nature of this idea shook him quite a bit and he
remained disquieted that he should be seriously entertaining it. He
sensed he might be on the path of building a closed theoretical system

and that he might even end up with a delusional product. Was he a bit mad to be giving serious consideration to such ideas? I replied that he had to have the courage of his own logic, which had indeed led him to strange conjectures. The question of madness would arise only so far as he ceased to look for evidence to confirm or disconfirm them. Freud, I went on to say, must have given himself some bad frights when he found the key concepts of psychoanalysis arising in his head for the first time; and who but Bion had propounded the view that doubt about what one was doing was part of normal life? The strain he was under was greater than I had sensed. The tasks of the war years had kept him close to empirical reality. Though he had performed major feats of reframing, he had not submitted them to systematic theoretical development. The rigour of doing just this was what he now found himself saddled with. He seemed unfamiliar with the conceptual side of himself and to distrust it. I had no inkling of his interest in or capacity for formal conceptual thought. This now turned out to equal his powers of clinical observation and his gift of seminal insight.

About this time he got the notion that the psychosomatic field might yield evidence about the proto-mental level. He did not think that the small group would be useful for this purpose but thought that epidemiological studies might be. He seemed relieved now that he had identified a line of possible verification. His conceptual crisis was over.

As the new line of thought turned his attention from micro to macro, he began drawing on his experience as a historian, which had retained far more importance for him than I had suspected. His ideas about the basic assumption and work groups underwent a sociological extension. He clothed them with the mythological and archetypal meanings spelled out in the later *Human Relations* papers. His penchant for mathematical formalism led him to the notion of the *duals* of the ba's. His treatment of the dual of ba D and the cognate concept of oscillation[22] brought him back to clinical observation. They were illustrated with great vividness in the therapy group I attended. The concept of schism[23] on the other hand seemed to be better illustrated in the dynamics of organizations and social movements. It was evident in the Staff Group he was conducting in parallel. During this phase it became apparent that Bion was using the word 'group' to mean, interchangeably, the face-to-face group and the wider society. For him there was one 'socio-'; and all socio- had a 'psycho-' dimension, all psycho-, a socio-dimension.

His second frame of reference, and its attendant hypotheses, was now complete — except that the dynamics of the alternation of the ba's remained unexplained. This problem he was to take up only some considerable time later when he sought an explanation in Melanie Klein's theory of the early psychotic phases of personality development. This was the beginning of his third conceptual round. What had begun as a practical enterprise in group therapy ended up by producing a theoretical construction which, if developed, promised to do for group dynamics what psychoanalysis had done for personality. Yet neither he nor anyone else has contributed much to its development since 1952.

There is another side to this whole experience that is relevant to report. The members of the patient group began to develop an 'extra-curricular' life, taking the form of giving parties in each other's houses and making expeditions together. These events were referred to from time to time in the group sessions and led to the patients presenting an invitation to Bion to come to one of their parties. He refused and explained why he thought it improper for him to go. But it was agreed that I could go — as a kind of intervening variable — and it was similarly agreed that a young psychiatrist from Oxford, whom Bion had invited to join the group, could go as well. The rules were that we would not initiate any discussion of therapy group affairs at the parties or of party affairs in the therapy group. The patients were free to do either but they never did discuss group matters when we were present at their parties. I doubt that they did when we were absent. A taboo had been established in the culture of the group.

My interest in attending these events was to discover their place in the wider life-space of the patients and what this itself was like. One of the social workers at the Clinic had started a patients' club that had been well attended and had generated a number of activities, but which had been stopped. The grounds for stoppage were that it was creating a false supportive environment that was militating against treatment and producing a closed society of neurotics that was acting as a protective barrier against their undertaking the more difficult task of establishing effective relationships in the 'normal' society. There was truth in this allegation, if the patients' club were regarded as a permanent community; but if it were regarded as a transitional community a very different prospect emerged. Connections could be established with a variety of outside organizations, and social therapists on the Bridger model could be used to help patients to select and develop activities and opportunities they would remain ignorant of or otherwise miss. There would be a flow of members out as well as in. I was too full of memories of the balance and mutual reinforcement of psycho- and social therapy at Northfield and CRUs to dismiss the idea of trying out a social therapy option under out-patient conditions and attempting to recover something of that balance and mutual reinforcement. The extra-curricular activities of Bion's patient group might provide a starting-point.

I found that the patients' field of social relations was restricted and impoverished. Their extra-curricular meetings, which had begun quite late in their life as a therapy group, could be looked on as a development rather than as a protective barrier. They represented a trial of themselves in more ordinary circumstances without the presence of Bion. They needed some additional resources to facilitate an expansion of their social field into other settings and prompt the capture of new opportunities. Any progress along these lines would have brought new material into the therapy group. Before I could present this plan to Bion, my attendance at the group sessions ceased. Stimulated by these I had incurred an obligation to carry a rather critical role in a relatives' group at a mental hospital. This now met at a time which prevented my continuing with the therapy group.

Faced with an immediate need for groups, others followed Bion's example and by the time the Clinic entered the National Health Service in 1948 virtually all consultants and registrars were taking groups. Ezriel (1950) made a modification in Bion's method in which he systematically interpreted individual contributions to 'the common group phantasy',[24] claiming that this was more effective therapeutically. Various personal styles of taking patient groups developed. There was not overmuch use of Bion's conceptual framework *in toto*. This has had more influence outside the psychiatric field, as in the Tavistock–Leicester Training Conferences on Group Relations and the A. K. Rice Institute in the United States. Nevertheless, he had led the way in establishing a practical method of out-patient group therapy which was reasonably successful according to repeated projective tests administered later in attempts at assessing outcome. As a by-product he had developed in outline a general theory of the human group which had implications for the whole of social science.

The Staff Group

The last task Bion took on before leaving the Tavistock was one of great delicacy that provided him with an experience of the dynamics of organization development. The Professional Committee that took over on the foundation of the joint organization had to decide how to implement the broad social psychiatric mission defined by the Planning Committee. It had to decide who should stay, go, or be recruited to carry it out. The Clinic had to be prepared to enter the National Health Service as an intact body. The Institute had to be established as an independent organization. As a result of the World War II social psychiatric developments it had been agreed that the organization would be explicitly psychoanalytic in orientation in the tradition of the object-relations approach which unified the psychological and social fields, and that undertaking a personal analysis would be made a condition of employment. The bulk of the staff would become full-time.

All this was a radical change from the pre-war Tavistock, which had been composed of a large number of part-time people who gave six hours a week to the Clinic while maintaining private practices. Apart from one or two social workers and the odd psychologist, they were all psychiatrists, but, though all psychotherapists, only one (Bion) had entered psychoanalytic training. Treatment had been entirely individual and no tasks were undertaken outside the medical area.

The process of transforming the old organization into the new became known as 'Operation Phoenix' (Dicks 1970). Some of those with the longest service and some with the highest public standing would not meet the criteria for inclusion that had been worked out and circulated. Two members of the committee would interview each member of staff. This process became one of great pain. Not only was there anger and depression among the staff, there was increasing conflict in the Committee. I remember a meeting where it was proposed (by Hargreaves) that we should all resign and ask the Council to appoint a new committee. The guilt over firing old friends and valued contributors and of giving key positions to newcomers was becoming unmanageable. There was a drawing back from the new mission, rising confusion and schism. It was at this point, when the group was in full flight from the W of its mandate, that Bion resigned from the Committee, the Chairmanship and from all active roles except that of taking his patient group in order to offer his services as a group therapist to the staff. His offer was accepted. The Committee decided to carry on.

He then set up the Staff Group which was open to all comers, whether professional or administrative. It used to meet late afternoons on Mondays for two hours; at first weekly, and later fortnightly when the major tensions became less acute. It remained in existence for the best part of a year. At first attendance was quite large, but it dwindled later.

Bion was the only person who could have conceived of such a group and the only person who could have conducted it. He was, as always, trusted by everyone. With his imperturbable patience he enabled us to get through masses of ill-feeling and sort out our personal agendas; to make up our minds whether the new mission was one we could espouse and if so whether we should seek inclusion; or whether we should attempt to persuade the Council to adopt another mission, or leave things alone to take their course. The literature on Organizational Development and Planned Change would suggest that this group of Bion's was at least ten years ahead of any other group in attempting such a task.

Three critical decisions made his task possible that showed his sensitivity to structural variables in an organizational setting. The first was his resignation from the Committee and his disengagement from all his active roles (including the Chairmanship) except his patient group, where he had a professional obligation to continue. This made plain to all that he had no stake in the future of the organization and could be accepted as a disinterested party. The second was to make the meetings of the Staff Group overall community meetings so that the old pre-war and the new post-war staffs, Committee and non-Committee members, could meet face to face, with professionals alongside non-professionals and those returning from the army alongside those who had remained civilians. He countered a situation in which many were being excluded with one in which everyone was included. The third decision was his strict adherence to a role of process consultation. Anyone could say anything and raise any issue; he did not contribute to content.

He had to deal with the questions of power and sovereignty that he regretted not having discussed in *Experiences in Groups*.[25] Anyone holding power would exercise both good and bad forms of power, and those over whom power was held would feel the effects of both forms which were also in themselves. As understanding of this duality became part of the group culture, there was less mutual antagonism between Committee and non-Committee members. Because of the bad component there was guilt over exercising power – this had almost wrecked the Committee. There were two faces of sovereignty: the good face that represented integrity, coherence and wholeness; the bad face that represented monopoly and exclusion. They were inseparable. It was very difficult to accept that we could not have one without some of the other in the change-process we were undergoing.

The presence of all interested parties made for a great variety of concerns which prevented monopolization by those with narrow pre-occupations. It limited the amount of projection that would otherwise have taken place on absent sub-groups and key individuals. As the discussions went on, quite a number of people privately made up their minds on their position; if it was to leave, they quietly withdrew. Others fought the psychoanalytic criterion or the broad social aspects of the mission or the substitution of multi-professional for medical control. In so doing they became aware of the degree of support for their position, which was not high. A problematic sub-group comprised a number of refugees who had played a major role in staffing the Clinic during the war. The exposure of this problem led to some healing compromises.

His interpretative comments, together with the structured setting he had created, prevented the formation of organized factions. These could have put severe pressure on the governing Council and thoroughly confused it. They could have sought support in several outside groups and, by drawing them in, produced one form of Bion-type schism, while the empowered military group by its purism produced the other. These twin processes could have brought the newly formed joint organization to a complete halt. The dynamic conservatism of organizations in Schon's (1971) terms would have triumphed over W.

Almost everyone became convinced that they would get a fairer deal as the result of the Staff Group meetings. Their proceedings had a beneficial effect on the interviews between Committee members and staff. An acceptable settlement was reached in the large majority of cases. As these settlements were made, attendance dropped. In the end six of us were left, including myself. Bion asked if there might not be something common about us. Investigation established that we were all for various reasons people who were at that time without homes — including Bion. He said that as we seemed to be making the group into a home he would not be at home to the group any more, for this was not the purpose for which the Staff Group had been established.

He was conducting the Staff Group at the same time as the therapy group I was attending. He was also seeing individual patients in his psycho-analytic practice. To be simultaneously experiencing psycho-social reality at the levels of the organization, the group and the individual was an ideal to which those who had been responsible for the wartime developments in social psychiatry and applied social science and who now provided the leadership of the joint organization were committed. We believed that something unique would emerge from the interpenetration of these levels of experience and professional activity. Bion embodied this ideal.

We did not know that his gift through the Staff Group of a better chance to survive as an organization would be his parting gift. After the Staff Group wound up, he came in from his rooms in Harley Street only for tea. Then he did not come in at all.

Some thoughts on California

I had expected that his exclusive commitment to psychoanalysis would be a very long haul, considering the magnitude of the task he had undertaken in advancing Melanie Klein's work on schizoid states. Yet I believed that in the long run he would find a way of returning to the social field — because he would need to relook at his psychoanalytic findings in a social perspective — to go on with the third round of conceptualization that he had initiated at the end of *Experiences in Groups*.

His decision after more than fifteen years of psychoanalytic London to go to Los Angeles seemed to me to provide the likely opportunity. Some members of the more orthodox (surprisingly enough) of the two Psycho-Analytical Societies in Los Angeles had become interested in Melanie Klein's ideas and had invited leading Kleinian analysts over to give seminars. Bion went over to give one such series. He was invited back to undertake training analyses of some of their members so that a beach-head for the Kleinian viewpoint could be established in the United States.

I was in Los Angeles myself at the time, teaching at UCLA. He said that when he experienced the dry climate and desert landscape of southern California it reminded him of northern India, where he had been born. His father had been a civil engineer engaged in irrigation projects. Until he was sent home to prep school in Norfolk at the age of nine, he had been brought up in the Punjab and the foothills of the Himalayas. Southern California felt like a homecoming. He had no particular reason to stay in London, he said. England to him was a rather wet place where he had been miserable as a boy.

By the mid-1960s he had written a series of articles and books which had greatly advanced the knowledge of primitive mechanisms at the psychotic level of the personality and proposed a new frame of reference, quasi-mathematical in its formalism, in which psychoanalytic theory and practice could develop. The mission he had undertaken seemed to have been fulfilled. Was it not time for a new journey?

I invited him to give a seminar to my UCLA faculty colleagues and our Ph.D students. It was a performance in which he excelled even himself. It excited all my (and their) hopes of his return to the social field. He spoke about the relations between the creative individual, the group and the Establishment — the theme that appeared in *Attention and Interpretation* (Bion 1970). This book did represent a come-back to the social field. Though it broke new ground it was not a full come-back, for he stopped short of undertaking empirical work or engaging with the problematic of the current scene in California, where, in the late 1960s (which it then was), contact could be made with the leading edge of almost every significant social, political, philosophical and spiritual movement and conflict of our times.

A cultural revolution was taking place. In Haight–Ashbury thousands gathered to celebrate their withdrawal from mainstream materialism by listening to the music of the Grateful Dead, while across the Bay the students faced the police in the wake of the Berkeley Free Speech Movement. With the Vietnam War tearing the society into bitter divisions that affected large numbers of families, the reality of a psychotic level to the human personality was made public as hundreds encountered bad trips in braving the drug scene. A vast movement of inward social learning was afoot at the cost of a high casualty-rate. The 'container' (Bion 1970) was not 'containing' the eruptive neoplasm brought forth by the younger generation during this social storm.

Fires were burning in inner city ghettoes in the long hot summers. Bobby Kennedy and Martin Luther King were assassinated, the former not very many miles from where Bion was living. Nor was America the only disturbed country. The phenomenon that Emery and I (1965) called *turbulence* was becoming persistent and pervasive across the world. Levels of stress were being experienced as higher, and forms of regressive behaviour were noticeably more frequent in individuals and groups.

There was a wealth of talented and stimulating people caught up in all this and trying to understand it. Too few of them were connected with psychoanalytical societies. Too few analysts were reaching out to them. Analysis in America was locking itself up within itself; it was no longer being experienced as the innovative contributor to the understanding of social conflict and change that it had been in the 1950s when the Group for Advancement in Psychiatry was at the height of its influence.

In *Experiences in Groups* Bion stated that the human individual was a group animal (albeit at war with his own 'groupishness'), to study whom one needed binocular vision. The individual required to be looked at from the position of the group and the group from the position of the individual. There was a 'socio-' and a 'psycho-' perspective; they were interdependent. This interdependence itself was what he was inquiring into.

The three basic assumptions derived from the group and represented the socio- perspective. In this perspective the dyadic relation of analyst and analysand appeared as a function of the pairing group. In the psycho-perspective, which begins with the individual, the phenomena of all three basic assumptions appear derived from primitive psychotic anxiety. In undertaking his psychoanalytic mission he went from the socio- to the psycho- perspective. To see with binocular vision he would have to return to the socio- perspective and include it along with the psycho-perspective. These were the necessary conditions for completing the third round of conceptualization.

In my belief, for him to have continued with the third journey would have entailed him in re-engaging empirically with the social field. He used to say that he depended on clinical experience; that he needed to have it continuously. Now it was fresh socio-clinical experience that he needed. This could not have been a repeat of what he had done during the 1940s. It would have had to be something else – some action research or therapeutic project, whether at the level of the group, the organization or the wider society (preferably all three) that would have yielded him direct experience of the contemporary problematic. He would have had to have worked out a process of social re-engagement – with the activities, methodologies, ideas and crises with which his California environment was replete and with the people, a number of them highly original, involved in them. He would have had to become directly correlated with the then moment of contemporary history just as he had been directively correlated with World War II and its immediate aftermath. The California scene contained elements calculated to stir someone with a valency for ba F. Needed was an action step to achieve this in a concrete engagement, out of which could have come a new conceptual breakthrough – for this was his pattern.

Attention and Interpretation was a rehearsal for the new directive correlation, the later works a literary substitute. In his own terms they belong to another 'vertex'. The result is that the third round of conceptualization remains at its take-off point in the last chapter of *Experiences in Groups.* The psychoanalytic and later writings which have established him in the eyes of many as the leader of a post-Kleinian era in psychoanalysis (Grotstein 1981) represent a fourth and fifth conceptual round. The third round, however, is missing.

Some people think this is because the ideas he had worked out by 1952 represented a closed system incapable of further development much as he had feared in his discussion with me on conceptual crisis night in the pub. Others (including myself) think of them as a gate-opening set which holds out one of the best prospects available for the development of a general theory of the human group and of the individual in relation to it. In this framework psychoanalysis appears as a special case generated by a dyadic relationship within the perspective of the pairing group. The more general framework is what his earlier work promised to develop. A perspective which regards the whole scene as generated from within – from the worm's eye view of part-object relations – smacks of reductionism. I say this without doubting (as a Kleinian analysand) the value of the contribution to general psycho-social theory to be made from this source.

The signal from the presentation Bion made at my faculty seminar was positive as regards his re-entry to the social field. I did not, however, immediately follow it up with attempts to interest him in on-going social projects. He needed some time to establish his practice and get going the training scheme he had been asked to inaugurate. I then left UCLA for the University of Pennsylvania and was not often back in California. There were, to my knowledge, many able people outside psychoanalytic circles or overlapping with them who were interested in drawing Bion into their affairs – and at least three Institutes (one in Berkeley, one in Santa Barbara and one in Los Angeles itself). Effective contact never seems to have been made.

There was something of a taboo about getting in touch with Bion. Rumour had it that he did not want to be disturbed, as he had a lot of work still to do with the individual (Banet 1976), which has led him to reframe classical metapsychology. On the other hand, he may have been waiting to be asked to re-engage collaboratively in the world of group projects in the 'here and now' rather than having to rely solely on his historical knowledge as he did in his later writing. He was a very modest person. Those who knew him could make allowances for this, but those whom he now needed most to work with were people he did not know.

As the active social re-engagement that might have occasioned a new conceptual breakthrough did not occur, it will take someone of equivalent genius to bring forward the ideas he left in *Experiences in Groups* to the stage where social scientists at large can elaborate on them and undertake the work of detailed verification and modification. Even now new empirical work could be undertaken to elucidate further than he did the conditions under which the various ba's and related processes operate. As it is, they have been left rather up in the air. A sign that new thinking is at last being undertaken is Merrelyn Emery's (1982) refreshing if controversial treatment of the constructive aspect of ba P in relation to creative group learning.

Notes

1 In *Experiences in Groups* Bion describes three systems of unlearned 'unconscious' group response which he refers to as 'basic assumptions'. These are basic assumption dependence (ba D); basic assumption fight-flight (ba F) and basic assumption pairing (ba P). They interfere with the group's accomplishing its work task (W), though in some circumstances they can assist it. For example, ba F is an appropriate response in wartime and the other ba's can also have positive roles. These ideas are discussed in the section on Therapeutic Groups.

2 The concept of directive correlation is developed by Gerhart Sommerhoff (1950) in his book *Analytical Biology*.

3 One of the first psychotherapists to hold an academic position in a British university – at University College, London.

4 Later to become Chairman of the Tavistock Institute, 1948–58.

5 The most socially oriented of the senior analysts of that period.

6 A copy of the Wharncliffe Memorandum has not been located in my files relating to the war period still at the Tavistock. It merits publication as a historic document if a copy can be located.

7 In her introduction to Rickman's Collected Papers (1957) Sylvia Payne quotes a passage by Bion in which he gives major credit to Rickman for the start made at the Wharncliffe. Rickman always gave it to Bion.

8 After the war to become Director of the Tavistock Clinic.

9 This was shown in a survey carried out by Dr John Bowlby.

10 This paper was not included in *Experiences in Groups*. Apparently the omission was unintentional, according to Harold Bridger who asked him about it. It shows, nevertheless, how far by 1961 he had left such interests behind.

11 The account given here reflects the legend which had grown up about Bion's World War I experiences in World War II. The more modest facts and how he perceived them have now been given in his autobiography, *The Long Week-end* (1982).

12 General Staff Officer, Grade One.

13 The French had no compunction about his retaining his Légion d'Honneur.

14 Ronald Hargreaves, who had been at the pre-war Tavistock, was the 'anchor man' in the Directorate of Army Psychiatry for most of the war. Later he became Deputy Director of the World Federation of Mental Health before becoming Professor of Psychiatry at Leeds.

15 By Dr Hugh Murray.

16 To make the best of this decision a scheme was developed at the Directorate of Selection of Personnel known as Exercise By-Pass. Unit Boards composed of officers (who might informally consult NCOs) were set up in Corps Training Centres to get as many candidates as possible to WOSBs before they went to field force units. The WOSB organization sent out staff to theatres of war to hold Boards with Divisions resting after battle, so that those with experience of action should not be lost. Follow-up studies directed

by John Bowlby showed that a satisfactory level of officer quality was maintained throughout the war. There seemed even to be some improvement.

17 The pre-war Medical Director of the Tavistock Clinic; later Director of the World Federation of Mental Health.

18 Later a founding member of the Tavistock Institute.

19 According to Hasan Ozbekhan (1969), normative planning is the highest and most fundamental level of planning and is concerned with identifying the ends of the organization and therefore centres on decisions about core values; strategic planning selects the means for pursuing the chosen ends; and operations planning selects implementive activities on an on-going basis.

20 The circumstances under which he resigned his chairmanship in order to free himself to take the role of staff therapist are described on p. 35.

21 The concept of Selective Interdependence was formulated by F. E. Emery (1976).

22 Bion's concepts of oscillation and schism have an affinity with Gregory Bateson's concepts of double bind and schismogenesis which merits systematic exploration.

23 See note 22.

24 Bion expressed increasing dissatisfaction with the results he was getting out of group therapy as compared with psychoanalysis. But he was comparing five individual sessions a week with one or at most two group sessions under out-patient conditions. There are other comparisons – with intensive periods in residential retreats which can be repeated at spaced intervals; settings in which social therapy reinforces psychotherapy; and settings in which either or both of these are linked to transitional situations. Apart from recalling Northfield and CRUs, in America I have taken part in schemes employing repeated residential retreats, sometimes alternating with weekly sessions, often under lay rather than medical control and emphasizing personal growth rather than being 'cured' from a 'disease'. Some of these schemes have been successful in bringing about a greater personal change than weekly out-patient régimes with which I have been acquainted.

25 The theoretical ideas summarized in this paragraph are inferences of mine from a number of interpretations he gave during group meetings.

Acknowledgments

Quotations from Bion (1946) and Main (1946) are by permission of the Menninger Foundation.

References

Banet, A. G. (1976), 'Bion interview', *Group and Organization Studies*, 1, 3: 268–85.

Bion, W. R. (1946), 'The Leaderless Group Project', *Bull. Menninger Clinic*, 10, 3: 77–81.

Bion, W. R. (1948a), Paper in *Proceedings of the International Congress on Mental Health, London*, vol. 3.

Bion, W. R. (1948b), 'Psychiatry in a time of crisis', *Brit. J. Medical Psychology*, 21, 2, 81–9.

Bion, W. R. (1952), 'Group dynamics: a review', *Int. J. Psycho-analysis*, 33, part 2.

Bion, W. R. (1961), *Experiences in Groups and Other Papers*, London, Tavistock.

Bion, W. R. (1970), *Attention and Interpretation: a Scientific Approach to Insight in Psycho-analysis and Groups*. London, Tavistock.

Bion, W. R. and Rickman, J. (1943), 'Intra-group tensions in therapy', *Lancet*, 27 November.

Bott, E. (1957), *Family and Social Network*, London, Tavistock.

Bridger, H. (1946), 'The Northfield Experiment', *Bull. Menninger Clinic*, 10, 3: 71–6.

Chevalier, M. and Burns, T. (1979), 'The policy field', in J. W. Sutherland (ed.), *Management Handbook for Public Administrators*, Englewood Cliffs, N.J., Van Nostrand Reinholt.

Curle, A. and Trist, E. L. (1947), 'Transitional communities and social reconnection: a follow-up study of the civil resettlement of British prisoners of war', Part 2, *Human Relations*, 1, 2: 240–90.

Dicks, H. V. (1970), *Fifty Years of the Tavistock Clinic*, London, Routledge & Kegan Paul.

Emery, F. (1976), *Futures We are In*, Leiden, Martinus Nijhoff.

Emery, F. E. and Trist, E. L. (1965), 'The causal texture of organizational environments', *Human Relations*, 18, 2: 21–32.

Emery, M. (1982), *Searching*, Canberra, Australian National University, Centre for Continuing Education.

Emery, M. and Emery, F. E. (1979), 'Searching – for new directions . . . in new ways', In J. Sutherland (ed.), *Management Handbook for Public Administrators*, Englewood Cliffs, N.J., Van Nostrand Reinholt.

Ezriel, H. (1950), 'A psycho-analytic approach to group therapy', *Brit. J. Medical Psychology*, 23: 59–74.

Fairbairn, W. R. D. (1952), *Psychoanalytic Studies of the Personality*, London, Tavistock; also as *An Object Relations Theory of the Personality*, New York, Basic Books, 1954.

Foulkes, S. H. (1946), 'Principles and practice of group therapy', *Bull. Menninger Clinic*, 10, 3: 85–9.

Grotstein, J. (ed.) (1981), *Do I Dare Disturb the Universe?*, New York, Aronson.

Gustafson, J. R. and Cooper, L. (1979), 'Unconscious planning in small groups', *Human Relations*, 32, 12: 1039–64.

Jones, M. (1952), *Social Psychiatry: a Study of Therapeutic Communities*, London, Tavistock.

Jones, M. (1968), *Beyond the Therapeutic Community: Social Learning and Social Psychiatry*, Yale University Press.

Jones, M. (1976), *Maturation of the Therapeutic Community: an Organic Approach to Health and Mental Health*, New York, Human Sciences Press.

Klein, M. (1948), *Contributions to Psycho-analysis*, London, Hogarth Press.

Klein, M. *et al.* (1952), *Developments in Psycho-analysis*, London, Hogarth Press.

Main, T. F. (1946), 'The hospital as a therapeutic institution', *Bull. Menninger Clinic*, 10, 3: 66–70.

Menzies, I. E.P. (1981), Statement at Memorial Meeting for Dr Wilfred Bion. *International Review of Psycho-analysis*, 8, 3: 8–11.

Ozbekhan, H. (1969), 'Towards a general theory of planning', in E. Jantsch (ed.), *Perspectives in Planning*. Paris, OECD.

Rickman, J. (1957), *Selected Contributions to Psycho-analysis*, New York, Basic Books.

Schon, D. A. (1971), *Beyond the Stable State*, London, Temple Smith; New York, Basic Books, 1974.

Sommerhoff, F. (1950), *Analytical Biology*, Oxford University Press.

Trist, E. L. (1977), 'A concept of social ecology', *Australian J. Management*, 2, 2.

Vickers, Sir Geoffrey (1965), *The Art of Judgment*, London, Chapman & Hall.

Weiss, J. (1971), 'The emergence of new themes: a contribution to the psycho-analytic theory of therapy', *Int. J. Psycho-analysis*, 52: 459–67.

Chapter 2
Bion revisited: group dynamics and group psychotherapy

J. D. Sutherland

I Personal recollections

During 1940-1, the darkest days of World War II for Britain and her allies, I was a psychiatrist in a hospital for the war neuroses. It was my good fortune to be working closely with W. R. D. Fairbairn (hitherto the only psychoanalyst practising in Scotland) during this period when the pressure of his creative ferment was coming to full fruition. Inspired by Melanie Klein's writings — his contact with her before the war had been limited because of his geographical isolation in Edinburgh and was now nil — and by the impact of several markedly schizoid patients, he was recasting psychoanalytic psychopathology. Instead of Freud's foundations on the vicissitudes of instincts, Fairbairn described the development of the personality from a state of infantile dependence to the mature dependence of the adult on the basis of the structuring of experience within personal, or object, relationships. To put it into the terms Bion was to use later, he had moved from Freud's vertex with its penumbra of nineteenth-century energy concepts in which the second law of thermodynamics was virtually the ultimate truth in nature, to one from which the person at the personal or psychological level could be viewed as an organism perpetually requiring, and seeking, personal relationships for his development and maintenance.

The war neuroses had been a valuable stimulus to Fairbairn in consolidating his views. By the end of 1941, the change in the war situation to one of lessened demand on the psychiatric hospitals along with an urgent effort to build up the armed forces led to my being asked to join an experimental unit in the army whose task was to evolve a model procedure for the selection of candidates to be trained as officers. Located in Edinburgh, there was a small staff of experienced army officers along with three psychiatrists to provide a professional psychological

47

component. The three of us were analytically oriented and, since I had been a psychologist before training as a psychiatrist, I acted as the psychologist for the first few months until Eric Trist could join the unit. My two colleagues were Eric Wittkower, later Professor of Psychiatry in Montreal, and who had been working in Edinburgh, and Wilfred Bion, whom I had not met before.

From the start we all got along well personally and our shared orientation to the task made work very congenial. Since Eric Trist describes the contribution Bion made within these early months, I shall confine myself to a few personal impressions, some of which will inevitably overlap with his. Bion had the great advantage of an imposing military presence. He was a large man wearing the ribbons of his distinguished record as a soldier in World War I — the British Distinguished Service Order and the French Legion of Honour. Apart from this visible record which, in the senior member of the technical team, was of enormous value in facilitating our acceptance in face of the widespread suspicion and underlying anxiety with which psychiatrists were generally received, he quickly made an impression on everyone of 'power' in the best sense. He was quietly spoken, unfailingly courteous and attentive to others, and always sensitive and thoughtful about their views. His remarks were usually brief and penetrating and he had the most delightful sense of humour expressed in dry pithy phrases along with occasional amusing personal anecdotes to make a point.

As Trist describes, there were at times tensions between the technical and the military sides in the early days when the latter, for instance, found it difficult to accept that an apparently competent man would be rated too low in the intelligence tests for the arm of his choice or when some psychiatric features were uncovered which cast doubts on the man's stability despite an apparently good impression. The shared work helped to lessen those difficulties within the unit group, though they would emerge when groups of senior officers came to see the new methods at work. At one such meeting a visitor questioned somewhat sarcastically our low estimate of the intelligence of a candidate who had been the successful trainer of some well-known race-horses. 'How could we account for that discrepancy?' Bion replied with a twinkle in his eye that 'perhaps the man thought like a horse!' Bion's strength, however, would appear when he felt a criticism had a malevolent tone. Challenged about a psychiatric opinion on a similar occasion, he replied with considerable acerbity that he did not propose to defend the professional status of himself or his colleagues, whereupon the retreat was both rapid and apologetic.

At that time, it was the common practice in applied psychology to think of a vocational selection task as requiring on the one hand a job analysis from which the qualities required could be identified and, on the other, the devising of tests to measure these traits or qualities. Such a view had little appeal to those of us who had come to understand personality functioning in a very different way. When Trist joined us he conceptualized the selection task as, first, describing the basic features of the candidate's personality with all its uniqueness and, second, matching this picture of the man with the demands of the army. An underlying philosophy of this kind had been there from the start and, indeed, had been one of the reasons for the psychodynamic psychiatrists being recruited. When I went with Hargreaves and Rodger,[1] to discuss with the Adjutant-General, Sir Ronald Adam, and the General Officer in Charge of the Army in Scotland, General Sir Andrew Thorne, I had been deeply impressed by the wisdom and acuteness of their minds. They were fully alive to the complexities of appraising people. Sir Ronald Adam said we must not be daunted by the complexity of the job; it was of the greatest importance and if we were not in time to win the war, the work might help to win the peace. General Thorne emphasized that no methods must go after stereotypes and so deprive the army of its eccentrics. It was clear to both of these top-ranking generals that a great range of personalities could not only make valuable officers but was necessary for creative developments within such a multifarious institution as the army.

Trist's conceptualization of the task highlighted the problem of how to get data on what was basic in the officer. The technical side could go some way towards this goal through their interviews and psychological tests; the military members had more difficulty in getting data on which to make an opinion. It was here that Bion's genius showed up. I knew well that Bion had been wrestling hard from the start with this problem. Although he was a very private person, as Trist says, he kept remarking on the need to judge the 'quality of contact' the candidate had with others. With his reserved way of communicating his ideas, and the highly condensed, almost cryptic, way in which he spoke of them, it took me some time to get at what he was after. I had learned early on that his terse statements stemmed from a great deal of hard thinking. He wanted to get at a crucial quality which, as his later words put it, 'a man's capacity for maintaining personal relationships in a situation of strain that tempted him to disregard the interests of his fellows for the sake of his own'. There was no doubt that his experience as a combatant officer in World War I, under the greatest of stress at times, was now fusing with his psychotherapeutic understanding. The popular way of trying to get some evidence on this general question, what kind of man was the candidate, was to ask in interview what he would do in certain imaginary situations. Bion's solution was the Leaderless Group method. Before it acquired this name, he tried it out by asking small groups to have a discussion. At first he was alone with the group, then he invited us one at a time to join him as observers. I can recall vividly how stunned I was by the simplicity of the notion, and yet what a stroke of genius it was to create in this way a living manifest sample of personal relationships in a situation in which the conflict between self-interest and a concern for others was an active reality. This was the man in actual open relationships with others and not within the constriction of the formal interview or test situation. As Trist points out, it had the added merit of making a radical change in the mode of working for the whole team because everyone could now relate opinions from a basis of shared experience of the candidate in spontaneous interaction. From the discussion group, the method was quickly used with other situations, especially with practical tasks out of doors as the kind of setting with which the military staff was most familiar.

When the unit moved to near London to facilitate the training of staff for the many new Boards being set up, Bion was naturally hoping he would have more opportunities for training and developing the work. The blow he received (see Trist) when he saw how he was to be cramped by the administrative arrangements angered him intensely. He felt there was a 'sell-out' of the real importance of the development of the work by a special staff group in its own experimental unit. The staff who had been involved were now to be more like 'sales representatives' or Inspectors, visiting other Boards to help them to use the 'right technique'. This was intolerable to Bion, who had to have his own thinking rooted in constant interplay with practice.

It was very difficult to understand why it had all happened. There were, of course, all the factors of the kind Bion was alive to, the envy and fear of creative ideas, etc. At the same time one had to ask whether he had contributed to the situation? There was only one way in which he may have done so; namely, in his own uncompromising attitudes on issues of this kind and in a reluctance to expand on the implications of his ideas so that it was not easy for the administration to work out their implementation with him. This is a very difficult issue on which to pass judgment. If the 'establishment' of an institution, the term he was to adopt later in relation to the acceptance of new ideas, is not ready for innovation, then it crushes the disturbing source in one way or another.

Not infrequently one argument used is that the creative innovator cannot be trusted to be 'practical' about the changes or to deal effectively with the people who would be affected.

Bion may have been labelled in this way before the Research and Training Unit left Edinburgh because there had been a growing strain between him and the President there. The latter had begun to complicate his own role by behaving increasingly like an 'amateur psychiatrist' — the term used by the soldiers as a cautionary 'what not to do' in their own role — e.g. in wanting various 'experiments' tried out to which Bion objected on the grounds that they were using technical staff time in unprofitable work. His rather self-contained attitude may also have made the central administration feel uncertain of how he would operate if given full scope. Rees and Hargreaves had had Bion as a colleague in the pre-war Tavistock Clinic and may have thought from this experience he was not 'extroverted' enough to win the support of the wide range of senior officers the occupant of the senior post in the new unit would have to meet. He was certainly totally uninterested in, if not actively hostile to, playing politics. Such doubts, however, were an inadequate justification for thinking that he might not have been a realistic manager of a project with which he was so identified, and particularly in view of his previous record as a combatant officer. Perhaps if his thinking about all those aspects of groups related to power and the resistance to inno-vation had been more advanced, some of the sabotage meted out to his creative and courageous endeavours might have been obviated.

For Bion, there was a limit to compromise if the new ideas were to be given an adequate opportunity, and his extraordinary sensitivity to the unconscious negative forces around him had convinced him that nothing would mitigate them enough short of debasing his work, whose urgent importance at this stage in the war he appreciated with deep passion. In other situations he would have been tolerant of such resistance as he met. I am reminded, for instance, of meeting him once in a corri-dor of the Tavistock Clinic after the war when various members of staff were 'taking groups' ostensibly following his inspiration. We were outside the door of a room in which a great deal of laughter was to be heard from a therapeutic group. Sensing the superficial use of his work that could be made even by close colleagues, Bion remarked, 'Now that's a "good" group — not like mine!'

I had been close to Bion during the whole of 1942; then, for the next three years, my contacts with him were few. The loss of his first wife in 1944 after the birth of a daughter was a dreadful blow. One felt fate was now carrying on the cruel experiences he had had. When he got his work established after the war he acquired a small house in the country with a housekeeper to look after the child. Though not an ideal arrangement, it gave him some quietness to find himself again and soon his extraordinarily resilient creative urge could be seen.

My contact with him resumed with the end of the war when the 'Tavistock Group'[2] began to plan its future. Again I leave further reference to Eric Trist's paper, and suffice it to say here that Bion's deep commitment to pursue his understanding of human behaviour began to surface through his mourning. He asked me to join Rickman and himself in a trial 'study group' (as it would be described later) with a membership of ten drawn from senior management in industry and other organizations by A. K. Rice, who was then working for the Industrial Welfare Society. Here I experienced Bion in action with a group that had few inhibitions about expressing its feelings, mainly very sceptical, for many months. Rickman and I felt ourselves lagging behind Bion's comments, yet we could appreciate how much his thinking had been developing. In spite of the denial mechanisms in the group, the impact was profound; two members got duodenal ulcer symptoms before the group finished and three decided to have personal analysis subsequently!

These effects served to bring out the depths of Bion's sensitivity and the validity of his conception of the close relation between the physical and mental at the primitive levels prominent in the group. His role was a stressful one much of the time and Rickman and I were not sufficiently on his wavelength to take the pressure off. He referred frequently in the group to the striking splits and denials in the perception of what was happening, splits that he was relating in his mind to the earliest levels of development. It was in this group I first heard him comment on the irrational attitude to time so typical of the basic assumptions. The keenness of his sensitivity was all the more remarkable for a man still coming to terms with the loss of his wife and the absence of a normal home background. Thus while he habitually kept his painful feelings to himself, I well recall a very poignant occasion at this period when he was visiting my home. He said quite spontaneously, 'You think you are out of it; then there is a day when everything brings it all back and you re-live it all again.'

On leaving the army, Bion resumed his training as a psychoanalyst at the London Institute. He continued to work with groups in the Tavistock Clinic though he did not wish to continue as a staff member, especially as it was to become a unit within the National Health Service. He had every reason to be chary of bureaucratic control and he seemed to be eager to give priority to his psychoanalytic work, for he did not stay within the independent Tavistock Institute either. His personal circumstances fortunately took a very favourable turn soon after he completed his analytic training. In 1952 his marriage began a sustaining relationship that brought him deep happiness. Also, he acquired the support of a group of Kleinian colleagues who, if not all sharing his interest in groups, did respond with active co-operation in his working out of some of the primary developmental processes in the individual. His creativity was very much the product of his own struggles and a group of even the most desirable colleagues could impose a certain pressure upon him, especially when he sensed there was a wish to keep him as a leader with the obligations that entailed. At any rate, that was the gist of some of the very last remarks I had from him shortly before he left for California in 1968. It may have been one element, if only a minor one, in the many that led to his decision to leave England.

Before turning to his work on groups, I should like to comment on Bion's apparent departure from the group field. It has often been thought that he gave up his interest in groups for the study of the individual in the psychoanalytic situation. I do not believe there was any break for him. Many years later he talked about Freud's remark on the 'caesura of birth' — that there is much more continuity in development than the impressive act of birth would have us believe. The change was essentially the next step he felt his work required.

Bion's switch from the group back to the individual

As with Freud, Bion's dedication was to the human condition, as can be seen from the extent to which he was steeped in history and philosophy. What he observed in the group and within the psychoanalytic situation constituted a binocular vision of the same phenomena. The basic assumptions in the group crystallized for him replicas of the emotions with which the infant related to the mother and, later, the family. He emphasized that, while they provided a convenient way of ordering some of the phenomena in the groups, they were the product of complex fusions of emotions and ideas. That they derived from the earliest levels of psychological development he inferred from the strength and the quality of the emotions, along with the fact that the psychic and somatic expressions were closely interlocked. There was also the striking avoidance of any learning that they induced when they were dominant. The group revealed these primitive developmental phenomena with great clarity. Indeed, Bion stated that he knew of no situation in which the hatred of learning was more striking than in the group when in the grip of these basic emotions. Nevertheless, for the elucidation of the factors from which the basic assumptions were created, it was for him the microscopic vision of the intrapsychic that would be most productive. Accordingly, it was eminently understandable for him to transfer his attention to where these early phases of development could best be studied, namely in the psychoanalytic pair. This change of focus certainly coincided with an increasing absorption in the earliest stages of psychological development because of his own analysis with Melanie Klein. When he came to review his group papers about two years after he had written them there was such a marked linking of his previous views with Klein's theories that it was sometimes thought her work had influenced him too much. This opinion has to be assessed against a background of several considerations.

In the first place, Bion's decision to have Melanie Klein as his analyst was based on a considerable knowledge of her work. She had made a revolutionary impact on the psychoanalytic scene in London before the war and his first analyst, John Rickman,[3] had had a period of analysis with her, although he never became a 'Kleinian'. Her writings on the child's inner world of phantastic 'objects' (parents and parts of parents), both good and bad, its intense emotional idealizations as well as its ruthless destructiveness, and the psychotic or splitting mechanisms used from the start in coping with the associated anxieties and impulses, could certainly make a profound appeal to someone all too familiar with the human scene from his psychotherapeutic experience, his knowledge of history, an intense involvement as a combatant in the most destructive war man had ever known, and now confronted with group behaviour, whose severance from reality made it describable only in terms of psychotic disorder. The splitting processes she stressed as characteristic of the earliest relationships with the breast-mother, with their projections and introjections, certainly fitted the savagery of the human scene. She also illuminated the way in which primitive internalized objects were projected into parts of the body, which then became the source of tension and anxiety leading to hypochondria and psychosomatic disorder. In short, her experience of these early processes as revealed in the phantasy play and behavioural difficulties of very young children matched closely what Bion felt when in contact with the primitive processes in groups.

Alongside her penetration into the role of the instinctive drives in the development of the infant's object relations, Melanie Klein in her writings had described the effects of disturbed emotional development on the child's 'epistemophilic instinct', her term for the dynamic origins of intellectual growth in relation to reality. The earliest object-relations greatly affected the child's capacity to use symbols and so were crucial in facilitating the child's general intellectual development, its whole ability to learn from an enriching experience with reality. To Bion, it was the activation of these earliest emotions in the group that blocked learning and development. Klein had made her advances through the analysis of the play of young children whose phantasy life was vividly open to the interested student, as well as being much less overlaid with the experience of many years of ever-widening involvement with reality. In her first formulations, chiefly concerned with the factors causing inhibitions in intellectual growth, she did not elucidate the processes in the normal acquisition of knowledge. In her use of the term 'psychotic mechanisms', however, she stressed a mode of relating to reality which was dominated by universal processes belonging to the inner world. While these are modified in the course of ordinary interaction with reality, they persist openly in the schizophrenic as the result of various mis-matches between the strength of the instincts and the failure of appropriate responses to them by the mother and, later, the family. Moreover, this persistence of psychotic mechanisms was much more widespread than was realized. Indeed, they were for Klein the chief underlying factor in the neuroses and character disorders, although commonly missed in the analysis of these conditions because of the degree of covering-up to avoid the intense anxiety associated with them.

In short, Melanie Klein's theories had a high degree of validity and relevance for Bion apart from any undue influence she might have exerted through being his analyst. It is true that her own pioneering courage and single-mindedness, qualities that appealed to Bion, were reflected in her associates, in whom she fostered inevitably a proselytizing zeal. Those qualities are necessary if new ideas are to be spread and developed, though the obvious danger is that there may be too little scrutiny of them. Bion was much too powerful and independent a person and a thinker to take up ideas without a deep critical evaluation of their relevance in making order out of the confusing phenomena of the earliest levels of psychological development. His appraisal of her views was his own and based on his own data.

There is one aspect that is at least of historic interest. He told me on the last occasion I saw him, not long before he left England, that, during his analysis and subsequently, he had felt Mrs Klein to be out of sympathy with, if not actively hostile to, his work with groups. She thought he was being diverted from more important psychoanalytic work. He could scarcely have convinced her, of course, of its value as a field for the study of psychotic mechanisms, bearing in mind her complete lack of clinical involvement with group phenomena — and, indeed, her tendency to underplay the role of the social environment in her theorizing. At any rate, Bion was not deterred from writing his *Experiences in Groups*!

When Bion did turn to the early levels of development, he soon focused on those around learning from experience problems for which there was no adequate psychoanalytic theory. The hatred of learning when the basic assumptions were active had struck him as a major impediment to work activity in the group, and further progress with his group studies would be held up because of this lack.

The readiest means of studying the most primitive emotions was in those adults in whom they overwhelmed ordinary rational thought, viz. schizophrenics. Bion accordingly took into analysis a few patients whose degree of disturbance had led to them being certified as psychotic. As he said later, had he known more of what he was going to be in for he would probably have decided against this course. His own 'epistemophilic drive', along with his extraordinary capacity to retain a sharp and objective sensitivity to what these patients were experiencing, saw him through in face of all his lonely doubts.

II Bion's first statement

Bion's account of his experiences with groups falls into two parts. The first contains the description of his method of work, the phenomena he noted by its use and his tentative theories evolved to understand these. While he regards his views as an extension of Freud's, his whole thinking has a quite distinctive character. Like Freud, he refers frequently to very different entities by the word group, e.g. to organizations, or institutions such as the church and the army, and to such an ill-defined grouping as 'the aristocracy'. These social references introduce so many complex factors that they are best left aside from our immediate concern. The fundamental features of human relationships are embodied in all social groups so that there is no question of the relevance of his references. His theories, however, stem from his observations in his 'laboratory', the small group, and it is against the background of this 'pure culture' that we have to appraise them.

Taking the origin of the group as the carrying out of its purpose, we note that he refers to two groups, each with a different task as perceived by the members at the start. In one, composed of 'non-patients', the accepted aim was to study group behaviour. In the other, the members were patients seeking help from a medical clinic. The actual situation was that, after an interview, the psychiatrist explained to each patient thought suitable that an understanding of their conflicts in personal relationships could help in the amelioration of their symptoms, because these conflicts were known to be at the root of many of these difficulties. Such under-standing was facilitated by meeting in a group in which relationships could be studied as they developed. (Most of the psychiatrists involved had worked with Bion in some of his groups. There is thus a rather tongue-in-the-cheek disingenuousness in some of his remarks about the staff's beliefs! His serious point, however, is that the latter were not always subjected to the questioning that he himself felt they should receive.) It is not always clear at the start which of these two groups he is describing, although their stated tasks are different. To Bion, the use of his approach, i.e. one in which the sole activity of the leader or thera-pist is to make interpretations of the phenomena in the group as these developed, made any difference between the groups irrelevant. The different expectations of members in the opening phase, however, are reflected in the groups. In fact his main references are to the therapeutic groups in which a strictly group-centred stance is stressed.

We readily recognize that the development of his method was in itself a major achievement. With a remarkable courage from his convictions, he showed that a psychoanalytic approach permitted the exposure of unrecognized, irrational and powerful relationships that were specific to the group situation. Bion was explicit on the highly subjective nature of his method, especially in its use of counter-transference feelings and in the detection of projective identification processes wherein the therapist picks up the feelings of the members through what he senses they are projecting into him. As in psychoanalysis, the observer learns to attend to two levels of mental activity; the manifest conscious and the latent sub-conscious and unconscious. It is its subjectivity especially of this degree that arouses so much antipathy in those who consider that 'scientific' research into human relationships can rest only on behavioural data, albeit the ephemeral impingement of many studies of this latter type is in notable contrast with that of Bion's findings. That he had described something that illuminated the depths of group phenomena was clear from the remarkably rapid and widespread interest in his observations. There was little doubt that his work had made a profound stir in the new field of 'group dynamics'. Nearly four decades later it continues to be as evocative as it was at the start — and a short scan of the history of theoretical views in psychology and the social sciences during the century readily shows that to be a quite unusual distinction.

To sustain the efforts of any group around its task requires in the first place a readiness to co-operate, which, for Bion, is a sophisticated product from years of experience and training. Next, the mental activity required to further the task must be of a particular kind, because judgments about the nature and origin of actual phenomena and actions designed to overcome difficulties presented by them have to be tested against constant interaction with reality. In short, as opposed to any magical solutions, it must involve rational thinking with consequent learning and development, i.e. ego-activity. It is this capacity to sustain task-focused activity that the unorganized group greatly alters through the persistent interference from competing mental activities associated, in Bion's view, with powerful emotional drives. These conflicting forces at first seemed to have little in common except to oppose the task by creating a group that would satisfy the emotional needs of members as these become prominent. This state of the group Bion termed 'the group mentality', and the way in which it might express itself, e.g. to find another leader, he described as 'the group culture'. These concepts, however, he soon found did not clarify sufficiently what his further experience perceived, namely, patterns of behaviour that gripped the group into a relatively specific group mentality in opposition to the work activity. Bion named these patterns 'basic assumptions' (ba's), of which he identified ba D (dependence), ba F (fight/flight) and ba P (pairing). In the *dependent group*, the basic assumption is that one person is there to provide security by gratifying the group's longings through magic. After an initial period of relief, individuals tend to react against the assumption because of the infantile demandingness and greed it engenders. Nevertheless, when he confronted the group with the dependence assumption taking over, Bion noted that a hostile response to any intervention by him frequently revealed more than a resentment against his refusal to provide the magical pabulum. A longing for a more permanent and comprehensive support was to be seen in the raising of religious themes, with the group feeling that its 'religion', in which the therapist is a phantasied deity, was being taken from it. *Fight and flight* appeared as reactions to what the group wanted to avoid, namely, the work activity that forced it to confront the need to develop by giving up primitive magical ideas. The ineffectiveness of these solutions led at times to a different activity, for which Bion postulated the assumption of *pairing*. Pairing occurred repeatedly in his groups in the form of two members, irrespective of sex, getting into a discussion. To his surprise, this was listened to attentively, with no sign of the impatience from members whose own problems usually pressed them to seek the centre of attention for themselves. There seemed to be a shared unconscious phantasy that sex was the aim, with reproduction as a means of meeting a powerful need to preserve the group as a group.

As mentioned, the group dominated by an assumption evolves an appropriate culture to express it, e.g. the dependent group establishes a leader who is felt to be helpful in supplying what it wants. Moreover, the assumptions can be strong enough for members to be controlled by them to the extent of their thinking and behaviour becoming almost totally unrealistic in relation to the work task. The group is then for each member an undifferentiated whole into which he is pressed inexorably to conform and in which each has lost his independent individuality. The individual experiences this loss as disturbing, and so the group is in more or less constant change from the interaction of the basic assumptions, the group culture and the individual struggling to hold on to his individuality.

Basic assumptions originate within the individual as powerful emotions associated with a specific cluster of ideas which compel the individual to behave accordingly and also to be attracted to those imbued with the same feeling with an immediacy that struck Bion as more analogous to tropisms than to purposive behaviour. These bonds Bion termed 'valency' because of this chemical-like nature of the attraction.

As primal motivating forces, the basic assumptions supply a fundamental thrust to all activity, yet the drive towards interaction with the real environment remains the more powerful dynamic in the long run, for, without that adaptive urge, survival would not be possible. The difficulties of reality interactions, however, are great. The physical environment may present insoluble problems; but it is the social factors that become prominent in their effects on the capacities of the individual when work demands co-operation with all the give and take that entails. The frustrations in sustaining work activity are thus perpetually liable to induce the regressed behaviour of the assumptions. The more the individual becomes identified with a basic assumption, the more does he get a sense of security and vitality from his fusion with the group, along with the pull back to the shared illusory hopes of magical omnipotent achievement inherent in the phantasies of the assumption. From all these sources there is derived what Bion described as a hatred of learning, a profound resistance to staying in the struggle with the reality task until some action gives the experience of mastery of at least a part of it, i.e. until development of new inner resources occurs.

The appeal of each assumption rests in the associated emotion which gets a characteristic quality from the specific phantasies and ideas it involves. The assumptions do not conflict with each other. Instead, they change from one to another and conflict occurs only between them and the work group. When one ba is combined with work activity, however, the other ba's are suppressed. A further observation Bion made was the way in which the ba group could change to its 'dual'. Thus the dependent group under the frustrations of the leader's failure to gratify its longings could reverse roles so that the group treated the leader as the one in need of help. In this connection, he also noted the tendency of the dependent group when left to its own devices to choose as leader the most disturbed member, as if it could best depend on someone of its own kind, as dependent as itself – the familiar 'genius', madman, or fanatic.

The interrelations of the ba's, plus the tenacity and exclusiveness with which the emotions and ideas are bound together in each ba, led Bion to what he felt was a theoretical impasse which no available psychological explanation could illumine. He therefore postulated a metapsychological notion that transcends experience in the form of a proto-mental system in which the prototype of each ba exists 'as a whole in which no part can be separated from the rest'. The emotion in each individual that starts the ba progresses to the psychological manifestations that can be identified.

The physical and the mental are undifferentiated in the basic levels of this system, a feature which led to his suggestion that certain illnesses, e.g. those in which a substantial psychosomatic component has long been recognized, might well be diseases of certain conditions in groups. To test such ideas needed much larger populations than the small group could provide, but he hoped it might be done in order to establish the basic assumptions as clinical entities.

Bion's concluding observations become increasingly concerned with aspects of group dynamics in general, e.g. the oscillations in attitudes to the leader as leader of the assumption group or of the work group, or splits in the group, according as members wished to cling to either of these groups. On the relationship of the individual to the group, he agrees with Freud that a group instinct is not primitive and that much of his groupishness originates in his upbringing within the family. Bion adds to these, however, from his observations the view that, while the group adds nothing to the individual, certain aspects of individual psychology cannot be explained except by reference to the matrix of the group as the only situation that evokes them. The individual loses his distinctiveness when he is in a basic assumption group, i.e. one in which his individuality is swamped by the valencies in these. Such a group has to change when it has to deal with realities, or perish.

Earlier I noted that most of Bion's references were to his therapeutic groups and he states how he believes their aim is furthered. His first and most emphatic view is that any help the individual may get from the group situation towards understanding himself more fully rests on the extent to which he can recognize himself as one torn between the pull of the basic groups and his membership of the work group which represents his ego functioning. For this reason, any interventions from the therapist directed to the psychopathology of the individual must be avoided because they are destructive of the experience of the basic group. He concluded that, by adhering strictly to his standpoint, individuals do become less oppressed by basic group activity within themselves. In other words, what he asserts is that by showing the group the ways in which it avoids its task through regressing to dependency, fight/flight, or pairing, it can become more work oriented and so further the development by learning of all members.

Much of the subsequent criticism of Bion's approach as a psychotherapeutic method arises, I believe, from a failure to keep his aims clear and especially to avoid the confusion which the use of the word therapeutic, and especially psychotherapeutic, has engendered. To those seeking to use the group situation in a psychotherapeutic way, i.e. to cope with the enormous diversity of neurotic behaviour and its unique configuration in every individual, then work has to be based on our understanding of psychopathology. The group processes must therefore be directly relatable to the latter. Bion's approach in fact originated in the problem of neurosis as a social one, i.e. how does the large organization cope with the failures of its members to comply with its work task. The opening sentences in his book make plain that, for him, 'group therapy' can mean the therapy of individuals in groups, in which case neurosis is the problem of the individual, but in the treatment of the group it has to be a problem of the group.

His conception of 'group therapy' may then be put as follows. The individual contains within his innate endowment certain potential patterns which are released in the unorganized group. This unorganized group is not a special kind of group identifiable by its external features, but a state of mind that can overtake any group. Once elicited, these patterns or basic assumptions bond the individuals together to give security by preserving the group as a unity and by seeking a course of action for it governed largely by magical phantasies. These patterns remove the individual's distinctiveness, i.e. his overall modes of dealing with his purposes as fashioned by his learning from the experience of reality. Because these modes, his ego functioning in short, are always present in some measure, a conflict between his ego and absorption in any basic assumption behaviour is never absent. Such group-determined behaviour is a serious limitation to the individuals in any group when faced with an unfamiliar task, because they then tend to feel in an unorganized group state and so with their capacity to tackle that realistically as a group to have become quite unreliable. (The commonest remarks after intensive exposure to the unorganized group situation at Group Relations Conferences run on the Tavistock model are those describing feelings of being 'de-skilled'.) To have developed a method whereby these group dynamics can be experienced in adequate depth, and to have shown some of the requirements in the leader for the application of this method, is an extremely valuable contribution to the whole study of group dynamics. His findings can assist those responsible for groups coping with tasks to note when their effectiveness is impaired by ba behaviour, and this kind of experience features prominently in many management training schemes.

It is a quite separate issue, however, to appraise the value of the principles underlying Bion's work in relation to the use of groups for analytical psychotherapy. The distinction between the study of group dynamics and group therapy has become a clear one in the courses developed by A. K. Rice and his associates, as was seen, for instance, in the staff attitude to any individual who got into serious personal difficulties during a conference. The staff naturally arranged to get the help needed, but it would not confuse its own role by attempting to provide psychiatric or psychotherapeutic help, especially when psychiatrists or psychoanalysts were members of the staff. The strict use of Bion's approach has never in fact been widely adopted by analytical psychotherapists, not even in the Tavistock Clinic. Many have, however, made more systematic use of the group situation in their interpretations than have most other therapists, in the sense of trying to base these strictly on the here and now dynamics in the group situation as a whole.

Although we can agree on a separation of these two tasks, we are left with many unsolved questions that affect our understanding of both. To state that the individual's groupishness is an inherent property in his make-up as a social animal has not really carried forward our understanding of its nature and origin. Are the phenomena of the basic assumptions as specific to the group situation as he asserts? There is no question that, when activated by them, individuals can show a remarkable capacity to abandon their distinctiveness. The group gives a prominence to these responses by intensifying them, yet they do not appear to be different from the primitive relationships that can be seen in individual treatment, especially in the light of our further knowledge of the earliest stages of the development of the person.

One feature of Bion's thought that is unrecognized by him, I believe, is his underlying adherence to concepts of energy as in the classical psycho-analytic theories of Freud. Thus basic assumptions originate as emotions which are viewed as sources of energy, and Bion is then puzzled by the specific clusters of phantasies around them. Phantasies are of imagined relationships, and if we take emotions to be the affective colouring accompanying any relationship, then their specific quality is determined by the specifics of the relationships. The dependence and pairing assumptions are much more complex in this respect than the others. They can be readily seen as the prototypes of human relationships, e.g. as infantile dependence in which the self and the object are not differentiated, becoming the more differentiated clinging or attachment to a differentiated object in ba pairing. Fight and flight are the basic responses of all animals to the situation that evokes pain or the threat of danger. Bion seems to sense the problem of the individual and the group as needing a good deal of further clarification, and the choice he made for his next step was to turn his microscope, to use his own metaphor, back to the earliest stages of individual development. This move leads to a major amplification in his understanding of the dynamics of all groups.

III The re-view of the first statement

In his re-view of the dynamics of the group, Bion 'hopes to show that in his contact with the complexities of life in a group the adult resorts, in what may be a massive regression, to mechanisms described by Melanie Klein as typical of the earliest phases of mental life'. This task of 'establishing contact with the emotional life of the group . . . would appear to be as formidable to the adult as the relationship with the breast appears to be to the infant, and the failure to meet the demands of this task is revealed in his regression'. The two main features of this regression are, first, a belief that the group exists as an entity which is endowed with characteristics by each individual. Distinct individuals become lost and the group is treated as if it were another person. Second is the change within the individual that accompanies his regressed perception of the group. For this change Bion quotes Freud's description of the loss of the individual's distinctiveness, with the addition that the individual's struggle to retain it varies with the state of the group. Organization helps to maintain work-group activity, and indeed that is its aim.

In the work group, individuals remain individuals and co-operate, whereas in the basic assumption group they are swept spontaneously by the 'valency' of identification, the primitive gregarious quality in the personality, into the undifferentiated unity of the group in which inner realities overwhelm the relationship with the real task.

Although starting his re-view with the regression in groups as their most striking feature, he emphasizes again the fundamental dynamic of the work group, which also has its combination of emotions and ideas, especially the idea that development and the validity of learning by experience is the impetus in the individual to possess the autonomy of his own mental life. It is as if there was a recognition 'of the painful and often fatal consequences of having to act without an adequate grasp of reality'. Despite the dominant influence of the basic assumptions over it at times, work activity is what takes precedence eventually – as it must. Freud, following Le Bon, believed the intellectual ability of the group was reduced, but Bion disagrees. His experience is that, even when basic assumptions are active, the group shows high-level intellectual work in the assimilation of interpretations. Although this work goes on in a segregated part of the mind with little overt indication, its presence has to be assumed from the way in which interpretations, ostensibly ignored, are nevertheless worked upon between sessions with subsequent reports from individuals of how they had been thinking of them, though they meant nothing at the time they were made. It is only in activity of the work group that words are used normally, i.e. with their symbolic significance. The basic assumption groups, by contrast, he thinks, use language as a mode of action and are thereby deprived of the flexibility of thought that development requires.

When he re-looks at the basic assumptions, there is considerable amplification in what he now discerns as presenting them. This development is apparently related to his much greater familiarity with primitive mental processes and their detection by an increased responsiveness to projective identification as described by Melanie Klein. He believes this method, which requires a psychoanalytically trained observer, is the only one that can detect the important subjective processes. Conclusions based on its use have to be appraised by the effect of interventions and by the experience of many observers over time.

In the dependent group, he adds to the expectation of treatment from the therapist, a much more primitive phantasy of being literally fed by him. At a less primitive level he again stresses the presence of a projected deity who is clung to with tenacious possessiveness. The sexual phantasies which characterized the pairing group, with the possible implication of reproduction as preserving the group, are now taken to be the result of a degree of rationalization. Nevertheless, Oedipal sexual phantasies are present much of the time in all of the assumptions. They are not, however, of Freud's classical type, but of the much more primitive nature described by Klein. According to her, the phantasies of very young children show, as the self is emerging in relation to its objects, themes of the parents mutually incorporating parts of each other with the hungry sadistic urges that the child attributes to one or both figures by its identification with them. The child can then experience a psychotic or disintegrative degree of anxiety from the fear of being the object of retaliatory attacks and so it splits off the part of its self involved in the relationship with an attempt, then, to get rid of it by projective identification. These primitive Oedipal relationships according to Bion are distributed in various ways among (i) the individual; (ii) the group felt as one fragmented individual with (iii), a hidden figure, the leader, used here by detaching him from his role as leader of the work group. A further addition to the Oedipal figures, one ignored in the classical formulation, is the sphinx — a role carried by the therapist and the work group. The curiosity of the individual about the group and the therapist evokes the dread associated with the infant's phantasied intrusions to get at and to devour what is inside the mother and what goes on in the phantasied primal scene.

The anxieties inherent in the primitive phantasies, sexual and other, are instinctively responded to by an attempt to find 'allies', figures with whom the feeling of a close contact can bring reassurance. Bion accordingly suggests this need as a powerful stimulus to the creation of the pairing group. Another factor in its establishment and maintenance, also operative with no regard to the sex of the pair, is the feeling of hope, not a phantasy of a future event, but a 'feeling of hope itself'. This feeling he takes to be the opposite of all the strong negative feelings of hatred, destructiveness and despair and it is sustained by the idea of finding a saviour, a Messiah essentially, an idea that must never be realized.

The fight/flight groups are, as would be expected, much less associated with complex phantasied relationships, since they have the relatively simple aim of getting rid of the threat of danger when no other assumption or activity seems appropriate. On this group Bion makes, almost as an aside, what I find to be a remarkable statement: 'The fight/flight group expresses a sense of incapacity for understanding *and the love without which understanding cannot exist*' (my italics). 1 do not think its full implications are taken up by Bion in regard to the emergence of any of the assumptions and to the role of the leader, topics to which I shall return.

Recognition of their more specific contents leads Bion to reconsider the status of his notions about the basic assumptions. There was no doubt they were helpful in ordering the chaotic manifestations in the group, but, in view of the primitive phantasies related to them, they now appeared as derivatives of these more fundamental processes. All the assumptions drive the group to find a leader, yet none of them is felt to establish a satisfactory state in the group. There is consequently perpetual instability with changes from one assumption to another with all those remaining opposed to learning and development. For all these manifestations, and for their very existence, Bion could find no explanation. The exposure of primitive phantasies and the anxieties they induce now made it clear that the basic assumptions were derivatives whose function is to defend the group against these anxieties becoming too intense. As defences, however, they are all inadequate because of their segregation from any reality-testing. For Bion, the dynamics of the group could now be adequately experienced and understood, therefore, only by the working out of these primitive primal scene phantasies as the factors underlying the basic assumptions and their complex inter-relationships.

With these developments in his thinking, Bion has moved back to the nature of the individual and his groupishness. The new views brought him again closer to psychoanalysis and it is perhaps significant that their original publication was in *The International Journal of Psychoanalysis* and not *Human Relations* with its social science readership. They were, of course, sought out, but their crucial position as the culmination of his work on group dynamics did not become widely manifest until ten years later, when they appeared in his book. The time-lag did not affect those students of group dynamics in close contact with his thinking. It helped to perpetuate, I believe, the separation of psychoanalysis and group dynamics when both disciplines needed each other. The obstacles to a wider acceptance stemmed from more profound sources. At the time of their appearance, Kleinian views were resisted among psychoanalysts in general, especially in the United States, and this rejection was scarcely needed to reinforce amongst non-analysts what they were eminently prone to do by their disturbing unconscious resonances.

Bion always kept Freud's views on groups in mind, and so he now looked at where he stood in relation to these. Leaving aside the references both made to complex social organizations such as the church and the army, he re-asserts his agreement with Freud in rejecting the need to postulate a herd instinct. For him the individual is a group animal by nature, yet at war with the group and with those forces in him that determine his groupishness. The latter is in no way created by the group; it is merely activated and exposed by it. The impact of the group on the individual's distinctiveness springs from the state of mind in the group, i.e. the degree to which its lack of organization and structure fails to keep work activity, a contact with reality, the dominant activity. In the organized group the bond between members is one of co-operation, whereas in an unorganized state the bonds become the valencies of the basic assumption states. Bion sees McDougall's criteria for the organized group as the conditions that suppress the basic assumption trends in the members by keeping them related to reality. Freud's statement that the individual's emotions are intensified in the group while his intellectual functioning is lowered is not acceptable to Bion. For him the apparent intensification is the effect of tension due to the suppression of the basic assumption emotions. Bion's comment, however, hardly applies to Freud, since he is referring mainly to mobs in which the primitive instincts are released from normal controls.

The bonding from valency is a more primitive process than that from libido, which Bion takes to operate only in the pairing group. Freud's view of the bond to the leader as almost entirely an introjection of him by the ego (Bion does not mention Freud's ego-ideal as a separate structure) is again only part of the relationship to a leader. For Bion, Freud does not recognize the much more potentially dangerous bonding that arises in the assumption groups. Here the individual does not introject a leader who carries power for him through his contact with external reality. The leader in the basic assumption exhibits features that appeal to the assumption state in the members, who therefore projectively identify with him. This leader is thus as much a part of the assumption state as the members and just as divorced from external reality, so that he leads as often to disaster as not. Freud's view of the leader as the ego-ideal led him to see panic in military groups as following the loss of the leader. Bion thinks this account is not right, for panic arises when the situation might as readily give rise to rage as fear. Intense fight/flight behaviour may resemble panic, but for Bion the group can well be still related to the leader on such occasions. Panic occurs when a situation arises completely outwith the purposes of the group and its associated organization.

Bion thus adds to Freud's views rather than refuting them. Freud saw in the group the kind of relationships present in the family when the individual has developed to the stage of the traditional Oedipus complex, i.e. its emotional features were neurotic in character with the main sources of anxiety being the fears of loss of love or of being castrated. Bion saw them as deriving from much earlier phases in which the fears are of disintegration, i.e. loss of the self or madness. His belief that the only feasible therapeutic help in the group lies in the individual experiencing its primitive emotions and attitudes to him is again maintained. Here we are into debatable issues which I shall return to when the aims of therapy can be considered.

Much as Bion has contributed, we are left with what seem to be the crucial questions about groups unanswered. What does the individual's 'groupishness' rest on? We have Freud's libidinal bonds supplemented by valencies from primitive projective identifications with a great deal about 'mechanisms', all manifested as the individual's distinctiveness is removed. This regressed state, moreover, can come and go with a high degree of lability. For Bion, this distinctiveness is placed in opposition to the 'groupishness' conceived as the expression of emotions with which the individual has to be at war. Freud, on the other hand, sees the conflict as between the id and the culture of the individual's society internalized in his super-ego and ego-ideal. Adult or mature groupishness, if we might put it that way, rests for Bion on co-operation, the sophisticated product of years of training. That is to say, it is like an activity imposed on the freedom of the individual to be 'doing his own thing' and accepted more or less reluctantly. How can such an achievement vanish within a few minutes in the unorganized situation of Bion's groups? Both Freud and Bion from their psychoanalytic studies have emphasized that individual and group psychology constitute the same field of study. If we accept that position we are a long way from understanding it. The intimate inter-relatedness of the individual with his social field strongly suggests to us that we are dealing with the individual as a highly open system maintained in his organization by appropriate input from a social field itself structured to provide this input. The phenomena seem to require the organization concepts of open systems, which neither Freud nor Bion had.

Freud, however inadequate his theorising may have been constrained by the scientific climate of his day, is universally recognized as a brilliant observer. I propose therefore to look back to what he said to see what can be taken from his observations.

Having eliminated the need for any such notions as a social or herd instinct, Freud stated that a psychology of the group had to answer three questions:

(1) What is a group?

(2) How did it acquire the capacity for exercising such a decisive influence over the mental life of the individual?

(3) What is the nature of the mental changes which it forces upon the individual?

The latter is the one that is best studied first, and it is the one with which observers of group phenomena such as Freud and Bion are most concerned. Freud's data were largely the writings of Le Bon, McDougall and Trotter, which he related to his own knowledge and experience of social behaviour, especially from the phenomena of transference. Groups brought together for the specific task of direct psychoanalytic observation had not yet occurred.

The changes made by the group were described by Freud in two different ways. At first, apparently influenced by Le Bon's description of mobs, he sees individuals in the group released from the inhibitions of civilization, with the consequent emergence of the unbridled instincts. He recognizes, however, that the same conditions can activate intense effort and self-sacrifice for the group's ideals. In other words, the group can convert the individual into one identified with all its members in the regressed expression of the repressed, or with its opposite, the repressing structure of the super-ego although the latter can scarcely be regarded as regressed, at least in the sense used about the id. These changes do not fit well into any notion of a social instinct, or behavioural system, activated or inhibited by a social stimulus. They represent more of an organizational change in the personality from the normal degree of integrated functioning to one in which intense emotions are prominent and shared by the group and in which identification is a dominant mode of relating.

On how the changes are made, Freud rejects the concept of suggestibility as tautological and brings forward his libido theory, libido being his hypothetical instinctive energy that impels people into all the relationships commonly described as love. In using this theory, Freud has moved away from loose aggregates or mobs to highly-organized, lasting groups in which he points out that role of leader is paramount. Thus in the Christian church or in an army, each individual has a bond of love with the leader and consequently all have a bond of identification with each other, that of brothers within the leader's family. The leader, moreover, may be replaced by an idea or an ideal. This move to the group with a leader alters the description of the changes forced upon the individual to the following: 'the individual, outside the primitive group, possessed his own continuity, his self-consciousness, his traditions and customs, his own particular functions and position, and he kept apart from his rivals. Owing to his entry into an "unorganized" group he had lost this distinctiveness for a time' (Freud 1922). Freud uses these two examples to bring out differences in the relationship with the leader and the associated characteristic of the behaviour when the group disintegrates. In the military situation, the loss of the leader can release 'a gigantic and senseless fear' progressing to a panic, a reaction that cannot be interpreted as always due to the increase in external danger. The religious group, with a corresponding loss or threat to the leader or his ideals, does not produce fear. Instead a ruthless hostility is mobilized to those not sharing the group's ideals.

While the role of the leader is undoubtedly central, the nature of the libidinal bonds between him and the group remained for Freud rather mysterious. He was struck by their close affinities to hypnosis as a libidinal bond without conscious sexual trends to the powerful father, yet he also recognized the paralysed feeling of helplessness in the hypnotic bond as closely resembling the submission of the child to its parent. And beyond that, the 'extreme passion for authority in the group' seemed to bring in the archaic residues of the dreaded father in the primal horde. With the bond to the leader being of the same nature as that of an idealized object, Freud defines the primary group as one in which the leader is put by all in place of their ego-ideal. The leader thus embodies the group ideal and is inextricably mixed with the aims of the group, both as the one who defines the task and as the one who will lead the group towards its successful resolution. The psychological situation within each member of these groups, however, is different. The soldiers are dependent on the actual presence of the leader for the survival of the group. On his disappearance, each member becomes totally disorganized and disconnected from everyone; and though this state may be seen as the response of any individual to an inescapable external danger, Freud points out that it happens in this group only as a result of the loss of the bond with the leader. This bond consisted in the replacement of their ego-ideal by the leader and we cannot but conclude that the organization of what is bonded to the leader in this situation resembles that of the young child to its parents in the quality of the powerful dynamic nature of the dependence on omnipotent parents. Without their manifest presence when stress has reached a critical point, the disintegration feared by the child increases with the terror of isolation. The inner situation of the group members, in short, is here that of a structural replica of this dependence which is too immature for them to function autonomously once it is not maintained by the reinforcement of the real external support. The ego-ideal has thus an immature status as well as the ego.

The bonding in the religious group has a different content according to Freud. Here the members are not only related to the leader or the ideal through these replacing their ego-ideal, they are also identified with him. The personality organization that is here tied to the leader has a more developed character in that it has assimilated the ideals so that they have become a part of this organized self. Moreover, the presence of the ideal is felt to be a matter of life or death in that its preservation has to be fought for at all costs, whether by the group or by the individual alone. The individuals in these two groups, as well as having different bonds, are in different situations externally and internally. What we see in the soldiers is a response from a group in which their distinctive identity has already been systematically diminished so that in the situation Freud describes there is a predisposed state of immature dependence. Functioning is conditional upon the support of a highly personalized relationship with the leader. The religious group is promised great rewards for a course of conduct prescribed by the ideals and so enhances the individual's distinctiveness, albeit in conditional ways. Freud does not elaborate on the implications of his observations, yet he has made fundamental comments on the integration of the individual and its maintenance. He has shown that the individual keeps his distinctiveness by having built into the structure of his personality an imago of his parents, i.e. an internalized representation of his social relatedness. Moreover, this inner imago has an open interchangeable relationship with external figures or ideas. The groupishness of the individual is thus placed as a dynamic within him which has developed from an early phase of almost complete dependence to one less comprehensive. Though stressing the highly tentative and limited status of his study of groups, Freud has reached conclusions of great significance. He has made it clear that what happens in any group is a particular instance of the relationship between the individual's inner world and his social world. Thus he has answered his questions about the group by expanding an answer to the unstated question of what is an individual. He had to advance the theory of the ego and its relationships by showing that a sub-system within the ego, the ego-ideal, entered into relationships that differed in character from those of the ego. Moreover, the most striking feature from his conclusions is the open and rapid dynamic transactions that can occur in the group whereby the individual, sensing his own inability and that of the other members to act effectively, can promptly alter the boundary of his self to internalize the leader as a part of it and so to surrender his previous distinctiveness in favour of a less mature organization of his self. Viewed in terms of Freud's metapsychology, and the meta-science available to him, with the dynamics of the person based upon the re-distribution of psychic energies, the phenomena could not be adequately conceptualized. We are clearly confronted again with problems of the organization of the individual as a highly open system in an environment which reacts with him in a correspondingly open way. Individual and environment are structured by, and within, each other.

To account for the group phenomena, both Freud and Bion have gone back to the dynamic structuring of the individual. Both have left many questions unanswered. Freud pays little or no attention to the individual's relationship to the common purpose other than to bring in McDougall's requirements for the organized group as the way in which he best furthers his contribution. Bion sees the grip of the reality task for the work group, like Freud's soft voice of the intellect, not resting till it has gained a hearing. His basic assumptions take over from the effects of 'valency', likened to a tropism, yet establishing a group mentality which has a much more purposeful quality than would arise in any lemming-like way. Both, of course, had views of the individual conditioned by their times. Recent trends in psychoanalysis, while not providing an agreed account, do give a different perspective on the dynamics of the individual in his groups. Of crucial importance for our evaluation of Bion's views in regard to therapy is how the experience of the 'individual's groupishness' relates to the psychotherapeutic task for which *the therapist has suggested his joining the group*. For·this purpose, I give in the next section a very sketchy and brief outline of the nature of his groupishness and of how his psychopathology enters into the group situation.

IV Recent trends in psychoanalytic conceptions of the individual and his social relatedness

Clinical work and child-observation studies of the last few decades have shown that the personality acquires the capacity to make effective relations with others only when there has been early experience of being treated as a 'person' by the mother, and the father later, with stimulating encouraging interactions conveyed with joy. The satisfaction of physical needs has to be supplemented by a social input that meets the need 'to become a person'. There appears to be from an early stage an overall Gestalt that gives to the potential self a feeling of 'things being right or not'. Bodily sensations and the affects accompanying many specific behavioural systems all contribute to the affective tone in the self, yet a general malaise, even to the point of death, can follow from a failure in 'being personalized' by appropriate mothering. Child studies show the dramatic results under certain conditions of deprivation, e.g. when a consistent maternal relationship is absent (see Spitz 1965). Clinical findings from the more seriously distorted personalities emphasize lifelong feelings of never having been valued for themselves as with cold or indifferent mothers or, more frequently, with mothers experienced as imposing preconceptions that denied powerful urges to develop autonomously (see Lichtenstein 1977). The self-system is thus structured by the internalization of the relationship with mother and child, undifferentiated at the start then progressively separated throughout the long period of human dependence.

Early structuring of the personality is inevitably dominated by the physical closeness in which the mother's attitudes are communicated through innumerable signals in her whole handling of, and responses to, her child. The emotional experiences are gradually cohered by consistent reliable mothering into a 'primary or central self'. This integration is a labile process with threats to it producing at times intense anxiety and aggression. Negative feelings from the inevitable frustrations are separated from this primary self, but with ordinary care these divisions are diminished so that a sufficiently coherent, resilient self becomes the dominant mediator in relating to the environment. The primary self remains the visible self, the one adapted to the mother. Should the latter have failed to facilitate development sufficiently well, this primary self acquires distortions of its capacity to relate, and when negative experiences have been strong enough, substantial divisions within the structure of the self-system are formed. These sub-selves embody frustrated needs, especially for unmet recognition as a valued person, and the aggressive reactions to the frustrating mother linked with fears of her talion retaliation. The self-systems each retain a self-pole and an 'object'-pole, with an imago of the kind of parent desired or feared and hated. The primary self relates to the outer world and so learns from its expanding experience. The sub-selves, while remaining highly dynamic as portions of the original self, have to find covert outlets – the processes described in the whole of psychopathology – because their aims have to be hidden from the feared parental attacks.

Defences or control measures are evolved by the central self in keeping with its reality pressures and incorporated into its patterning. When the urges cannot be managed in this way then they constitute a secret self in conflict with the central one. Stabilizing factors such as family and work, or selected social groups, all assist in their control though the precarious balance shows when the functioning of the central reality-related self is altered as by drugs or by changes in the social environment. The central self ordinarily copes with changes in sections of the latter but removal of security-pinnings from it rapidly leads to the emergence of sub-system dominance.

When the imagos constituting the object-poles in the inner relationships are facilitative, then the impact of infantile sexuality is worked through without undue trouble. Marked divisions in the self make for serious difficulties because the new urges to closeness are dealt with in their terms, e.g. hostile imagos evoke anxieties about rejection and retaliation and so lead to the fusion of aggression and sexuality in sadistic and perverse expression in which the object becomes in varying measure de-personalized.

The essential change in this way of conceiving the person is from one based on theories of psychic energies to one dealing with the organization of experience of relationships in an open system interacting with the social environment. Because of the incomplete differentiation of self and object, relations in the primary self are characterized by identifications and urges to have omnipotent magical control with regressive clinging to objects for security against the threat of 'going to bits'. With growing appreciation of reality and differentiation of self and others, the primary self is progressively superseded by a strengthened definition of the self through satisfactions from talents and skills. Attachments to others changes to relationships based on shared activities. Goals and purposes become organized, and values add to the integration of the self. The personality acquires its characteristic configuration, i.e. its identity (see Erikson 1959), and in keeping with the uniquely evolved patterns from its specific experience, the individual requires constant affirmation from the social milieu. The constant need for this 'psycho-social metabolism' in maintaining a normal degree of effective integrated functioning is readily exposed when sections of the environment are removed, quite apart from any interference with the biologically rooted sexual and pro-creational needs. Populations displaced from their usual cultural setting show widespread indications of disorganization as in the rise of illnesses of all kinds, not only psychiatric. Again, when individuals lose a feeling of personal significance in their work, similar stress manifestations occur (see Trist and Bamforth 1951). These deprivations disorganize the most developed adaptive functioning of the social self leading to the increased dominance of the primary self with its insecurities and more primitive compulsive relations. Such regressive disorganization is almost universal. With individuals whose sub-systems are a constant threat, the loss of their usual sources of relative security confronts them with the extra dangers of their 'secret' selves being exposed.

The origin and nature of the individual's 'groupishness' is thus no problem. From the very start he cannot survive without his needs for social relatedness being met.

As happens so often, Freud makes a remarkable description of the individual in relation to the group. He notes McDougall's conditions for the organized group as (1) a continuity of existence; (2) the individual should know the nature, composition, functions and capacities of the group; (3) the group should interact with other groups partly similar and partly different in many respects; (4) it should possess traditions, customs and habits, and especially such as determine the relations amongst members; and (5) the group should have a definite structure, exposed in the specialization and differentiation of the functions of its constituents. As stated previously, Freud (1922) takes these as precisely the features that characterize the individual and which are removed by the unorganized group. In short, although he could not fit it into his theories, he apparently sensed that the group and the individual structure each other in the closest possible way.

There is no phase in the life-cycle in which man can live apart from his groups. Bion's statement that the individual is at war 'with himself for being a group animal and with those aspects of his personality that constitute his "groupishness"' therefore has to be examined.

V Group dynamics and group psychotherapy

Group dynamics

From the view of the individual I have sketched, the important questions about groups are those devoted to the conditions that take away the factors in the social environment that ordinarily keep his self-system in its normal integration. Bion stated that the basic assumptions are states of mind the individuals in the group get into. He then described these states and what seemed to constitute them. What he uncovered was the emergence of the primary mechanisms of relatedness, those of the developing infant to the breast/mother, and it is the intense anxieties associated with these mechanisms that drive the group into the assumptions. The individual's state of mind in them, however, remains a more developed organization than would pertain exclusively to their earliest phase. In the latter, differentiation of external objects hardly exists, whereas in the assumptions there are intense needs to relate to a leader and to each other. The phase in development that appears to be activated here is that of separation–individuation (Mahler 1975). As described earlier, this phase extends over several years, and a range in the depth of regression is to be expected. The dominant characteristic of this early self is its primal 'instinctive' type of relationship, the precursors of the maturer ones in which the external reality of others is appreciated. The more the developmental elaborations around the earliest structures are put out of action the more primitive the levels that are exposed. Ba dependence can be interpreted as the re-emergence of this stage in which the need for closeness gives to identifications a considerable urgency and immediacy; and the phantasy clusters around them represent the ways in which this is evoked, e.g. by being fed, or protected, or held in parental security. Fight/flight responses similarly show this level of identification to provide security. As Bion described, the urgency of the identifications can make the whole group an undifferentiated object within which the greatest security is to be found. Pairing is clearly a more developed state in which more precise definition of the self is sought in the relationship with one other. At the deepest levels it can activate the mother–child pair, in which case the attraction affirms the existence of the self. As he puts it, an ally against the dreads of isolation in face of mounting anxiety is then provided. The fact that the rest of the group preserves it by giving the pair their rapt attention suggests that for them it has become their security, either from the primitive relationship or by this combined with the parental sexual couple, by identifying with the pair.

Regression to these stages represents the removal of the influence of later structuring and an inability to recover it. The awareness of the group remains in its regressed form because the group is there and so restrains further disintegration which would be tantamount to psychotic states, an eventuality that the early structuring of the self also resists desperately. The problems of group dynamics thus become those of how the normal affirmations of the self system are removed. The situations of groups in this respect are of almost infinite variety. Thus when Bion said that certain illnesses might originate as diseases of the group, he thought specific illnesses might prove to be linked to specific states of the group. So far this has not been established, though there is much evidence now to show that disruptions of some areas of their normal relatedness, as in groups displaced from their familiar environment, lead to increased illness of all kinds, physical and psychological. In view of this complexity of factors, it is best for present purposes to consider Bion's groups only. Here the most prominent stem from the task. Although there may have been some nominal description such as 'to study group processes', none of the members has any clear notion of what that task involves. There is therefore immediately a considerable loss for the self of its ego anchorage in reality. Important also is the realization that the task, in whatever form it emerges, will involve members in some exposure of their private and even hidden self. This factor I believe to be important in the 'group dynamics' group, although much more so in the therapeutic one. Since the origin of the secret self was its unacceptability, there is a great deal of anxious suspicion among members, alleviated only as each member demonstrates his participation in the task by the freedom with which he expresses some of his feelings about the situation. Likewise the intense curiosity about the leader derives from wondering how he is going to help them with the task at its reality level and from the fears of what he will 'read into their minds' and how persecutory or rejecting he will then be.

What characterized Bion's method of work is his waiting for developments to occur spontaneously no matter what the pressures on him 'to help'. There is no doubt his stance exposed the regressed basic states with, at times, considerable intensity and persistence. For him it is imperative that members should experience the primitive nature and power of these states, and to have contact with these layers of his personality contributes a great self-integration in that the boundaries of his self understanding are thereby extended. By focusing exclusively on the group, however, it is only those features in the shared assumption states that are noted. Such recognition is essential, but to learn more about how they are brought into being is as important.

Freud had noted early in his experience how individuals will only with the greatest reluctance give up a source of gratification. The group's hatred of learning has this quality for Bion when he confronts them with clinging to assumption behaviour instead of learning to cope with reality. In emphasizing this reaction we have, however, to balance it with the impetus to develop, the impetus which in the work group Bion notes as eventually overcoming the irrational resistances to it. We may then ask if Bion fosters an exaggerated degree of basic assumption behaviour by not giving help sooner. This is a question not easily answered. I referred earlier to his almost incidental remark on love as a necessity for understanding, i.e. in this context, some fostering assistance. Bion was an extremely caring person and so one is left wondering whether he was in part fascinated by the assumption behaviour to the neglect of this aspect of how much help from the leader the egos of the members required to be re-asserted for the learning task.

The assumptions made about the leader's role is that the group will by itself progressively learn to tackle the reality of the task through the leader pointing out what it is doing. Since, however, much of the overt behaviour is determined by the need to avoid unrecognized feelings, these must require more explicit interpretation than Bion gives. Interpretations would seem to need more of 'a because' clause – an attempt to identify what it is that is feared. Without this 'help' the work group cannot function effectively. A group met to study its dynamics is like any other task group, a socio-technical system and here, as elsewhere, the technical job has to come into the sphere of the ego's resources for mastering and using it. The specific complexity of this situation is that undoing the 'depersonalizing' of the members because of their lost ego-involvement is itself the aim of the 'technology'. A degree of understanding does go on much of the time, but it has to be asked whether it is at optimal proportions; especially when once in the grip of the basic assumptions it is all the more difficult to get back to normal ego-functioning. It thus seems that, as in analytical psychotherapy, a simultaneous relationship with the members' egos and the regressed state has to be kept alive.

When Bion referred to the struggle of the individual against his groupishness, we can put this in another way. The groupishness he describes is clearly that of the regressed separation–individuation stage from which the individual has developed to inhabit his adult distinctive identity. This new development, however, has its own needs for group relatedness, namely, in groups in which his identity is affirmed and enriched by the extent of the ego's reality involvement in them.

The situation created in Bion's groups takes away the anchorage of the adult self-identity and it has to be asked then whether the groupishness that is resented is so because of this loss. The self-identity requires identification by others of its ordinary status plus the engagement with the task in a meaningful way. The organization of the group has to match the nature of the work, and if the latter presents a puzzle the group does not see how to cope with, then the leader has the task of both dealing with the tendency of the group members to regress as well as enabling them to see that their belief that they have no resources is not entirely founded in reality. The experience of the latter, i.e. of regaining ego-function, brings back the work capacity.

Group psychotherapy

As Bion mentions at the start of his book, this term is itself ambiguous as to whether it means therapy of the group conceived as an entity and so concerned with facilitating the group to overcome barriers from its internal conflicts to its effectiveness as a work group or whether its purpose is therapy of the individuals comprising it. In practice, the latter purpose would be more accurately described as analytical psychotherapy in groups.

When Bion says that his method of work cannot be called psychoanalysis he means that the fundamental principles of psychoanalysis do not apply to it. There is here a source of widespread differences of view even amongst analysts. Both the classical and Kleinian analysts believe that a comprehensive exploration of unconscious processes is possible only in the traditional setting with the analyst preserving a somewhat distant stance in the interests of objectivity, maintaining a certain intensity in the conduct of the process, usually five times per week, and avoiding any other activity than the analytic one, e.g. no reassurances of any kind nor advice and only offering understanding of the unconscious solely by interpretation. The value of this approach is not in question. What is, however, is the common assumption that other less intensive and rigorous approaches are relatively poor substitutes and, in short, 'not analysis'. Analytical psychotherapy on a less intensive pattern than the standard psychoanalytical one has in recent years altered this view considerably to the extent that it is widely practised by analysts themselves with the conviction that it can be of considerable help for the individual. Many unconscious factors in the personality can be exposed and their disturbing effects ameliorated in a range of patient–therapist settings. The critical factors are not so much the latter as the therapist's understanding of the unconscious and the extent to which he focuses on that.

The general aims of analytical psychotherapy are the same as those of psychoanalysis, namely, to bring into consciousness the unconscious relationships structured from early experience and then segregated within the self with varying degrees of emotional distancing from awareness because they are not permitted by the opposing parental imagos reinforced frequently by further rejection by the ego. The work of treatment is to bring out in the transference relationship with the therapist both the forbidden aims and the defences against them. Because these conflicts are structured into divisions within the self from very early phases, the personality as a whole is damaged by them. Their roots cannot be extirpated or exorcised. We do not talk of cure but of achieving degrees of freedom for the person by lessening their power in relation to the central self. All psychotherapy, therefore, from intensive analysis over years to much less intensive and shorter-term treatments is ameliorative to varying extents. There is at present no accepted means of appraising the functioning of a personality in a comprehensive objective way, such as would be comparable with the assessment of the physical state of the person that the doctor makes by his examination of the main bodily systems. Careful interviewing can give some assessment of change, but even here the particular bias in any judge of what is important in the person limits the status of the findings. The important point about these familiar comments is that beliefs about what is and is not adequate therapy have to be evaluated by broad considerations.

The psychotherapeutic factor in Bion's method — again to be recalled as directed towards group dynamics — can be considered if we take one of his examples, the events in a group occasioned by a woman talking about a fear of choking in restaurants or, on a recent occasion, of her embarrassment during a meal in the presence of an attractive woman (Bion 1961: 182). About half of the group responded by saying they did not feel like that, and the others were indifferent. Bion notes that in analysis such a statement would have evoked various possible interpretations, none of which he felt could be regarded as appropriate to the group. What he did point out to the members was that the woman's difficulty was also theirs, although in repudiating it they made themselves superior to her. Moreover, in doing so they made it difficult for any member to admit any problem because they would then be made to feel more inferior and worthless. From an analytic point of view he appreciates that the woman got no help and is left in discomfort because in fact group treatment is the wrong treatment. He then adds that her manner of speaking suggested that she felt there was a single object, the group, that had been split into pieces (the individual members) by her eating and that being the recipient of the members' projective identifications was her fault and so reinforced her guilt which, in turn, made it difficult for her to grasp how the actions of the others had affected her. For the other members, they have not only rid themselves of the woman's troubles as part of their own, but they have also got rid of any responsibility for her by splitting off their caring parts into the therapist. The result of this process is akin to a 'loss of individual distinctiveness' through the basic assumption state of dependence. The group dynamics are clear; the psychotherapeutic effect is not only nil, it is negative.

The question then is why Bion could not have made an interpretation along the lines he indicated in this reflection about the situation, at least to the extent of conveying the woman's hunger (perhaps felt as greed), destructive to the group, with the latter attacking her, as they did to these feelings in themselves. Also, by treating each other's problems in this way they were perpetuating the feeling there was no help to be had from the group, only from the therapist. The precise interpretation is not so important as long as enough of the underlying dynamics of the total situation are articulated. By focusing exclusively on the group as a whole, certain awareness of group attitudes is made possible. Has that been as helpful as it might have been for the development of each individual? Kleinian analysts frequently use the term 'the correct interpretation'. It is doubtful if such an achievement is ever possible, especially in the group situation, so that a degree of metaphoric latitude helps to catch some of the wide range of processes going on in each individual. Psychotherapeutic change is a developmental process requiring considerable time, and Bion mentioned, as evidence of intellectual work going on in spite of its covert nature, the fact that patients came back to his comments in later sessions. In other words, reflection on what is happening in the group with delayed assimilation is a necessary part of the individual's 'work' activity. The therapist's task, I believe, is to further this by giving each individual as much awareness of all sides of his responses in the group situation, including especially the apparent reasons for abandoning his 'distinctiveness' when faced with his intolerance towards his own unconscious processes. In my own experience with groups over thirty years, I have never ceased to be impressed by the importance that members attach to their group meetings, even though only once per week. It is common after only a few months for them to remark that what goes on in the session plays a prominent part in how they feel for the rest of that week. By commenting along the lines I believe Bion could have done in the light of what he described, he would have avoided in some measure in at least some of the members the depressing feelings of the badness of the group as almost inevitable.

In regard to pairing, he again warns against concentrating on the possible unconscious contents of the pair interaction. Here too, however, it is not at all difficult to comment on the group's interest in this interaction and in what this interest might consist. I have heard reports frequently in groups that certain sessions with marked pairing on which interpretive comments were made, were recalled vividly for long periods as having been particularly helpful.

Bion likened the problem of the individual coming to terms with the emotional life of the group as closely akin to that of the infant in its first relationship, viz. with the breast-mother. In his later analytic work he spelled out the nature of the infant's task in overcoming frustration, i.e. when instead of the expected breast there was a 'no breast' situation. For this achievement he took the mother's role as a 'container' to be crucial. This is perhaps an inadequate term for the active contribution of the mother in making her comforting and 'encouraging' presence felt. It could readily be said that, for the group therapist, Bion advocates a role of considerable withholding.

The importance of Bion's strictures can be granted and that the essential aspect in all these issues is whether or not enough of the total dynamics in the group are being brought to notice when an individual is being referred to. Basic assumption behaviour occurs in groups, whether the task is explicitly therapy or not. But when the aim is therapy, the individuals need to understand much more of themselves than the tendency to regress to the primal self of their separation–individuation stage of development. I have stressed that the paramount consideration is much more our understanding than using an assumed correct technique. Understanding the unconscious is notoriously subject to individual bias. Increasingly over recent years my 'bias' has been a much greater focus on the state of the self that underlies the particular expression of the unconscious motives. Thus, to revert to the example just quoted, one can ask whether Bion's reluctance to use the individual in the group situation is influenced by the Kleinian view of greed as stemming from a high degree of oral sadism. I want to emphasize at once that Melanie Klein is far from ignoring object relationships, yet she retained the view that aggressive phantasies were mainly the product of the death instinct. If one takes the view that the most profound aggression arises from the universally desperate struggle to maintain the self — a view that Freud took, as I mentioned earlier — then the greed of the patient might well be seen as a primitive expression of her attempt to get possession of the object she needs to maintain a security in her self. In this case the social relevance of her symptoms, and hence its importance for the group is different from that were her greed to be taken as a problem of excessive oral sadism.

The need to cope with anxieties over the self can be seen in another of the examples he quotes (Bion 1961: 144). The members discuss a suggestion to use Christian names — three are for it as a good idea that would make things more friendly. Of the other three, one doesn't want her name to be known because she dislikes it, another suggests pseudonyms and the third keeps out of it. I do not want to make unjustified use of the example, especially as Bion mentions only certain aspects of the episode to make his point. What he takes up is the way the group seems to regard friendliness or pleasant emotions in the group as a means of cure, as a contribution to their work group. Perhaps more immediately relevant to the work group is the anxieties about whether or not the self of the three dissidents will be secure if it begins to be looked at by the others.

The disadvantages of groups as a therapeutic medium are well known. They do, however, have several advantages. The sharing of humiliations, shame and guilt is a different experience for many when they receive sympathetic understanding from other members. Also, whereas the projective identification of self-objects from the segregated sytems has to be done mainly one at a time with the therapeutic pair, the projection of several around members of the group is active much of the time and its recognition can be used by all.

The individual in psychotherapy has to learn about his split-off relationships, his wishes, from maternal love for the infantile self that felt deprived to the full repertoire of sadistic coercion to get power, gratification or revenge, and all his anxieties and despair about these inner situations. This task can become a life-long one for every individual. Therapy, as in other learning, has to give enough capacity to carry on the work. Psychotherapy in groups has to make much more of a contribution to this capacity than can be done through confining attention solely to the group dynamics equated with the basic assumptions.

Bion, like so many creative thinkers, confined his study of the work of others to relatively few. Perhaps he felt, as Winnicott once said to me, 'I did not pay close attention to Fairbairn as I was too absorbed in my own pregnancies at the time.' I never heard Bion discuss Foulkes, and I do not think he knew much about his work because he had left groups by the time Foulkes was publishing his accounts of it. He was not given to disparaging the work of others if it differed from his own; for him, experience would eventually find its survival value. Foulkes was convinced the total group interactions had to be used in therapy, and I believe that Bion, had he done more group therapeutic work, would have accepted that position though he would have insisted on what might be loosely put as more rigour and more depth, more attention to the primitive relationships.

None of Bion's Tavistock colleagues engaged in group therapy, in contrast with those concerned with group dynamics, adhered to his view about the sole use of the latter in their work. Ezriel's formulation (1950) of using a common tension in the group once it could be identified as coming from the wish for a specific relationship with the therapist, and adding to its exposure by showing how each individual dealt with it, was considered to be more appropriate. Revisiting both led me to conclude that Ezriel's views could not account for the group dynamics in general, and I believe our understanding of the individual should be such as to account for both. It has seemed to me for some years that a theory of the organization of the self is the emerging task for psychoanalysis and so I used my own rather rough and ready gropings in this direction. Analytic group psychotherapy has usually been considered by its users as a valuable therapeutic medium in spite of the negative findings of Malan and his colleagues (Malan 1976). Perhaps we expose here the inadequacies in our concepts of the nature of psychotherapy as well as our means of assessing change. Because of my interest in the self as an independent variable in the therapeutic task, Gill and I (1970) carried out an exploratory trial using spontaneous sentences as an indication of conflicts within the self system. Significant changes in patients after eighteen months of treatment were found, so Malan's criteria seem to have referred to different processes.

When Dr Pines asked me to contribute to this volume I had thought a brief personal memoir of Bion and his creation of the Leaderless Group method would be appropriate. Eric Trist's paper, with its splendidly detailed and accurate recall of so much that I had forgotten of those times when the three of us had worked together, ended my rather modest project. For me Bion has always been the *preux chevalier* making his doughty forays into the confused tangles of psychoanalytic thought and the complexities of human relationships. His power to look at phenomena with fresh challenges remains a permanent questioning legacy. I started out by referring to Fairbairn as one of the first analysts to seek a conceptual basis for psychoanalysis that freed it from the shackles of nineteenth-century science. Fairbairn and Bion met on several occasions in Edinburgh, though in the circumstances of war with little chance of much sharing of work. It was a strange chance for so much creativity in psychoanalysis to be germinating in that city, so remote from Vienna and London and, in spite of its brilliant intellectual traditions, with a climate of opinion at that time not a little hostile to the new understanding of man that was being furthered in psychoanalysis. It is perhaps even stranger that the contributions of each can be seen now as needing that of the other and each, with its tough theoretical work, drawing its inspiration from the intuitive genius of Melanie Klein.

Notes

1 The former from the Tavistock staff, and now the major innovative mind in the War Office psychiatric group under Brigadier J. R. Rees, and Rodger, a socially oriented psychiatrist with whom I had worked in Glasgow and now the psychiatrist to the Army Command in Scotland.
2 The term applied to those members of the pre-war Tavistock Clinic Staff who had been most involved in the development of the psychiatric services in the army along with a few recruits to the group who had no previous connection with the Tavistock, mainly Trist, Bowlby and myself.
3 Rickman had a keen interest in field theoretical concepts in his understanding of the individual. He had been in a Quaker ambulance unit in Russia in the latter part of World War I, where, although a non-combatant, he had been on the point of being shot after the Revolution started. They were both large impressive men who shared many attitudes and views, although I doubt that he was a major creative influence on Bion's thought; he was more a kindred soul. He had a more maternal component in his personality than Bion which often made me think of him as the father of all mother, and Bion as the mother of all father figures. He published many psychoanalytic papers and collaborated with Geoffrey Gorer, the well-known anthropologist, in writing a book *The Peoples of Great Russia.*

References

Bion, W. R. (1961), *Experiences in Groups*, London, Tavistock.
Erikson, E. H. (1959), *Identity and the Life Cycle*, New York and London, Norton.
Ezriel, H. (1950), 'A psycho-analytic approach to group treatment', *Brit. J. Med. Psychol.*, 23: 59–74.
Freud, S. (1922), *Group Psychology*, Standard Ed., vol. 18, London, Hogarth.
Hartmann, H. (1964), *Essays on Ego Psychology*, New York, Int. Univ. Press.
Jantsch, E. and Waddington, C. H., (eds) (1976), *Evolution and Consciousness*, Reading, Mass., Addison-Wesley.
Lichtenstein, H. (1977), *The Dilemma of Human Identity*, New York, Aronson.
Mahler, M. S. *et al.* (1975), *The Psychological Birth of the Child*, New York, Basic Books.
Malan, D. (1976), 'A follow-up study of group psychotherapy', *Arch. Gen. Psychiatry*, 33: 1303.
Spitz, R. A. (1965), *The First Year of Life*, New York, Int. Univ. Press.
Sutherland, J. D. and Gill, H. S. (1970), *Language and Psychodynamic Appraisal*, London, Karnac Books.

Trist, E. L. and Bamforth, K. W. (1951), 'Some social and psychological consequences of the longwall method of coal-getting', *Hum. Relat.*, 4: 3-38.
Winnicott, D. W. (1958), *Collected Papers*, London, Tavistock.

Chapter 3
Northfield revisited

Harold Bridger

(*A review of Wilfred Bion's unique experiment at Northfield Military Hospital; some antecedents, implications and successors.*)

> ... how any given man was reconciling his personal ambitions, hopes and fears with the requirements exacted by the group for its success.
> ... the basic principle of all the Leaderless Group Tests.[1]

> If we do not learn from history we shall be doomed to repeat it — George Santayana

Introduction

To the many who find it difficult to understand Wilfred Bion's writings because of their 'condensed' character I would strongly recommend two of his lesser-known communications. The first,[1] from which the above quotation is taken, is a short succinct article in which he compares the essential features of his contribution to the use of group methods in the selection of officers with those of his approach in dealing with the Rehabilitation Wing of a large psychiatric hospital during World War II. Not a word or a sentence is wasted and it is a brilliant example of communicating the symbiotic relationship of concept and experience — something of the quality which Bion admired so much in the poets.[2] At some point prior to his leaving for the USA, he remarked that he had included all his writing in book form and I reminded him that he had omitted this article. He did not immediately recall it and I sent him a copy.

A similar quality of communication occurs in the spontaneity and directness of his responses in the much later interview with Anthony G. Banet Jr.[3] He does not actually 'discuss' anything with the interviewer

87

even when there is a clear or implied invitation to 'fall in with' or argue against a certain statement or point of view. Bion states what he thinks and where *he* is on the matter — leaving the interviewer with his 'own work' to do. In this meeting, too, Bion's comments are more forthcoming and 'of a piece' than those deriving from the larger public meetings in which he responded to a wide range of issues, frequently with little connection between them. The reader has a fine opportunity to follow Bion's thinking through and then discover where he himself stands.

In this interview it is clearly apparent that Bion's approach to his professional work, whether related to groups or to individuals, was quite consistent with the values he held in other aspects of his life and relationships. Especially was this true for those of us who were privileged to know him as a friend and colleague 'heretic',[3] both during World War II and after it. He always endeavoured to be his 'own man' and did not look for followers or disciples. He distances himself from the interviewer when such inferences are offered and clearly shows that this is not his idea of commitment to a common cause.

It is to be regretted, however, that in certain 'schools' of group therapy and many forms of group relations work in Europe and in the USA there is a tendency to 'reproduce' Bion's style and even his theories as if they constituted *the technique* to use. He demonstrated his own determination not to be captured in the literal or metaphoric sense[4] and was always at pains to distinguish between commitment to a common cause and building political or tactical groupings. He was never at ease in any of the professional bodies and other institutions where these latter tendencies were far from infrequent. Nor did he attempt to sway others to his point of view even when their professional or institutional antagonism was likely to be detrimental to his own endeavours — as will be shown later in this article. For him, it was the individual's responsibility to find his own way towards that commitment to the common cause.[5] The group work of a real-life situation, combined with the insights which might be gained in exploring the intra-group tensions arising in pursuit of tasks and goals, were the essentials he looked for. He did not seek to 'capture' reluctant recruits to his cause but expected to gain colleagues who recognized and respected his efforts even if they differed strongly from what he was attempting. Yet it must be said that Bion made few concessions and I do not recall him ever 'bargaining' or negotiating.

For a worth-while cause, however, he would do his utmost. When, in the early 1960s, the Tavistock Institute was beset with bitter internal splits, Wilfred and Francesca Bion were two of the very very few people who took any step — not to heal — but to provide a basis for re-exploration.

We are all aware of the difference between sharing an experience with a colleague who is recounting what happened in his first session with an individual or group, and one who is endeavouring to communicate what happened in his n th. The earlier the situation under discussion the better we can share and, even though the data are less, we can anticipate, speculate, build options and predict together more readily. In addition, it is, in my experience, frequently evident that all the data were actually embodied or implicit in the earliest session if only those present, including the consultant, had the means of identifying or reaching it. Of course, we also know that this is part of the work to be done, and that time, facilitating steps and working through are common features in education, therapy and development generally.

The series of inter-related early experiences which will be the subject of this contribution took place, however, between thirty-five and forty years ago. My opening comments may yet remain true, and besides a kind of 'archaeological' interest, the sequence of creative developments which led to the design of the first therapeutic community experiment will be traced. Although seldom acknowledged, the basic design remains the model for the many applications in many countries and cultures. At the core of the work was the study of a group's 'internal tensions in a real-life situation'.[6]

Out of this personal, historic description some key principles and dimensions will be drawn which affect the purpose and functions of therapeutic communities and institutions when considered as part of, and interacting with, the wider society. I will also try to distinguish such principles and dimensions from those which govern a community or institution endeavouring to operate as a relatively 'closed system', i.e. one regarded 'as sufficiently independent to allow most of its problems to be analysed with reference to its internal structure and without reference to its external environment'.[7] In effect, I am distinguishing the more limited therapeutic community, based on established firm boundaries between it and its environments, from one conceived and developed as an open system.

The experience to be revisited was, as far as I am aware, the first attempt at actually creating a therapeutic community as an open system by intention and not just by accident, and came to be known as the 'second Northfield experiment'. Wilfred Bion's was the first. Both were conducted during World War II and developed as an integral part of the army's medical operations. I shall be reviewing both endeavours, their antecedents and implications, however, with the insights, knowledge and experience of the years which have followed that beginning. The Northfield experiments have also been chosen because the opportunities provided at that time were unique and the lessons have not really been exploited to anything like their real potential.

The country-at-war emphasized an environment which, at one level, could not be denied by the professional staff and patients of a hospital. Yet returning people to health in that hospital setting posed quite considerable problems and difficult decisions for both staff and patients. All were military personnel with the professional staff in various therapeutic roles. The paradoxical issues were not dealt with explicitly but appeared in various stressful and rationalized forms, such as when decisions were made concerning the return of men to the armed forces or to civilian life. Correspondingly, it was important to consider how far the professional staff member's own purpose, values and approach to treatment was affected by that environment and by organizational aims and functions. In the community and organizational life of today those choices, problems and decisions may not appear so sharply, but they are just as real and critical. In fact, the personal and organizational issues are even more fundamentally difficult today than in 1939-45. Dilemmas of values and standards, environmental uncertainties, overall complexity and increasing interdependence are always besetting our thinking, planning, decisions and actions. In a word, the environment today can be acknowledged just as well as a war climate — but much more easily denied.

The War Office Selection Boards for officers

At the outbreak of World War II I was head of a Mathematics Department in an English school, but not long after taking up my military command I was sent, with others of the same and allied disciplines, to learn about the secret weapon called radar. I mention this because on return to our various units, we were soon faced with the effects this new technology was to have on our organizations in terms of structure, manpower, methods of working and patterns of leadership. Of course, we did not speak in such terms at that time, but with all the brilliant clarity of hindsight it is now possible to connect such developments with the corresponding initiative which was taken in devising new methods for selecting officers, i.e. for leaders who could take responsibility for more complex combinations of manpower and technical development. My interest and attempts at reorganizing my Battery to meet the demands of technology led me to be seconded (for mixed reasons, I suspect!) to a very active research and development body exploring leadership for new forms of organizational life. This was the War Office Selection Boards, comprising many of the professional staff from the Tavistock Clinic and others who later conceived and set up the Tavistock Institute of Human Relations.

Increasingly throughout the war, the quality of demand on leadership was of a very different order from that required in World War I with its near-Crimean philosophy of 'theirs not to reason why . . . ' The new Officer Selection Board, through its three- or four-day series of experiences, was much more than a test of stamina and of the virtues of personal courage and authority. Through a wide variety of group tasks, for the large majority of which no nominated individual was appointed to the overall leadership role, candidates were observed coping with the normal tension system in working groups: i.e. needing to co-operate for the achievement of the group purpose or goal, yet competing with others to demonstrate both a distinct personal identity and a competence for leadership.

This method was originally, and inappropriately, called the Leaderless Group approach.[8] I say inappropriately because, while no one was actually appointed to the role, the group tasks were specifically designed so that opportunities could be taken for functional leadership to be displayed by group members. Selection under such conditions entailed .observing candidates' readiness to take responsibility for thinking, decision-making and actions; to show ability and devote effort in gaining commitment from others; to earn the right for trust in one's judgment, and to be accountable for committed outcomes, etc. It was as much a training and developmental opportunity as it was a selection one. In identifying those who might best lead in such a series of changing situations there was also an increasing importance on interdependence and communication; on taking into account technological and complex considerations; on balancing shorter-term benefits against longer-term hazards. In effect, new dimensions were required beyond the traditional qualities of courage and inspiring confidence in members of one's team, and beyond the readiness to lead one's men out of the trenches against enemy targets.

The Officer Selection Boards are not the subject of my paper. It was, however, their design, operational success, further research and evaluation, and application to so many later endeavours, that contributed some basic concepts and practices to a therapeutic community which was itself to go far beyond just providing a haven for recuperation, occupational activity for skills, regaining individual confidence or even a facilitating climate for individual therapy. Real-life situations, i.e. community and task-oriented groups involving self-management and self-study, were to be developed as a basic feature of organizational and community life.

The elucidation of the dynamics of groups facing tasks which demand realistic appreciation of internal resources and leadership needs in a rich diversity of situations owed much to the original theoretical and design contributions of Rickman and Bion, whose work is well known.[9] The developmental and experiential extensions of their ideas by Sutherland,[10] Hargreaves, Trist and Morris, and further original ones of their own, created a network organization of planned Boards and the systematic dissemination of procedures, staff training, selection criteria and methodology. Bowlby's follow-up field evaluation of the Officer Selection Board outcome is a classic of its kind, and Morris's[11] later evaluation, after the war, of performance and results not only showed the great strides forward achieved in selection but essentially identified and demonstrated many of the critical features in community and organizational life which make for the development of responsibility, maturity, commitment and leadership in individuals and groups.

The US was quick to see the tremendous social and technical step forward taken by the British army at a time of crisis. The group approach as well as other features were applied successfully for selection in their OSS and other spheres of work. More recently, even, the notion of Assessment Centres also owes its origin to the Officer Selection Boards.

As experience grew, further innovative programmes and techniques were developed for different fields of activity and professions. For example:

- The application to other public services, such as the Fire Service, Palestine Police (at the time of the Mandate), were early derivatives.
- The selection and development of young people who would be capable of undertaking a university course to be followed by military or naval commission, opened up a new approach to vocational and career guidance and, after the war, Sutherland and Bridger designed the first application to graduate selection for industry and commerce.[12]
- Probably the best-known application was the development of the Civil Service Selection Board for the Administrative Grades of the Civil Service. This was designed towards the end of the war and, with modifications, continues today.

The central point I wish to make about all these applications and many more besides is that because of the attention to the dynamics of individual and group development involved, and universality of the original concepts, there was what one might call an organismic diffusion to many other aspects of life — not just for wartime activities but for society generally. The opportunity had arrived for designing the introduction of change processes and methods to meet the needs and/or aspirations towards change on the part of the community or institution concerned. We were, however, at that time, only dimly aware in practice of what it meant to begin such processes in situations where the need might be perceived from some external source but not from within; where the readiness to face the implications of such changes, and the form of pain and anxiety incurred, might be accepted intellectually but not politically or emotionally; where the attitude to power and authority within and outside could determine the manipulation of forces to produce and effect a form of change or defeat such a purpose; and above all, where their introduction would expose differing personal, professional and social values among the different functions and specialisms involved.

Again, with hindsight, the great accident in the development of these endeavours, bearing in mind the inherent resistance to such ideas even in an army at war was, predominantly, having two remarkable men in the key positions at the same time; one in the critical executive role and the other in the critical functional role. Without this 'accident', little might have been achieved by the people who are so well known today — despite their brilliance and, in some instances, near-genius. The first, the late Sir Ronald Adam, was the Adjutant-General of the British army throughout the war. This is not the place to speak of him at length but, although not mentioned with more than a passing comment by all the generals rushing into print, his contribution was greater than most. He it was who had the foresight, sense of strategy and breadth of vision to encourage and maintain these developments. The other, the late Ronald Hargreaves, was a rare psychiatrist with intuitive and administrative and political sensibility who initiated, supported and nurtured key projects until they got off the ground. Only when we look closely into things do we realize that we neglect

(a) the appropriate kind of sanction, and

(b) the implications of an open-system approach

at our peril. I shall return to these points in reviewing Bion's experiment.

In considering the various potential observations of the normal group's tension system for identifying and comparing an individual's behaviour, attitude and competence in relation to various kinds of relevant group tasks, an increasing awareness of the forces operating within a task-oriented group became apparent. Without elaborating on the theories which Bion[13] explores in his book *Experiences in Groups*, I would particularly mention here his original emphasis on the way the group develops a life of its own in the course of achieving the tasks it sets out to do. Values and norms develop, partly as a result of those introduced by individual group members and partly as a consequence of their modification and adaptation during the course of working together on tasks. At any one time, therefore, the group may be operating 'as if' it is endeavouring to fulfil its tasks while actually, consciously or unconsciously, behaving on quite a different basic assumption. For example, disagreements within or seeking a scapegoat outside might, on occasion, be less concerned with the current reality than with avoiding responsibility for seeing the task through. Since the individual's relationship to the task-oriented group was defined as 'reconciling his personal ambitions, hopes and fears with the demands made by the group for its success', it can be seen that the wish to make use of the 'as if' group is not infrequently sought. Each of us, in fact, has developed his or her own preference or predilection for a particular basic assumption in coping with group demands which do not suit our more intra-personal needs.

Wilfred Bion's Northfield experiment

While Bion and Rickman were developing their ideas with their colleagues at the War Office Selection Boards, and exploring their implications for therapy and training, some serious problems were affecting military psychiatric hospitals dealing with breakdowns in battle and in Units. It was being discovered that the automatic withdrawal of psychiatric casualties back to base and then to hospital seemed to be associated with a growing high proportion of patients being returned to civilian life. It was as if 'getting one's ticket', as it was called, had replaced one of the objectives of hospital treatment, which was to enable healthy officers, NCOs and men to return to the army. Even at one of the largest hospitals, Northfield Hospital (800 beds) near Birmingham, where the military medical staff who had been appointed to head wards and develop their own treatment methods were highly qualified psychoanalysts and psychiatrists, the Rehabilitation Unit to which patients were transferred for review before leaving for the army or 'Civvy Street', seemed to have no better statistics than the rest.

Wilfred Bion was appointed to the command of the Rehabilitation Unit at Northfield to develop his own approaches to the problem, based on the learning and experience gained in WOSBs. He undertook a double role as Officer Commanding that Unit, and as psychiatrist helping his men face the working-through of issues following their treatment and make decisions about their future — including that of returning to military duties or to civilian life. Returning to the army might, of course, contain various possibilities, including changes of role, unit and conditions of work. Inevitably either course entailed confronting not only the conscious and unconscious attitudes and desires of individuals, but the values and norms which had been established in the Rehabilitation Unit and hospital over time. It is clear from many accounts that the notorious indiscipline, slackness and untidiness of the Unit of which Bion took command was one form of showing him, and the Review Panel, how unsuitable it was for returning any of its members to the army! T. F. Main, in the First Annual Lecture founded in memory of S. H. Foulkes,[14] gives a lively description and goes into some detail on Bion's approach to his Unit. He omits, however, one key factor in the situation which leads him to ascribe Bion's departure ('sacking') after only six weeks of work with his Unit to the inability of the Commanding Officer of the hospital and his professional and administrative staff[15] to tolerate the early weeks of chaos which accompanied the self-management and functional leadership responsibilities demanded of the Unit by someone who, as the men were trying to insist, should have taken over those responsibilities himself. Main was only partially correct. Bion was essentially facing his Unit and the hospital professional staff with the task and responsibility for distinguishing between their existence and purpose as a military organization, and their individual inferences (in the majority of cases) that health entailed a return to civilian life. In addition, more fundamental issues were at stake, as I hope to show later.

The degree of success Bion achieved in that six weeks amply demonstrates not only the validity of the principles he and Rickman had evolved but says even more for the 'double' professional approach he had employed. He was in uniform, an officer in the organization (i.e. the army) confronting his men with the state of their Unit and morale; he was also a professional psychiatrist consulting with these same men in assessing their health and direction of choice during a time of the nation at war.

Two of the critical lessons to be derived from his 'sacking', however, which I was later to define when succeeding Bion to the command of

the Rehabilitation Unit at Northfield and making my own analysis of
the situation, were:

(a) That while he had established his own professional and technical
approach to the situation and the Unit, he had not sufficiently appraised the effect it would have in its contrast with the psychiatric
and organizational approaches of all the other psychiatrists and administrators (including the Commanding Officer) in the hospital. In
my personal discussions with him between the time of his leaving
and my appointment, it became clear that Bion's philosophy, value
system, technical and organizational appreciations were poles apart
from those of others such as Foulkes and Bierer, who were operating
under quite different principles and values. This was not to say that
it was Bion versus the rest. There were differences between the
others' approaches too, but, in general, they were consistent in
their aims of fulfilling the expectations, resources and future life
needs of the individual regardless of hospital, army or war needs. I
can well remember the expressive comments with which both
Rickman and Bion voiced their total disagreement. It was encap-
sulated in an experience which they had had when given the
opportunity of observing Foulkes in a first group session. Foulkes
had opened that session by saying, 'I want you to look on me as
you would the doctor in a white coat and not as someone in
uniform.' In addition, Foulkes at that time utilized the group
approach more as a way by which the work with any one individual
could be observed and reflected on by the others. It was a setting
rather than having a dynamic life of its own in the Bion/Rickman
sense.[16] Later, after my appointment, I was able to enlist Foulkes's
collaboration in working with actual *activity* groups – and then the
strength and persistence of the forces operating towards the attainment, distortion or avoidance of group goals demonstrated their
relevance to him. But I shall be referring to this development later.

Referring back, however, to Bion's quite distinctive approach in
conceptual form and in professional/technical practice, it is no
wonder that a high degree of rivalry and even less desirable emotions
were fuelling the hospital climate at that time.

In effect, therefore, the introduction of change processes requires
a search for common understanding of both purpose and methods.
While only a few of the likely consequences of any such change might
be predictable, it is important to engage in exploring the implications
of any steps envisaged even if the outcome is unknown. It is equally
important to set up the equivalent of a forum or 'mini-scientific

society' in which a collegiate climate can be established in exploring common problems and different ways of approaching them and resolving them. It is necessary to have that opportunity of adapting to change under conditions and in circumstances which are 'good enough' (to use Winnicott's term) to effect the transition.

(b) That while Bion was fully aware, both in his organizational role and in his professional one, of the central importance of the country-at-war as a critical environmental force which had implications for the internal worlds and defences of his men, he neglected – and was indeed somewhat disparaging of – the more immediate environments of the hospital and traditional reactions of the bureaucratic aspects of the military machine.

The Commanding Officer at that time was, by profession, a psychoanalyst who perceived his task as maintaining co-operation between the professional and administrative functions in the hospital. Bion, in contrast, really demanded that the external organization, as the environment of his Unit, should stand and tolerate the forces and pressures which his efforts and ideas might release in the struggle with his Unit and with the hospital mission he was endeavouring to fulfil. He expected people to see for themselves that what was happening was, in essence, a microcosm of the tasks and problems facing military hospitals as a whole. As a Major commanding tanks in World War I and a psychiatrist in World War II, Bion showed his own range of capabilities. He could also, however, expect too much of his wider environments. In addition, he did not recognize, or perhaps not accept, that it was equally his business and part of his task to take these environments into account, just as much as he had taken the army and the country-at-war so very seriously. In passing, and without taking one iota from his great insights and creative work, I believe that Bion was not at ease with the group as an open system, i.e. he was not at home with what I have referred to as 'the implications of ecological change in groups, institutions and communities'.[17] In this respect Foulkes and Bierer were even less concerned – it was not their philosophies or compass.[18]

While all three, and others at Northfield and since, showed high regard for the immediate environment of the individual, they differed, depending on their values and perceptions of the therapeutic task, in the way they used that environment of the group, and in the expectations and demands they expressed in the context of the wider environments. Rickman, on the other hand, had a much greater anthropological sense in his awareness of societal forces and perception of group tensions. He has never really had the credit he merited for communicating and working collegially and unsparingly with others in these developments. He wrote little, but his 'coffee-pot' sessions to those of my generation who were fortunate enough to take part in them were unforgettable experiences.

The second Northfield experiment: the 'therapeutic community'

1 *Orientation*

So far as I am aware, the term 'therapeutic community' was first coined in connection with this second experiment which I initiated over the period 1944–5. Over the course of time an increasingly large number of people contributed to its development, not least the transient population of officers, NCOs and men who learned to take responsibility over time for their own return to health, and in so doing, found that *the process* of creating and developing the community was a critical constructive ally for the various disciplines and resources available to them.

Following Bion's departure from Northfield, Ronald Hargreaves had approached me and discussed the possibility of my taking over the role of commanding the Rehabilitation Unit. It was recognized that I am not a psychiatrist or a psychologist but had held a command, was an educationalist and teacher by profession, and had extensive experience of the various approaches developed at the Selection Boards. I had been seconded originally to understand more of the group and organizational processes and, although it was not remotely like the field command from which I had come, here was the chance to test out the ideas and experience I had gained in an organization with a very different mission! In one sense, I welcomed the opportunity and challenge; in another sense I was quietly terrified, since I had no idea of what a mental hospital was like and felt, as in all such changes, as if I had been suddenly de-skilled.

My actual posting was to take place only when the last Commanding Officer had been replaced by a medical C.O., professionally a pathologist, but with regular army command experience. For those who do not know the culture of the army, it is important to note that when trouble in any form arises in a Unit involving transfer of the central figure in the 'storm', it is almost invariably accompanied by the transfer of the accountable officer or NCO concerned. I remember thinking that the hospital staff — whoever they were — might also be wondering what was likely to happen when a regular officer and a field officer were replacing the psychiatric specialists who had occupied these roles before — and what kind of a bargain they had let themselves in for. As I discovered later, they had certainly expected a 'law and order' campaign!

In the meantime, I was to be given the chance of acclimatizing myself by visiting a selected number of other military psychiatric hospitals, by the opportunity to meet and talk with a variety of people who I felt might be able to help my orientation — and not least, by a copy of the book on the 'Peckham Experiment'.[19] This last made fascinating reading, since it described the development of an *unintentional* therapeutic community which had grown in Peckham, south London, following the attempt by biologists, physiologists and others to monitor over a long time a number of factors and elements in members of all those local families who were prepared to volunteer for these regular tests. Originally a swimming-pool was the main 'draw' and one could join only if the family unit did so. In the course of the 1930s the community development exceeded expectations and created what has been referred to previously as 'a life of its own', while fulfilling its part of the bargain in relation to the tests. I was struck, in this account, by the emphasis on

(a) working with those who are prepared to work with you — and not just attempting to use some established form of sampling technique; and at the same time

(b) using the swimming-pool, consciously or unconsciously, as a focus for the district families who accepted. These families and the development process they set up represented the *community as a whole at any one time.*

My discussion with Bion encouraged me to build on my own capabilities and experience and certainly not to attempt a follow-on of his experiment in the restricted area of the Rehabilitation Wing. I decided to work *in some dynamic form* with the *institution as a whole*, while also being prepared to consult and collaborate with those parts of the organization which showed a readiness for responsibility in attempting to achieve the health of an enterprise however small, or to create some entity which could grow.

In the teaching of mathematics, that frequently unpopular subject, I had always searched for growing-points on which to build and had innovated various kinds of institution which could both draw on real-life interests and yet have mathematical thinking inherent in them: e.g. a school Stock Exchange. Similarly in my Battery Command we had overcome the difficulty of getting men to read and digest Battery Orders by publishing them, accompanied by 'Battery Disorders'. The latter were a set of cartoons prepared by a talented corporal, but they could not be appreciated without reading the Orders first. Only later did I come to learn how these transitional systems linked up with Winnicott's work in psychoanalytic theory and treatment.

Of the many other experiences which contributed to my orientation I would like to compare two – which, in turn, also influenced the strategy and practice I eventually formulated. The first, Mill Hill Hospital, seemed to me a large hive housing a conglomerate of every type of treatment, physical (which seemed all too popular), psychotherapeutic (Ezriel) and psycho-socio-therapeutic (Maxwell Jones). In his own small empire, Eysenck was developing approaches and methods about which he has long since published in various forms. Maxwell Jones's work at that time was the most interesting in what I considered to be a large 'therapy-market place'. In general the patients seemed incidental. In Maxwell Jones's ward everyone was taking part and shared in the various therapeutic tasks – but it was what I have referred to as a relatively closed system and centred on Maxwell Jones himself. I was later to reflect on and compare his approach to that of Joshua Bierer, who also used a dependency closed-system relationship in his ward at Northfield as the setting for his therapeutic work with individuals and with groups. After the war, of course, Maxwell Jones had much more scope to develop hospital-wide activities of which he has written fully.[20] It is only sad that in private he has frequently acknowledged his debt for the ideas and dynamics he drew from Northfield I and Northfield II but has not, to my knowledge, done so publicly in his many books.

The second hospital, Dumfries in Scotland, was not as large but it seemed more like the well-managed workshop or depot. Although not the C.O., the person at the centre of things was Major Elizabeth Rosenberg, later better known as Elizabeth Zetzel, the psychoanalyst. She encouraged activities in every form, and specially those which patients could run themselves with the help of central resources – a hospital newspaper, for example.

There was, however, a certain guiding control over the range of activities. In addition, it was noticeable that care was taken to encourage what one might call the 'recovering' patient to draw the newer ones into the various groups – when they were ready for it. This experience certainly reinforced my choice of the 'hospital-as-a-whole' approach as an essential component in the work to come. Bion had certainly tackled both his 'Unit as a whole' and his consultations with individuals or groups when they were ready to do so. I decided to adopt what I called the 'double-task' approach, but with one task located with the hospital as an institution and with the other task at the level of those parts which showed leadership in developing some relevant creative work. This leadership had also time to include a readiness to perceive, reflect on and review the way that group or part was working.

2 *Entry and joint planning*

I reported to the C.O. of Northfield with some trepidation, wondering whether some of the half-formulated ideas would ever take root, let alone bear fruit. Tom Main, in his account,[21] writes that we arrived about the same time. Actually he arrived quite some time later to replace the two divisional psychiatrists Emmanual Miller and Alfred Torrie, who had already given me every support in getting the design started. The new C.O. and I had, together, to settle down, to meet the professional staff of the different disciplines and learn about the hospital as a whole. Foulkes and others generously and constantly invited me to observe their group sessions; I had discussions with nurses, social workers, administrators, occupational therapists and indeed every section of staff in the hospital, including building and maintenance engineers. Learning about the various systems, and the roles of those who operated them in whatever form or level, certainly allowed me to appreciate the prevailing and distinctive conflicting cultures. Obviously I could not know at this early stage how they all hung together, but it was important even to experience the confusion of a newcomer and gain some sense of what the whole place was about. I learned, for example, that while devolution to wards in almost every respect had its advantages, the atmosphere of 'live and let live', of some wards being more privileged than others in different ways, of undercurrents and 'politics' within and between the various functions of professional and administrative staff and so on, left much to be desired. A further extended discussion with Ronald Hargreaves, the Commanding Officer, Torrie and Miller led to agreement to the proposals I outlined earlier. One part of the double-task role would, however, be quite different from that which Bion had occupied. I would take command of the Rehabilitation Unit but also undertake a functional role for the 'hospital-as-a-whole'. A psychiatrist who was just about to leave, Martin James, had held responsibility for the distribution of all the recreational material sent out to wards for the activity and skill sections with their respective staff, NCO craftsmen or artists in charge, and for any external development from which it was felt patients might benefit. I suggested that my functional role in the 'hospital-as-a-whole-institution' would be that of Social Therapist to distinguish it from my Unit command role and that I would be responsible in that capacity for Martin James's activities. The respective offices for myself and the staffs associated with each of those two roles would also be distinct and separate in the hospital.[22] In particular I proposed a drastic reformulation in the hospital layout. Influenced by the Peckham Experiment and recognizing the 'socio-psychological gap' in ward, professional and administrative relationships, I suggested, without necessarily reducing the number of beds, that the ward in the very centre of the hospital be cleared and named 'The Hospital Club'![23] It would start as a 'gap' with no furniture, equipment – or rules. A meeting of representatives from each ward to explain the move and to suggest that they discuss equipment and organizing methods was to be the only other positive action regarding the Club itself. My Social Therapy office was, however, close by, and so were the offices of my staff related to that role. I explained that I wished to create some identifiable equivalent of the 'hospital-as-a-whole-with-its-mission' and this would be represented by, for example:

- Staff seminars to explore and discuss what was intended and what the implications were likely to be.
- Independent professional discussions according to the particular discipline or function – e.g. psychiatrists, nurses, and so on.
- Ward meetings when requested for exploring the implications of external effects and the impact of internal stresses in the wider environment.
- The Hospital Club, with its deliberate emptiness but allocated space for potential development, also represented the patient's own personality and social gaps within his 'life space'.
- Greater emphasis to be placed on all activity supervisors on changing the pattern of relationships with patients to one of watching for initiatives on *their* part and responding to them. Previously the effort had been more in the direction of teaching skills and well-meant instruction-centred methods.

After very full discussion and when the various steps were agreed, the series of staff discussions were begun and gradually, over a period, the empty Hospital Club made its presence felt. It took a little while for the representatives' meeting to be arranged — not because of finding appropriate people within the wards, but because everyone knew, among other inter-ward considerations, that one of the main matters for discussion would be what each ward might contribute from their 'recreational armoury'! Already, however, in the intervening period between the official opening and the date of the meeting, talk and feelings were beginning to flow within and between the wards. The various staffs ranged in their attitudes from the highly sceptical to the equally highly interested members.

The first Hospital Club meeting was hardly an electric affair. All waited for me to organize the whole thing, including the meeting. There was no appointed or elected chairman and I refused to act as one. It was as though the meeting had suddenly become vaguely aware of an earlier comment of Bion's that 'it was first essential to find out what was the ailment afflicting the community, as opposed to the individuals composing it, and next to give the community a common aim.' And again, 'the apparatus of the psychiatric hospital, huge buildings, doctors, nurses and the rest, together provide a magnificent smoke screen into which therapists and patients alike disappear when it becomes evident that someone may want to know what social function is being fulfilled, in the economy of a nation-at-war, by this aggregate of individuals.'[24]

The weeks that followed brought more 'sight-seeing parties' to the Club and a series of enquiries to the Social Therapist and his staff:

'When is it going to start?'

'When are the games equipment and furniture going to arrive?'

The replies were equally succinct:

'When any of you want it to happen.'

'They are already here, but they are on your wards.'

During this period, staff were encouraged to arrange for any patient on their wards to come for discussion about the kinds of things he might want to try out either for leisure, interest or work. The allocation to activities to keep someone occupied or for like reasons was stopped, and patients were encouraged to find early curiosities of what it would be like to do this or that, and to revive earlier 'passions' which had been pushed aside. Patients were encouraged to help each other in this respect and it was not long before we were asked to help a group activity, e.g. a band. The Austin Motor Company (now British Leyland) was sited almost across the road — and the wish of many to try themselves out there had to be negotiated with unions as well as management.

Nothing happened at once or symmetrically. Growth was horticultural and the activity patterns across the hospital were much more tree-like,

with branches in all directions, than representing any tidy, ordered cur-
riculum or programme. Even when an eventual richness of societal
endeavours became established, perhaps then to fall into decline, to be
abandoned or wrecked and then rebuilt, depending on the population
and the different needs or states of illness, there was never any time or
chance to say 'Now we have arrived!' In that sense the therapeutic
community as an institution became far healthier than many businesses/
organizations. The individuals comprising the former might be sick,
mad or bad; those of the latter might be sane and physically healthy,
but institutions are not the same as the sum of the individuals comprising
them — and we were continually learning and relearning this at Northfield. A much fuller and detailed account is contained in the *Menninger
Clinic Bulletin* (10, no. 3, May 1946), attempting, inadequately, to give
a review of the community's state only eight months after its beginning.

Returning to the Club, the cumulative awakening of interest eventually led, not to a meeting of ward representatives to reach some business-
like arrangement mutually agreed, but to a protest meeting which I was
summoned to attend. The protest, with full and prepared arguments,
was to ask why we were wasting public money and space in wartime —
money and space that could be put to so many good uses! I agreed, and
suggested that we work out what could best be done with it and how,
since it was ours to do with as we wished. And we certainly could use it
for the war effort quite directly.

Without giving a blow-by-blow account it is difficult to convey the
tremendous energy and directive ability which can be generated when it
is possible to find the transitional setting/experience through which the
insights of therapy, derived from their treatment, could be allied with
social purpose and satisfaction in identifying with institutional forms,
infra-structure and activities. By the same token, of course, in such a
society the growing Club and its facilities (which eventually won the
day against other proposals) was equally frequently damaged, despoiled
and even smashed up on occasion. Perhaps one of the most critical and
probably the most important boundaries crossed in the development of
the therapeutic community was when the apparently inevitable ebb and
flow of social change led, more positively, towards serious patient-
community efforts in those 'recovering'. A critical step forward was
made when they began to share responsibility for those entering the
Admission Ward and to care, in the earlier phases, for those who might
benefit from empathy and the experience of those who 'had been
through it' themselves. The growth and development of the newspaper
'Mercury', the external schools' repair teams and many others not only

facilitated the interaction between outer society and inner struggles towards health, but were themselves 'workshops' for self-review for the forces and emotions affecting the life and work of the groups.

I have said little so far about the hospital professional and administrative staff groups, but they too developed many different directions of interest and enquiry. For example, the nurses, in particular, explored over a long period the nature of their role in such a therapeutic community. Previously, they would all have been able to work according to the principles governing hospitals accepting patients with physical illnesses despite the fact that there was only one medical ward as such in the place. Now, there emerged the problem of discovering the role of the nurse in the therapeutic community institution where only a few patients were in the ward all day – let alone in bed! Their patients were out in Birmingham schools (learning as well as doing), repairing toys at a department store stand to develop cash for charity or hospital activities, in the car factory opposite the hospital, in the Club, etc., and in many additional types of treatment sessions with psychiatrists. There was only one way – for the nurse to learn more and to be with her patients in a different role, and where *they* were. Above all, the force-field of therapeutic functions could be more clearly seen to have changed. The therapeutic task now involved far greater inter-disciplinary practice of all kinds. The Admission Ward became a joint patient/staff project; skill and creative activities became media for therapy in groups at work; hospital and environmental endeavours involved collaboration between professional therapeutic staff and social practitioners from a variety of functions. A few months earlier, the boundaries between them had been distinct and their tasks regarded as separate. And, in turn, the greater the orientation of the hospital to the core mission, the more ready the Rehabilitation Unit was to face its own purposes and decisions of its members.

When Tom Main arrived, the psychiatric scene developed still further. He showed his support for the developments taking place and his own enthusiasm and skill with his colleagues enabled many steps forward to be taken. This change was perceived in our daily meetings with the Commanding Officer, and when there really were explosions in the course of community growth we were able to develop a strong collegiate group to work things through. The Social Therapy staff too were not just dedicated tolerant soldiers. Theirs was a most stressful set of responsibilities – and not only as regards the patients. Professional and other staff could be very demanding and inter-ward rivalries quite destructive. The study of our own intra-group tensions had to be seen as an essential part of our activities.

It was demonstrated over the course of time that there was a need to gain sanction in appropriate quarters through collaborative work and inter-disciplinary competence. The development of key resources within a system to appreciate and share perceptions with consultative initiatives from without is an on-going necessary part of any dynamic community – whether with a therapeutic mission or another. To balance and optimize the forces and resources from within and without is the strength of the open-system approach.[25] The price we pay for that is the increased demand on inter-dependence and the management of complexity, conflict and uncertainty. With the relatively closed system the price we pay – much more, particularly today, than in the 1940s – is really exemplified by what happened to Bion at Northfield – and to others elsewhere. One method is not good or the other bad. Depending on the characteristics of the institution, its mission, people, methods and technologies, values and standards etc., within its various relevant environments, there is a price or cost for any particular choice made in the way it is run, structured and developed. We cannot have the choice or option without the price that goes with it.[26]

Notes and references

1 Bion, W. R. (1946), 'The Leaderless Group project', *Bull. Menninger Clin.*, 10: 77–81.
2 Bion, Francesca (1980), 'Wilfred Bion', *Bull. Brit. Psychoanalytical Society*, March.
3 Banet, Anthony G., Jr. (1976), 'Interview with W. R. Bion', *Group and Organization Studies*, 1, pt 3: 268–85.
4 Anonymous (1981), 'Bion: an appreciation', *Old Stortfordian Newsletter*, January.
5 Towards the end of World War II when various 'civvy-street' careers were being compared and discussed, Bion remarked: 'Well, in the final resort I can always put "Clinic" over the door – and wait!'
6 Bion, F. (1980).
7 Emery, F. E. and Trist, E. L. (1965), 'The causal texture of organisational environments'. *Hum. Relat.*, 18: 21–32.
8 Bion (1946).
9 Bion, W. R. and Rickman, J. (1943), 'Intra-group tensions in therapy: their study as the task of the group', *Lancet*, 2: 678–81.
10 Sutherland, J. D. and Fitzpatrick, G. A. (1945), 'Some approaches to group problems in the British army', *Sociometry*, 8: 443–55.
11 Morris, B. S. (1949), 'Officer selection in the British army', *Occ. Psychol.*, 23: 219–34.
12 Bridger, H. and Isdell-Carpenter, R. (1947), 'Selection of management trainees', *Industr. Welf.*, 29, no. 315: 177–81.

13 Bion, W. R. (1961), *Experiences in Groups*, Tavistock.
14 Main, T. F. (1983), 'The concept of the therapeutic community: variations and vicissitudes', in Pines, Malcolm (ed.), *The Evolution of Group Analysis*, Routledge & Kegan Paul.
15 Actually by no means all the staff were of the Commanding Officer's mind at that time. Some who were interested in Bion's work and that of the Selection Boards, understood this better than others. The 'chaos' reason alone, however, would never have occasioned the 'sacking'; the rest of the hospital was far from peaceful!
16 Bion (1961).
17 Bridger, H. (1980), 'The implications of ecological change on groups, institutions and communities, with particular reference to membership, leadership and consultative roles', Proceedings of VII International Congress of Group Psychotherapy, Copenhagen, 1980 (in M. Pines and L. Rafaelsen (eds), *The Individual and the Group*, New York, Plenum, 1982).
18 Tom Main, however, who was later to take over a Division at Northfield and who then re-developed the Cassel Hospital after the war, certainly had this gift. He was also able to encourage and develop others to recognize its value in practice.
19 Pearse, I. H. and Crocker, L. H. (1943), *The Peckham Experiment*, Allen & Unwin.
20 Jones, Maxwell (1968), *Social Psychiatry in Practice*, Penguin Books.
21 Main, T. F. (1946), 'The hospital as a therapeutic institution', *Bull. Menninger Clin.*, 10: 66–70.
22 Bridger, H. (1946), 'The Northfield experiment', *Bull. Menninger Clin.*, 10: 71–6.
23 I had become convinced that 'the enemy to be faced', as Bion refers to it, was primarily at the level of the 'hospital-as-a-whole'.
24 Bion (1946).
25 Bridger, H. (1980), 'The kinds of "organizational development" required for working at the level of the whole organization considered as an open system', in Trebesch, K. (ed.), *Organization Development in Europe*, vol. 1A: *Concepts* (Proceedings of the First European Forum on Organisational Development Aachen, 1978), Berne, Paul Haupt Verlag.
26 Bridger, H. (1981), *Consultative Work with Communities and Organizations: Towards a Psychodynamic Image of Man*, Malcolm Millar Lecture, 1980, Aberdeen University Press.

Chapter 4
Major Bion

Patrick B. de Maré

Both Bion and Foulkes started off believing that the larger group context, in this instance manifesting itself as a nation in a state of war, was an essential dimension in the handling of neurosis. For Bion, matters of morale, esprit de corps, discipline, punishment and communal responsibility were prime considerations, and led him to raise serious doubts about the suitability of a hospital milieu for psychotherapy; he suggested the name 'training unit' or 'training wing' instead. He wrote: 'the neurotic is commonly regarded as being self-centred and averse to cooperative endeavours; but perhaps this is because he is seldom put in an environment in which *every* member is on the same footing as regards interpersonal relationships'. Then follows his cryptic comment: 'The experiment was interrupted by the posting of personnel, so I cannot give clinical or statistical results.'

In all, the first Northfield experiment conducted by Majors John Rickman and Wilfred Bion lasted six weeks.

Later, Lt-Colonel Tom Main was to remark that the hospital machine unfortunately produced a 'desocializing effect', and he described how the traditional hospital milieu produced a refugee culture that was not appropriate for the treatment of war casualties since it produced a passivity and depending atmosphere of 'patients grateful to the presiding psychiatrist, himself educated to play a grandiose role among the sick.' Main suggested the term that was more appropriate which was 'therapeutic community'.

The crucial issue that was discussed by Rickman, Bion, Foulkes and Main was the link between the deepest 'vertical', intrapersonal axis with the transpersonal 'horizontal' of the social and cultural context.

Following the ending of hostilities, a slowing-down of this dynamic approach to large group issues developed; this occasioned Foulkes to write in 1964: 'It happens that much of my earlier experiences and experiments were conducted under military conditions, in conjunction with the introduction of group psychotherapy into the psychiatric services of the British Army. What has been a cooperative effort during the war lost its unity afterwards.'

This first flush of enthusiasm lost its initial momentum as a result partly perhaps of Rickman's untimely death, and partly because of Bion's gradual withdrawal from the group field altogether. The groups conducted at the Tavistock Clinic fell dramatically from about forty a week to, at one point, only five, and there was a gradual tilting towards the psychoanalytic model from the social therapy of the two Northfield experiments towards an increasing emphasis on individual psycho-dynamics.

An example of the original enthusiasm occurred in 1945 when a commission of American psychiatrists, who made a three-thousand-mile tour to investigate the psychiatric resources of the Army Medical Services in the European theatre, eventually stayed for a period of several weeks as guests of the British War Office. Karl Menninger wrote in 1946 in the *Bulletin of the Menninger Clinic*: 'All the members of the commission fell in love with England and its people. One of the things that impressed us most was the skillful use of the principle of group psychology ... which carried the application of these principles much further than is common in American psychiatric practice ... It is not as yet the method of preference in the leading psychiatric hospitals of America whereas it actually is in England.'

The insistence of Bion was that the situation had to be a real-life situation, and this he carried out subsequently in the technique he and Rickman evolved in the War Office Selection Boards, wherein potential officers were tested, not in a free-for-all competition with other candidates, but as members of a group of eight or nine people with some such programme as building a bridge. These were called 'Leaderless Group tests'.

Referring to the first Northfield experiment, Bion wrote in 'The Leaderless Group project' in the same *Bulletin*: 'The flight from neurotic disorder had to be stopped; as in a regiment, morale has to be raised to a point where the real enemy could be faced.' 'To this end discussions were carried out with small groups ... As soon as a sufficient number of patients had in this way been persuaded to face their enemy instead of running away from it, a daily meeting of half-an-hour was arranged for the whole Training Wing, consisting of between a hundred and two hundred men. These meetings were ostensibly concerned only with the organisation of the activities of the Wing ... ' 'Thus occupational therapy had been given a new meaning. The therapeutic occupation of the group was the study of its own internal tensions in the real life situation, with a view to laying bare the influence of neurotic behaviour introducing frustration, waste of energy and unhappiness in the group . . . ' 'The therapeutic occupation had to be hard thinking and not the abreaction of moral indignation.'

In describing the psychiatrist's problem in stopping a 'rout', he wrote: 'Outside Nazi Germany psychiatrists are not likely to be shot for doing their job, though of course they may be removed from their posts.'

Bion's attitude towards the large meeting was more radical than the subsequent handling of Foulkes in the second Northfield experiment. Foulkes was more gradualistic in his approach. Bion saw the large meeting of a hundred to two hundred people as the main trunk of the tree which could explore the tensions of the smaller activity groups – once he could persuade them to meet – which he arranged, partly by persuasion through small group meetings of chosen members, and partly by simply issuing an order to parade that would be held every day at 12.10 p.m. for making announcements and conducting other business of the Training Wing. The result of this radical approach was that it produced a cultural clash with the hospital military authorities. The fear that Rickman's and Bion's approach would lead to anarchy and chaos occasioned War Office officials to pay a lightning visit at night. The chaos in the hospital cinema hall, with newspapers and condom-strewn floors, resulted in the immediate termination of the project. Majors Rickman and Bion were posted, and set up War Office Selection Boards elsewhere.

Foulkes, in contrast to this, developed the small group meetings with official approval from the Commanding Officer, which took a period of at least a year to prepare. There was then a gradual viewing of the large groups in the form of ward groups of from thirty to eighty men. But he was insistent that 'more is needed, however. The patient needs insight . . . Therein lies the limitedness of a large meeting of thirty to eighty men; the patient's reactions cannot be brought to light, voiced, described, realised or brought home to him by others. For this the more intimate setting is essential. Seven or eight people at a time has proved a good number. They meet regularly from once to three times a week for a set period of one to one-and-a-half hours.'

I personally helped Rickman and Bion to pack. Clearly, Bion was put out by these events. Rickman, on the other hand, merely exclaimed unrepentantly and unperturbedly: "Pon my soul!', in the high-pitched tone he sometimes adopted in mock surprise.

I was fortunate in having witnessed both the first Northfield experiment of Rickman and Bion, and also to have co-operated with Foulkes in the second experiment. I have already described these experiences with Foulkes in 'Michael Foulkes and the Northfield Experiment' (1983). I was first posted to Northfield Hospital in December 1942, having been a Medical Officer attached to a Battle School at Hay Tor in Dartmoor, a most bleak setting, in the late autumn of 1942. It was with some relief that I found myself, on the grounds that I had had a year's psychoanalysis and had worked for eleven months at Shenley, and had taken the first part of the DPM, posted as a Trainee Army Psychiatrist to a three-month course held at Northfield, Birmingham, conducted by Major Rickman. The course was arranged as a series of lectures and seminar meetings. There were altogether ten trainees, of whom five were British, four were American and one was Polish.

After a week or two Rickman was joined by his friend and colleague Wilfred Bion. They were both psychoanalysts, and at that time spoke frequently of the findings of Melanie Klein, which Rickman compared to the acceptance and tolerance of 'lumps in the porridge', referring to 'good' and 'bad' objects. They, like Foulkes, had both seen service in World War I, Foulkes in the German army, Rickman as an ambulance driver in a Quaker unit (he was a conscientious objector) in Russia, and Bion as a very young officer in the Tank Corps.

The seminars conducted by Rickman were extremely thoughtful and lively. He was much the older man — large, grey-haired, bright-eyed, moustached, balding, bespectacled, with sensuous lips, continually smoking a pipe, with a gentle caustic manner, soft-voiced. Everything and everybody seemed to provoke an attitude of a first encounter, with a very slight sense in him of wonder and surprise. He continually referred to the findings and happenings of Freud and of his earlier followers. At the very first meeting of our seminar he announced in soothing terms that this course was to give us all the opportunity to have 'a breather, as if we were at a university', and to take a look at psychiatry in wartime. Coming from a Battle School at the height of the uncertainties of the war, this attitude was enormously consoling and did indeed enable us all to do some hard thinking rather than become paralysed by anxiety.

Bion, on the other hand, was a good deal younger, a Boswell to Rickman's Johnson. He too was a massive man, balding with a thick black moustache, high-coloured cheeks, thick-lensed gold-rimmed spectacles, smoking a large Sherlock Holmes pipe. He looked very much the officer of the 'old school' and indeed came from an upper-class Edwardian background with British Raj connections. He was an extremely shy man, which was belied by his imposing presence. He rarely spoke, and when he did so it would always be in the form of cryptic comments. In the seminars which he conducted separately from Rickman, he would sit in the circle in profound silence, smoking his pipe and occasionally, after someone had vouchsafed a comment, would emit a loud prolonged sniff which was somewhat disconcerting, since it was ambiguous. What could it all mean? Indeed he would only rarely reveal his thoughts, seated ostensibly as an unobserved observer, but always the centre of unvoiced attention. I remember one comment was that 'the working class is always in a state of war', and on another occasion that a Tank Officer in the previous war had been seen to be wearing a bullet-proof waistcoat under his uniform, which comment was followed by a contemptuous sniff with the inference that the offender was regarded by fellow-officers as a 'poor type', clearly not a 'good man', terms which were rife at that time. In contrast to this approach much talk centred on the Gestalt quasi-Marxist approach of Kurt Lewin and Brown. In fact the Russians at that time were much favoured by many of us, including Rickman and Bion, and Stalin was referred to as 'Uncle Joe'. This was shortly after the retreat by the Germans from Stalingrad, the first sign of a break-through for the Allies.

The overall impression of those fraught three months was an unforgettable atmosphere of stimulation, thoughtfulness and interest. Thank you, John Rickman, thank you, Wilfred Bion! I shall never forget you and to this day I continue to miss you both. The lively meetings were the forerunner to much that subsequently evolved and which was intensively followed up at the Tavistock, at the Cassel, at the Maudsley, at St George's Hospital, above all by Michael Foulkes at the Group Analytic Society, Institute and Practice. Of the four, Foulkes was the least 'élitist'. Perhaps this accounts for his work having flourished more, even though at present the writings of Bion seem to have become more widely published. In a nutshell it can be said that Bion was more aware of large group and cultural forces than Foulkes, but Foulkes was more radical in seeing the small group as taking on its own therapy, rather than Bion's approach which continued to recommend ambiguously that the conductor is essentially a work group leader. Perhaps if Rickman and Bion's large group project had not been so summarily terminated, history might have taken a very different course. Certainly, in Bion's book, *Experiences in Groups*, one gains the impression that he often handled small groups as if they were large. To my knowledge neither he nor Rickman ever again attempted a large-group approach.

References

Bion, W. R. (1946), 'The Leaderless Group project', *Bull. Menninger Clinic*, 10, 3.

Bion, W. R. (1961), *Experiences in Groups*, London, Tavistock.

Foulkes, S. H. (1948), *Introduction to Group-Analytic Psychotherapy*, London, Heinemann.

Foulkes, S. H. and Anthony, J. (1957), *Group Psychotherapy*, Penguin Books.

Maré, P. B. de (1983), 'Michael Foulkes and the Northfield experiment', in *The Evolution of Group Analysis*, ed. M. Pines, London, Routledge & Kegan Paul.

Chapter 5
Research with Bion's concepts

Herbert A. Thelen

For five years, 1951-6, my graduate students and I worked intensively with Bion's seminal ideas as set forth in the first five or six 'Experiences in groups.'[1] We were immensely stimulated not only by his concepts of group cultures and individual valency but also by his contextual meta-theory which directed the use of the concepts and gave them great force.

The underlying proposition was that the group can be regarded and treated as an organism – in contradistinction to the group as a super-individual or as a collectivity. The organismic conception faces two central theoretical problems: what to postulate as the group's organizing principle (the overall assumptions that maintain the organism through co-ordinating the experiences of the quasi-autonomous members), and what to postulate as the dynamics of group reconstruction of experience and growth. Bion saw that the group at any time exists in some (hope-fully identifiable) state, e.g. the 'emotionality-work' pattern; and that over time each state gives way to the next through interaction of the members' valencies with the group's state of being. Thus the group is a 'state-determined system'[2] in which the tensions generated by its own operation lead to system-wide adjustments in both structure and process. Bion brought these concepts to life by his vivid descriptions of events in therapy groups, and they resonated deeply with our own experiences since 1948 in T-groups.

We decided to do research with and on Bion's conceptions and I think that some of our efforts may be regarded at least as footnotes to his explanations. I welcome this opportunity to recall some of these studies and to place them in the context of social practice and research at that time.

The exciting work that gave birth to group dynamics as a new science was political in its intent. Kurt Lewin was a refugee from Nazi Germany.

114

He wished to demonstrate experimentally and scientifically that life is much better under democracy than under authoritarianism. He proposed that small groups might represent society and that a carefully trained leader might be able to produce democratic or authoritarian atmospheres in such groups. But the finding that excited students of groups was that experimentally-produced leadership 'styles' could indeed predictably influence members' behaviors and attitudes. The Lewin–Lippitt–White[3] studies opened up group phenomena to experimental study. Experimenters composed groups (even of strangers), gave them work to do, set up and supervised the treatments, and assessed the outcomes.

These activities broke sharply with the descriptive clinical and historical methods of Cooley, Simmel, Weber, Freud, and others whose 'subjects' were 'natural groups' with long histories, traditions and social functions. The new experimenters had to face all sorts of questions: Can valid research be done on any laboratory group? Can results from such artificial groups have value for 'real' on-going groups? There was resistance to the heretical view of leadership as a function distributed among all the members rather than as a preserve of the leader. There was even the suggestion that those who study group processes must have a yen for power and that their findings would encourage exploitation of groups by would-be dictators and manipulators. There was doubt that objective results could emerge from studies in which the experimenter himself administers the group treatments. And there was serious questioning as to whether the enterprise of group study might not contribute to the destruction of individuality by converging on some restrictive ideal of 'the good group member' to which all persons should conform.[4]

The researchers were also involved in conflicting views of the proper nature of the social sciences. The conflict was (and still is) between 'hard' and 'soft' conceptions of scientific inquiry and of 'truth'. The hard position was exemplified by 'quantitative' inquiry which was said to be rigorous, objective, paradigmatic, analytical and positivistic. The soft position was that of the humanists or intuitionists – sloppy, subjective-phenomenological, heuristic, insightful, quasi-philosophical. (If you liked Bion, you were a humanist.) Sociology and economics tended toward the quantitative and mathematical: anthropology and psychology leaned toward the humanistic. The adherents of the respective positions could make them fit because they could, at will, define and select the aspects of society or groups that they cared to respond to. But group dynamicists had more trouble – as well as more conceptual opportunity because they wished to study not arbitrarily chosen *aspects* of group life but rather the group as a *whole* entity, organism, or society. But how do you apply molar concepts of society to the face-to-face inter-acting group? None of the disciplines then current, with the possible exception of the beginning systems theories, had the methodological or substantive scope for such studies.

Given the openness and the vigor of dialogue in those days (in which 'schools' of psychology vied for recognition), each toiler in the group vineyard had to figure out his own position, role, and loyalties in this elusive new field of inquiry. There were plenty of options and their very diversity stimulated or even demanded that one make his conceptual preferences explicit — prematurely so, in the opinion of S. Koch.[5] In 1953 Cartwright and Zander[6] classified the various approaches as follows:

Basic dimensions. Cattell advocated the fundamentalist-reductionist belief that the proper research strategy should be to establish basic conceptual and mensurational 'dimensions of groups' first and then find out their relationships in experiments. His instrument of inquiry was factor analysis, whose mathematical ability to reduce many variables to a few was thought somehow to provide a mystical pipeline to the significant and universal. His dimensions represented three kinds of variables having to do with individual characteristics, group structure as organized in status hierarchies, and group performance. This work was a logical sequel to L. L. Thurstone's earlier efforts to define 'primary mental abilities'.

Interaction. Bales, Homans, Chapple, White, and Arensberg had a common interest in the way the group develops and changes as a result of interactions among members and between the group and its environ-ment. Bales's theory related patternings of twelve behavior categories to the processes of developing group structure. Homans showed how the complex of activities, interactions, and sentiments develops the internal and external systems in relation to each other and the environ-ment.

Organizational leadership. Stogdill, Shartle, and Hemphill considered the organizational aspects of group life: the functions and responsibilities of individuals with reference to achievement of group goals. There are both formal and informal networks of relationships among these factors. The formal network defines expectations of role performance. The informal network defines actual role performance. Leadership influences both networks and finds problems in the discrepancies between them.

Psychoanalytic. Scheidlinger, Slavson, Redl, Bion, and Ezriel were seen working with Freud's notion that 'group cohesiveness arises through common identifications of the members with one another'. The meaning of a particular behavior to the actor has to be understood both as fitting into his genetically developed mode of adjustment and as involving him in present reactions to the external world. 'Personality' is the habitual mode of synthesizing into a pattern of adjustment, the aims of drives, conscience, and physical and social reality (environment). Personality develops through social interaction, especially in the family. Opportunity for needed social interaction is also found in other groups which form through common identifications such as with the leader. Redl has identified ten types of 'central persons' with whom, under various conditions, members of the group may identify and thus maintain the group. According to Bion's notion of 'valency', at different times unconscious subgroupings form through 'combination' in support of a particular emotionalized mode of group operation. The group ethos is the organizing principle through which individual strivings are coordinated in common effort. Role differentiations and social structure are produced in accordance with the capacities of individuals for interaction in the group.

Sociometric. Moreno, Jennings, Barker, Criswell, and others postulate that the 'social space' within which an individual lives is delimited by his range of interaction with others, and that this space is structured by his feelings of attraction or repulsion for others. Such feeling bonds are the bases of groups. Groups may be formed spontaneously from free choices of others (psychegroup) or they may be formed by social demands that require people to work together (sociogroup). The working out of interpersonal needs, as reflected in the choice pattern, is a major aspect of group process, and the choice pattern at any time reveals significant cleavages, subgroups, and group structure in general.

Force field. Kurt Lewin,[7] often considered the founder of 'group dynamics', saw that behavior arises out of the 'life space' of the individual (cf. 'social space' above). The life space contains perceptions of behavioral alternatives such as different activities in which the individual might engage. Some alternatives are definite and clear (structured), others vague and unstructured. The alternatives have different degrees of attractiveness and repulsion (valence) depending on their usefulness in meeting current needs. In addition there may be permeable or impermeable 'barriers' to 'locomotion' into the chosen activity region and these barriers also have a negative or positive valence. Thus the individual, represented by a point in his life space, is subject to a variety of forces which tend to influence him in a variety of directions. Applied to groups, these concepts led to the notion that the distribution of leadership depends on the degree of overlap or communality of the individual life spaces; cooperation and competition are viewed (e.g. by Deutch[8]) as conditions under which the efforts of an individual to locomote into a chosen activity region either facilitate or hinder similar efforts by other individuals. The primary data for studies within this frame of reference have been perceptions by members of themselves, each other, their group, and its activities.

In our laboratory at the University of Chicago, work with small groups began in 1947. At that time the research team felt unsure of how to decide among the large array of current theories and approaches to research. Accordingly our earliest work was concerned with empirical matters: what kinds of data about groups can be collected, recorded, and counted on? The first year was devoted to a wide range of techniques for collecting data: time-lapse photography, noise level, feeling intro-spection, and so on. From experiences with such techniques and, of course, with the classroom and other groups on which the techniques were employed, two decisions emerged for further work. First, that we would work with sequential analysis, looking at each event in relation to antecedent and subsequent events; and second, that we would try to identify feelings or affects as basic data of experience during meetings, rather than sticking only to objectively-defined overt behaviors.[9] A brief characterization of our research follows:

In 1948 and 1949, the experiments of Withall,[10] Flanders,[11] and Perkins[12] demonstrated the importance of affective communication between teacher and students. Affect was seen as a concomitant of the 'intent' of the communicator and was found to influence recall, anxiety, perceived 'feeling', and a number of physiological measures. During this period, Rehage,[13] in an experiment on teacher-class planning, noted the importance of the teacher's response (or lack thereof) to feelings expressed by students; and he also found marked development of cohesion in the sociometric pattern of a class that had shared intense feelings.

The effort to understand why teachers (and other leaders) responded as they did to the feelings of others led Glidewell[14] to the experimental study of interpersonal anxiety as related to the behavior of the leader. The four members of the group were trained to play the roles of people who had been identified through clinical study of the leader to be either anxiety-producing or anxiety-allaying. They were trained to make 'supportive' or 'threatening' statements, and observers correctly spotted these two types of statements by noting their consequences in the deterioration or the 'strengthening' of the subject's style of leadership.

About this time (1950) Thelen[15] published a methodological analysis of the postulates required for research on groups, and this forecast with some accuracy the direction of succeeding work in the laboratory.

In the same year deHaan[16] attempted to use Bion's emotion and work concepts as a basis for sequential plotting of group interaction. The results, although crude, were encouraging and led to considerable further effort at refinement and systematization of the method. During this period there were several other tests of the usefulness of the concepts of emotionality and work tendencies in personality. Thus Stock[17] had fair success in predicting sociometric choices; D. McPherson[18] showed that an individual emotion-work sentence completion test was more useful than the TAT for predicting emotion and work behaviors in the group. In connection with some research with the Air Force, J. McPherson[19] showed relationships between emotionality-work personality patterns and tendencies to distort the meaning of close-to-self written materials; B. Sarchet[20] used the same personality data to predict roles of groups of officers. Working under the same contract,Glidewell[21] showed that certain characteristics of the solutions to problems, worked out by fifty different twelve-man groups of officers, could be differentially predicted from knowledge of the emotionality-work patterns of the group and from knowledge of the group's standards controlling the expression of feeling (e.g. labile, constrictive, integrative). The notions of control, incidentally, have yet to be worked into the overall system. In the same year, Freedman[22] studied the way eight different teachers dealt with emotionally charged discussion following presentation of a provocative dramatic story to their class, and related their 'styles' both to their anxieties and to lack of congruences between the perceptions of the teacher and his students.

Beginning in 1951 an experimental program was begun under the auspices of the Group Psychology Branch of the Office of Naval Research. This work was brought to a close officially in July 1956 and was summarized in two monographs. The first monograph[23] reports on research methodology: the development and validation of the basic emotionality-work assessment instrument (the Reactions to Group Situations Test) by the Gradolphs, Stock, and Hill; the development of the method of sequential analysis and interpretation (Behavior Rating Scheme, minute-by-minute graph, the Work-Emotionality Field Graph), a variety of unitizing procedures by Stock, Thelen, and Ben-Zeev; and a method for studying inter-subgroup dynamics by Stock and Hill. The second monograph[24] gives the substantive findings of Stock, Gradolph, Hill, Glidewell, Lieberman, and Mathis with respect to the behavior of individuals in groups, group composition, 'trainability', and productivity. In 1956,

Thelen[25] published an analysis of the methods, findings and theories developed in the project, and in 1964 Stock[26] presented the major findings of the project within her resumé of all group dynamics research between 1947 and 1963.

During this whole period the recognized 'capital of the world' of Group Dynamics Research (at least in the USA) was the Research Center for Group Dynamics, founded by Kurt Lewin at the Massachusetts Institute of Technology in 1944-5. Lewin represented group dynamics as a field for research on 'the forces and behaviors that facilitate and resist change in groups'. This definition was immensely appealing to many of the new professional social and public health workers whose occupations originated in the dislocations of the Great Depression of the 1930s. They sensed the possibility of a new science of change and of leadership and management, and when Kurt Lewin and Ronald Lippitt of the Research Center joined forces with Leland Bradford (of the Adult Education department within the National Educational Association) and with Kenneth Benne (then at the University of Illinois) to launch the National Training Laboratories, a great new movement began.

Human relations training

The National Training Laboratory in Group Development, with its summer workshops in Bethel, Maine, from 1947 to the present, initiated literally thousands of professional workers, managers, graduate students, and beginning professors into the culture and climate of group study and group leadership.

The most potent vehicle of training was the human relations training group, known first as the 'Basic Skills Training Group' and then as the 'T-group'. The T-group contains twelve to twenty-five adults who have come together to learn 'what goes on in groups' and how to participate more effectively in groups. The groups usually meet for two or three hours at a time and they usually hold ten to fifteen sessions during the two- or three-week workshop or laboratory. Frequently there is an assistant trainer, and the relationships between him and the trainer often contribute to the 'dynamics' (I am tempted to say 'problems') of the group. Probably the most useful and widespread learning of members is that they can operate at a much lower level of anxiety in groups and thus give their native intelligence more of a role in their performance.

In the original conception the T-group was to be an educational laboratory in which members would learn about social systems by consciously participating in developing one, namely their own face-to-face T-group. The staff 'trainer' would serve as teacher, counselor, and resource person. Among his resources would be not only a great deal of knowledge of group dynamics but also understanding of how to utilize the 'laboratory method' of inquiry. Described in terms of facilitating opportunities for learning, the laboratory method bears considerable resemblance to John Dewey's specifications of inquiry. Thus, according to Bradford, Gibb, and Benne,[27] members are to have opportunities to test and discover their dissatisfactions with and in the group, test congruence between goals and action (behavior of self and others); set directions for change in the operation of self and group; determine pathways, through experimentation, for change in behavior; assess effectiveness of new behavior; and practice, internalize, and apply new behavior.

Within these generally-agreed-upon expectations there were great differences in operation, especially with respect to three dimensions: (a) the group being the inquirer with the trainer serving as consultant versus the trainer setting the agenda and directing the group through its activities; (b) the extent to which the client of training was seen to be the group as distinguished from a collection of individuals — and hence the extent to which leadership would facilitate culture-building versus 'helping' individuals to move closer to some definition of 'the good group member'; and (c) the extent to which members' perceptions of each other were invited and interpreted within the context of carefully described group activities versus having no context beyond the subjective usually unrevealed and defended motives of individuals.

By the third summer of operation, the various differences of the trainers tended to be mobilized around two conceptions of the group's *raison d'être*: the group as a supportive milieu for giving therapy to individuals or the group as a collectivity attempting to develop itself into a society and culture in which members could be more self-realizing and effective. Those to whom the therapeutic image appealed tended to adopt roles consistent with Rogerian therapy; those who emphasized cooperative inquiry and culture-building tended to look to the ideas of Lewin, Dewey, and, increasingly, W. R. Bion.

Regardless of the orientation of the trainer, the groups were very revealing subjects for study. In the course of their own transactions they talked about their perceptions, feelings, diagnoses, and goals — exactly the sort of data most useful to the researcher–observer. Operating as a 'cultural island' free from the usual home institutional constraints, the processes by which 'felt' problems are identified and translated into explicit agreed-upon purposes could be charted. Within their three-week life, changes in the course of group development and growth were dramatic and describable, and could be used to illuminate cause–effect hypotheses.

In 1948 Bion's 'Experiences in Groups' started appearing in *Human Relations*, a new journal published jointly by the Research Center for Group Dynamics and the Tavistock Institute. By the time of the seventh installment in 1951, our little band of earnest inquirers was pretty well committed to his concepts. Probably the main reason for this decision was that his concepts spoke directly to certain convictions that our experiences both as trainers and researchers had led us to. These were formulated as follows.[28]

1 That groups do have periods in which they are dominated by different moods.
2 That the concept of group *qua* group rather than as group *qua* collection is essential to our thinking and reacting as social beings.
3 That the 'laws' governing group life will be 'laws' of change; that is, they will (when developed) be concerned with the continually shifting balance of forces in the group and with the continually shifting 'culture' (in the sense of unconscious values and purposes) of the group.
4 That affective behaviors communicate directly and non-verbally and are sensed directly, i.e. that 'emotion' should be recorded as primary data rather than be inferred from so-called objective behavior.

These convictions led to specifications for research; (a) for sequential analysis, or analysis of 'flow' of experience through time, (b) for finding concepts that would fit the group as a whole – and by this I do *not* mean simply analogies to individual personality, (c) for seeing in the group a dynamic interplay between conflicting tendencies, i.e. for looking for some dynamic, dramatic theme in group life, and (d) for categorizing emotion directly through paying attention to our own visceral responses to goings-on in the group.

These four convictions pointed us toward a 'psychiatric' approach to group dynamics as distinguished from sociological, perceptual, sociometric, and other approaches noted above. In Bion's stimulating articles we found many of the concepts we needed. Bion's terms fight-flight, pairing, dependency, and work were utilized to describe the moods that groups sustain at different periods. The notion of applying these terms to characterize specific individual behaviors was not suggested by Bion; he was primarily concerned with group modalities and individual tendencies.

To us, the concept of group as group was more convincingly explained by Bion than by any other theorist we knew. Especially useful were his ideas that the individual in some sense always reflects the needs of the group. At least during some periods it is as if the group was speaking through many voices and the particular individual whose vocal chords are thus utilized may be functioning primarily on behalf of the group. Moreover, the notion that at times different persons seem to be central — as spokesman, for example — in the group seemed in Bion's thinking to be extended and generalized to cover a great many possible roles. It also appeared that Bion's concept of unconscious identifications as the basis for subgroups which attempt to maintain or promote particular basic assumptions (of emotion-work) made room for a subgroup structure which fitted the facts of group life more adequately than do more socio-logical or sociometric concepts (although these clearly are useful at times).

We were indebted to Bion for his coherent imagery of the group as organism. His explanations of its various states of being, of how all the members (even those who denied it) apparently participated in and supported these states, of how each state — through the group's experi-ence of it — ran its course and was supplanted by another, and of how to explain different roles of individuals — all seemed economical and elegant to us. I especially liked the broad evolutionary sweep encom-passed in fight-flight (animal stress reflex), dependency (family protec-tion for growing up), and pairing (creation of new relationships and, through them, new group capabilities). These dynamics seemed intuit-ively satisfying because fundamental; and they endowed the group organism with a richness of capabilities and nuances that seemed to have been squeezed out of more 'scientific' theorizing.

Moreover, Bion was easy to connect to other exciting work. Weston LaBarre's *The Human Animal*,[29] appearing about the same time, devel-oped the evolutionary context and seemed to confirm the shrewdness of Bion's emotionality terms. I felt that Bion's 'work' concepts, which others, too often, limited to task efforts rather than broadened to the seeking of reality through understanding — exactly complemented and even further explained Hannah Arendt's distinction between labor and work in *The Human Condition*.[30] Thus Bion in a way represented not only himself but LaBarre and Arendt, too. As for Bion's conception of the observer role, that was easily assimilated to Dewey's conception of the inquirer. His notion of persons 'combining' in valency subgroups which had different degrees of centrality at different times seemed — function-ally at least — to be a neat equivalent of Fritz Redl's[31] conceptions of group formation through identification with central persons. And his handling of need-meeting by individuals seemed entirely consonant with Lewin's[32] ideas of individual locomotion within the force field — but without the difficulty of trying to explain the nature of psychological 'forces'. Finally, because I was deeply committed to sequential recording and unitizing as a major research tool, I was pleased with the ready applicability of the emotionalities to periods as short as a gesture and as long as several meetings. The emotional modes made sense both microscopically and macroscopically and the possiblity of talking about a macroscopic fight period which was sustained by microscopic level interplay between the impulses of pairing and dependency (for example) seemed to me properly to respect the psychological richness and complexity of group process.

Bion not only presented insightful constructs; he demonstrated their power for focusing recognizable and significant events in group life. His revelations of how he 'experienced' groups helped sensitize us to form and style; and his discussion exemplified and clarified the nature of the intellectual quest for comprehension of group life. My major works,[33] on theories and methods of classroom instruction, owe much to Bion.

The researches

The best concise account of our 1951-6 researches is, I think, that given by Dorothy Stock[34] (Whitaker) in her chapter in Bradford, Gibb, and Benne (eds), *T-Group Theory and Laboratory Method*. I have extracted some key points from that account:

In two groups whose development was studied over fourteen sessions, one group moved through identifiable stages toward effective work and the adequate control and utilization of affect, while the second remained stuck throughout its life in a stage of routine exploration, alternating between flat and explosive affect (Stock and Ben-Zeev[35] and Hill[36]). These differences in development seemed related to composition. The first group, regarded as more effective, was composed of persons fairly similar in preferred atmosphere and mode of interacting, while the second was composed of two incompatible subtypes vying for control of the group, and a third subtype of withdrawn members.[37]

The possible importance of composition was pursued in two further studies, both of which involved deliberately composing groups to include varying combinations and weightings of individual valencies (based on members' pre-group responses to a sentence-completion test).

Ida Gradolph compared four six-member groups composed respectively of work-pairing members, flight members, and (two) half work-pairing and half flight members. All groups worked on the same two assigned tasks. Members of the flight group were uncommitted and uninvolved and completed the task quickly and cursorily; members of the work-pairing group also completed the task but were more involved and expressed more affect of all kinds; neither of the mixed groups completed the second of the two tasks and both expressed frustration and anger. This work suggested that groups homogeneously composed with respect to individual valence are likely to behave in ways which are direct expressions of the emotional orientations of members. Groups composed of two different types of valency found it more difficult to find a common and satisfactory way of approaching tasks.[38] Lieberman studied two differently composed T-groups: one which included equal numbers of persons with primary tendencies to express fight, flight, pairing, dependency and counterdependency; and one which omitted pairing persons. Observers tabulated the amount of fight, flight, etc. behavior actually expressed during the three-week life of these groups and found that the first group expressed the same relative amount of pairing throughout while the second expressed little pairing at first but gradually built up to the same level as the first group. In the second group much of the pairing behavior was provided by the leader. The second group expressed far more counterdependency at first but gradually reduced this to the level of the first group, which had been steady in the amount of counterdependency expressed throughout its life. This study suggested that a range of affective valencies supports group functioning, and that when certain valencies are unrepresented in the composition some persons in the group may try to fill the gap by modifying their usual behavior.[39]

Three studies suggested that the affective preferences (valency) of the leader plays a part in the character and development of a group: by offering behavioral models for group members,[40] by being located (in valency terms) in one or two warring subtypes and consequently being in a poor position to help members to resolve conflict.[41] Leaders may also be pressed into behaving in particular ways in response to pressures generated by the composition, as in Lieberman's study, where the leader displayed more pairing behavior than he considered typical,[42] and in a study by Stock and Luft where the leader of a group whose members preferred a high degree of structure pressed more than usual for process analysis while the leader of a group whose members preferred low structure found himself pressing for interaction.[43]

In a study of the relation between sociometric choice and pattern of participation, Ben-Zeev hypothesized that members would tend to co-participate with persons whom they liked. Results were mixed. Ben-Zeev then examined his findings in the light of personality data acquired by a Sentence Completion test. This clarified matters: persons with preferences for expressing warmth and friendliness tended to interact with those whom they liked; persons with preferences for expressing hostility and anger seemed most stimulated to participate with those whom they disliked, i.e. under conditions of conflict and controversy.[44] Compatible findings emerged from a study by Stock, which attempted to predict sociometric choice from an analysis of each member's 'need system' (assessed in valency terms from self-perceptual data by means of a Q-sort). As in Ben-Zeev's study, the results were unclear at first, but fell into place when one took into account whether or not persons were conflicted with regard to their preferred emotional mode of operating. Those who were unconflicted preferred those who facilitated operation in their preferred mode; those who were conflicted preferred those who supported preferred defenses.[45]

In a study which compared 'most change' and 'least change' members of a large T-group, Stock found that 'least change' members were like one another in perceiving themselves as warm and work-oriented. 'Most change' members were more diverse but shared an unclear, less well established sense of the kinds of persons they were. One possibility is that these 'most change' members utilized the T-group as an opportunity to explore and to some extent to resolve internal inconsistencies.[46]

Mathis developed a 'trainability index' in an attempt to predict an individual's potential for learning and change through a group experience. This index was a ratio between 'adient' and 'abient' indicators. 'Adient' characteristics were the existence of intrapersonal conflicts plus tendencies toward the free expression of fight and pairing. 'Abient' characteristics were indications of immobilization plus tendencies to express dependency and flight. Of fifty persons for whom a trainability index was calculated, the ten highest scorers differed from the ten lowest scorers in showing greater increases in the integration of work and emotionality, in their ability to predict sociometric ratings among fellow-members, and in their confidence in their acceptance by other members of the group.[47] Lieberman's study, already reported,[48] also bore on the issue of individual change, and suggested that group culture is a factor. The two groups which he studied differed in climate or group culture: one displayed an atmosphere of warmth and of easy relationships with the leader; the other was marked by a struggle for leadership. Persons showed personal change in both groups, but in the first group it was persons with tendencies toward counterdependency which changed most and persons with tendencies toward pairing and dependency changed least. In the second group dependency members changed most and counterdependency members changed least. Lieberman suggested that in the first group, in which counterdependency was an inappropriate way of behaving, counterdependency members were forced into another mode of behavior. Similarly, the prevailing atmosphere of counter-dependency in the second group pressed dependency members to shift their preferred mode of operating.

In the course of conducting these various studies the research team gained considerable experience in trying to operationalize Bion's concepts and in applying them to a range of issues having to do with the overall character of a group, composition and its consequences, group development, and individual behavior, perceptions and change. We remained convinced that Bion's fundamental insight — that the group as a whole can be seen to operate on certain shared assumptions which lie outside awareness — remains viable and transcends the specifics of his theory.[49] The same can be said of the basic idea that group events can be seen as the varying and fluid interaction between cognitive and affective aspects of group life.

The concepts of dependency, pairing, and fight-flight seem viable but somewhat subject to oversimplification. Similarly labeled group cultures can in fact take quite different forms. There are times when the group situation is confused and cannot be described clearly in terms of a single basic assumption culture, as when one emotional modality may be used to express concern over another. For example, warmth and friendliness may be used to avoid getting at real issues. Pairing behavior and flight (unconscious) are both present, but at different levels of awareness and expression.

The theoretical framework has been useful in exploring both com-position and development. The composition of the group, defined in valency terms, has something to do with its working style, with the range of affective issues explored, and with the sort of context it provides for individual growth and change. The development of the group may use-fully be described in terms of a succession of group cultures and with respect to how far the group moves toward a mature state in which emotionality and work are effectively integrated.

Bion suggested that each basic assumption culture carries its own rewards and threats and that when the threats associated with a particular culture accumulate, a shift occurs. That such shifts do occur has been demonstrated in our research, but the question of just what anxieties are specific to each of the cultures, and how individuals may contribute to the shift, has yet to be explored.

All of the above has to do with group phenomena. The theory has also been applied to subgrouping. Pairs or small groups may collaborate in support of each other's activity and/or in formation of interpersonal (sociometric) relationships. Ben-Zeev's work[50] showed that a particular basic assumption culture may be 'carried' by a certain subgroup; and that as one culture gives way to another a different subgroup may become dominant. This occurrence was so consistent that Ben-Zeev was able to develop a formula for dividing a group session into successive phases corresponding to distinguishable participation patterns. Applying the concepts of valency to sociometrically chosen subgroups proved to be more complex. An attempt to predict sociometric choice from modality preference worked for some members but not for others, depending on the nature of the underlying conflict. To remain within the terms of the theory and at the same time satisfactorily account for sociometric choice patterns, one has to attend to three distinguishable aspects of valency — affective approach, culture preference, and area of concern — and to the dynamic relationships among them.

With regard to individual dynamics and the relationship of the individual to the group, we found the theory less useful and in need of more elaboration. In order to identify personal change in valency terms — a plausible idea — it was necessary to differentiate three aspects of valency and to accept that valencies could operate in combination and at different levels. For example, two persons might change with respect to preferred affective approach — let us say dependency. However, one might have used dependency as a vehicle for expressing pairing and for establishing closer interpersonal relationships. As his capacity for intimacy developed, dependent behaviors became less useful and tended to drop out. Another individual might have displayed dependent behaviors in consequence of censoring out from his behavior all hostility and even assertiveness. As his capacity to tolerate his own hostile feelings developed, counterdependent or independent behaviors more frequently replaced his dependent ones. In general, in order to describe the uniqueness of each individual and the ways in which he or she changed, it was necessary to invoke concepts of conflict and defense as well as concepts of valency. Much of the behavior of leaders who press their members to change in their image may be organized by the notion of narcissistic needs — another concept that is outside Bion's formulations.

In sum, the attempts of the research group to operationalize and apply Bion's concepts proved useful and deserving of further attention. These purposes include studying group composition; group development; and the more microscopic flow of group events, particularly with regard to functioning and the shifts from certain shared preoccupations to others; the relationships between composition and group development and problem-solving; and subgroups or combinations of persons supporting one another to establish, maintain, or dissolve particular emotional cultures. Bion's theory is most fundamentally a set of deep insights into the group as an organism and it includes intuitions about the part of individuals in this organic whole. But it is less complete and adequate when we address it to more person-centred questions, for which it was not specifically designed.

The proper nature of human-social science

One of the appealing features of Bion's articles was their relaxed and speculative tone. Even when he discussed his furthest-out conjectures he remained calm. Nature, inquiry, and good sense spoke through him by virtue of his openness but it was his thoughtfulness that made the expression so elegant and meaningful. His personal example as creator of the articles is a model of reflective inquiry and was a by no means unimportant contribution to the dialogue of the time.

I wish I could end this piece in the same thoughtful and meditative mood that Bion sustained so well. I would like to ruminate on the nature of our experiences in researching Bion's ideas; and about the proper study of human-personal-social systems. I would like to consider what social science would look like if we were to start with the idea, explicit in Dewey and implicit in Bion, that the most valuable outcome of research is the participants' experiences of the inquiry — as distinguished, say from the demonstration and organization of objective findings. The knowledge to which human social research contributes most meaningfully is within the personal culture of inquirers; and, as they interact and 'combine' with others in the joint enterprises of living (including therapy and T-groups), insights from their personal cultures tend to become shared and communally internalized within the culture of the social system — as Bion has so well explained. Basic assumption cultures act as central themes which organize the group's way of life, and the society's repertoire of ways of life constitutes its adaptive potential. These concepts jibe well with Lewin's[51] idea that the state of major variables in the group's life is that of a quasi-stable equilibrium maintained as a balance of centripetal and centrifugal forces or tendencies. The quasi-stable equilibrium, like Bion's basic assumption culture, persists as long as it serves the survival and growth needs of the system. As these needs are met, others develop, making the condition maladaptive and straining the equilibrium 'beyond its parameters'.[52] After a period of transition a new quasi-stable equilibrium, steady state, or basic assumption culture takes over.

I shall refer to a body of propositions such as the above by the term 'metatheory'; and the particular body listed above will be further differentiated as a 'systems' metatheory — as distinct, say, from a 'machines' metatheory to be discussed later. Metatheory is the body of agreements we have with ourselves as to how we shall look at, approach, and comprehend the existential universe we are investigating. Metatheory substantially influences experimental designs because it pretty well forecasts the epistemological problems of the inquiry. How you as a social scientist go about getting knowledge — and what knowledge you need to get — depends on your overall sense of the nature of society. And this is just as true for the practical inquiry of trainers and therapists as for the theoretical inquiry of scientist–researchers.

We felt that our experiences as trainers and researchers were mutually facilitative. Bion's systems metatheory helped us as trainers to understand what was going on and how our projected interventions would affect group life; and the same concepts generated both variables and hypotheses for us as researchers. The more dramatic events in training groups suggested authentic experimental situations and the carefully-described and thoroughly explicated research treatments (e.g. *re* group composition and leadership) furnished prototypes for role-playing and models for 'significant incidents' in training groups. Thus the orienting or metatheoretic concepts for training and research had much in common; and so also did the sense of meaningful problems to be coped with in training and explicated in research.

In our own studies, we used Bion's metatheories as the subject-matter to be investigated. We showed that basic assumption cultures do present themselves, that they do shift, that individuals 'combine' in subgroups, and that inter-subgroup dynamics do provide very satisfactory content for metatheoretical scenarios. I don't feel that we went very far beyond Bion in the sense of adding much to his organismic picture — nor was that our intention. We did fill in some new details, especially about the three senses of valency.

What we confirmed were *patterns of behavior and affects* suggested by Bion to be characteristic of the different basic assumption cultures.

Such macro-level patterns cannot, of course, be given directly by the data of observation because such data are necessarily on the micro-level of utterances and acts of singular persons. Our processes of inference from the level of observations to that of broad propositions called for a kind of indirect reasoning that I now feel is the very essence of social research. I shall present these processes later as the agenda for the 'diagnostic conference'.

The diagnostic conference operated *a posteriori* and therefore could not at that time be considered 'scientific'. Most of our other studies, however, could be represented as 'scientific' because the research methods conformed to the scientific canons of the time. These canons in turn reflected the dominant societal–cultural assumption that the model for all events, whether human–social or physico–chemical, is the machine. The machine is composed of parts, each of which has its special function. The functioning parts are observable – or at least detectable – by technical means. The properties of the parts determine the capabilities of the machine. The output of each part provides the inputs for other parts. Understanding is complete when all of the machine's operations are demonstrated to be completely determined by how the parts operate.

This machine metatheory, like the systems metatheory above, recognizes part–whole relationships. But the dynamics of these relationships are entirely different: in the homeostatic systems model the operation of the parts is coordinated by the shared basic assumptions which confers on the whole the properties of an organism. In the machine model, coordination is programmed by an intelligence external to the machine; there is no shared basic assumption; and the way to understand the machine is to trace the flow of energy or goods from the environment, through the works, and back to the environment. Each component of the machine can be considered a separate small input–output unit, with the input seen from the standpoint of the part as an independent variable and the output as a dependent variable, with the two connected by the conception of a fixed technical rule of operation which might be called an 'intervening' variable.

It follows from this machine metatheory that the method of experimentation is to establish relationships among independent and dependent variables – that is, between component causes and effects – and that the ideal way to do this would be to show one-way 'concomitant variation'. If every change of A is followed by a change in B, then A is the 'cause' of B. If at the same time, every change B is followed by a change in A, then B is the cause of A, and we have association rather than causation. About the only 'independent' variables we can be sure of as 'causes' are those that are intentionally controlled by the experimenter. One can change the composition of the group, the way he treats the group, and the demands he imposes on the group – and at least some of the consequences will be identifiable.

But when all the variables are internal to the group as organism, the question of independence and dependence tends to be moot. By the time of *Psychology: a Study of a Science* (1959), the editor, Sigmund Koch, concluded that the paradigm of independent-intervening-dependent variables was seriously eroded although it was by no means clear what would replace it. But the machine metatheory with its cause–effect or input–output linkages dominated the scientific strategy of the day. Hopefully, in good Baconian fashion, each researcher would establish a few 'significant' connections between variables, and, after enough research has been done in more or less similar situations, the accumulated knowledge of relationships can be fitted into the fabric of an elegant explanation or theory. Thus the first question to ask of a researcher was what 'statistically significant' relationships were found among variables, next, how well did the findings fit the hypotheses; and finally, what is the researcher's opinion of which parts of the reasoning behind the hypotheses can be said to be supported or 'confirmed' by the experiment. Now, twenty-five years later, scrutiny of some of the relationships that we were able to establish, as well as some we weren't, suggests a good deal about the proper nature of social science – one, as it turns out, that more accurately reflects the 'systems' metatheory.

First, then, the more nearly alike were the variables being correlated, the higher the correlation. 'Alike' tended to mean two aspects of the same construct, such as the expression of emotionality valency on a private sentence completion test on the one hand and in a friendly face-to-face group on the other. Under certain conditions, the private and group situations were equivalent with respect to the impulsive expression of emotion, but in other group circumstances the correlation was low. One sees that the fruitful question for investigation is *not* how strong is the relationship but rather under what conditions in the group does the relationship show up? This would be consonant with our systems metatheory which would say that as the state of the group changes so also do the component relationships.

Another kind of consideration is illustrated in our effort to predict sociometric choices from valency patterns of individuals and in the effort to predict group problem-solving performance from the averaged valency patterns of the members. In both cases the expected tendencies were found to be weak (e.g. 'significant' at 'only' the 20 per cent level) and the relationships 'complex', which we took to mean that we had not sufficiently comprehended the 'whole' system. We found that the tendencies could be strengthened by taking account of additional variables – the threat–defense mechanisms of the individuals and the control mechanisms of the group (labile, constricted, integrative). Here we become aware of the metatheoretical proposition that predictions of behavior depend on knowledge not only of inherent tendencies but also of the means by which their expression is controlled in the experimental situation. Presumably the next step suggested by such weak relationships would be to see what implications about control we could derive from Bion and other sources and then to design a more complete experiment. And the 20 per cent level, discarded by 'rigorous' researchers, converts our effort from technical exercise to genuine inquiry.

The third sort of relationship we found was substantially zero for both size and significance of the correlations among variables. Assuming that we believe our procedures to have been sound, such a finding invites us to re-consider our reasons for thinking a relationship should be found. At this point, Bion's reasoning about groups as systems demonstrates its power. For if we assume that the group maintains itself as an organism through shifts in the whole pattern of its dynamics (as when it moves from one basic assumption culture to another), fixed relationships among pairs of variables would destroy the homeostatic, compensatory, or adaptive capabilities of the group. Hence we should not expect strong relationships among variables operating at the micro-level of utterances, feelings, and overt behaviors which are the signs of modality-maintaining interactions. On the other hand, at the macro-level, two aspects, characterizations or properties of the modality as a whole may show a strong relationship. Thus the participants active during a period dominated by pairing may be consistently different than the participants active during fight-flight. Similarly, one would expect strong relationships between style of leadership and the basic assumption culture capable of legitimating the group's relationship to the leader.

Because of the unpredictability of microlevel activity – the specific details of life – a fully deterministic social psychological science is impossible. The proper method of social science is akin to history. Each group – even in therapy – 'writes its own history' and the task of historical research is to 'reconstruct' the life and culture of the group and give an account of it. The warrant for the account is determined by the method it is arrived at, and this method has been aptly called 'the cross-examination of testimony by doubt'. This corresponds quite well, I think, to the method of inquiry by which a Bion, listening intently to the members, forms an opinion about the underlying commonality to which, in accordance with his metatheory, they 'must' be responding.

In our own inquiries we made deliberate use of the 'diagnostic conference'[53] whose mission was to construct a theory (or reconstruction) of 'what happened' in such terms as to make clear why each participant presumably 'had' to act the way he did in the observed situation. For success, we obviously had to have salient information (such as valency about each participant's characteristic reactions to the situational problematics); and the information had to be sufficiently precise that the solution (organizing assumption) would be uniquely determined.

One of our own researches may illustrate, at least partially, the required method of inquiry for inferring macro-level theoretical modes from micro-level observables. Presumably at times there would be discernible in the group a good percentage of utterances and affects expressing fight-flight, pairing, or dependency, along with some level of work. But how would we know which of these modes the group was in? Modes are macro-level characterizations and they cannot be measured directly. Certainly a fair share of expressions in the micro-level of the same mode would serve to cue one's intuitions. But what about contradictory expressions of other modes by some individuals? With more 'testimony' from previous knowledge of these individuals, we find that the emotionality in question has other valency meanings for them, not for reactive expressions of affect in this situation but rather as something to be concerned about — with their reactions being to their concern — or as a quality of the milieu which invites personal private need-meeting not possible in other group circumstances. Thus even the apparently contradictory data can be called into account, the behaviors of seemingly 'deviate' individuals is found to be entirely reasonable and actually supportive of the mode they seemed to contradict — and some further insights for further investigation are created as elaborations of Bion's metatheory.

What we are calling the diagnostic conference in research exemplifies the conscious use of dialectical processes in the quest for truth. In general terms, the group develops each option, point of view, action suggestion, or interest as fully and sympathetically as it can. Then it compares them with each other, noting the comparative costs and benefits, weaknesses and strengths, advantages and disadvantages. Then the group imaginatively creates a further option that best captures those aspects of common reality that all the others, each in their individual ways, were apparently responding to. Such conclusions, arrived at in this way are, I think, the nearest approximation that we can hope for of 'the facts' in the human-social realm. It follows that 'truth' is local, emergent in each situation, experience-based, and partially warranted by the quality of the dialectical processes and the metatheoretical assumptions employed in its construction. Ultimately, the major warrant for such truth is the same as in psychoanalysis — that it resonates with intuition and facilitates changes in character, commitments, and action. Dewey thought of such learnings as being toward the experiencing of 'higher value' which, in our context, could mean a more harmonious and effective internalization of realities.

Such thoughts about dialectical inquiry invite speculations about the nature of a proper human-social science. It cannot generate principles capable of predicting specific micro-level behaviors in singular situations. The principles that the new science can develop and organize and teach lie not at the level of 'scientific' part-part theories but at a higher organismic or wholistic level. The principles will be of two closely intertwined but distinguishable sorts: the metatheories that help us to see what data to look for and the epistemology of dialectical inquiry through which recorded and experiential data are turned into evidence for the local or situational conclusions. Every inquiry thus will have two sorts of products: the practical, personal, and cultural understanding sought by the participant-subjects and the increasingly sophisticated metatheory and epistemology sought by the new breed of scientists. One might say that the participants will carry on a dialogue with nature in natural or experimental training situations in order to gain practical wisdom and more informed policies for coping with such situations; and that the scientists will carry on with the dialogue in order to discern and formulate policies for improving its dialectical, educational,[54] and therapeutic effectiveness. The new human-social science will be a philosophically-oriented (to metatheory and epistemology) quest for better policies of inquiry and action.

Let us now bring these ruminations to a close. Even though we cannot nail down the epistemology and method of the new science with very much precision or completeness, we can, thanks to Bion's clarification of work and emotionality cultures within his systems metatheory add some richness to our bare-boned concepts of dialectical inquiry. The new science would be about human conduct rather than overt behavior. Emotion and cognition would be understood as aspects of intentionality rather than as separate subsystem domains. The changing pattern of the way of life would be both the central object of investigation and the context for making sense in less wholistic studies. The unit of action would be a coherent dramatic event rather than a single utterance or a specified time period. Activity would be interpreted as the outward sign of experiencing, rather than as 'outputs'. Conflict would be seen more in the service of growth through dialectic than as a disturbance in an otherwise 'stable' *modus vivendi*. And the efforts of groups to learn to work and act in their conjoint interest will become the prototypes for the urgently needed reconstruction of the technical society into a world-wide humane community.

Notes and references

1 Bion, W. R., 'Experiences in groups', I: *Human Relations*, 1, 314–20, 1948; II: *Human Relations*, 1: 487–96, 1948; III: *Human Relations*, 2; 13–22, 1949; IV: *Human Relations*, 2: 295–303, 1949; V: *Human Relations*, 3, 3–14, 1950; VI: *Human Relations*, 3, 395–402, 1950; VII: *Human Relations*, 4: 221–7, 1951.

2 Ashby, W. Ross (1960), *Design for a Brain*, New York, John Wiley.

3 Lewin, K. and Lippitt, R. (1938), 'An experimental approach to the study of autocracy and democracy; a preliminary note', *Sociometry*, 1: 292–300; Lewin, K., Lippitt, R. and White, R. K. (1939), 'Patterns of aggressive behavior in experimentally created "social climates"', *J. Social Psychology*, 10: 271–9.

4 Thelen, H. A. (1961), Review of *Autocracy and Democracy* by Lippitt and White, *Harvard Educational Review*, 31, no. 3, summer: 327–34.

5 Koch, S. (1959), Epilogue, chapter in Koch, S. (ed.), *Psychology: a Study of a Science*, vol. III, New York, McGraw-Hill.

6 Cartwright, D. and Zander, A. (eds) (1953), *Group Dynamics*, Evanston, Ill., Row Peterson.

7 Lewin, K. (1947), 'Frontiers in group dynamics: concept, method, and reality in social science: social equilibria and social change', *Human Relations*, 1, 5–41; Lewin, K. (1951), *Field Theory in Social Science*, New York, Harper.

8 Deutch, M. A. (1949), 'A theory of cooperation and competition', *Human Relations*, 2: 129–52.

9 Thelen, H. A. (1950), 'Educational dynamics: theory and research', *J. Social Issues*, 6, no. 2: 1–95.

10 Withall, J. (1951), 'The development of a technique for the measurement of social-emotional climate in classrooms', *J. Educational Research*, 45: 93–100.

11 Flanders, N. A. (1951), 'Personal-social anxiety as a factor in experiment learning situations', *J. Educational Research*, 45: 100–10.

12 Perkins, H. V. (1951), 'Climate influences group learning', *J. Educational Research*, 45: 115–19.

13 Rehage, K. J. (1951), 'A comparison of pupil-teacher planning and teacher-directed procedures in eighth grade social studies classes', *J. Educational Research*, 45: 111–15.

14 Glidewell, J. C. (1949), 'Prediction of some aspects of group leadership behavior', unpublished Master's essay, University of Chicago; Glidewell, J. C. (1951), 'The teacher's feelings as an educational resource', *J. Educational Research*, 45: 119–26.
15 Thelen (1950).
16 deHaan, R. (1951), 'Graphic analysis of group process', unpublished doctoral dissertation, University of Chicago.
17 Stock, D. (1952), 'The relationship between the sociometric structure of the group and certain personality characteristics of the individual', unpublished doctoral dissertation, University of Chicago.
18 McPherson, D. (1951), 'An investigation into the nature of role consistency', unpublished doctoral dissertation, University of Chicago.
19 McPherson, J. (1951), 'A method for describing the emotional life of a group and the emotional needs of group members', unpublished doctoral dissertation, University of Chicago.
20 Sarchet, B. (1952), 'Prediction of individual work role in two adult learning groups', unpublished doctoral dissertation, University of Chicago.
21 Glidewell, J. C. (1953), 'Group emotionality and productivity', unpublished doctoral dissertation, University of Chicago.
22 Freedman, M. (1952), 'The effects of the teacher's role on the group's willingness to participate in problem solving', unpublished doctoral dissertation, University of Chicago.
23 Thelen, H. A., Stock, D., Ben-Zeev, S., Gradolph, I., Gradolph, P. and Hill, W. F. (1954), 'Methods for studying work and emotionality in groups', University of Chicago, Human Dynamics Laboratory (planographed).
24 Stock, D. and Thelen, H. (1958), *Emotional Dynamics and Group Culture*, National Training Laboratories, New York University Press.
25 Thelen, H. A. (1956), 'Emotionality and work in groups', in White, L. (ed.), *The State of the Social Sciences*. University of Chicago Press: 184–200.
26 Stock, D. (1964), 'A survey of research on T-groups', in Bradford, L., Gibb, J., and Benne, K., *T-Group Theory and Laboratory Method*, New York, John Wiley: 395–443.
27 Bradford, Gibb, and Benne, op cit.: 15–44.
28 Thelen, in Koch (ed.) (1959) (see note 5).
29 LaBarre, Weston (1954), *The Human Animal*, University of Chicago Press.
30 Arendt, Hannah (1958), *The Human Condition*, University of Chicago Press.
31 Redl, Fritz (1942), 'Group emotion and leadership', *Psychiatry*, 5: 573–96.
32 Lewin, K. (1936), *Principles of Topological Psychology*, New York, McGraw-Hill.
33 Thelen, H. A. (1954), *Dynamics of Groups at Work*, University of Chicago Press; (1960), *Education and the Human Quest*, New York, Harper & Row; (1981), *The Classroom Society: the Construction of Educational Experience*, London, Croom Helm; New York, Wiley.

34 Stock (1964).
35 Stock, D. and Ben-Zeev, S. (1958), 'Changes in work and emotionality during group growth', in Stock and Thelen (1958).
36 Hill, W. F. (1955), 'The influence of subgroups on participation in human relations training groups', unpublished doctoral dissertation, University of Chicago.
37 Hill, ibid.; Stock, D. and Hill, W. F. (1958), 'Inter-subgroup dynamics as a factor in group growth', in Stock and Thelen (1958).
38 Gradolph, I. (1958), 'The task-approach of groups of single-type and mixed-type valency compositions', in Stock and Thelen (1958).
39 Lieberman, M. A. (1958), 'The relationship of group climate to individual change', unpublished doctoral dissertation, University of Chicago.
40 Back, K. (1948), 'Interpersonal relations in a discussion group', *J. Social Issues*, 4: 61–5.
41 Hill (1955); Stock and Hill (1958).
42 Lieberman (1958).
43 Stock, D. and Luft, J. (1960), 'The T-E-T design', unpublished manuscript, National Training Laboratories.
44 Ben-Zeev, S. (1958), 'Sociometric choice and patterns of member participation', in Stock and Thelen (1958).
45 Stock, D. (1952).
46 Stock, D. (1958), 'Factors associated with change in self-percept', in Stock and Thelen (1958).
47 Mathis, A. G. (1955), 'Development and validation of a trainability index for laboratory training groups', unpublished doctoral dissertation, University of Chicago (abstracted in Stock and Thelen) (1958).
48 Lieberman (1958).
49 This section is slightly revised from Stock and Thelen (1958).
50 Ben-Zeev (1958).
51 Lewin, K. (1947).
52 Ashby (1960).
53 Sarchet, Jeremy (1951), 'The applicability of the analytical staff conference to the study of group development', unpublished doctoral dissertation, University of Chicago.
54 Thelen (1981), *The Classroom Society*.

Chapter 6

Beyond Bion: the basic assumption states revisited

Victor L. Schermer

It has been a little over two decades since the publication of W. R. Bion's *Experiences in Groups* (1961), a work written in three phases, beginning with his work as a British army psychiatrist in World War II. The book was both revolutionary and controversial. Like much of the work of Freud, Bion's work on groups markedly deepened our understanding, yet was subject to important methodological, clinical, and theoretical criticisms, for example by Yalom and by Gibbard. Stock and Thelen attempted a detailed empirical study of the basic assumption states, finding some grounds for the notions of valency and group culture while having difficulty operationalizing Bion's theory and using somewhat different definitions of the ba states (I shall use the abbreviation ba to refer to the basic assumptions in what follows) than did Bion himself. Bion's conceptualizations have always had a way of quite intentionally bursting the bubble of experiment and rationality. In his own later terminology, he strove to keep his concepts 'unsaturated with preconceptions.' He wanted his ideas to facilitate a continual sense of newness and 'growth through experience.' He regarded the group therapist as someone who required a special 'fearlessness' to remain above the demands of the group and to see what could not be seen. He would likely not have objected had someone understood group mentality in an entirely different way than he himself, so long as that person had acquired what mystics might call a vision. Bion's was a unique and provocative blend of religious purity and scientific perversity, of standing back gently and of greedily plundering the graves of heroes and martyrs, of devils and angels.

It was my original intention to depict the broad scope of Bion's later thinking as it might apply to his largely pre-analytic theory of groups. (Only the last chapter of *Experiences in Groups* was written following his Kleinian training analysis and his appointment at the Tavistock Clinic,

139

where the group relations approach emerged and was then extended to a variety of practical applications.) The original task cannot be accomplished here for a variety of reasons, the least of which is time and the most important of which is that I do not feel prepared to attempt such an endeavour. So the more limited and practical problem of re-evaluating the nature of the three basic assumptions will be undertaken. Nevertheless, it will prove necessary and useful to some of Bion's later psychoanalytic writings to grasp the paradoxes inherent in his group psychology.

One last brief historical comment. Bion's group theory arrived on the scene concurrently with Lewin's and others' group dynamic approaches. It was as if the time had come to regard the group as an entity unto itself within the field of psychology. In addition, developments in ego-psychology and systems theory took hold shortly thereafter. Such multifaceted approaches incorporated consciously or unconsciously Bion's concepts of the group mentality or culture and of the basic assumptions. There are thus two avenues of approach to understanding Bion's group theory. One is to view Bion *in context* and the other is to free him *from* it. In his own words, this will provide distinct 'vertices' from which to understand the basic assumptions.

Kernberg, in a paper entitled 'Leadership and organized functioning: organizational regression' offers a description of the ba states which is not too divergent from Bion himself and to which most current workers would probably concur but for minor details. One can do no better than to quote him at some length:

> Bion . . . has described the regression that takes place in group processes in terms of basic emotional assumptions . . . The 'fight-flight' assumption, the 'dependency' assumption, and the 'pairing' assumption [see Table 6.1]. These assumptions constitute the basis for group reactions that potentially always exist but are particularly activated when task structure breaks down.
>
> The 'dependency' group perceives the leader as omnipotent and omniscient while considering themselves inadequate, immature and incompetent. This idealization of the leader is matched by desperate efforts to extract knowledge, power and goodness from him in a for-ever dissatisfied way. The failure of the leader to live up to such an ideal of perfection is at first met with denial, and then with a rapid, complete devaluation of him and a search for substitute leadership. Thus, primitive idealization, projected omnipotence, denial, envy and greed, together with defenses against these, characterize the dependency group, and its members feel united by a common sense

Table 6.1 Characteristics of basic assumption states

	Dependency	Pairing	Fight-flight
Predominant defense mechanisms	Introjection Idealization Devaluation	Denial Repression	Splitting Projection
Object relations	Leader as 'container-breast' Object hunger/object loss	Condensation of Oedipal and pre-Oedipal object relations *via* the primal scene	Bad, externalized object is pervasive Internal world is objectless
Narcissistic features	Over-idealization of leader is defense against narcissistic injury	Narcissistic self-object merger with the pair	Primary narcissism Narcissistic rage
Mythic features	The leader is anti-hero, prophet, and deity	Messianic myths; myth of the Birth of the Hero; Creation mythologies	Struggle between good and evil 'Paradise Lost'
Roles	The 'dual' of the leader Dependents and counterdependents	'Mary and Joseph' Overpersonal and impersonal	Fight leader Flight leader
Biogenetic core	Child-rearing and bonding	Reproduction and production	Protection of group from danger

of needfulness, helplessness, and fear of an outside world vaguely experienced as empty or frustrating [i.e., the infant's relation to the bad or absent breast: VLS.]

The 'fight-flight' group is united against vaguely perceived external enemies, as well as to protect the group from any in-fighting. Any opposition to the 'ideology' shared by the majority of the group, however, cannot be tolerated, and the group easily splits into sub-groups which fight each other. Frequently, one subgroup becomes subservient to the idealized leader, while another subgroup attacks the first one or is in flight from it. The group's tendency to forcefully control the leader or to experience itself forcefully controlled by him, to experience 'closeness' in a shared denial of intragroup hostility, and to project aggression onto an outgroup, all are prevalent. In short, splitting, projection of aggression, and 'projective identification' are predominant, and the search for nurture and dependency characteristic of the dependency group is here replaced by conflicts around aggressive control, with suspiciousness, fight, and dread of annihilation prevailing. [Clearly, Melanie Klein's paranoid position *en masse*. Note also that the 'bad' internal object seems omnipresent and the dynamics of the group reflect a continued ineffectual attempt to extrude it.]

The 'pairing' assumption leads the group to focus on two of its members — a couple (frequently but not necessarily heterosexual) to symbolize the group's hopeful expectation that the selected pair will 'reproduce' itself, thus preserving the group's threatened identity and survival. The fantasies experienced about this selected pair express the group's hope that, by means of a 'magical' sexual union, the group will be saved from the conflicts related to both the dependent and fight-flight assumptions. The pairing group, in short, experiences generalized intimacy and sexual developments as a potential protec-tion against the dangerous conflicts around dependency and aggression (which . . . have a pre-genital character, in contrast to the genital one of the pairing group). [Kernberg is not clear what he means by 'genital' in this context. Bion and observation are both convincingly clear that pairing involves pre-Oedipal part objects, most closely approximated by the notion of the 'primal scene' rather than Oedipal incest and rivalry.]

. . . The general implication is that a breakdown in the effective-ness of work created by various internal factors and relationships between the organization and the environment induces regressive group processes first, and regression in the functioning of the leadership later. If these group processes remain undiagnosed, only their end-product may be visible, in the form of what appears to be primitive, inadequate leadership and, more specifically, negative effects of the leader's personality on the organization.

Kernberg then goes on, in his typically lucid way, to show how the basic assumptions operate within an organizational context, making the ba states understandable in clear systems terms which are useful to the organizational administrator or consultant.

In keeping with this systems approach, Kernberg, following Miller, Rice, and Turquet, regards the ba states as 'the basis for group reactions that . . . are particularly activated *when task structure breaks down*' (italics mine; VLS). Here, he raises a most important question concerning primitive basic assumptive mental states in a group: are they fundamental, omnipresent variables, or do they enter the picture primarily under conditions of group or organizational malfunction? Unquestionably, Bion leaned more and more towards the former position in the three essays that comprise *Experiences*. The notion of organizational function and dysfunction seems in that light to be a result of the work ethic and of socioeconomics: God is such that one can always fix things up and build a better mousetrap, organization, or therapy group. In Bion's particular theology, however, God is omnipresent and tarnished and work is exploration of a transcendent sort, not a verbal or material or monetary construction. From that perspective, the notion of mechanistic regression from a state of operational boundaries and tasks would appear as utopian technology and thus reflect the operation of ba pairing and ba dependency.

This Bionic vertex is insightful in a particular way to which later discussion will be addressed. At this point it is pertinent to note that a compromise formation between the systems approach and the Bionic visionary approach has emerged, particularly in the work of Graham Gibbard and of Phillip Slater as well as the current presenter. Such a point of view results from a confluence of psychoanalytic developmental psychology with a concept of group phases which emphasize fantasy themes, role differentiation, and boundary differentiation as the 'invariants' (Bion's term) or states of equilibration (Piaget) in group development. Correspondingly, patterns of defense mechanisms, object relations, and narcissism in the members can be seen on closer scrutiny.

Gibbard emphasized the themes of Utopianism and messianism as they apply to ba D and Ba P respectively. His conceptualization of roles is artful, and he regards them as essential to the evolution and dynamics of groups. Particular role assignments propel the group to change its boundary conditions so that the basic assumption themes are both modified and return in higher forms of ego-development. Bion's concept of roles (e.g. the fight-flight leader) offers little hope for change and growth. He places his bets on a return to a mature work group on the leader's interpretations and on the limited capacity of the group to think thoughts rather than to return to the Procrustean bed of 'proto-mental,' anonymous, psychotic-like communication. 'The voice of intellect is a soft one' (Freud). In fact for Bion it is silence itself, the 'absence of memory and desire.' Yet the Bionic leader is paradoxical in this respect, as one is forced to recognize the capacities of the membership as bearing some resemblance to that of the leader, if not in quantity then in quality. To deny the capacities of the membership is simply to collude with ba dependency. Hence, with Gibbard and others, we recognize roles and role differentiation as potential growth elements in a group, despite their frequently defensive functions (cf. also Bennis and Shepard's dependent and counterdependent roles, etc.).

There is a particular denial of Eros in Bion's group psychology, as he portrays the group forever enmeshed in returns to the ba states, *à la* the repetition compulsion or the death instinct. This despair is not quite so dominant in his later writings, where he seems to have found life in thought itself, and where he sets as his task the elaboration of what he calls 'transformations in O,' O being the 'thing in itself' or the elusive object of scientific scrutiny. By transformations he means change at the deepest, almost inaccessible, areas of the personality. Here, knowledge will not do, only 'experience' of a particular sort, involving the creation of what he calls psychoanalytic objects, object referring to the creation of a mythic model and its resultant abstractions, overlapping with but different from the Kleinian notion of object relations. Such objects incorporate *sensa*, *myth*, and *passion* (their felt connotations fairly approximating to Bion's abstractions). Essentially, Bion's later works challenge the group psychologist to question at the most fundamental level the function of groups in human existence and the goals of therapy and training groups.

Slater, whose *Microcosm* represents a precise and yet human description of the evolution of a small group, emphasizes the theme of the group revolt, which can in no way be equated with Bion's fight-flight mentality, although it can be said to swallow it up in its more gradual, concerted, and growth-producing attack on the leader. The protocols which Slater so accurately records for us reveal something important about the ba states. One comes not so much to see them as states (static, stable) as what might be termed 'metabolites' of the group process. They fuel the group motor, as it were, but the motor itself is a continually operating paranoid 'influencing machine,' the goal of the group being to escape this unknown but feared quantity and the end-product being paradoxically the attainment of the depressive position and the rather successful resolution of separation–individuation and mastery of Oedipal problems. (This would of course be an ideal group composed of college students or psychiatric residents!?) The above paradox may be resolved in Freud's terms by noting that the essentially paranoid orientation of the nascent ego and superego towards the id is precisely what causes the ego to join forces with reality.

Slater's evolutionary approach seems to be the most adequate developmental theoretic setting for the ba states that we have to date. One may add here that ba's are not only energic forces, but also represent bio-genetic object relations templates, as it were, and which motivate the group organism, along specific lines in much the same manner as a hormone. But the development of this organism depends upon its ability, *via* its communicative nerve network, to move adaptively within its surround (cf. especially Foulkes). That is, we must continue to postulate and research the microscopic and macroscopic events in a group which are involved in its birth, life, and death.

As an aside, one can venture a guess as to why the Slater groups displayed this upward psychic mobility, whereas the Tavistock-type groups seem to drone on endlessly like a fugue of three notes in the bass with infinite variations in the treble. Although Slater seems to have followed Bion's rule of making group interpretations only (at least on the record), the leader's comments were less interpretative and more in the form of investigative queries. In addition, there are indications of a certain amount of maternal holding by the leader. Books were assigned (transitional objects) and the leader seems to have been uncannily aware of the sensitivity to narcissistic injury in the group. In Winnicott's terms, Slater and his associates seem to have provided an optimal holding environment for the group's symbiosis, rapprochement crisis, and separation. If the regression was not as deep in the Tavistock group, the therapeutic and, in the Dewey-an sense, educational potential may have been greater.

This leads us, *via* a detour, to what for the present writer may yet turn out to be Bion's most important contribution to group psychology, particularly as his later writings filter back to the group field along with newer conceptions in linguistics, anthropology, and what Piaget has called 'genetic epistemology,' that is, knowledge as it develops and emerges, which not incider⁺ally was a major interest of Bion, although from an entirely different perspective than Piaget.

The basic assumption states are the 'heart of darkness' of the group. They have a mysterious, unspoken quality about them. Acted out on a societal level, they lead to well-oiled social institutions (Bion emphasizes the army, church, state, and aristocracy, curiously omitting the technocracy of which he was a part). But due to the very primitive splitting mechanisms inherent in these institutions (cf. Fornari), the ba's lead also to group psychoses, war, religious fanaticism, mindless bureaucracies, and over-population. Perhaps this is too extensive a use of a psychological construct, but in any case it is not the main point here.

The question ultimately posed by Bion is how to enter into these states in such a way as to promote positive transformations in O, or more simply expressed, illuminate the darkness (oddly, for Bion, with beams of darkness) and, as far as possible, resolve the splitting which inhibits the development of the group and promotes social pathology. The problem of how a group may gain insight into its own processes while at the same time regressing deeply enough to allow manifestations of the most primitive, psychotic-like undifferentiated group phenomena is precisely the dilemma of the Tavistock consultant. That the dilemma is yet to be resolved is evidenced by cogent criticisms of the Bionic group (with its restriction of interpretations to group-as-a-whole phenomena, etc.) as psychotherapy, along with empirical evidence (Malan) suggesting less than desirable outcomes.

One among several approaches to this dilemma is to look at Bion's later writings on the psychoanalytic process, which in this context may be understood to mean the process whereby that sort of insight which leads to deep personal growth may be attained.

In his elements of psychoanalysis (see Table 6.2) he develops the idea of a grid, a two-dimensional space in which all the elements of a psychoanalytic session could be potentially located. The two dimensions are (1, horizontal axis) the potential actions taken by both parties in the psychoanalytic session. Here, he emphasizes a quantum leap that must be taken from the realm of falsehood to truth and scientific study, (2, vertical axis) movement from uncontained thoughts through the alpha-function which contains them and then on to abstract thought and what he calls algebraic notation, meaning something very different from the mathematical use of that notation, apparently referring to his own ideas of the point and the line, etc., a type of purest metapsychology, something akin to Plato's ideal world which we know indirectly through the senses.

Table 6.2 The Grid

	Definitory Hypotheses 1	Ψ 2	Notation 3	Attention 4	Inquiry 5	Action 6	...n.
A β-elements	A1	A2				A6	
B α-elements	B1	B2	B3	B4	B5	B6	...Bn
C Dream thoughts dreams, myths	C1	C2	C3	C4	C5	C6	...Cn
D Pre-conception	D1	D2	D3	D4	D5	D6	...Dn
E Conception	E1	E2	E3	E4	E5	E6	...En
F Concept	F1	F2	F3	F4	F5	F6	...Fn
G Scientific deductive system		G2					
H Algebraic calculus							

The fulcrum of the vertical axis is *myth*, because myth, according to Bion, performs the role of relating the various parts of the mind (and of the group?) to one another. For example, the Oedipus myth relates themes of love and incest to themes of aggression, murder, and guilt, and, *via* the Sphinx, to knowledge. One might add that myth relates the individual to the group through the equation of dream myth with legend (collective dream). In this view, it would be necessary to address the roles of individuals as well as the group mentality in order to flesh out fully the myths implicit in the basic assumptions.

Bion – and here he is moving into the educative function – makes a sharp distinction between knowledge of facts and learning from experience, by which he means very deep movements in the unconscious. It is the combination of sensa, myth, and passion which is at the root of learning from experience. That is, awareness must be of feelings and sensations, connected emotional imagery and their anxious anticipation, and a passionate search for the truth.

It is through his own subsequent work that one can see that Bion's formulations of the group and of leadership functions were incomplete. The leader must not only describe and interpret that which is occurring outside the conscious awareness of the members, he must also develop an activity in the group, one which is akin to psychoanalysis, namely that process of emotional insight which includes sensa, myth, and passion. On re-reading *Experiences in Groups*, I found Bion's example of his own group interpretations to be obsessional and intellectualized in character, particularly in comparison with his later writings where he moves fluidly between virtually autistic, psychotic thinking and highly abstract meanings, thus exemplifying in his narrative style the process he means to examine.

Implicit in what I have said is a specific educative, therapeutic, and research task for the consultant of group relations workshops and also for group psychotherapy. The task is to study the style of their interpretations and role modeling. This is a linguistic problem of meaning, of the message both as sent and as received and understood, which bears directly on the capacity of the group and its members to grow. It has to do with the fullness of the experience, of the group container, its endowment with sensa, myth, and passion, so that the group not only oscillates between work and primitive basic assumptions, but also moves towards a resolution of the split between emotion and intellect, between all-good and all-bad, and between alientated subgroups.

One can conclude with an observation concerning the viability of the basic assumption states themselves. Questions have been raised about the cyclical quality of the ba states and it has been suggested that one ba state may be a defense against another. These must remain questions until further scientific scrutiny answers them. More to the point, Gibbard, Stock and Thelen, and others have taken exception to Bion's tripartite model of dependency, pairing and fight-flight. They point to a distinction between fight groups and flight groups and to various admixtures and heterogeneities of the basic assumptions. Yet it may be Bion who is ultimately vindicated in this regard, as these basic assumptions so closely approximate three biological imperatives of human groups, particularly in their primordial onogenetic and phylogenetic state. These imperatives are child-rearing/bonding to the social group (ba dependency), reproduction of the species (ba pairing), and protection of the group from internal and external danger (ba fight-flight). Perhaps Bion, despite his confusion, was able to perceive in the unstructured group the fundamental and wired-in (instinctive) aspects of our group-ishness. Some day we may recognize that Bion was the first to recognize the biogenetic components inherent in group life.

References

Bion, W. R. (1961), *Experiences in Groups*, New York, Basic Books.

Bion, W. R. (1962), *Learning from Experience*, London, Heinemann.

Bion, W. R. (1975), *Attention and Interpretation*, London, Tavistock Publications.

Bion, W. R. (1977), *Two Papers: The Grid and Caesura*, Brazil, Imago Editora.

Foulkes, S. H. (1964), *Therapeutic Group Analysis*, New York, International Universities Press.

Fornari, F. (1974), *The Psychoanalysis of War*, New York, Doubleday.

Gibbard, G. (1972), Bion's group psychology: a reconsideration, unpublished paper.

Kernberg, O. (1978), 'Leadership and organized functioning: organizational regression', *International Journal of Group Psychotherapy*, January, pp. 3–25.

Lyth, O. (1980), obituary: Wilfred Ruprecht Bion (1897–1979), *International Journal of Psychoanalysis*, vol. 61, pp. 269–73.

Miller, E. J. and Rice, A. K. (1980), Selections from 'Systems of Organization' in A. D. Colman and W. H. Bexton, eds, *Group Relations Reader*, Washington, A. K. Rice Institute, pp. 43–68.

Slater, P. (1966), *Microcosm*, New York, John Wiley.

Stock, D. A. and Thelen, H. A. (1966), *Emotional Dynamics and Group Culture*, New York, New York University Press.

Yalom, I. D. (1970), *The Theory and Practice of Group Psychotherapy*, New York, Basic Books.

Acknowledgment

The quotation from Kernberg's paper appears by permission of the American Group Psychotherapy Association.

Chapter 7

Basic assumption groups and working groups revisited

Karl König

Regression is a concept central to Bion's view of groups. A group in the state of basic assumption acts irrationally because of regression. Basic assumption states are ways of dealing with impulses so as to satisfy the defensive needs of group members: they are compromise formations between impulse and defence which make do with a state of ego-functioning regressed to an infantile level. Later authors (Brocher 1967; Heigl-Evers and Heigl 1979; König 1980; Mentzos 1976) described more mature compromise formations which also occur in daily life, that is, outside a minimally structured therapeutic setting.

Indeed, social norms can be shown to result from psycho-social compromise formations which have become habitual. Thus the chairman of a scientific or business meeting by calling speakers in chronological order may prevent aggression in a rivalry situation from becoming too manifest. A therapy group may evolve a norm which makes turn-taking mandatory; one of its members will perhaps watch over the proceedings: we then observe the formation of a social habit which is already very similar to proceeding in a more formal meeting or a falling back on such a habit. Of course the therapist's task would be to interpret such a group habit as a defence: it is not conducive to therapeutic work, which makes use of the emotions arising in a situation of rivalry or envy.

Regression in groups is triggered by a lack of structure: the group leader refuses to act like a chairman, and since norms of behaviour in a meeting require the chairman to act in a way consonant with them, the group leader's behaviour makes them inoperative. The group is then perceived as an unstructured and therefore confluent global object, which comes to represent the mother of a very small child, who is so much bigger than her baby. This kind of transference activates a state of the self in each of the group's members which, to a certain extent, corresponds to the state of self of a baby.

151

Whereas the group leader does not give structure in the *usual* way; he does so in an *unusual* way (Argelander 1972). By refusing to behave like a chairman, he creates a situation conducive to therapy. At the same time he remains a representative of rationality. He does not tell group members how to behave, but he tells them how to look at their behaviour and how to think about it, and he also shows group members how their behaviour is motivated: both consciously and unconsciously. Change then comes as a result of all this: change in the group, but also outside the group, when patients transfer the memory of what they have experienced in their group, and also the way of looking at their own behaviour and at the behaviour of others they have learned in the group, into their daily lives.

The group leader, by his interpretations, also helps group members to switch from a state of experiencing in regression to a state of rational reflection and vice versa. In order to do this, the group leader must presuppose what Sterba (1934) has called the therapeutic splitting of the ego into an experiencing and a reflecting part. He will form an alliance with the reflecting part of the ego of each of the group's members: the therapeutic working alliance (Greenson 1967). If such a state of the ego and such an alliance exist, group members will feel safer to regress without too much fear. Regression will be in the service of the whole ego; or of self.

Since the relationship a therapist establishes with the members of a group serves as a model patients can identify with, they form therapeutic alliances with one another, not only with the therapist; this is indeed a main difference between individual and group therapeutic work (König 1974; 1979). However, the therapist will have to watch out: some members tend to emulate the therapist not only as a model of psychoanalytic reflection but also by abstaining from self-disclosure; such behaviour will of course have to be taken up and interpreted as a resistance.

In looking at social compromise formation in small groups, we look at the group as a more or less structured whole; in looking at therapeutic small groups we more specifically perceive them to form a network of mature working relationships. As part of this network of working relationships, each member must be able to identify with the others, but also know himself to be separate and different from any other person, to be an individual with his own life and his own personal history: this will also enable him to link what happens in the group to what occurs outside the group. While the network of working relationships persists, regression can be used therapeutically. If, however, regression becomes so deep as to paralyse rationality to a point where the network of working relationships becomes ineffective, if the reflecting part of the ego of each of the group's members becomes helpless to deal with the powerful emotions engendered by very regressive transferences, there will be no way, at least in the session when this happens, to use regressive phenomena therapeutically. Of course, this will most often happen with groups composed of members whose egos have been weak to start with, as in some neurotic or borderline conditions where much splitting into good and bad objects makes for very intense transferences.

The stronger the network of working relationships, the deeper the regression can be allowed to develop. In a group with a weak network of working relationships, the therapist will be well advised to limit regression by early interpretations.

The larger a group, the more structure a therapist will have to establish in order to keep it therapeutically useful. It may become necessary to permit and even foster the evolution of norms, which in a small group would have to be taken up as a resistance, just because they prevent regression from becoming *deep enough*. Thus, therapeutic large groups more than therapeutic small groups may mirror the evolution of stereotyped ways of behaviour in society. They may thus serve as training for citizenship (Maré), while at the same time remaining useful for dealing with pathological internal conflicts that come out into the open when, under the influence of regression, they determine interpersonal behaviour.

However, at times it may be quite difficult for a large group to evolve functioning social structures. Perhaps this can be explained by just assuming greater complexity in large groups than in smaller ones. However, there also is the matter of previous experience. In Europe, children usually grow up in small families during the first few years of their lives: even in kindergarten, groups are modelled after a nuclear family with many sibling children. More complicated social structures are experienced at school and later at work. In every situation which has not been experienced before, similarities to previous situations are looked for. In a large group, the global object 'group' is very large; thus, an unstructured large group may be very powerful in evoking the early mother–child situation. The need for familiarity (König 1980) of each of the group's members will thus be dealt with by projecting an early mother object or, if more information about other group members is already available, members may experience the group as divided into subgroups. Then the group may cause members to project other members of the nuclear family, thus obscuring the group's complex reality.

The projection of internal objects corresponding to members of the nuclear family even occurs, however, in fairly mature social compromise formations. The chairman of a meeting may be used to project father or mother objects; the other attendants of the meeting may be used to project sibling figures.

This can be explained by the fact that we all have experienced our nuclear families at a stage of our development when the core of our ego structure was formed. More complex social systems are therefore experienced in the light of earlier events, and our world of early inner objects serves as a frame of reference which structures later experience. If we possess an innate 'generative grammar' for social learning in more complex situations, it cannot be imagined separate from the core internal world derived from our nuclear family; both would influence behaviour in all social situations. In stranger groups, we try to manoeuvre the other group members into positions which correspond to our internal objects, the more so when we are in a state of regression; that is, when our perceptions and relational dispositions are closer to the past, when our ways of perceiving and relation are tinged by transference. Then a transference to a global large object, the group, may, by the regression that accompanies it, affect our transference dispositions: earlier transference dispositions become active.

Social compromise formations, both in a therapeutic group and in outside life, may become relatively stable if they satisfy the need for familiarity. Thus, a scapegoat may repeat a role he has taken on in his nuclear family, or at least certain aspects of that role. He may have been in the centre of attention in some other way. The group members scapegoating him may project bad internal objects or bad parts of self in order thus to deal with their inner conflicts, or just plainly to satisfy their need for familiarity. Other social compromise formations may deal with sibling rivalry, as does turn-taking. Small groups present quite a powerful trigger for sibling–parent situations. In large groups, turn-taking seems to occur less often than in large therapeutic groups. The large group as a very powerful trigger for the transference of very early good or bad maternal objects, may call for other ways of structure formation.

If we look back at what has become of Bion's concepts in today's group analytic practice, we find a differentiation of the concept of basic assumption groups reaching into more mature forms of group behaviour. On the other hand, there is an extension of the concept of the working group back into the basic assumption state. Deep regression and strong working relationships may coexist. A mature network of working relationships can thus be preserved in a state of the group where the experiencing egos of all members seem to fuse into one common ego, giving rise to very primitive phantasies.

Future theoretical work might be directed towards examining Foulkes's (1964; Pines 1979) concept of a group matrix in order to see whether it contains the socially mature non-regressive communicating channels of the group and also, more specifically, the network of working relationships described in this paper. The therapeutic splitting of the egos of the group's members would then permit the mature channels of communication to melt away in deep regression while, supported and fostered by the therapist, the network of working relationships could continue to function. The mother aspect of the matrix might correspond to the group as a global object, serving first as a transference trigger which induces regression, and, later on, more mature stages of the mother object being transferred to it during the course of group development. The mother object transferred would then be the chief determinant of the depth of the group's regression, thus causing more or less mature aspects of other internal objects to be transferred to the therapist and to other group members. With the increase of information about other group members, the group as a global object would separate into the individual persons with salient personal characteristics, permitting the multiple transferences of the Oedipal and adolescent stages of development to be deployed.

References

Argelander, H. (1972), *Gruppenprozesse: Wege zur Anwendung der Psychoanalyse in Behandlung, Lehre und Forschung*, Reinbek bei Hamburg, Rowohlt.

Brocher, T. (1967), *Gruppendynamik und Erwachsenenbildung*, Braunschweig, Westerman.

Foulkes, S. H. (1964), *Therapeutic Group Analysis*, London, Allen & Unwin.

Greenson, R. R. (1967), *The Technique and Practice of Psychoanalysis*, vol. I, New York, International Universities Press.

Heigl-Evers, Annelise and Heigl, F. (1979), 'Die psychosozialen Kompromissbildungen als Umschaltstellen innerseelischer und zwischenmenschlicher Beziehungen', *Gruppenpsychotherapie und Gruppendynamik*, 8: 152–66.

König, K. (1979), 'Arbeitsbeziehungen in analytischen Gruppen', in Annelise Heigl-Evers (ed.), *Die Psychologie des 20. Jahrhunderts*, Bd. VIII: *Lewin und die Folgen*, Zürich, Kindler: 790–4.

König, K. (1980), 'Le travail thérapeutique dans l'analyse de groupe', *Connexions*, 31: 25–34.
Maré, P. B. de, personal communication.
Mentzos, S. (1976), *Interpersonale und institutionalisierte Abwehr*, Frankfurt, Suhrkamp.
Pines, M. (1979), 'S. H. Foulkes' Beitrag zur Gruppentherapie', in Annelise Heigl-Evers (ed.), *Die Psychologie des 20. Jahrhunderts*, Bd. VIII: *Lewin und die Folgen*, Zürich, Kindler: 719–32.
Sterba, R. F. (1934), 'The fate of the ego in analytic therapy', *Int. J. Psycho-analysis*, 15: 117–26.

Chapter 8
After basic assumptions: on holding a specialized versus a general theory of participant observation in small groups

James P. Gustafson and Lowell Cooper

Introduction

There are several traditions which share the premise that social life can be understood more deeply and improve if people participate in groups designed to study their own behavior. However, such groups may go very well or very badly, as with any social invention. There are many dangers, and there are many routes for the development of groups. Hence, an adequate mapping of these possibilities could serve groups and their leaders or their consultants to find their way to the learning about society that is desired.

Whether these groups are called 'study groups,' 'T groups,' 'culture circles' or something else, the common endeavor is participant observation. In general, the members of these groups need to make useful observations for themselves and they need to participate in the interaction so that there is something to observe. Thus, an adequate map or theory for consultants or potential leadership of these groups has to explain (a) What will help the members to make the observations they need to? (b) What will bring about their deepening participation in the interaction?

We suppose that people already have intuitive or unconscious mapping of this social reality in small groups. An explicit, conscious map or theory could either improve on intuition, or betray it. A very specialized map, such as one which located all the firearms in the neighborhood, could work for better or worse in daily life. It might help, as in civil defense, but it could also be quite a distraction in routine visits with the neighbors. Most individuals would probably fare better without such a specialized map.

Thus, we are interested in having a theory of participant-observation in study groups which does not overly occupy us with the special case.

It would be better to have a *set* of special cases, of groups with particularly memorable sequences of events.[1] Still better would be a general theory whose domain includes the full set of special cases, but which can explain the relationships between these possibilities.

If we confine ourselves to the Tavistock tradition of study groups, there are two theories available for these practical problems. One is the set of ideas first used to interpret such groups by Bion (1959). It is hardly fair to call these ideas 'Bion's theory,' since he proposed them in a very tentative way, after some few experiments, and then left the field. It is extremely doubtful that he would have kept these hypotheses for very long, as he was always thinking up new ones. We shall then refer to this set of ideas entertained by Bion for a brief period as the basic assumption theory of small groups. Most consultants utilize only this theory.[2]

For the past five years we have written a series of articles (Gustafson and Cooper 1978a, 1978b, 1979; Cooper and Gustafson 1979a, 1979b, 1983; Gustafson *et al.* 1981a, 1981b) most of which have appeared in *Human Relations*, identifying unsolved problems in small groups, the limitations of the basic assumption theory, and gradually proposing an alternative theory which we shall refer to as the unconscious planning theory of small groups. Although the person interested in the practical problems of consultation might read through this series of articles and arrive at his own systematic comparison of the two theories, most people do not want to go to this trouble. Thus, the alternative theory in systematic form has never been available.

These two theories have one major idea in common, which is the basic working hypothesis of psychoanalysis transferred to the field of groups: they both agree that groups of people share *unconscious* ideas, assumptions or theories, which restrict participant observation and which can be demonstrated. Beyond this working hypothesis, they differ completely over: (1) What unconscious ideas are most restrictive? (i.e., content); and (2) What kinds of interventions are most useful for freeing up observation and participation? (process)

Given this dramatic difference in predictions, it is quite possible to test the utility of one theory against the other. We offer the reader the opportunity to carry out the experiment himself. First, we consider what unconscious ideas each theory attends to, and then summarize the differences. Then, we consider what interventions are implied by each theory. Finally, we consider the evidence favoring the unconscious planning theory and the evidence favoring the basic assumption theory.

To anticipate the conclusion, we may say that the basic assumption theory generally assumes that there is only one rational work group within a small group, while that which opposes it is denigrated as being irrational, anonymous and opposed to development.[3] This bias of the theory makes it completely unsuitable for handling serious differences of people in groups, the most everyday problem. It is a very specialized map, which is applied as if it had general relevance.[4] This makes it very misleading, awkward and even dangerous.

On the other hand, we argue that the unconscious planning theory is a general theory of small groups, which is able to provide consistent intelligibility for the range of phenomena to be encountered, and able to predict what interventions will and will not be helpful. Within this general theory, the specialized theory of basic assumptions can be comprehended as a special case. We believe that *this* kind of conscious mapping of small groups is consistent with the wide variety of unconscious mappings carried on by individuals. It is not a substitute for the latter, but we think it augments the unconscious bearings, and so it does more good than harm.

Unconscious planning theory: the relevant content

According to the unconscious planning theory, everyone has personal unconscious theories about what to expect in groups, what we call 'unconscious social theories' (Gustafson and Cooper 1981; Gustafson *et al.* 1981a,b). Such an individual theory includes ideas about what situations in group life are likely to be dangerous, threatening to take the individual back to traumas that have been recurrent in his group experience; and it contains ideas about what conditions in groups are likely to be protective.[5]

If a new group offers the opportunity to differ freely, the group is likely to align itself into two subgroups,[6] each very roughly representing one subgroup of members with parallel social theories, each pushing for conditions in the group which favor the development of its own subgroup. One of the most common alignments is that described by Bennis and Shepard (1956) in which one subgroup pushes for conditions of reliable dependence, while the other subgroup pushes for conditions favoring maximum autonomy and independence. Another (Gosling 1979) poses a subgroup wanting a very loose rein, allowing for free play of associations, against a subgroup needing a very tight rein, staying close to task. A third possibility is a group where the primary battle is over tempo, one subgroup wanting to push deep and fast, while the other subgroup wants to protect the right to move slowly and resist in good conscience (Gustafson *et al*. 1981a,b). In general, the unconscious planning theory states that the alignment of the members into subgroups may occur over *any major condition for the group's work*.

Let us consider one of the types in more detail, namely that in which the alignment is between a dependence subgroup and an independence subgroup. The subgroup pushing for conditions of mutual dependability as a first step does so in accordance with an unconscious idea or plan, that once dependability is proven, further risks can be safely ventured, such as becoming aggressive, since they may always fall back upon dependable comfort. One might also state this shared idea in the negative form: that people in groups are often undependable, so that one ought to venture nothing further, until this threat of being cut off and alone and uncared for is demonstrated to be set aside. In other words, this 'dependence subgroup' is a set of people with a shared unconscious social theory, very restrictive for participation, until the theory is disconfirmed for a particular new group. There may be a large number of differences between their individual versions of the shared social theory, but this much that we stated is held in common.

The subgroup pushing for conditions of maximum independence as a first step does so in accordance with an unconscious idea of plan, that once independence is shown to be safe and fully allowable, further risks such as affection or attachment can be safely ventured. One might also state this idea in the negative form: that groups often do not allow independence or autonomy of thought and action, so that one ought to venture nothing further, until the threat of being stifled or smothered is set aside. In other words, this 'independence' subgroup is a set of people with a shared unconscious theory, very restrictive for participation, until the theory is disconfirmed by particular conditions. Again, within the independence subgroup are apt to be individuals with quite different versions of the shared subgroup theory.

In summary, the unconscious planning theory sees the small group as an *inter-group* event, a struggle between clashing work groups with contrary unconscious plans, who try to push the small group towards conditions favorable to the development of their own subgroup.[7] It is important to add that the play of the two work groups with the situation is not the result of any particular education. It is something that can be observed in groups of children, who dispute vigorously over what form their play group will take. Some of the children may need to play house, while others insist that it be war. Both subgroups are engaged in developmental work activity.[8]

Basic assumption theory: relevant content

On the contrary, in the basic assumption theory there is ordinarily but one 'work group', for which schooling and conscious decision making is necessary. According to Bion, 'The [work] co-operation is voluntary and depends on some degree of sophisticated skill in the individual. Participation in this activity is possible only to individuals with years of training and a capacity for experience that has permitted them to develop mentally' (1959: 143).

When the 'work group' starts to cooperate within a particular new group, such as by exchanging names or bringing up their problems for discussion (Bion 1959: 144, 145; 51, 52), what opposes this 'rational' work group is an *undergroup*, which is opposed to development, hates to learn by experience, preferring the comfort of anonymous magical ideas, namely, its basic assumptions: that it need only wait for its single sustaining leader (basic assumption dependency); that it need only attack or flee some kind of dangerous object (basic assumption fight-flight); that it need only participate in the creativity of a pair of individuals to reproduce a savior or saving idea (basic assumption pairing).

This content of the undergroup is restricted to these few unconscious ideas. It shifts between these ideas, as any one of them threatens to remind the members of some primitive part-object relationship (e.g., dependency becomes equated with being swallowed), so that one of the others is more tolerable.

Bion suggested that an individual can gauge the presence of such an undergroup by how he feels about the group, how one or two of its members respond to him, and by nonverbal complicity of the others with the few who speak.

Comparison of the two theories: relevant content

When a 'work group' starts a form of cooperation, such as exchanging names or problems, and is met by difficulty from another subgroup, the two theories diverge completely in the perspectives they offer. The basic assumption theory, noting the disruption threatened by the second subgroup, views it as an undergroup. The unconscious planning theory takes the second group as a rival work group, which needs to begin by pushing for different conditions than the first work group. According to the planning theory, any demotion of the second group is a result of the bias lent to the situation by the consultant. He is like the colonialist who watches the natives start some civilized procedure. When some of them balk, they are being primitive, rather than having their own ways of working.

The basic assumption theory considers the undergroup to be an eternally recurrent, regressive posture, a-historical like the id. Its unconscious ideas are very simple minded and few.

The unconscious planning theory considers the second group to emerge to be a rival work group to the first established work group. It proposes that the unconscious purposes of each work group stem from the histories of the members in previous groups. The dispute about work conditions is not over a few possible matters, but over any conditions that can be decisive in individual and group development.

The basic assumption theory is very simple to remember as a guide to observation of unconscious content. One need only wait for the under-group to show one of its characteristic three faces. The unconscious planning theory, by contrast, directs observation toward what work conditions are in dispute, noting that there are a great many possibilities. It is less parsimonious, having a much larger set of possible dimensions.

When we pose the content interests of the two theories like this, it is quite likely that many readers will think that both offer some way to make sense of group phenomena, some method of rendering the complexity intelligible. Bion himself felt that the basic assumption theory lent only occasional intelligibility. He made very modest claims about this. He wrote: 'My attempt to simplify, by means of the concepts I have adumbrated, will prove to be very misleading unless the reader bears in mind that the group situation is mostly perplexing and confused; operations of what I have called the group mentality, or of the group culture, only occasionally emerge in any strikingly clear way' (1959: 57). On the contrary, the unconscious planning theory claims to offer a steady reading, of how one interaction is linked to another. Still, it is difficult to evaluate competing theories on the basis of the intelligibility they provide, unless the interpretations offer prediction and possible control through interventions. Retrospective intelligibility is of less interest.

Both theories then offer a bridge between their observations and practical intervention. Both claim to predict interventions that will deepen the participation and learning capability of the members. Bion hedged on this a great deal, however, noting how often his efforts were met with more difficulty. He liked to measure the effect of his remarks, not in terms of immediate effects (which were often negative), but in terms of subsequent meetings. The unconscious planning theory suggests that the effects of interventions can be measured in the immediate segment following when they are made. The group will either become bolder and more insightful, or it will become more cautious and dulled, or it will show no effect at all. Both the immediate-effect and late-effect methods for judging interventions have something to be said for them, but proving a late effect is very much more difficult and open to skepticism. In any case, we now turn to each of the theories for its account of how groups deepen, and how each predicts useful intervention to bring this about.

The unconscious planning theory: on deepening observation and participation in groups

The unconscious planning theory holds that individuals and individuals in alliance, i.e. subgroups, restrict participation as long as their unconscious social theory, in its negative form, is confirmed. They offer up behavior continually as *tests* of whether or not the theory is still confirmed. There are at least five modes by which an unconscious theory may be tested in a group situation (Cooper and Gustafson 1983). One of the most common is a direct transference test.

For example, a subgroup which holds that dependability of other members is often not available in small groups may offer up some small need for depending on others, either on the consultant or one another, to see if it is taken advantage of or exploited. A member or a subgroup of members may complain of being confused, to see if others are contemptuous, belittling or cold. It is a direct transference test, in that others are directly tempted to repeat the traumatizing behaviour predicted by the unconscious theory, in which case the past transfers directly into the present. If others do not repeat this trauma, deeper reliance on others may be ventured.

A second common mode of testing unconscious theory in groups is to give others, either other members or the consultant, the difficult state which one is afraid will be traumatic, hoping that they or he will demonstrate how to manage it. Again, if the member or subgroup of members believes that open dependency is dangerous, the need to be taken care of may be imputed to the consultant, for example, while he is belittled by these very people for his need for care or help. This is called a passive into active test (Weiss *et al.* 1980), in that it undoes the danger of being passive and traumatized by becoming active and traumatizing! To continue the example, this subgroup of members may deprive the consultant of any data, to demonstrate his dependence on them for data to do his job. The test might be passed if he can admit he needs their contributions to be of use, while keeping his dignity and self-respect. If he can show how to do this, then they may be able to admit they need help, when they do need it. They can take that risk, knowing they have a way of warding off people who try to attack them for their need.

Basic assumption theory: on deepening observation and participation in groups

Basic assumption theory holds that there is a part of (almost) every member that wants to participate in the work group. However, each is pulled by the larger part of himself into the regressive forms of shared fantasy we have discussed, into the undergroup.

The temporary cure for this descent is to identify it vigorously. In the clear light of interpretation the magical idea is exposed as inadequate, and its spell is broken. The members can then resume making observations, thinking, and so forth.

Thus, if the members of a group who can be observed show some signs of helpless waiting on their leader for some period of time, it will be assumed by the consultant that they may be very hard to wake up. Bion's extended example in chapter 1 (1959: 29-40) shows how the recommended interpretation made ten times in one session produced nothing but outrage. This, Bion suggests, is common. Bion himself minded this very little, as it allowed him to continue his demonstration of the phenomena, his chief interest. He pointed out that he was not concerned with being helpful. Thus, the principal method for intervention proposed by the theory has a relatively weak effect on the basic assumption phenomena to be observed.

Evidence favoring the unconscious planning theory

In summary, the unconscious planning theory says that a subgroup deepens its participation and study when its tests are passed, wherein behavior designed to tempt trauma (predicted by the subgroup's social theory) does not bring on the trauma, but clearly shows protection against it. The basic assumption theory, however, views regressive behavior as something that needs vigorous opposition in the form of interpretation.

Consider a group, for example, that appears to be helplessly dependent. In one theory the behavior is considered to be testing behavior, in the other as uncontrolled regression. Within the planning theory, helpless dependent behavior could be in the service of various tests of social theory. For example, if a subgroup is concerned about whether they can show their difficulties openly to get help, the helplessness shown is a way of finding out whether further dependent behavior will be attacked or disparaged. On the other hand, if a subgroup is wanting to know whether it can use its full strength without threatening other members or the consultant, helplessness might be shown to see if others prefer this weakness to make themselves feel superior.

Now if the consultant operates within the basic assumption theory, his one line of approach to the helpless group is to interpret the helplessness as evidence of a basic assumption that is irrational: namely, the 'the group is acting as if it only need wait for a god-like leader to have its problems solved,' etc. According to Bion, such an interpretation often will have little effect, although on other occasions it might help the group to resume perceiving and thinking. The basic assumption theory cannot predict when its one recommended intervention will be useful and when it will not be useful.

However, it is possible to explain whether or not the interpretation of a basic assumption will work within the logic provided by the unconscious planning theory. If the group were wholly made up of members who were testing to see whether they could use their full strength, by offering helplessness to see if it were needed to make the consultant feel needed, then telling them that they were acting dependent 'as if they only needed to wait for a god-like leader' would be a very welcome comment, which would pass the test. In effect, it would say: 'No, I don't need you to act helpless, and I am sure you can use your own heads.' This disconfirms the social theory that others (e.g. the consultant) are comfortable only when you are weak.

If the group were wholly made up of members who were showing helplessness to see if they could openly show more of their dependent needs, without fear of injury, the interpretation would justify their worst fears. It would confirm their social theory that you cannot show what you need from others in groups. They would become more uncooperative or withdrawn.

More often than not, any given small group will have members with varying social theories, not uncommonly dividing into the two subgroups defined. What then would be the effect of the interpretation that they were behaving 'as if they only need wait for a god-like leader to solve their problems (basic assumption dependency).' Half of the group would become aroused and begin to act more vigorously. The other half would become more withdrawn. If this event occurred within the first meeting of a study group, it would have the effect of telling the 'independent' subgroup that their work would be supported, while it would tell the 'dependent' subgroup that their work would be denigrated. It sets up some members to succeed, others to fail. In other words, the intervention implied by the basic assumption theory will be useful to all group members only in the very special case. Otherwise, it will discourage participation, or it will advance some members at the expense of others. Of course, what we have described is the result of a thought experiment, of seeing whether one group can explain what is missing in the other, and from the results of our own experiments in practice. The reader would have to test it out in actual group situations for himself.

Thus, we think it is hazardous to have only one method of intervention predicted by a theory to approach a given group situation. It is like the surgeon who only knows how to do an appendectomy. When his bell is rung and the patient is brought in, he proceeds to do the thing he knows. The results at times are spectacularly good. More often than not, they are poor.

Just as serious as his limitation of thought is his limitation to giving interpretations, for the consultant operating with the basic assumption theory. His characteristic posture is giving vigorous interpretations *ex cathedra*. Indeed he allows himself no other form of interaction with the group members. Consider situations where members hold a social theory that predicts that those who are in authority want to intrude and inject their own ideas and terms on others, to use this as a mode of domination (Freire 1970).

This *ex cathedra* pronouncing confirms the expected trauma. The members may mouth the words forced upon them, but their actual being withdraws into a 'culture of silence' (Freire 1970). The actual sequence of events might begin as follows. The testing behavior, exhibited in the first meeting, might be to tempt the consultant to pronounce on minimal evidence or participation, especially for him to be scathing about the apparent regressive stance of the members, who seem to be taking little responsibility.

How might this particular test be passed? According to Freire (1970), who has worked extensively with people dominated in this fashion, the most reliable method is to avoid strictly any pronouncements, but rather to limit oneself to posing problems. For example, in the situation we have described, one might say: 'I feel tempted to take over, but I can see that it won't do you any good. It isn't clear what you want this group to be about.' Or one might say, 'Isn't this the kind of situation where you get jumped on?'

In general, we have found this particular test so pervasive that we find a problem-solving stance, in starting with a group, to be almost always required. For us it is routine consultation to invite group members to give their own interpretations, prior to stating our own. This also disconfirms the pervasive social theory that consultants in authority want to arrogate interpretation to themselves in order to dominate.

Now even if one should avoid the *ex cathedra* posture and the narrow logic of exposing basic assumptions, one is still left with a major difficulty as a small group consultant. According to the unconscious planning theory, one is likely to be faced with at least two subgroups with very different tests to pass for their participation. If reality is this complex, how is one to keep in mind the differing requirements of the two subgroups? The constant danger is of being captured by one of the subgroups, helping it to advance, while neglecting the other. Of course, it helps some to have a formulation in mind of the two subgroups and their different needs, to manage more even-handedly. The theory directs one toward this kind of intellectual balancing activity.

Even so, the consultant operating within the perspective of this theory will find it difficult to stay in contact with one of the subgroups. He finds himself favoring the conditions of one subgroup, while the other is going dead. This may have to do with his own unconscious developmental needs. This is not only a matter of thought and verbal statement. At the most basic level, both subgroups must find him available, non-verbally, by tone, as well as by what he selects to attend to. This is what we call the *steering problem* (Gustafson *et al.* 1981a, 1981b).

Sooner or later, it will get even worse. He is likely to be put in a position where to be with one subgroup is to abandon the other, and vice versa. Inactivity doesn't help, either, because one of the subgroups is able to exclude the other. We call this a 'steering contradiction.' It is the most high-powered test available to members in a group situation, because the consultant is put in a position where to pass the test of one subgroup fails it for the other. It taxes him to the utmost, whether he can keep in mind what both require, since he will be so tempted to sacrifice one to the other.

For example, given the alignment between dependent and independent subgroups, a common steering contradiction arranged by the group members would be: several members skipping a critical meeting of the study group when they were expected. If the consultant jumps on this absenteeism as a flight from 'the task,' he invites the independent sub-group to consider him as attacking what is most essential to its develop-ment, i.e., the right to make its own decisions. If the consultant ignores or passes over lightly the absence, he invites the dependence subgroup to consider him as in collusion with allowing members to let one another down, most traumatic to the sense of security necessary to development for the dependence subgroup.

Within the basic assumption theory, this extreme test is sure to be failed, as the consultant locates one of the two groups as the 'work group,' failing the other. Indeed, this is what did happen in the example cited, as the consultant interpreted that the group 'was acting as if it only need to flee the room (basic assumption flight).' Cooperation broke down completely.

Within the unconscious planning theory, the simplest advice that can be given, to have a participating group, is to ride down the middle between the two subgroups. It is less important what you say, what you interpret, than that you occupy this position. Still, here is a situation where the middle position does not exist.

One must understand how to solve this particular technical problem: how to pass this double, contradictory test of the subgroups. In general the solution is to admit that one cannot but fail one of the subgroups, given the conditions. In the example cited, one would need to explain how either approach to the absenting members fails half the group. This disconfirms both negative social theories, and leads to vigorous joining in of both subgroups. They then work out for themselves a suitable compromise, for example, regarding absences from meetings.

Interestingly enough, there is a side to Bion's own thinking in which he tried to avoid seeing the group in one way. He looked for what he called the 'dual' of any particular hypothesis (1959: 86-90), which is a technique for constantly changing one's point of view. He said that to remain (with the group) within one basic assumption was to become lost. One must have the ability to 'shake oneself out of the numbing feeling of reality' (p. 149). Indeed, he suggested that an important way to shift out of a numbing basic assumption is to *act* within another basic assumption. Thus pairing activity may break the bond of helpless dependency (p. 72). Indeed, he argued that the sophisticated work group uses one basic assumption, as in this example, to control another (e.g., pairing may delimit dependency, fight may help control pairing, etc.) (pp. 96-8). These ideas would come very close, at least in their practical implications and recommendations, to those of the unconscious planning theory. At least they would lead to some of the elementary principles of technique: e.g., steering between the subgroups, avoiding capture by any one.

But this side of Bion's thinking is relatively minor and completely unknown to most people who use the basic assumption theory. In most of his examples, Bion actively fostered the regressions he loved to keep demonstrating. He found evidence from several members of a regressed attitude, and apparent complicity from others, and interpreted this as an entire group regressed (pp.57-8). He handled some obvious dependent behavior with contempt, as if members had no reason to look to him for help (pp. 29-40). If a certain number of members started to work in a particular way, by exchanging names or problems, he viewed the others who did not want to start in this way as some sort of undergroup (pp. 144, 145; pp. 51, 52). In these ways, he actually failed to take a 'dual' view.

Evidence favoring the basic assumption theory

This can be put very simply. It must be true that sometimes groups actually are struggling to do sophisticated work, while, in spite of themselves, falling into one magical idea or another. It surely does happen. Let us use W1 to refer to the first apparent grouping or alignment, and W2 for the second alignment to appear. Within the basic assumption theory, if the second grouping is around some magical idea, W2 is simply a basic assumption, work-avoiding group, ba (D, P, or F). This is the simplest way to put it. The simplest intervention might be to call a spade a spade, inviting the members to stop it and resume work.

The unconscious planning theory would appear to be misleading in such special cases. For it treats *all* group alignments as in the service of *some* kind of work, particularly the work of testing unconscious social theories. Thus, W2 is also a work group, however regressed it may appear, because it is in the service of testing the situation, the other members or the consultant. Conceivably, this could lead consultants to be overly tolerant of patent nonsense (ba D), noxious irresponsibility (ba F), or utopian dreaming (ba P). It could. But this would be a misunderstanding of the unconscious planning theory. What it invites is a consideration of the *possible* testing implied by the behavior. It does not mean that every subgroup alignment is progressive. Subgroups often act badly, to test whether others want them or need them to continue doing stupid things. The unconscious planning theory invites consideration of the several different tests that might be implicit in an alignment that is apparently regressive. It is a general theory which provides alternative lines of thought in complex situations.

Conclusion

What needs to be explained is how a theory built on a very special case could be used as a general theory at all. How could the basic assumption theory become the rationale for the Tavistock tradition of small study groups? By Bion's own admission, it only explains occasional events, and it implies intervention with little power to alter the events it is interested in.

If so little is offered to study group members, how could a tradition be sustained? Indeed, in America, it doesn't produce people who want to be members. It mainly results in people who want to play the part of the consultant. There must be something useful in this role that people want the experience for themselves.

What is the role, essentially? As we have analyzed it in this article, it amounts to: considering oneself at the head of a rational work group beset by an undergroup. Presumably taking the part of consultant would mean getting practice at carrying this off, while offering assistance very occasionally.

But why would this be interesting to people? It must serve many different functions, as there are many different kinds of people who have wanted the role. It could serve for many different lines of development, like any particular role or behavior. But it is also fair to say that the ability to carry off such authority, while offering so little, is a talent for rising in the world, for taking one's place as a part of the governing class.[9]

By contrast, the unconscious planning theory is a general theory of participant observation in groups, which has the potential for helping people manage serious differences, so that various routes for development can be worked out within the same group. This capability for cooperation in groups, for democratic management, is not so much in demand as it once was. Like Mann's paper (1975), this theory could be considered a very late effect or response to the problems and the hopes we experienced in the 1960s. At present, democratic, cooperative groups are less evident.

We assume that the unconscious planning theory will be widely misunderstood. Previous versions of it came back to us in very distressing forms. For example, when we wrote a paper on 'collaboration' in small groups (Gustafson and Cooper 1978a), we found that it was assimilated to fit with the axioms of the basic assumption theory, namely, that we were talking about desires of the group as a whole, and that we meant that it be interpreted. Thus, we were taken to mean that groups held some kind of shared wish for collaboration, as if the lion and the lamb did seek to lie down together. This would be a familiar discredited humanism. We were also taken to mean that a new topic for interpretation had been introduced. This led to a repetition of the word 'collaboration,' such that we wished we hadn't mentioned it.

We *are* interested in how groups become cooperative, but neither of these methods is what we had in mind. Cooperation is a result, not a place to start. Indeed, one of the most serious dangers for members, which they attempt to protect themselves against by unconscious testing, is that people will seem to share identical developmental interests, when they do not in fact, the problem of pseudo-mutuality (Gustafson 1976). The only adequate protection against this, according to our theory, is an outlook and a technique thoroughly devoted to clarifying how different and divergent members' interests are. Only when these clashing interests are fully appreciated can people make dependable compromises with their antagonists.

This paper was presented April 4, 1981 in Washington, D.C., at the 5th Scientific Meeting of the A. K. Rice Institute.

Notes

1 This metaphor (or theories as maps) may remind us how a good theory may be a matter of life and death. Garrett O'Connor, in his discussion of this paper at the 5th Scientific Meeting of the A. K. Rice Institute, said that Bion's theory had been that critical for him. It reminded him of the fact that sailors in the middle ages used to bring back crude maps of their voyages which they called 'rutters.' These rutters, however simple, could be invaluable.
2 As with any oral tradition, there are pure and mixed forms. There are some who keep rigorously to Bion's original point of view. Most others have added various *ad hoc* principles. A common variation might be as follows: The consultant orients himself to the 'work' of the group in terms of its 'primary tasks' and 'task boundaries' (Miller and Rice 1967; Rice 1955). He may observe the group's departures from its task and from its various boundaries as occasions for the

interpretation of irrationality. He will look for the forms of irrationality in terms of the basic assumption theory. However, he will also be watching for any kind of projective process, whereby disturbances from one part of the social system may be induced in other parts, utilizing the broader Kleinian concept of projective identification. In this variation, both the 'work group' and the 'basic assumption group' of Bion have undergone some elaboration, but the substantial ideas are these same ones. Although those who practice this and other *ad hoc* variations are mindful of the improvement in practice brought about by their additional concepts, it is also possible that this 'improvement' holds back scientific progress. It is always easier to add an *ad hoc* principle than to change, revise or throw out the original theory. Thus, we believe it is essential to go back and subject the original theory (of Bion) to full criticism. What we have to say about this applies, with minor adjustment, to its later cousins.

3   It is not possible to provide all the necessary qualifications of broad statements at once. We shall return at length to some of the important exceptions in Bion's thinking. For now, it must suffice to say that he claims that, occasionally and very transiently, there are situations in groups which are 'schismatic,' in which two subgroups war for control. Each has half of what the 'work group' needs. This is the main exception to the pervading conception of one work group, versus an irrational undergroup (Bion 1959: chapter 7).

4   We do not intend to fault Bion for failing to do something that he did not intend. Bion involved himself for a brief period with groups, as a kind of literary adventure, something like Hemingway in Spain, or Henry Miller in Paris. He wanted to see if he could demonstrate how groups could act as an entity. He openly acted towards the given group as if he were studying its activities for his own curiosity, definitely not out of any interest in being helpful, which he disdained. He developed a very specialized map, which predicts what such an adventurer is apt to run into. Note very carefully: This kind of map or theory does not predict what is useful to the *group members*, but rather what gives some coherent shape to the events that follow upon a certain line of behavior for an *experimenter* with groups of this peculiar kind. Bion himself, in his essays, was very tentative about the value of his observations, staying close to the context in which he made them. However, he also wandered into wider speculation, which certainly has encouraged others to construe his specialized theory as a general theory. Our objection is to those who make Bion's observations into a general theory, and utilize it as if it were adequate general theory, not to Bion's original purpose, which was daring and imaginative.

5   As discussed thoroughly in previous articles (Gustafson and Cooper 1979; Cooper and Gustafson 1979a, 1979b), our theory of groups is an extension of the control-mastery theory of Weiss (Weiss *et al.* 1980) and Sampson (1976) beyond the domain of individual psychoanalysis.

6   By a 'second subgroup' we mean a second alignment of members for

a common purpose. It is possible for some members to participate in both alignments or subgroups. For example, in the basic assumption theory, some or all members could be part of the work group and the basic assumption group.

7 This sentence glides between two complementary different worlds, with hardly a pause, but we should mark it carefully because it is of great importance for a theory of groups that is more general than the theory of *study* groups. It appears that most work groups in society have a work task put upon them by a larger organization, by a dominant social class. These organizational plans tend to be interiorized, so that individuals and subgoups become over accommodated to them (Gustafson and Cooper 1981). Individual and subgroup plans that contradict the organizational plans continue in the shadows or on the margins of the work group. In any case, the work group dominated by the organizational plan is a ubiquitous phenomenon, very important for a general theory of groups and social organization. However, we have limited ourselves here to *study* groups (T-groups, etc.), wherein all members are offered an equal opportunity to make use of the group for their own study. This contractual equality, when it is backed up by democratic leadership, allows the free divergence that we are describing in this paper. Given this relatively equal strength of the group members, balanced by the democratic commitment of the consultant, the battle between two subgroups over the working conditions of the study group becomes the central problem. Since different subgroups will have different interests for how they want to learn and develop, the group will become engaged in the politics of learning. Of course, we do not mean to be literal about the necessity of only *two* subgroups, when more are possible. It is simply the most common form. In summary, we have offered in this paper a general theory of the world of participant observation groups, which are *decentralized* by definition. A general theory of all small group must explain the phenomena of the small group dominated by organization or centralized power as well as decentralized groups. For discussions of the more general theory, and the transition between domination and equality in groups, see Gustafson *et al.* (1981a, 1981b).

8 We do not want to be misunderstood in our emphasis on subgrouping. We *do* think that the group as a whole can be more or less coherent in its agreements. These shared agreements will be partly conscious, in so far as a work task and an arena for that task has been negotiated. They are also apt to have unconscious agreements, as to how the *divergent* plans of subgroups and individuals will be managed. These divergent problems are, as E. F. Schumacher writes (1973), the 'true problems of living – in politics, economics, education, marriage, etc. – which are always problems of overcoming or reconciling opposites. They are divergent problems and have no solution in the ordinary sense of the word' (1973: 97–9). It is equally possible to see the divergent work groups as built up from divergent individual or subgroup plans (as a synthesis of smaller units), *or* as a strain within a

larger general system (which is played out in terms of two particular subgroups). We are indebted to Larry Hirschorn and Jim Krantz for discussions on this latter point. Hirschorn and Krantz differ with us, in preferring the general systems alternative. We prefer to be able to consider the divergence from either starting point.

9   The politics of the Tavistock tradition deserves an entire essay of its own, as it has been an interesting alliance of a number of interests, with a somewhat different composition in America than in England. However, the dominant, organizing constructs from the original conference organization, the Tavistock Institute of Human Relations, focus upon the problems of boundary control by management. The 'primary task' of an organization is that which it must do to 'survive' (Miller and Rice 1967). Within this managerial outlook, Bion's theory of the work group versus its undergroup is utilized as a way of conceptualizing control of small groups by management (to keep small groups 'on task'). This is not to say that the tradition lacks, altogether, concern for and consideration of the dilemmas of workers or clients. For example, a common viewpoint in this tradition is that group members are vulnerable to charismatic authority, which group relations conferences dramatize and help members to recognize and protect themselves from. It is usually conceptualized as a matter of protecting the task from these incursions of madness, or, in the language of Weber, protection of bureaucratic authority from charismatic authority. What is largely in the shadows is that members may need to be protected from the 'task system' itself of the new, prevalent bureaucratic authority. This single-minded 'rationality' is hardly questioned, for the 'work groups,' by definition, is the embodiment of what is good. Meanwhile of course, we remain fascinated by what is *not* in the work group, and some of us can even get romantic about it.

References

Bennis, W. G. and Shepard, H. A. (1956), 'A theory of group development', *Human Relations*, 9: 415–37.
Bion, W. R. (1959), *Experiences in Groups*, New York, Basic Books.
Cooper, L. and Gustafson, J. P. (1979a), 'Planning and mastery in group therapy', *Human Relations*, 32: 689–703.
Cooper, L. and Gustafson, J. P (1979b), 'Towards a general theory of group therapy', *Human Relations*, 32: 967–81.
Cooper, L. and Gustafson, J. P. (1983), 'Conflict in group therapy, management of individual differences', in *Group and Family Therapy, 1982* (ed. L. Wolberg and M. Aronson), New York, Brunner/Mazel.
Freire, P. (1970), *Pedagogy of the Oppressed*, New York, Herder.
Gosling, R. (1979), 'Another source of conservatism in groups', in *Exploring Individual and Organizational Boundaries* (ed. W. G. Lawrence), New York, Wiley.

Gustafson, J. P. and Cooper, L. (1978a), 'Collaboration in small groups: theory and technique for the study of small group processes', *Human Relations*, 31: 155–71.

Gustafson, J. P. and Cooper, L. (1978b), 'Toward the study of society in microcosm: critical problems of group relations conferences', *Human Relations*, 31: 843–62.

Gustafson, J. P. and Cooper, L. (1979), 'Unconscious planning in small groups', *Human Relations*, 32: 689–703.

Gustafson, J. P. and Cooper, L. (1981), 'Over accommodation', presented at the 5th Scientific Meeting of the A. K. Rice Institute, April.

Gustafson, J. P., Cooper, L., Lathrop, N., Ringler, K., Seldin, R. and Wright, M. K. (1981a), 'Cooperative and clashing interests in small groups, part I: 'Theory', *Human Relations*, 34: 315–37.

Gustafson, J. P., Cooper, L., Lathrop, N., Ringler, K., Seldin, F. and Wright, M. K. (1981b), 'Cooperative and clashing interests in small groups', part II: 'Group narratives', *Human Relations*, 34: 367–78.

Mann, R. D. (1975), 'Winners, losers and the search for equality in groups', in *Theories of Group Processes* (ed. C. Cooper), London, Wiley.

Miller, E. J. and Rice, A. K. (1967), *Systems of Organization*, London, Tavistock.

Rice, A. K. (1965), *Learning for Leadership*, London, Tavistock.

Sampson, H. (1976), 'A critique of certain traditional concepts in the psychoanalytic theory of therapy', *Bull. Menninger Clinic*, 40: 255–62.

Schumacher, E. F. (1973), *Small is Beautiful*, London, Blond & Briggs.

Weiss, J., Sampson, H., Gassner, S. and Caston, J. (1980), *Bulletin* no. 4, Psychotherapy Research Group, Department of Psychiatry, Mount Zion Hospital and Medical Center, San Francisco, (available on request from Ms Janet Bergman, San Francisco Psychoanalytic Institute, 2420 Stutter Street, San Francisco, California, 94115).

Chapter 9

Bion's contribution to the understanding of the individual and the group

León Grinberg

Wilfred R. Bion was, above all, a creative psychoanalyst. His capacity to observe and to give meaning to his observations, together with his magnificent intuition, which he postulated as essential functions in psychoanalytic work, constituted precisely the basic elements of his creative attitude. Based on Kant, he maintained that intuition, which is blind, and the isolated concept, which is empty, can be integrated in such a way as to form a complete and mature thought. This is the type of thought essential for the 'psychoanalytic function'. Few analysts have been able to achieve the maturity of thought which he reached and the extraordinary clinical acuteness which transcends all of his work, characterized by the originality, profoundness and systematization with which he developed his ideas.

Bion's devotion to truth was one of his greatest merits and one of the most valuable contributions which he has left us. Following Freud's (1937) statement that 'We must not forget that the analytic relation is based on a love of truth; that is, on a recognition of reality, and that it precludes any other kind of shame or deceit', Bion also stated that the search for truth is as essential for mental growth as food is for the growth of the biological organism. Without truth, the mind does not develop; it dies of starvation.

But we all know that insight, based on the 'love for truth', the principal goal of psychoanalysis, awakens, in the majority of cases, the most powerful resistances. Bion (1978) pointed out that 'we have to alter to a point where we comprehend the universe in which we live. The trouble is that supposing we reach that point, our feelings of fear or terror might be so great that we could not stand it. So, the search for truth can be limited by our lack of intelligence or wisdom and by our emotional inheritance. The fear of knowing the truth can be so powerful that the doses of truth are lethal.' The analyst, during his work of investigation, disclosing the secrets of the patient's mind, often stumbles against not only the barrier which the patient has put there as a resistance to achieving insight, but also his own barrier which is determined by the anxiety which this getting closer to truth and insight means. Frequently, therefore, both resistances join together and gain strength to avoid facing up to the psychic pain associated with the acquisition of insight. This collusion can be demonstrated, sometimes, through mutual idealizations and adjudication of omnipotence, the use of intellectualization and of pseudo-insight and other defensive mechanisms. On the other hand, the learning which has been achieved through true insight will help to diminish the psychotic anxieties and will produce changes and remodelling of the ego which will continue spontaneously in the analysand, allowing the application of the acquired understanding to all subsequent experiences. He will begin to develop his greater capacity for discrimination, reality thinking, and creative potential in an autonomous and separate way, and he will feel able to work through his irrecoverable losses.

It is my opinion that the concept of insight is related to that knowledge which stems from the patient's experiences, which have been lived in an emotional and deep way, of all the unknown of himself manifested through the multiple transformations which he goes through in the psychoanalytical process. Some of these transformations are linked to 'knowing about something', while others are related to experiences of deep change and mental growth, helping the patient to get near to 'being that something'. The transformations which are related to 'knowing about something' correspond to what Bion (1970) called 'Transformations in K' and result in a kind of intellectual knowledge. On the other hand the 'Transformations in O' are related to experiences of deep change, mental growth, insight and 'becoming O'. According to Bion, reality cannot be known by definition but has to be been. There should be a transitive verb for 'to be' expressly for use with the term 'reality'. He calls this 'becoming O'. The analyst is concerned with the patient's personality in such a way that he goes beyond 'knowing about it', even though this knowing (K-link) is an important part of the analytic process. The 'Transformation in O' which would correspond to authentic or real insight is feared and resisted because it is the equivalent of 'being oneself one's own truth' with the need to accept the corresponding responsibility; so, for example, it is not enough that a patient knows that he has envy, but rather that he should feel that he *is* envious and should be able to tolerate it. It is important, naturally, to differentiate such insight so close to getting near to the truth, from all other types of intellectual knowledge or 'pseudo-insight' which tends towards the opposite; that is to say, the avoidance of truth.

According to Bion, the analyst's function is to psychoanalyse. It can be like being a mirror held up to the patient which would help him to see all of what he looks like. In accordance with what he has stressed several times, instead of being 'just like', both parties might start 'becoming'. Trying to teach the patient psychoanalysis or psychoanalytic theories is a part of education, not psychoanalysis. If the analysis effects an introduction of the patient to himself, it seems to initiate 'growth'. After patients have spent their life up to date trying to be 'just like' somebody else, the analyst is suggesting that they should be themselves, whoever they are, because they may have some redeeming features. He added that, in psychoanalysis, two people dare to ask questions about what they have forgotten and about what they do not know and, at the same time, must be capable of living in the present. As a result, they do get stronger. The analysis itself is done in the present. It cannot be done in anything else whatever. Nostalgia and anticipation are important because they exist in the present. The ideas of the past and the future, although they are feeble ideas, are emotionally strong.

Bion pointed out that if psychoanalysis is to survive and develop, there has to be contact with the reality with which we deal. That is why the practice of psychoanalysis is dependent on the analyst and the analysand being able to contact the psychoanalyst is a fact. Feelings are one of the few things, as it were, which analysts have the luxury of being able to regard as facts. The patient is feeling angry, or frightened, or sexual, or whatever it is. At least one can suppose that this is a fact. The analyst can say: 'That which you have just expressed in ordinary language is what I call evidence of envy.'

On the other hand, one fundamental matter with which we are all concerned is tension. Sometimes there can be so little tension between two people that they fail to stimulate each other at all. At the other extreme, the differences in outlook or temperament are so great that no discussion is possible. The question is, can the society or group or pair find the happy mean which is tense enough to stimulate but belongs to neither extreme — either lack of tension or too much?

Another dilemma is the one which confronts every one of us in this tiny universe which is the universe of ourselves; a universe which seems to be rather bigger than what, if we could fall back on anatomy and physiology, one could say was 'oneself'. A person could have a good idea of who he is if he were allowed to consider that his boundary is the same thing as the boundary of his skin. But he may wonder whether his mind is really inside his skin with the rest of the works. If we have this psychoanalytic prejudice, which is based on the theory that there is something which it is worth calling the human mind, and that it is worth investigating, it may be as important as all these radio interferences which are worth while attending to instead of the program which our betters have decided is what we ought to listen to.

Freud has mapped out a great number of characteristics and periods which can be seen to be recognizably human; characteristics of a human mind and a human personality. That very work now makes it possible to see certain periods in greater detail. Practical psychoanalysis is what we would call actually experiencing some period or state of mind of that kind, either one's own or that of another person who comes to share the analytic experience. A person in the adolescent period experiences survivals of childhood thoughts, feelings and ideas which have not died. They are vestigial, but they survive with a great deal of vitality. In language, a wonderful invention as Freud supposed, there are vestiges of its generation. Grammar displays some of these; for example, metaphors. Some are dead, some are still alive. If someone says, 'I smell a rat; I will nip it in the bud', those are two metaphors, both all right in their context, but bring them together, and dead clichés, these dead metaphors, become alive and the result is ludicrous. Some of these dead or dying states of mind survive with sufficient vitality to accord well, but some do not accord with coming states of mind, post-adolescent states of mind which are also coming alive. So what with the states of mind which are supposed to be dying, and what with the states of mind which are supposed to be coming into existence, a confusing situation is produced. It is not easy to say whether the state of mind at which we are looking, or which we are studying, is falling into decay, or is coming to maturity. That is what makes a period like adolescence so difficult both for the adolescent and for the observer.

What Freud and psychoanalysis have investigated are phenomena. The human mind is an important element; but, sometimes, it is also an obstacle. For example, it is not easy to see a stream which is flowing smoothly without any obstacle to disturb it because it would be so transparent. But if we create a turbulence by putting in a stick, then we can see it. Similarly, the human mind may set up a *turbulence*, and some sensitive, intuitive, and gifted mind, like the one we call Leonardo da Vinci, can draw pictures of turbulence reminiscent of hair and water. He can translate this turbulence and transform it by making marks on paper and canvas which are clearly visible to us. But we may not so easily 'see' this turbulence in the world that we call the mind. If we can, then it becomes possible that there is such a thing as a human personality in the world of reality, and such a thing as an underlying group in the universe of which we know nothing, only phenomena.

The analyst must be able to tolerate the expanding universe that appears in front of him through his relationship with the patient. He could, he thinks, pass from nothingness to interpretation, but by the time he has finished talking, the universe has expanded beyond its own perception, and the 'unknown' comes back.

Bion has studied the problems related to the learning process and the acquisition of knowledge. He reformulated the existing theories about the process of thinking, postulating original concepts based on the consideration that 'thinking' is a function of the personality which arises from the interaction of a variety of factors. In order to be able to develop his hypothesis, he proposed a 'theory of functions' which, articulated with the use of models, can be applied to analytic situations of different kinds, giving psychoanalytic theory and practice a greater flexibility. The theory of functions and the 'theory of alpha-function', in particular, must be considered instruments in the psychoanalytic task which allow the analyst to work without having prematurely to propose new theories. The area of investigation in which he applies the concept of 'alpha-function' (intentionally devoid of meaning) includes thought processes as they manifest themselves in their end products, such as gestures, words, or more complex formulations. The theory of 'alpha-function' includes the hypotheses that explain how these processes are produced and can be applied to the study and understanding of the capacity to think and of disturbances of thought. In his clinical practice, the therapist can observe the different functions operating in the verbal and non-verbal behaviour of his patients and can deduce the factors that play a part in each of them. Factors are elements of a function. The theories and hypotheses that appear as factors must be expressed and applied with rigorous precision.

The theory of 'alpha-function' postulates the existence of a function of the personality which operates on sense impressions and on perceived emotional experiences, transforming them into alpha-elements. These, unlike the perceived impressions, can be used in new processes of transformation for storing. Alpha-elements are, then, those sense impressions and emotional experiences transformed into visual, auditory, olfactory, or other images in the mental domain. They are used in the formation of dream thought, unconscious thinking during wakefulness, dreams and memories. Bion called beta-elements those sense impressions and emotional experiences that are not transformed. These elements are not appropriate for thinking, dreaming, remembering or exercising intellectual functions usually related to the psychic apparatus. These elements are experienced as 'things-in-themselves' (viz. Kant) and are generally evacuated through projective identification.

Bion also proposed the term 'contact barrier' for the group formed by the proliferation of alpha-elements that cohere and demarcate, contact and separate between conscious and unconscious with a selective passage of elements from one to another. This 'contact barrier', being in a constant process of formation, performs the function of a semi-permeable membrane which separates mental phenomena into two groups. In this way, it provides the capacity to sleep or be awake, to be conscious or unconscious, and to have a notion of the past and future. The 'contact barrier' can be compared with the function of dreaming as protecting sleep; it prevents fantasies and endopsychic stimuli from interference from a realistic view. In turn, it protects contact with reality, avoiding its distortion by emotions of internal origin. In the context of the same theory, Bion introduces another concept – the 'beta-element-screen' – which he used to explain those mental states in which there is no differentiation between conscious and unconscious, sleep and wakefulness. Analogous to the 'contact barrier', the 'beta-screen' is formed by beta-elements considered 'things-in-themselves' which do not have the capacity to relate to each other. Therefore, the 'beta-screen' is a product of the agglomeration of beta-elements, more like an agglutination than an integration. Nevertheless, these can achieve a certain coherence that manifests itself by provoking certain emotional responses in the object, which can be clinically observed. (This hypothesis has many points in common with the concept which I have developed under the rubric 'projective counteridentification' (Grinberg 1962)). The 'contact barrier' is the basis for the normal relation to reality, and to the internal and external world, while the 'beta-screen' is a characteristic of the psychotic part of the personality.

Bion's theory of thought and thinking is also a theory about knowing, about learning from experience and its disturbances. He developed concepts about the origin and acquisition of knowledge, as well as some formulations about 'psychoanalytic knowledge'. He took into account the evolution of the individual's knowledge about himself and others, the learning relationships of the individual in the group and those of one group with other groups.

The theory of knowledge which can be discerned in Bion's work is a theory that assumes that all knowledge has its origin in primitive emotional experiences related to the absence of the object. Characteristics that are inherent in this emotional experience sometimes intervene in an attenuated form in the later experiences of discovery, learning, and formulation of new ideas in any field, whether scientific, aesthetic, or psychoanalytic. He proposed to discover similar configurations in very dissimilar experiences; i.e., to point out invariants or equivalent structures every time the individual, group, or society is faced with a problem of knowledge.

As I pointed out above, Bion assumed that the ultimate reality of the object is unknowable in the Kantian sense of the term. The object of knowledge in psychoanalysis is one's own or another person's psychic reality. The investigation of it poses various problems. One of the main problems is related to the fact that this object of knowledge, psychic reality, is not an object in the physical sense. The basic emotions the psychoanalyst deals with – anxiety, love, fear, fate – cannot be apprehended with the sense organs (they cannot be touched, heard, or seen), but verbal and bodily transformations of them can be distinguished. The problem posed by psychoanalytic experience is, in a sense, the lack of an adequate terminology to describe such events and resembles the problem that Aristotle solved by supposing that mathematics dealt with mathematical objects. Bion suggested that it is convenient to assume that the psychoanalyst deals with 'psychoanalytic objects'. (The term 'psychoanalytic object' is not related to the word 'object' as used in psychoanalytic literature. Here, it means an 'object of knowledge'.) The psychoanalyst tries to detect them in the course of psychoanalytic treatment and, through successive abstractions and transformations, he attempts to find a way of communicating the nature of these objects.

This process of intuition, abstraction, and transformation is similar in some of its characteristics to the process of discovery and abstraction that Bion assumes takes place in the infant's mind during development. Thanks to his alpha-function, the infant deduces from his first emotional experiences the models and concepts he will use as hypotheses in his contact with internal and external reality. From constant evolutive interplay, his conceptions, concepts, vocabulary and language will arise, allowing all possible developments and uses.

During this developmental process, the personality comes across the problem of bearing the frustration inherent in the experience called the K-link. The word 'link' describes the emotional experience that is ever present when two people or two parts of a person are related to each other. Bion selected three of these emotions – love (L), hate (H), and knowledge (K) – as intrinsic to the link between two objects, as the requisite for the existence of a relationship. The sign K is used to refer to the link between a subject who tries to know an object and an object which can be known. The K-link can also typify the individual who tries to know the truth about himself through introspection. It also characterizes the psychoanalytic relationship between an analyst and a patient. Knowing the truth about oneself is a function of the personality. Bion suggested that Freud implicitly attributed this function to consciousness when he defines it as 'the sense organ for the perception of psychical qualities' (Freud 1900). The development of this function of the personality is achieved through multiple emotional experiences where the operations Ps ↔ D and ♀ ↔ ♂ (see below) intervene. According to Bion, an apparatus for thinking thoughts is formed in the infant's mind with the intervention of these two mechanisms: a dynamic relation between the paranoid-schizoid position and the depressive position (Ps ↔ D) and the dynamic relation between something which is projected, the contained (♂) and an object with contains it, the container (♀). This function of perceiving psychic qualities is basically related to the knowledge of psychic reality and is called by Bion the 'psychoanalytic function of the personality'. This function exists from the beginning of life and is developed by the psychoanalytic method.

The attitude called 'knowing' is the activity through which the subject becomes aware of the emotional experience and can abstract from it a formulation which adequately represents this experience. The process of abstraction is essential to the emotional experience of the K-link, because the abstracted elements can be used for learning from experience and for understanding. It is necessary to distinguish between the 'acquisition of knowledge' as the result of a *modification* of pain and frustration in the K-link (in which case the knowledge acquired will be employed for further discoveries) and the 'possession of knowledge' that is used to *evade* the painful and frustrating experience. The latter can be found to predominate in the omniscient part of the personality. The establishment of a K-link and, therefore, of learning through emotional experiences is precluded. This evasion of pain and frustration can be at the service of an activity called 'minus-K-link' (−K), an emotional state in which all the factors suggested for K are reversed. The emotional factors in −K are envy and greed, and, in terms of a container-contained, they constitute a relation which is mutually spoiling and destructive, where meaning and emotion are actively denuded of vitality and sense so that discovery and development become impossible. The −K link substitutes morality for scientific thought. There will be no function in this approach for discriminating between true and false, between 'thing-in-itself' and representation. In describing this link, Bion is defining the domain of the psychotic personality or the psychotic part of the personality. This link can also be called parasitic and takes place between two objects which relate to one another in a manner that will produce a third one destructive for all three.

Bion proposed to approach the Oedipus myth by searching for elements related to the K-link, that is to say, to the problem of knowledge, considering this — at least — as basic in the human being as the L (love) and H (hate) links. Psychoanalysis has found in the Oedipus myth an illumination of the details of sexual development, as Freud demonstrated through his use of the theory of the Oedipus complex. Investigation of the Oedipal situation in its multiple and changing realizations has proved valuable for promoting the development of patients in analytic treatment. It also nurtured the development of psychoanalytic theory, as for instance, the formulation of the early stages of the Oedipus complex. Psychoanalytic discoveries, in turn, allowed for a richer understanding of myths.

Myths have been a source of knowledge for very diverse disciplines. Myths can be compared with a many-sided mobile polyhedron which, according to the angle we see it from, or the view from which we observe it, demonstrates different faces, vertices, and edges. Some myths have deeply influenced psychoanalytical thought, particularly the understanding of the early human emotional experiences. One example of this, as I said before, is the Oedipus myth, told with mastery in Greek tragedy and which was elaborated upon by Freud and his followers in his theory of the Oedipus complex. Myth, tragedy and theory are, without a doubt, important elements in the understanding of a number of repressed situations, repeated and reactualized, in an 'undesirable, faithful' way, in the relationship between the analyst and the patient, and allowing its clarification, and the lifting of the repression, and filling of the mnemic lakes and the modification of symptoms through the analysis of transference. It is known that psychoanalytic theory has placed the Oedipus complex as the central nodule of neurosis and as a foundation for the bringing to light of love, hate, jealousy and rivalry as essential aspects of sexual development of the individual. Bion tried to approach the Oedipus myth from a vertex which looks at those other elements which were displaced by the emphasis given to the sexual components of the myth, although it does not exclude the essential importance of the latter. The riddle of the sphinx is for him an expression of the curiosity of man directed towards himself. But that curiosity is also represented by the determination with which Oedipus pursued his investigations into the crime against the warnings of Tiresias. According to Bion, psychoanalytic research has its background in a respectable ancient history, because curiosity regarding the personality is a central feature in the story of Oedipus. Significantly, that curiosity has the same status of sin in the Oedipus myth, in that of Eden and in that of the Tower of

Babel. In other words, he found a common underlying structure related to the K-link in these three different narrative myths. The common elements are the following: an omniscient and omnipotent god, a model for mental growth through an attitude of curiosity and challenge and punishment related to the prohibition against curiosity and the search for truth. In the Eden myth, the challenge consists of eating the forbidden apple from the Tree of Knowledge, an act punished by expulsion from earthly paradise. Oedipus' curiosity about himself is represented by the riddle of the sphinx; the challenge resides in the arrogant and obstinate manner in which Oedipus carries out his investigation despite the warnings of Tiresias, and the punishment consists of blindness and exile. In the Babel myth, curiosity and thirst for knowledge (to reach Heaven) meet the challenge by construction of a tower, and a city is punished by the confusion of languages and the destruction of the capacity to communicate.

The underlying confuguration of these myths is identical in relation to 'knowing'. Stimulated curiosity searches for knowledge: intolerance to pain and fear of the unknown stimulate actions and these actions tend to avoid, cancel out or neutralize the search and the curiosity. Myths give a narrative version of the problem; each of the three describes the drama of the relationship of the individual to the group with respect to the search for self-knowledge.

Bion suggested that the Oedipus myth is part of a primitive apparatus which operates as a preconception in the infant's mind. This preconception refers to the parental couple and will be realized through contact with real or substitute parents. The 'Oedipal-myth-preconception' is a precursor of knowledge or psychic reality. Therefore, Bion postulated the 'private Oedipus myth' formed by alpha-elements and suggested that it is an essential part of the learning apparatus in the early stages of the child's development. This private 'Oedipus-myth-preconception' is thus a factor in the 'psychoanalytic function of the personality'. The private myth, which allows the infant to understand his relation with the parental couple, can suffer destructive attacks from envy, greed and sadism, which are constitutionally present. The consequences of the destructive attack are fragmentation and dispersion of this preconception, obstructing the evolution of the intuitive dimension of an apparatus for learning from experience. In consequence, the development of the psychoanalytic function of the personality will be impaired.

To follow with the same subject of curiosity, Bion mentioned Maurice Blanchot's remark that 'La réponse est le malheur de la question' — 'the answer is the misfortune or disease of curiosity' — it kills it. He went on to say that 'experience brings it home to you that you can give what we call "answers", but they are really space stoppers. It is a way of putting an end to curiosity — especially if you can succeed in believing the answer is *the answer*.'

On one occasion, he was asked if 'the answer lies in the group'. Bion said that it was a convenient idea because it restricts the area of search. On another occasion, answering a question about the possibility of a group having an unconscious, he said he would not want to abandon that idea; nor would he want it to obscure the discovery of what else the group has.

Bion maintained that he continued to pay attention to group work, which he had always found extremely interesting. For him, group psychotherapy was not a lessened form of psychoanalysis, but rather a kind of different therapeutic technique, with a specific terminology and concepts related to the group's dynamic. He pointed out that it was necessary to develop a capacity which would be able to find out which was the common emotion of the majority of the members of the group. Group analysis would, therefore, depend on the evaluation of the 'essential' of a manifest emotion.

Commenting on some of W. Trotter's ideas about the functioning of a group, Bion made the following remarks:

> For example, take a group like this: We have a combined wisdom which is extraneous to the little that each of us knows, but by analogy we are like individual cell bodies in the domain which is bordered by our skins. I think there is something by which this combined wisdom makes itself felt to a great number of people at the same time. We like to think that our ideas are our personal property, but unless we can make our contribution available to the rest of the group, there is no chance of mobilizing the collective wisdom of the group which could lead to further progress and development. [On the other hand], the body has the intelligence to resist an invasion of foreign bodies like bacteria — or even plants, cocci — and mobilizes phagocytes to deal with these invading objects. Is it possible that we can organize ourselves into communities, institutions in order to defend ourselves against the invasion of ideas which come from outer space, and also from inner space? (1980)

Following on the same line, about the way in which the individual or the group can react facing the appearance of certain ideas, Bion stated:

Let us imagine that when a number of people collect together like this, there are stray thoughts floating around trying to find a mind to settle in. Can we, as individuals, catch one of these thoughts without being too particular about what race or category it is, whether it is a memory or an intuition, and however strange or however savage or friendly it might be, give it a home and then allow it to escape from your mouth — in other words, give it birth. To put it in other terms, can we catch a germ of an idea and plant it where it can begin to develop until it is mature enough for it to be born? We do not have immediately to expel the wild thought or the germ of an idea until we think it would be viable if it were made public. (1980)

Another important concept related to group dynamic is the one which Bion (1970) has called 'catastrophic change'. This term (with its elements: 'violence', 'invariance', and subversion of the system) describes the constant conjunction of facts that can be found in diverse fields, among them the mind, the group, the psychoanalytic session and the society. These facts can be observed when a *new idea* appears in any of the areas mentioned. The new idea contains a potentially disruptive force, which violates — to a greater or lesser degree — the structure of the field in which it appears. Thus, a new discovery violates the structure of the pre-existing theory, a revolutionary the structure of society, an interpretation the structure of the personality. Referring in particular to the facts as they occur in therapeutic groups, the 'new idea' expressed in an interpretation or represented in the person of a new member promotes a change in the group structure.

The group needs to preserve its coherence and identity; efforts to do so are manifested in conventions, laws, culture and language. It also needs the exceptional individual who brings the new idea and, therefore, needs to make provision for him. Groups are friendly or hostile, favourable or unfriendly, to the development of the new idea. Bion used the term genius or *mystic* to refer to exceptional individuals in any field, whether scientific, artistic or religious. Genius has been said to be akin to madness. It would be more true to say that psychotic mechanisms require a genius to manipulate them in a manner adequate to promote growth or life. He also used the word 'Establishment' to designate those who exercise power and responsibility in the state or other institutions, and to refer to whatever exercises these functions in the personality or in the group. The 'mystic', bearer of a new idea, is always disruptive for the group. The 'Establishment' tries to protect the group from this disruption; but, at the same time, has to find and provide a substitute for genius. The 'mystic' is both creative and destructive. The 'creative mystic' formally claims to conform to or even fulfil the conventions of the Establishment that governs his group; and the 'mystic nihilist' appears to destroy his own creations. The problem of the relationship between the mystic and the institution has an emotional pattern that repeats itself in history and in a variety of forms. The 'mystic' needs the Establishment and vice versa. The institutionalized group (work group) is as important to the development of the individual as is the individual to the work group. The group, as a container, should find some way of expanding itself in order to contain this new phenomenon, not to attack the new idea nor to drown the mystic. But the group should also avoid fragmentation or being exploited by the mystic or the messianic idea.

The relationship between the group and the mystic may belong to one of three categories. It may be commensal, symbiotic or parasitic. The same categorization may be applied to the relationship of one group with another. In the commensal relationship, the mystic and the group co-exist without affecting each other; the existence of each is harmless to the other. In the symbiotic relationship, there is a confrontation and the result is growth-producing, though that growth may not be discerned without some difficulty. In the parasitic relationship, the product of the association is something which destroys both parts to the association. The group–individual setting is dominated by envy.

To sum up, the recurrent configuration in these descriptions is one of an explosive force within a framework which tries to contain it. In the case of the group, this configuration takes place between the 'mystic-genius' and the 'Establishment' with its function of containing, expressing and institutionalizing the new idea provided by him and of protecting the group from the destructive power of this idea.

Before finishing this paper, I should like to refer briefly to some of Bion's contributions to the theory of technique.

We know that the aim of psychoanalytic treatment is mental growth. This is the psychoanalytic vertex from which Bion approached the practice of psychoanalysis and that of group psychotherapy. Bion's suggestion about working 'without memory or desire' – which, in my opinion, constitutes an extension and a deeper application of the concept postulated by Freud of 'floating attention' – can produce confusion and perplexity in the reader. It leads itself to misunderstandings which distort its true spirit. It proposes an internal attitude rather than a real modification of the analyst's technique with the patient. Instead of using the memory which refers to that aspect of the experience predominantly related to sensuous impressions, Bion particularly wishes to encourage that quality of functioning on the part of the analyst (the 'evolution') which will facilitate the full use of his intuition. He meant by this, that it is better for the analyst not to be influenced by his previous knowledge or his *a priori* judgment so as to avoid contaminating his evaluation of what is happening in the 'here and now' of the analytic session. In this way, he can more fully grasp the new elements and shades that always exist in each separate encounter between analyst and patient. This implies giving up the conscious use of 'memories' and 'desires' that may not be linked with the patient's material and rejecting the defensive use of his theoretical knowledge. Bion does not want to give the erroneous impression that he considers it would be good for the analyst to multilate his personality in suppressing his memory and desire. But he thinks the analyst can be sufficiently trained so as to retain his capacity to free himself *temporarily*, only during the session, whenever they appear as disturbing mental phenomena and threaten the profitable use of the analytic session. This implies an ability to embark on the experience of each session with a free, unprejudiced mind so that observation is fully efficient and 'evolution' or intuition can develop.

However, Bion wondered which was the most convenient mental state for the analyst if memory and desire were not. He then postulated an active position which restrains memory and desire and provides a mental state which he represents by the term 'faith' which allows him to get near the psychic reality that cannot be known but can 'be been'. It is a scientific 'act of faith' quite different from the religious meaning ascribed it in conversational usage; it has an unconscious and unknown event in its background. In this way, the analyst's intuition can be increased. This intuition consists in the ability specifically to recognize the emotional states of the patient and forms part of the 'psychoanalytic function of the personality'. This will help the analyst to reach the mental level in which he becomes more receptive to 'O' and also to have 'evocation' or 'evolution' instead of using memory and desire. The 'evolution' can be compared to the 'substance of dreams' and corresponds to psychic reality. It shares with dreams the 'quality of being totally present or inexplicable or rapidly absent'. 'Evolution' implies being able to join together by sudden intuition a series of incoherent and non-related phenomena which, in this way, acquire the coherence and meaning which they have previously lacked. In practice, this means an important step towards the 'at-one-ment with "O"'; that is to say, the capacity for 'unification' or 'being one' with the material of the patient.

Elsewhere, Bion (1977c) comments on the following sentence of

Freud (1926): 'There is much more continuity between intrauterine life and earliest infancy than the impressive caesura of the act of birth would have us believe.' Of course, there are many kinds of 'caesuras'. How can they be got over? It is during the course of changes from one position to another when people appear to be more vulnerable, as for example during adolescence. The problem consists in how to get over the caesura when one is 'moving from one mental state to another', how to overcome the different obstacles throughout the period of psychological development. Paraphrasing Freud's affirmation, Bion said that 'there is much more continuity between autonomically appropriate "quanta" and the waves of conscious thoughts and feelings than the impressive caesura of transference and countertransference would have us believe. Then . . . ? One will have to investigate caesura: not the analyst, nor the analysand, not sanity nor insanity. But the caesura itself, the link.' That is to say, Bion stresses the importance of studying the link and the caesura which involves the passing from one link to another.

Finally, I do not imply that analysts should now work with the technical ideas which Bion suggested. Even if we wanted to, we know that it would be very difficult to incorporate the technical attitude of 'without memory or desire' or the 'act of faith' or the 'at-one-ment with "O"' of the patient. Nevertheless, I think that, if we could acquire these mental instruments, they would provide a useful way to understand the patient's material in a deeper sense and reach being the 'O' of his evolution. I pose this because I feel that a change in our technical attitude would be another caesura or transcendental change equivalent to the caesura in the birth process. But I also believe that there would be much more continuity between the systematic analysis of transferential fantasies and the 'at-one-ment with "O"', than what the impressive caesura of the change of technical attitude would have us believe.

Let me express my gratitude to Dr Wilfred Bion because he placed psychoanalytic and group psychotherapy theory and practice in a new dimension, thus opening up new ways of psychoanalytic thinking, stimulating the development of intuition and helping the investigator to get himself into what we would call 'the state of discovery'.

References

Bion, W. R. (1961), *Experiences in Groups*, London, Tavistock.
Bion, W. R. (1962a), 'A theory of thinking', *Int. J. Psychoanal.*, 43.
Bion, W. R. (1962b), *Learning from Experience*, London, Heinemann.

Bion, W. R. (1963), *Elements of Psycho-analysis*, London, Heinemann.

Bion, W. R. (1965), *Transformations*, London, Heinemann.

Bion, W. R. (1967), *Second Thoughts*, London, Heinemann.

Bion, W. R. (1970), *Attention and Interpretation*, London, Tavistock.

Bion, W. R. (1973), *Brazilian Lectures*, vol. 1, Rio de Janeiro, Imago Editora.

Bion, W. R. (1974), *Brazilian Lectures*, vol. 2, Rio de Janeiro, Imago Editora.

Bion, W. R. (1975), *A Memoir of the Future*, Book I: *The Dream*, Imago Editora.

Bion, W. R. (1977a), *A Memoir of the Future*, Book II: *The Past Presented*, Imago Editora.

Bion, W. R. (1977b), *Two Papers: The Grid and Caesura*, Imago Editora.

Bion, W. R. (1977c), 'On a quotation from Freud', in *Borderline Personality Disorders*, ed. P. Hartocollis, New York, International University Press.

Bion, W. R. (1978), *Four Discussions with W. R. Bion*. Perthshire, Clunie Press.

Bion, W. R. (1979), *A Memoir of the Future*, Book III: *The Dawn of Oblivion*, Perthshire, Clunie Press.

Bion, W. R. (1980), *Bion in New York and Sao Paulo*, Perthshire, Clunie Press.

Freud, S. (1900–1), *The Interpretation of Dreams*, Standard Ed., vol. 5.

Freud, S. (1926), 'Inhibitions, Symptoms and Anxiety', Standard Ed., vol. 20.

Freud, S. (1937), 'Analysis Terminable and Interminable', Standard Ed., vol. 23.

Grinberg, L. (1962), 'On a specific aspect of countertransference due to the patient's projective Identification', *Int. J. Psychoanal.*, 43.

Grinberg, L., Sor, D. and Bianchedi, E. T. de (1977), *Introduction to the Work of Bion*, 2nd Ed., New York, J. Aronson.

Chapter 10
Bion and Foulkes: basic assumptions and beyond

Dennis G. Brown

Introduction

Wilfred Bion is justly famed in the world of group therapy for his studies of groups in the years 1948-57. Although subsequently he did not work with groups himself, these papers, which were brought together in 1961 in the book *Experiences in Groups*,[1] continue to stimulate and worry those of us who do.

Bion took groups very seriously. His ideas are challenging, and some, which I shall come to at the end of this chapter, profoundly helpful. It is my wish here to contribute something towards threshing the chaff of Bion's contribution from the corn. For some of his ideas are, I think, ultimately inadequate and misleading as a basis for therapy, particularly the unmodified concept of basic assumptions which is dealt with in the main body of the chapter, after the Introduction.

Bion asserted that these primitive states of mind tend to dominate groups and interfere with their declared task. He related the emotional attitudes organized in these states to unconscious basic assumptions of dependence, fight-flight, or pairing. At different times a group will behave as though satisfaction, safety and the future require respectively that the group depends on a succouring leader, fights or flees from a common enemy, or waits for some pair to create together the where-withal for the group's salvation. Few of us have not been grateful to him for helping us to understand something of why our institutions and committees get stuck. Dependence on the chairman, blaming the absent saboteurs, or hope that a fruitless discussion between two will provide a perfect answer for all, can often alert us to the need to do some work ourselves or sink further into collusive evasion of reality.

Yet, in contrast to those studying group dynamics in training and research settings,[2] many therapists find that attempts to use the concept in a clinical setting encounter serious problems, theoretical and practical. This is perhaps particularly so for those of us working on group-analytic lines originally developed by S. H. Foulkes.[3] We rarely speak about basic assumption states or use them as guides in our work. Why is this, when seemingly related phenomena can be observed in our groups at times? An attempt to answer this question and to differentiate and reconcile the two approaches may throw light on both of them.

Before examining the concept in more detail, it may be helpful to look at several of Bion's related ideas, some unexceptionable, some confusing, following roughly their development in his book to the point where they culminate in the idea of basic assumptions.

He wrote early on that 'the group is essential to the fulfilment of a man's mental life – quite as essential as to that as it is to the more obvious activities of economics and war' (1961: 53). He went on to demonstrate his view of the interpenetration of individual and group in putting forward the scheme that 'the group can be regarded as an inter-play between individual needs, group mentality, and culture' (1961: 55). What did he mean by group mentality and culture?

Bion conceived of *group mentality* as 'the pool to which anonymous contributions are made' (i.e. contributions disavowed by individual group members) 'and through which impulses and desires implicit in these contributions are gratified' (1961: 50). To become part of the group mentality any individual's contribution has to enlist that of others. Bion seemed to expect that group mentality would be opposed to the avowed aims of the individual members of the group. Moreover, he appeared to imply (1961: 103) that the level of deep interaction between members of a group is what he called 'proto-mental', corresponding to a developmental stage in the infant before differentiation of body and mind, i.e. in the preverbal first few months. This is the level of functioning in which Bion went on to locate basic assumption phenomena.

How he conceived of *group culture* is less clear. On the whole, the term seems to signify the group atmosphere and the way members relate to each other, including the therapist. However, at some points in his writing, it seems to merge with the idea of group mentality. At other points, group mentality and culture seem to differ in that the former concerns 'bad' and unconscious processes, the latter 'good' and more conscious ones (1961: 60). Indeed Bion wrote:

My attempt to simplify, by means of the concepts I have adumbrated, will prove to be very misleading unless the reader bears in mind that the group situation is mostly perplexed and confused; operations of what I have called the group mentality, or of the group culture, only occasionally emerge in any strikingly clear way (1961: 57).

In my view Bion's major errors may have been, first, considering 'group mentality' as composed only of disavowed aspects of individual members — a sort of pool of projective identification — and secondly, separating so sharply consciousness and unconsciousness as manifested in individual and group. Indeed, Bion himself stated that he did not find the three concepts of 'group mentality', 'group culture' and 'individual' useful in practice (1961: 61), though what he came to call basic assumption states were described as happening when the group culture was dominated by states of group mentality which interfered with its explicit task. He now saw group behaviour as involving three sets of conflict: (a) in the individual, between wishes to belong and to be independent of the group, (b) between individual and group, when aims of group and at least some members seem discordant, and (c) between the explicit task of the group and its 'basic assumption tendencies'. In an analytic group, conflicts (a) and (b) can indeed be discerned. But it would be misleadingly simplistic to imply that all the resistance to analytic work can be attributed to the group's 'basic assumption tendencies', or that bringing them into the open by interpreting them would itself ensure the dissolution of resistance. In the final section of the chapter I shall propose that a more practical theoretical framework is provided by Foulkes's concept of the 'group matrix' and his view of therapy as involving the promotion in it of communication at all levels. It is based on a greater appreciation of the positive as well as the negative consequences of group membership. It recognizes the interpersonal basis of individuality, conscious and unconscious, external and internal, from mother–infant dyad, to family group and beyond. It is summed up in Foulkes's idea of the group as the matrix of the individual's mental life.

Bion's first paper in *Experiences in Groups*, written during World War II with John Rickman on the basis of their short spell of work in the rehabilitation wing of a military neurosis hospital (where they were succeeded by Foulkes), attempted to define the qualities associated with 'good group spirit'; that is, the positive aspects of group culture. They found these to include (a) a common purpose, (b) common recognition of group boundaries in relation to larger units or groups, (c) capacity to absorb new members and relinquish old ones without fear of the group disintegrating, (d) freedom from rigid internal sub-groups, (e) recognition of the value of each individual for his contribution, and (f) capacity to face discontent and cope with it in the group. At the end of this first paper, fresh and modern though written forty years ago, Bion and Rickman assert that 'there is a useful future in the study of the interplay of individual and social psychology, viewed as equally important interacting elements' (1961: 26). They also rightly pointed out that 'psychology and psychopathology have focused attention on the individual often to the exclusion of the social field of which he is a part', but in his subsequent work on groups, Bion seems to have over-reacted against this tendency.

Although the rest of the book struggles with fascinating complexities, it appears to dwell on the negative aspects of group functioning and to offer a one-sided view of the interplay between individual and social psychology as we see it in therapeutic groups, a view that can be misleading both theoretically and in practice. Bion stated his belief that groups are essential to the fulfilment of mental life yet, paradoxically for a psychoanalyst and unlike Foulkes, he seemed to be in danger of losing sight of the individual in his attempt to discern that which was characteristic of groups. Focus on individual dynamics and the subtlety of the network of interaction in the group, was sacrificed in favour of grasping another layer of phenomena.

It seems to me that this overemphasis on the group, to the neglect of the individuals who had come to therapy for their own pressing individual needs, combined with a therapeutic stance derived from a particular form of *individual* psychoanalysis — formal and hieratic — may explain the prominence of frustration as a characteristic of the groups Bion reports on in his book. He attributes the frustration and the consequent resentment in part to the nature of any group to deny some desires, e.g. the wish for privacy, in satisfying others, such as the wish for company. This is indisputable, but it is not so easy to follow his proposition that most resentment is caused through 'expression in a group of impulses which individuals wish to satisfy anonymously, and the frustration produced in the individual by the consequences to himself that follow from that satisfaction' (1961: 54). He suggests that the power of the group to fulfil the needs of the individual is challenged by the group mentality, and that the group meets this challenge by the elaboration of a characteristic group culture. Though this seems to belong to a different level of group dynamic from that of Ezriel's required, avoided and calamitous relationships',[4] or of Whitaker and Lieberman's 'focal conflict theory involving disturbing and reactive motives and restrictive and facilitating solutions',[5] his emphasis on the negative and defensive aspects of group culture is noteworthy. In terms of Ezriel's ideas, such a culture would be dominated by required relationships; in terms of focal conflict theory, by reactive motives and restrictive solutions. Working through these are everyday group tasks.

So rather than their being inevitable and major features of groups, alternative or additional explanations of the degree of frustration and resentment he observed are Bion's unwitting promotion of a group culture that neglected the individual, and his simultaneous implicit devaluation of the group's potential to foster individual fulfilment. It is true that Bion granted that the group is potentially capable of gratifying some of the individual's needs, excluding those that can be obtained in solitude or in family life, but by concentrating on those manifestations of group mentality he dubbed as basic assumptions, the bulk of his book does not allow for the positive and facilitating aspects of groups, therapeutic or other. Thus it might be that some ambivalence to groups as well as his style of working may have contributed to the prominence of the phenomena he described. I never saw Bion working in groups, but have observed groups conducted by therapists influenced by him. This suggests to me that his attitude and style in the group may well have been remote and oracular, as he himself seems to have recognized. Writing about a particular group session, he states: 'Before the patient began to alarm the group my interpretations might have been oracular pronouncements for all the ceremonious silence with which they were received' (1961: 56). Ultimately the very different sorts of individuals Bion and Foulkes were must have influenced the way they conducted groups, and therefore the way the groups developed, and their own influence on the world of psychotherapy. Perhaps they could provocatively be termed Shaman and Anti-Shaman.

Let me turn in more detail to the manifestations of group mentality that Bion is most widely known for, the *basic assumptions*. (a) First I shall describe them briefly; (b) then attempt to link them with individual as well as group psychology, and (c) try to integrate them with the Foulkesian group-analytic view which I believe does greater justice to the interplay of individual and group life. Finally, (d) I shall attempt to answer the question posed earlier, why is it that group-analysts rarely invoke and use the concept of basic assumptions, and offer some thoughts about the light the Bionian and Foulkesian models throw on each other.

Brief description of basic assumptions

Bion described basic assumptions as primitive states of mind which are generated automatically when people combine in a group. These states are inevitable because of the dilemma created by the dual pulls of man's individuality and of his groupishness; as Bion put it: 'The individual is a group animal at war, not simply with the group, but with himself for being a group animal and with those aspects of his personality that constitute his "groupishness"' (1961:131). They develop instantaneously and involuntarily as a result of the individuals' possession of a hypo-thetical 'valency' springing from a primitive proto-mental system existing in early infancy before body and mind were differentiated (1961: 153). The fantasies and emotional drives associated with these basic assumptions unconsciously dominate a group's behaviour in a way that is apt to interfere with its explicit work task and so prevent under-standing and development. In the case of a therapy group, the basic assumption organization interferes with exploration by the group of the feelings and problems of individuals in it. Appropriate leaders are drawn in by the basic assumption states, by no means necessarily the formally designated leader, and can be inside or outside the group, a person, a book of laws or history.

While leaving open the question of how many basic assumption states there might be, Bion named three: *dependence* (expecting solutions to be bestowed by the therapist/leader; *fight-flight* (fleeing from or engaging in battle with adversaries, particularly outside the group), and *pairing* (encouraging or hoping for a coupling of individuals which could lead to the birth of a person or idea that would provide salvation). As the philosopher of science Michael Sherwood[6] has pointed out, basic assumptions seem not to be observed phenomena or even empirical propositions, but either *a priori* premises or descriptive labels. What is basic to each form of organization is an emotional state — respectively of dependency and awe; or of hostility and fear; or of optimism and hopefulness. The 'as if' basic assumption follows from this and is an attempt to explain it in the absence of its overt expression, even when the group may be acting on it.

The three basic assumption states, Bion suggested, are institutionalized respectively in the church, the army and aristocracy. In these 'specialized work groups' (1961: 156) the basic assumption states tend to foster their work task; respectively to organize dependency on a deity, to defend the realm, and to ensure the next generation of superior leaders. In other groups the basic assumptions tend to interfere only with explicit work tasks with which they are discordant. However, it is difficult to follow Bion's bald assertion that there is a sharp distinction between the reality adjustment of basic assumption and work group states. It is also difficult to accept that basic assumption states do not co-exist at times rather than 'inevitably' alternate, as he states. Indeed at one point (1961: 64) he states: 'A group which shows itself intolerant of activities that are not forms of fight-flight, will nevertheless tolerate the formation of pairs. Reproduction is recognized with fight-flight in the preservation of a group.'

Individual and/or group

As will be seen in the next section, Bion came to use Kleinian ideas about primitive mental mechanisms and the early infantile stage of the Oedipus complex in individual development to explain the basic assumption states. However, he started trying to restrict his view of what went on in groups to the group context alone, as though 'indivdual' and 'group' are not mutually interacting systems. Nevertheless it is not difficult to relate his ideas about basic assumptions to concepts originating in other psychoanalytic theories, as stated elsewhere.[7] The relation between basic assumption and work groups imply (1961: 99) an analogy to that between primary and secondary process thinking. Further it is possible to imagine the three basic assumptions of dependence, fight-flight and pairing as linked by fantasy systems associated with the oral-dependent, separation-individuation and Oedipal stages of individual development. In terms of the erotogenic zones of early psychoanalytic instinct theory these would be related to oral, anal and phallic stages of development. However, like group analysis, modern psychoanalytic thinking is more concerned with the vicissitudes of the emerging self and 'object relationships' and with motivational systems rather than instincts. As George Klein[8] put it:

> The essential clinical propositions concerning motivation have nothing to do with reducing a hypothetical tension; they are inferences of *directional* gradients in behaviour, and of the *object relations* involved in these directions. They describe relationships needed and sought out, consciously or unconsciously, and how they are fulfilled through real and conceptual encounters, symbol and action. The key factors then, in the psychoanalytic clinical view of motivation are relational requirements, encounters, crises, dilemmas, resolutions and achievements — not a hypothetical 'tension reduction.'

The individual is part of a group from earliest infancy – initially a group of two, the mother-infant dyad, then a group of three or more as the existence of father and siblings have to be accommodated – later a series of overlapping family and social groups. These co-exist in eternal reality *and* the developing individual's internal world.

The caricature Kleinian[9] interpretation tends to reduce all psychological processes to their supposed most primitive infantile origins. It is apt to see the infant in the adult, not the person struggling to develop from infant to toddler to school-child to adolescent and onwards. Anna Freud's developmental lines and Erikson's psychosocial stages are reductively telescoped into what many would see as an over-simplified scheme. Despite the fact that Kleinian analysts such as Jaques[10] and Menzies[11] have illuminated the more primitive anxieties and defences active in institutions, it remains true that most Kleinian analysts tend to view man's social existence through eyes which do not look beyond the crib (even if the reality of the crib is allowed). The reality of the individual's changing context is minimized or denied by them. This contrasts with the view of others, including group analysts, that fantasy and external reality dance together and that individuals seek to be true to themselves and part of groups larger than themselves. As George Klein wrote:[12] 'Two components of selfhood must be recognized: a centrifugal assertion of personal autonomy, and a centripetal requirement for being an integrated and needed part of a larger, more encompassing entity or social unit. The reconciliation of this dual requirement as a condition for integrated selfhood itself creates one of the most basic sources of potential conflict'.

In a sense though, this is what Bion meant; but his decision to avoid viewing basic assumptions within the context of individual development blinds him in one of his two eyes, for man is both an individual *and* a social being. Bion's decision accords with his emphasis on treating the group rather than the individuals in it. It also reflects his Kleinian id-psychology, with its seemingly sharp distinction between primary and secondary thinking. Because of this we read a lot in Bion's writings about 'basic assumption groups', and relatively little or virtually nothing about the psychological processes involved in the work of the 'work group', which we ourselves might describe in terms of enabling individuals to discern and overcome the blocks to their continuing search for autonomy and relatedness. Rather less than 10 per cent of the book concerns itself with work group functions (notably 1961: 98–113 and 143-6), and in fact says next to nothing about them. Instead Bion writes about the relationship between work group and basic assumption functions, the supposed origin of the latter in a proto-mental level of development, and speculation about their relation to psychosomatic illness and economics.

Bion seems to imply that if the group is told when it is not working, it will know how to and get on with it. But psychotherapy is a form of education in the fullest sense of the word. A good teacher would not be satisfied with only telling his pupils to get on with it; he needs to sustain the working process and in a sense embody it as Foulkes did. Ezriel, the other main influence to the Tavistock Clinic approach to group psychotherapy, as described by Heath and Bacal,[13] at least includes 'because . . .' clauses with his interpretations. His interpretations of the required, avoided and calamitous relationships with the transference figure of the conductor, suggest to individuals why they may be behaving and experiencing in a certain way. Yet, as Heath and Bacal remark, restricting interpretations to the 'here and now', and expecting individuals to make the link with their current life outside and with their past 'presupposes capacities that possibly not all patients have'. (Robin Skynner's[14] ideas about the importance of modelling as well as of interpretations in therapy, especially for more deprived, non-verbal or chaotic people, are clearly relevant to this problem.) One might add that the Tavistock approach – unlike that of group analysis, which encourages analysis by the group – because it emphasizes interpretation by the therapist, would seem to foster 'basic assumption dependence' and excite feelings of frustration. These factors may have contributed to the disappointing results found by Malan and his colleagues[15] in their study of outcome of group psychotherapy conducted at the Tavistock Clinic, contrasting with the much better results described by Barbara Dick,[16] who used a technique based on group analytic methods. The few in the Tavistock series who did particularly well were people who had had previous individual therapy. That is, they might be presumed to have learned already how to apply psychodynamic ideas to their own personal problems, and thus to be less confused and frustrated by a technique that seems to ignore them.

A Foulkesian interpretation

The fact that a concept, on its own, is a poor basis for effective therapy, does not invalidate it. How can the idea of basic assumptions be integrated into a more useful scheme such as Foulkesian group analysis? We would probably all agree that, as in a family, the reality of belonging to a therapeutic group demands that we face up to jealousy, envy and a considerable degree of frustration of dyadic dependency wishes. It also requires us to play an active role in our own salvation, and eventually to eschew the defence of blaming external agencies, including siblings and parents. Within the group matrix, both reality and fantasies can be discerned, talked about and eventually understood. What fantasies underlie basic assumptions? In his final chapter Bion himself suggests that the basic assumption theory may be inadequate. 'I have drawn attention already to the fact that these three states of mind have resemblances to each other that would lead me to suppose that they may not be fundamental phenomena, but rather expressions of, or reactions against, some state more worthy of being regarded as primary' (1961: 162–3).

He goes on to trace the basic assumption states to defences against or reactions to psychotic anxieties, and mechanisms of splitting and projective identification springing from an extremely early and primitive primal scene (1961: 164). I believe that the primal scene is the archetypal provoker of feelings of exclusion. If the reality of belonging to a group does involve facing up to jealousy, envy and the frustration of dyadic dependency, it is not surprising that primitive fantasies and anxieties of this type are stirred up in an analytic group. If these are regarded as related to the narcissistically painful recognition by the child of separateness from mother and of the real relationship between parents, then defences against recognition of the primitive Oedipal situation can involve any of the (at least) three basic assumptions. Pain, experienced by the self as a result of frustration or disillusion, evokes rage and fantasies of punishment and destruction associated with paranoid or depressive anxieties. Following, but modifying, Bion's view of the importance of the 'primal scene' in basic assumption states, one might propose something like the following:

1 In the 'basic assumption dependence' there is regression into the state of 'merging' of the early mother-child nursing dyad, in which there is no room for the reality of an intruding father or sibling – it is denied. According to Mahler *et al.*[17] the psychological birth of the infant takes place in the second or third year of life, as he emerges from the symbiotic phase into a phase of separation and individuation. (This involves successive sub-phases: (a) differentiation and development of the body image; (b) practising of autonomous functions; (c) a rapprochement crisis in which attention is redirected to mother; finally, (d) consolidation of individuality and beginning of constancy of objects and the self.) It is in the space created by the realization of separateness that the Oedipal triad

comes to be recognised and internalized, and the capacity to cope with the Oedipal crisis laid down. This emergence into the family network marks, one could say, the beginning of the *social* birth of the infant.

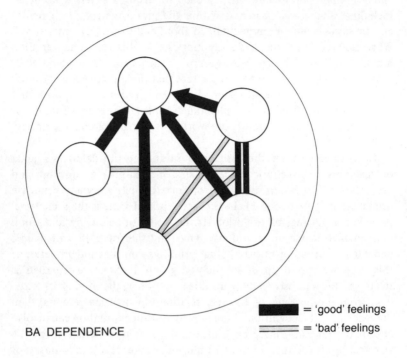

= 'good' feelings

= 'bad' feelings

BA DEPENDENCE

Figure 10.1

2 In the 'basic assumption fight-flight', an intruding threat is challenged or fled from. There is no time for maternal succouring, but equally none for the fear of parents nor for passive contemplation of their sexuality or 'favouritism' towards siblings. It is as though an apparent identity of interests blurs differences in the group; separation and individuation are avoided within the group, but emphasized in at least some crucial external relationships. Ambivalence within the group is avoided through excessive use of projection. In massive social manifestations of the basic assumption, such as war and political upheaval, the reality of external threats can overshadow the reality of internal fantasy.

3 In the 'basic assumption pairing', the sexual theme is most nearly explicit, but passive contemplation is maintained through idealization,

in which a mood of hopefulness prevents the emergence of destructive rage. This characteristic of the 'basic assumption pairing' contrasts with more mature renunciation and resolution of Oedipal rivalry through

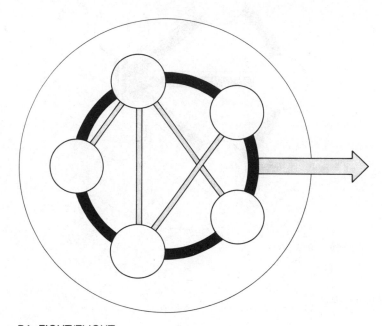

BA FIGHT/FLIGHT

Figure 10.2

identification. As pointed out by the sociologist Talcott Parsons:[18] 'The parents' erotic solidarity thereby forces him to a higher level of value-internalization than that governing *any* dyadic relationship within the family and prepares him, in his latency period and in subsequent orientations outside his family to internalize still higher-level patterns of value.' Revolutionary zeal could be viewed as a reaction to the fruitfulness of tradition, linked with the idea of parental fruitfulness; we often come back to traditional values when we in turn are challenged by the fruitfulness of our own children. Equally, blind traditionalism may be a manifestation of 'basic assumption pairing'.

A composite hypothesis based on these ideas would be as follows: the group dominated by a basic assumption is one which avoids reality

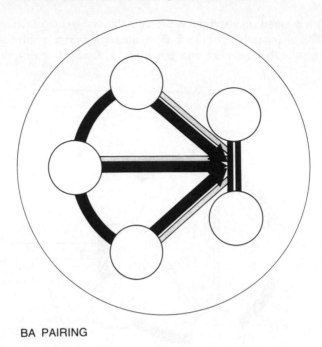

BA PAIRING

Figure 10.3

testing of those elements in it which embody creative strength and self-reliance, as well as of those involving hatred and despair. In the dependency group strength resides in the leader, in the fight-flight group badness resides in the outside enemy, and in the pairing group rage and despair are kept at bay only by hopeful illusion. In the dependency group, there is no chance for integration of the group's own strengths because of 'depressive anxiety', with fear of destructive feelings. In the fight-flight group, adoption of the 'paranoid position' avoids testing out the essential ambivalence of relationships. In the pairing group, assertive feelings cannot be mobilized in a way that makes the defeat of rage and despair less dependent upon hopeful illusion. Perhaps pairing is an inter-mediate state, defensive against both depressive and persecutory anxieties (in the Kleinian sense). I shall give examples of each type of basic assumption group encountered in group-analytic practice, and hope to illustrate some of this hypothesis with clinical material.

'Basic assumption dependency' group

An underlying shared attitude of dependence on the conductor is usual in the initial stages of all groups. The group analyst accepts this, but does not encourage it, so that the group members feel safe enough, in due course, to turn away from him in disappointment towards a more active involvement with other group members. Dependence is more characteristic of some individuals and groups, especially in regressed states. It has to be allowed but also, eventually, challenged and worked through, as in this example.

A pre-break session in a group of hospital out-patients, all originally referred because of psychosomatic disorders, was dominated by a mood of sullen isolation which left activity to the two co-therapists. It could be viewed as a group dominated by the 'basic assumption dependence'. This appeared to be confirmed, following a comment by one of the therapists that members seemed to be avoiding feelings about differences between them as well as about what they have in common at this time, by J. admitting to disturbing feelings of jealousy which she had become increasingly aware of recently. She asked for 'offerings' to explain their origin. This patient had originally complained of extreme lassitude which overlay an impenetrable repression of sexuality and of jealous resentment within the family, and which had begun to lift as she came to realize her jealousy and envy in relation to a brother born when she was four. L. and M. began to talk of their hatred of each other because of things said on a previous occasion. R. described how she had recently asserted herself by finishing with an unsatisfactory boyfriend, and no longer needed the group which she felt to be unresponsive and dead like a brick wall. M. revealed that he had experienced pain in the stomach following the last session, in which he had attacked L. for expressing indifference to him; he had replied that he would therefore never care for her. R. responded by saying that she had felt the same sort of pain when trying to hold things together with her boyfriend, and also at the age of four when she had seen her mother feeding her newly arrived infant sister. L., a compulsive eater, reported a bad week, cut off from feelings. She had had a nightmare of being with a young god-child who was (in the dream) a diabetic like herself. She had to give her insulin, but 'accidentally' gave her the same dose as she has herself, i.e. a massive overdose. Commenting on it, L. said the godchild was herself; she neglected herself by taking risks with her own diabetes control. Moreover, turning of aggression on herself could be linked with the birth of a sibling shortly after she was weaned at the late age of two.

The group finished with a recognition of each person's avoidance of strength out of a fear of omnipotent destructiveness, leading — until it was faced — to a regression to an undifferentiated state. When it was faced, L. was able to see a little more clearly that she avoided her own strength because of her fear of murderous jealousy, and M. because of his fear that if he were to be an unqualified success in his life, this could lead to envious attacks by others. Finally, recognition of their shared rage at the therapists for leaving them, and their fear of the consequences of its expression, allowed them to repeat their resolve to have a session together during the break as they had discussed previously, and then decide they did not need to. Disavowed destructive sibling and Oedipal rivalry no longer blocked the path to co-operation, nor did they need to rely on 'manic' denial and 'acting out'.

Comment: In retrospect it seemed that denying the reality of bad feelings towards siblings and parents (fellow patients and therapists in the group) cut members off from the support and solidarity with the 'good enough siblings and parents' in the group, and prevented their moving through ambivalence towards freer interchange and interaction with each other at a non-transference level. (The history of this slow-open group was marked by a striking difficulty in welcoming newcomers.) Both their comments about the avoidance of differences and similarities in the group, and the therapists' style of not behaving like 'brick walls' seemed to promote therapeutic change. This involved the ability of the group to face differentiation and the fear of their own strength, so that defensive weakness could be transcended. Feelings about transference relationships in the group — towards the therapists and each other — came to be expressed and explored rather than somatized, displaced or turned on the self as formerly.

'Basic assumption fight-flight' group

This phenomenon has been vividly evident at times in groups composed both of patients in private practice and of students in an associated training institute having their training group analysis. The mixture usually works well, to the mutual benefit of both sets of group members, despite the envy of each for the supposed advantages enjoyed by the other. For example, trainees may envy the patients their freedom from the 'expectation' to be healthy and mature, and their chance to be a 'real' patient; patients may envy trainees their supposed greater health and special relationship with the therapist, etc. The institute or particular supervisors and teachers may be reacted to as an intruding and even persecuting superego, awesome and vengeful parents or part-objects.

Following a summer break, during which I had made a few changes in the furnishings of the room we met in, these were not reacted to overtly, even the large, rather flamboyant 'double' couch. What did emerge was the hidden rage that one trainee had felt for some months over an apparent leakage of confidentiality. Some group material had seemingly come to the notice of his female supervisor, implying that we were talking together behind his back. Strong feelings were mobilized in the group about the intruding and unfair relationship I had with the institute as a whole, which became, as it were, a scapegoat. The members of the group seemed united in indignation against it.

It was not until the next session that the changes in the room came into focus, with fantasies of my being different, and of the pictures (the same as had always been there) having been painted by my wife. Much Oedipal material emerged, with expression of impotent rage at the primal scene. A patient who had despised the paintings in the room as dull and obsessional, and was sure they had been painted or chosen by my wife or, if not, by me, came to express powerful disappointment in her sensual and erotic strivings towards her deserting father. Contrasting with the unthinkableness, for some, of sexual activity with father was the excited enjoyment of a man who openly maintained an erotic intimacy with his teenage daughters. The group managed to contain these discrepancies, and allowed space for thinking to representatives of each extreme position.

Comment: The scapegoating of the Institute, with the group led in basic assumption fight-flight by the seething trainee, could be seen as displacement, allowing avoidance of ambivalence in relation to the conductor, who had 'failed' them in the break and, by changing the room in their absence, provoked primal scene fantasies. The trainees and non-trainees were united in their sense of injustice. It was not necessary to draw the group's attention to the basic assumption, or even the scapegoating. The Oedipal theme and ambivalence emerged spontaneously in many forms, contributed to by several members, and involving for many their relationship with the conductor. Jealous rivalry and ambivalence towards the conductor were now containable within the group.

'Basic assumption pairing' group

Pairing is often observed in groups. Collusion by the rest of the group is obviously necessary, and any resentment may be left to the conductor's countertransference, e.g. a feeling of being excluded.

The session to be described was the fourth after a short holiday break, seven months after the start of the group. Issues of jealousy had come out in the first session after the break, and in the session before the one concentrated on here, a good deal of covert hostility to the oldest woman patient. (She is a professional who had had a lot of physical ill-health and at times in the group she was imagined as having a special relationship with me.) One of the older male patients was away.

At the beginning of the session in question, he returned, explaining that he had had a bad attack of colic. Anxious enquiry was then made about the health of the oldest woman, and she spoke movingly of her own infuriatingly offhand treatment at the hands of the specialists. As these two members revealed themselves as suffering, burdened by bad parental introjects and guilt, they struck up a pairing relationship. The rest listened apparently passively but unresentfully as they intimately shared feelings about their very similar family backgrounds.

It was only after I had pointed this out to the group, *and* asked about the two *most* silent members, that the underlying material emerged. This was about destructive projections and introjections. One of the silent members said he had been waiting and sulking. He recalled, when three or so, attempting to detain his mother after she had tucked him in for the night; when she insisted on rejoining father in the parental bedroom, he momentarily hallucinated her to be a giant beetle. This resonated. The other most silent member said she felt *herself* to be a beetle, especially in relation to a group member who she thought must see her as a beetle. It emerged that she specially liked him, but he was having to leave the group in a few months' time. He, in turn, responded with a rush of energy that dissipated the sleepiness he had been feeling. Linking this with the profound sense of loss and guilt over the early death of his father, he told how he empathized with the hero of Kafka's story 'Metamorphosis'.

In the following session very powerful material emerged. The beetle-hallucinator revealed he had felt intense jealous rage at being excluded. This focused on the imagined relationship between the oldest woman and me, but brought alive 'autistic' non-specific feelings of despair and painful exclusion as a child, and his passive attempts to get either of his parents to engage with him. Now, in the group, he became sadistic and scathing towards each of the others in turn. Later material from some of the women related to wishes for merging, and pain and rage at the loss of perfect 'permanent' love. An interpretation made sense to many that they were reacting to the premature shattering of the experience of symbiosis, and the fear of ambivalence and autonomy.

Comment: These powerful feelings had been kept covered by the 'group defence' of pairing. This seemed to be relatively superficial, but had to be brought to the group's notice before it dissolved to allow exploration and sharing at a much deeper level. Perhaps this is because of the intensity and primitiveness of the feelings and fantasies which seemed to involve both depressive and persecutory anxieties. One wonders if it required some indication from the conductor that he could approach and contain these before the rest of the group could follow suit.

It will be noticed that there is much overlap in the clinical material just quoted from three different groups illustrating each of the three basic assumptions. This confirms Bion's modest statement in his concluding chapter (1961: 165-6):

> there is much to suggest that these supposed 'basic assumptions' cannot be regarded as distinct states of mind. By that I do not mean to claim that they are 'basic' explanations which between them explain all conduct in the group . . . but that each state, even when it is possible to differentiate it with reasonable certainty from the other two, has about it a quality that suggests it may in some way be the dual or reciprocal of one of the other two, or perhaps simply another view of what one had thought to be a different basic assumption . . . It may be difficult to see because the presenting emotional tone is so different. Anxiety, fear, hate, love, all, as I have said, exist in each basic assumption group. The modification that feelings suffer in

combination in the respective basic assumption group may arise because the 'cement', so to speak, that joined them to each other is guilt and depression in the dependent group, Messianic hope in the pairing group, anger and hate in the fight-flight group.

Bion and Foulkes: an integration

Finally, let us return to the questions raised at the beginning of this chapter. Why are basic assumption states seldom commented on in group-analytic groups? And what light does this throw on the nature of the group-analytic approach to groups as opposed to that of Bion?

The apparent absence or unobtrusiveness of basic assumption states in groups conducted on group-analytic lines is probably due to two things. First, the encouragement of spontaneous interaction and communication at *many levels*, which discourages their development. Second, the role of group analyst, which is not that of a sphinx-like therapist. It aims at a flexible attitude which conveys both an analytic and a democratic spirit, through modelling as well as by interpretation. My impression would be that the mere interpretation of basic assumptions could perpetuate them and not lead to group work on the basis of mutuality and joint endeavour. In fact, as stated earlier, it is striking how Bion failed in his writing to state what work a psychotherapeutic group should do. Following Foulkes, we would see it as developing members' autonomy and relatedness, within themselves and within the group, fostered by working towards ever more articulate forms of communication and communion. This involves relating in all senses of the word: making oneself understood and trying to understand the communications of others, seeing yourself in and through others and discovering them in and through yourself, recognizing both similarities and differences, and respecting and enjoying both. Though members are in the same boat, they are so for different reasons. Perhaps particularly in slow-open groups, individual members not only switch into and contribute to the group culture, they also to varying degrees hold back from it, consciously or unconsciously, for reasons of their own (Bion's 'anonymous contributions'). They are at different points of individual development and group involvement. If this is not recognized, the individual is likely to feel coerced and depersonalized by an emphasis on group phenomena. (Training group experiences of the Leicester Conference type[19] are perhaps less harmful as they involve 'normal' people in short-term closed groups and do not aim at helping individuals except in a limited work-centred way.)

What light do group analytic concepts throw on Bion's formulations? The two-dimensional nature of Bion's scheme is highlighted by Foulkes's multi-dimensional view of the therapeutic task as one of *widening and deepening communication at many levels*: (a) the level of current adult relationships (or 'working alliance'); (b) the level of *individual* transference relationships; (c) the level of projected and shared feelings and fantasies, often from early pre-verbal stages of development (prior to separation and individuation from symbiotic merging); (d) a primordial level of archetypal universal images. 'It will be seen that these levels range from the more conscious objective "everyday" relationships to increasingly subjective and unconscious fantasy relationships; from more to less clearly differentiated and individual relationships.'[20] Bion's relative neglect of the group's ego functions and its work task, and his failure to discuss where and how it is achieved, are made good by Foulkes's central concept of the *matrix* as the place in which group communications are made, distortions are corrected and group culture develops. It is in the matrix that interpersonal problems come to be located and where the individual can question his boundaries and re-establish his identity.

Foulkes defined the matrix as 'the hypothetical web of communication and relationship in a group. It is the common shared ground which ultimately determines the meaning and significance of all events and upon which all communication and interpretations, verbal and non-verbal, rest'.[21] He likened the relationship of manifest and latent content of communications to that between manifest and latent dream thoughts, and stressed that 'the group matrix is the operational basis of all relationships and communications. Inside this network the individual is conceived as a nodal point. The individual, in other words, is not conceived as a closed but as an open system.'[22] In the matrix, group processes are transpersonal. Psychological processes are seen as taking place in the matrix, 'while at the same time involving the various individuals in different specific ways and constellations. Just as the individual's mind is a complex of interacting processes (personal matrix), mental processes interact in the concert of the group (group matrix). These processes relate to each other in manifold ways and on a variety of different levels.'[23] Foulkes went on to explain that he saw it as the therapist's task to remain equally attentive to what was happening in the individuals and in the group.

Foulkes's concept of *resonance*, through which group members react to what occurs at different levels of consciousness and regression, *according to their needs and preoccupations*, seems an essential ingredient of group work; in order to co-operate in discovering their autonomy, individuals need freedom to discover themselves at their own pace. (In contrast, having always to accommodate oneself to a group interpretation of basic assumptions must be like being coerced into a Procrustean Great Bed of Ware. It forces a false choice between the polarities of schizoid isolation or 'false self' compliance.) After all, Foulkes always stressed the treatment of the individual; 'the individual is being treated in the context of the group with the active participation of the group'.[24] Group analysis is 'psychotherapy *by* the group, *of* the group, including its conductor'.[25]

Thus Bion and Foulkes put forward very different pictures of individuals interacting in groups. Bion's seems two-dimensional — individuals are either alienated or falsely co-operative, the group is either working on some superficial or imposed task or is avoiding genuine encounter. This is perhaps a caricature, and it could be argued that simplification is necessary to explain a new and fundamental idea. And no one could

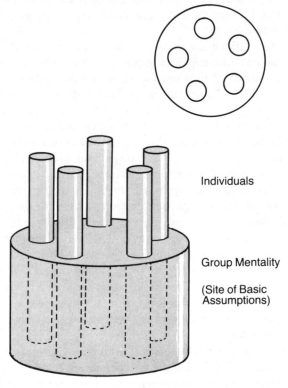

Individuals

Group Mentality

(Site of Basic Assumptions)

Figure 10.4

sustain a general criticism of Bion's views as simple, in any sense of the word. In contrast, Foulkes's picture is multi-dimensional, complex, and at first glance could be judged as woolly and lacking the bite of paradox and pessimism. But he did not underestimate the difficulty of analytic work and the powerful resistances it has to encounter, both individual and group. However, he believed in and fostered the group's own therapeutic and analytic power. Figures 10.4 and 10.5 attempt to illustrate the two different pictures, projected from the conventional circular cross-section.

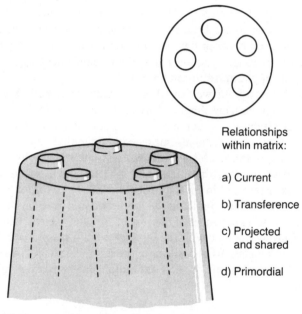

Relationships within matrix:

a) Current

b) Transference

c) Projected and shared

d) Primordial

Figure 10.5

Ultimately the choice of approach must depend on their explanatory and predictive value in the clinical setting and on their therapeutic usefulness. This must include their ability to deal with basic assumption phenomena. If these do exist — and I believe that something corresponding to them can be observed in all types of groups, and can seriously obstruct work in groups operating badly at a deep level — the analytic task is to recognize them in order to help the group to transcend them. In practice, pointing them out is rarely necessary. Concentration on them seems less desirable than understanding and working through the resistances to acknowledging and communicating the underlying conflicts and anxieties within relationships in the group matrix. These are manifested in and through the *individuals* in the group, as well as the group as a whole. Individuals speak for the group and the group for individuals. Individuals personify aspects and attitudes of the group, often initially disavowed by others, and represent polarities which may later become reconciled within individuals and the group as a whole.

Perhaps we have, in their constant attention to the individuals within the context of the group, the main explanation of why basic assumption states are seldom seen and commented on by group analysts. Foulkes understood the need for balance in man's paradoxical struggle for both individuality and belonging. His background in psychoanalysis and interest in social forces brought new meaning to Gestalt observations of the interaction between figure and ground. The analytic group allows individual and group to discover that their complementarity is at least as real as the opposition stressed by Bion.

From this viewpoint we can wholeheartedly agree with Bion's statement in his summarizing chapter, 'Group dynamics: a Review', that 'the adult must establish contact with the emotional life of the group in which he lives', and with his subsequent rider that 'this task would appear to be as formidable to the adult as the relationship with the breast appears to be to the infant, and the failure to meet the demands of this task is revealed in his regression' (1961: 141). I think it is likely that this rider applies particularly to those who have failed to cope adequately with experiences at the breast, or with the entry into social life which involves coping with the impingement of the parents' relationship and of siblings. What we cannot accept, except as a paradox, is Bion's subsequent assertion that the group does not exist in reality. He states:

> The belief that a group exists, as distinct from an aggregate of individuals, is an essential part of this regression, as are also the characteristics with which the supposed group is endowed by the individual. Substance is given to the fantasy that the group exists by the fact that the regression involves the individual in a loss of his 'individual distinctiveness', indistinguishable from depersonalisation, and therefore obscures observation that the aggregation is of individuals. (1961:142)

Such may be the nature of regression in the supposed basic assumption states, but I have no doubt that regression also takes place in groups in a way that is not so psychotic. Individuals can regress, as can groups as a whole, in an 'as-if' way that keeps in touch with the reality of the group and of other members in it. They can be experienced as womb, breast, mother, others in the family, aspects of the self, part-objects etc., without their real existence, at another level, being lost touch with. The statement that implies that the group does not really exist only makes sense at the level that, for a baby, its mother does not exist as a separate person, and therefore the 'group of two' does not exist. Even a group of strangers meeting for therapy for the first time exists. Bion's assertion that the group is a delusion is like insisting that transference is *always* psychotic, never neurotic or even normal. This view could accord with that of Ada Abraham[25] who has powerfully challenged the notion put forward by Bion, Jaques and Menzies that the conscious or unconscious fantasy systems connecting group members are psychotic phenomena. She points out that this level of communication occurs in normal groups, including those functioning well. As she states, fantasy activity may endorse as well as disturb group development, and promote healthy processes such as cohesion. Normal groups are not just work groups, their role is not the destruction of fantasy relationships, but a change in their quality and their free communication. 'This is achieved by forming a communicative system in which the individual feels free and learns how to move back and forth fluidly between the conscious and unconscious aspects.'

Beyond basic assumptions

To summarize my main argument in this chapter, Bion's view of a sharp dichotomy between basic assumption states and work group functioning provokes both theoretical and practical objections. On the *theoretical* side, these states may owe their existence in large part to the conditions imposed on the group by Bion himself, resembling hierarchical institutional structures; and they are inferred from a viewpoint which is far from clear, but is based on a Kleinian approach to mental functioning that is preoccupied with primitive processes to the relative neglect of more mature ego functions. Hence Bion neglects the work group functions of an analytic group; he sees them as opposed by the more primitive functions, not developing out of them and gradually superseding them. This leads to the *practical* objection that the recognition of basic assumption states can only be a sign that analytic work is called for. If they predominate over work group functioning or a group keeps getting stuck in a basic assumption state, it might be right to deduce that the group and its conductor are struggling unsuccessfully against resistance. But the clinical examples given earlier (pp. 205-9) suggest that the resolution of such resistance does not require that the basic assumption states be a focus of therapeutic intervention. And in the simple form in which they were described by Bion, they do not guide us in our therapeutic work. They might be more helpful if we can relate them to more dynamic relationships such as that proposed here (pp. 201-3), and operating in the group both within individuals and between them.

Basic assumptions apart, several of Bion's other ideas are of great value in understanding what goes on in any therapy situation, individual or group. Colin James[27] has recently drawn attention to the value in group therapy of Bion's ideas on thinking, projective identification and the relationship of container and contained. These concern the genesis of thought in infancy from the raw data (β-elements) of primitive, un-differentiated somato-psyche ('proto-mental') experience; the development of frustration tolerance as a consequence of mother's receptivity to projective identification without inappropriate impulse discharge (retaliation, panic, etc.); and her capacity to contain, and so feed back to the child her perception of his experiences in a more tolerable and less persecutory form. These ideas throw light on the group's developing capacity to think, communicate and tolerate frustration; as a result, these capacities grow in individual members who have become more accepting and understanding of themselves and others. Unlike the basic assumptions, these ideas can be seen to be constantly at play in psychotherapy, and are entirely compatible with the group analytic approach of S. H. Foulkes. As Bion wrote in a later book, *Attention and Interpretation*:[28] 'The psycho-analytic problem is the problem of growth and its harmonious resolution in the relationship between the container and the contained, repeated in individual, pair, and finally group (intra and extra psychically)'.

We may need to digest and replace Bion's original concept of basic assumptions — grasp what it contains and modify what is distorting in it — if we are to integrate fruitfully the practical contributions of Bion and Foulkes. We could relax in the hope that Bion and Foulkes will do this themselves in posthumous pairing, or start to work on it ourselves.

I would therefore like to finish with some preliminary propositions. Crystallizing from the material I have presented is the notion that unmodi-fied basic assumptions result in groups from avoidance of genuine personal encounter, so that difficult feelings in relationships are dis-avowed. They are therefore more likely in settings where personal contact is forbidden, inappropriate or best avoided — e.g. committees, large groups, and work situations where disturbed or fragile personalities have to coexist or be supported; and I suspect, therapy groups run on strictly Bionian lines. A leader, an enemy, or a Utopian idea may seem the best solution to all problems.

But in settings which promote genuine contact, such as well-functioning therapeutic groups and the positive phases in therapeutic communities (they too, of course, can operate on basic assumption principles), the facing up to problems and differences, and the expression of feelings however awkward, prevent the emergence or persistence of basic assumptions, at least those discordant with the main purpose of the group. Our task as group analysts is not to promote them in order to study them, but to see that they do not manifest themselves or persist.

We could ask whether basic assumptions are the same, or used in the same way, in different group settings. The hypothesis I have put forward, that basic assumptions can be viewed as small group defences against primal scene fantasies and anxieties might be seen as supported by the clinical examples I gave earlier. However, the function, form and underlying content traced there may be connected with the nature of the group-analytic setting, in which intimacy is both sought and feared; intimacy involving openness and contact between people in the field of vision of other people (Foulkes's 'Model of Three').

It could be that in work groups with other tasks, e.g. committees, or in large institutions and wider social groups, basic assumptions more often offer a way of keeping a group together in the face of chaos and feared loss of control and individuality. And the individual in these settings is perhaps not threatened so much by primitive jealousy and feelings of exclusion, as by loss of power and autonomy. He is tempted to withdraw − to fall asleep in committees or opt out of communal life − unless he contributes to the idea of primacy of the group's work task, or a basic assumption more or less concordant with it. My impression is that basic assumption phenomena are more common in these larger, less psychotherapeutic settings; that of dependency particularly so where members are selected for dependency, e.g. psychiatric units, where people go for help, or in states where individuals are reduced to feelings of hopelessness and helplessness; those of fight−flight and pairing in political parties and scientific and psychotherapeutic societies in search of power, Utopian solutions and ultimate answers. One would doubt that primal scene fantasies are the best guide to what is going on here, rather than some more socially and culturally determined variant dealing with the issues of authority and faith, like the myths of Prometheus ('Forethought') and Pandora (wife of Epimetheus − 'afterthought'), the

Garden of Eden, the Tower of Babel, or the Crucifixion, Resurrection and Second Coming; myths which may be squeezed into infantile inter-pretations, but which are more resonant within particular social contexts. Relationships exemplified by such myths may have more relevance than the 'primal scene' to our understanding of social institutions such as church, army and aristocracy – and political ideals and forms such as marxism and monetarism and the various interpretations of democracy.

This way of thinking could contribute to a 'metasociology' that I believe we need to complement and balance, on the other side of object relations theory, psychoanalytic one-body 'metapsychology'. We could then integrate our clinical experience, wider analytic understanding, and the contributions of social psychology within a completer view of Man in relation to society and culture. This would include the effect on personal and social development of different social structures and con-texts (and vice versa), analogous to but transcending mother's holding and containing. Bion's ideas about basic assumptions, like Foulkes's concept of the matrix, may turn out to be early attempts to establish such a 'metasociology'.

This chapter is a development of ideas originally proposed in 'Some reflections on Bion's basic assumptions from a group-analytic viewpoint', *Group Analysis, International Panel and Correspondence*, 12, no. 3, 1979: 204–10.

Notes and references

1   Bion, W. R. (1961), *Experiences in Groups and other papers*, London, Tavistock.
2   Rice, A. K. (1965), *Learning for Leadership*, London. Tavistock; Bennis, W. G. and Shephard, H. A. (1956), 'A theory of group development', *Human Relations*, 9: 415–37; reprinted in Gibbard, G. S. *et al.* (eds), *Analysis of Groups: Contributions to Theory, Research and Practice* (1974), San Francisco and London, Jossey-Bass: 127–53.
3   Foulkes, S. H. (1948), *Introduction to Group Analytic Psycho-therapy*, London, Heinemann; Foulkes, S. H. (1964), *Therapeutic Group Analysis*, London, Allen & Unwin; Foulkes, S. H. (1975), *Group Analytic Psychotherapy: Methods and Principles*, London and New York, Gordon & Breach; Foulkes, S. H. and Anthony, E. J. (1973), *Group Psychotherapy: the Psychoanalytic Approach*, 2nd ed., Penguin Books: 16; Pines, M. (1978), 'The contribution of S. H. Foulkes to Group analytic psychotherapy', chap. 3 in *Group Therapy, 1978: an Overview* (ed. Wolberg, L. R. *et al.*), New York, Stratton International.

4 Ezriel, H. (1952), 'Notes on psycho-analytic group therapy, II: Interpretations and research', *Psychiatry*, 15: 119–26.
5 Whitaker, D. S. and Lieberman, M. (1964), *Psychotherapy through the Group Process*, New York, Atherton.
6 Sherwood, M. (1964), 'Bion's experiences in groups: a critical evaluation', *Human Relations*, 17: 113–29.
7 Brown, D. and Pedder, J. (1979), *Introduction to Psychotherapy: an Outline of Psychodynamic Principles and Practice*, London, Tavistock: 127.
8 Klein, G. S. (1976), *Psychoanalytic Theory*, New York, International Universities Press: 47–8.
9 Kleinian here refers to the school of Melanie Klein, not George Klein.
10 Jaques, E. (1955), 'Social systems as defence against persecutory and depressive anxiety', in *New Directions in Psychoanalysis* (ed. Klein, M., Heimann, P. and Money-Kyrle, R.), London, Tavistock.
11 Menzies, I. E. P. (1960), 'A case-study in the functioning of social systems as a defence against anxiety', *Human Relations*, 13: 95–121.
12 1976: 36.
13 Heath, E. S. and Bacal, H. A. (1972), 'A Method of Group Psychotherapy at the Tavistock Clinic', chap. 2 in *Progress in Group and Family Therapy* (ed. Sager, C. J. and Kaplan, H. S.), New York, Brunner/Mazel.
14 Skynner, A. C. R. (1979), 'Reflections on the family therapist as family scapegoat', *J. Family Therapy*, I: 7–22.
15 Malan, D. R., Balfour, F. H. G., Hood, V. G. and Shooter, A. M. N. (1976), 'Group psychotherapy: a long-term follow-up study', *Arch. Gen. Psychiat.*, 33: 1303–14.
16 Dick, B. M. (1975), 'A ten-year study of out-patient analytic group therapy', *Brit. J. Psychiat.*, 127: 365–75.
17 Mahler, M. S., Pine, F. and Bergman, A. (1975), *The Psychological Birth of the Human Infant*, London, Hutchinson.
18 Parsons, T. (1964), *Social Structure and Personality*, London, Collier-Macmillan: 101.
19 Rice (1965).
20 Brown and Pedder (1979): 129.
21 Foulkes (1964): 292.
22 Foulkes (1964): 118.
23 Foulkes (1975): 130.
24 Foulkes and Anthony (1973).
25 Foulkes (1975): 3.
26 Abraham, A. (1973), 'A model for exploring intra- and inter-individual process in groups', *Int. J. Group Psychotherapy*, 23: 3–22.
27 James, D. C. (1981), 'W. R. Bion's contribution to the field of group therapy: an appreciation', chap. 4 in *Group and Family Therapy, 1981* (ed. Wolberg, L. R. *et al.*), New York, Brunner/Mazel.
28 Bion, W. R. (1970), *Attention to Interpretation: a Scientific Approach to Insight in Psychoanalysis and Groups*, London, Tavistock.

Chapter 11
The space of madness

Salomon Resnik

Introduction

This article is dedicated to W. R. Bion, whom I met in 1955 during an international psychoanalytic congress in Geneva. People working with groups in different countries took this opportunity to meet and exchange ideas regarding groups and psychoanalysis. The two leading figures were Foulkes and Bion.

I had not been to Europe before, so it was the first time that I had the opportunity to see and listen to some of the pioneers in a field in which I was particularly concerned. At that time, my main interest was in psychosis and I was working as a psychoanalyst with individual schizophrenics and with a group of very chronic psychotics in a mental hospital in Buenos Aires. I remember asking Bion, being myself already interested in Melanie Klein's work, what he thought was the relationship between psychosis, object relationships and groups. He answered that at present he had given up groups because he was more interested in delving into a more profound, deeper psychoanalytic understanding of psychotic thinking. It was during this congress that I decided to come over to Europe and study with Melanie Klein, Bion and H. Rosenfeld. In 1957 I arrived in London and for the following ten years I was able to attend Bion's seminars at the Institute of Psychoanalysis and at his home. I also had the privilege of having personal supervision on my own work with psychotic patients for two years. The traces that his creative impact left on my personality were crucial for me. He not only helped me to understand my patients and myself but also stimulated me towards my own personal way of thinking: he helped me to be myself and I shall always be grateful to him for this.

I thought that to write a paper in 1982 on chronic psychotic patients in groups would be the best way to talk to him again, in a place which I have kept carefully and affectionately in my inner world.

Space and 'madness' are two aspects of being with which I have been concerned for a long time. What does it mean to be an individual? What does it mean to be in the world and what about the world itself? A being is not a thing, not merely an object, but mainly a subject. Being a subject, to be one's self, to be a person means to have a 'living body', a moving body, a thinking body. To be means to have a place of one's own, to experience one's body and mind as a living element in space and time. To live means to experience time ('*temps vécu*' in Bergson's view) and the passing of time (becoming) as part of existence.

My interest in psychotic patients has to do with my own ontological preoccupations about existence: what it is and what it means.

In 1954 I wrote a paper on 'Personalization' concerning a patient who used to say: 'I am not a person. A person is somebody who is somewhere, who people can see, and who is able to see other people. A person is somebody who has a body, and to have a body means to see, to look at others and to be seen; means also to stand on one's own feet and to know that one is standing, to speak and to be entirely oneself. Those who are not persons remain closed and silently exterior to everything, or saying perhaps something different from what they feel.'

To be a person means to have one's own mask, a mask that reveals the true inner self. The Latin word 'persona' is derived from the Etruscan 'phersu', which signified the actor's mask, the character. 'Phersu' corresponds to 'prosopon' (Greek: προσωπον, face as container) from which derives 'prosopeion' (προσωπειον, mask).

A person's mask is a particular mean of communication, a way in which an individual being reveals his or her own inner self. The face is a visual externalization of an inner order or disorder. The mask originally represented the divine or demonic side of the human being. Through the mask, through the mask of the entire body, its covering as well, people in all cultures reveal something about themselves. The way in which the self appears and 'acts' portrays his being. It is part of a personal and social language which play a very important role in the understanding of cultural anthropology and the theatrical aspect of ritual, religion and daily life.

To have a body means to be aware that one is living matter and form. Malinowski described the matrilineal structure of the Trobriand Islanders where the matrilineal kin became part of one's unique body. The father is the stranger, different and outside of the maternal space. He introduces the concept of diversity among the lineage. The father introduces the idea of matter or substance. He represents the link in space (communication) and time (chronology). He also introduces the notion of law and boundaries. In Melanie Klein's view, in the beginning the father is conceived of as inhabiting maternal space: combined parents.

Identity and diversity are two extremes of a dynamic space where narcissism and socialism (as Bion used the word) are questioned.

Why 'Space of Madness'? Space is not mad, but mad thoughts take possession of space and time and lead to a strange life which cannot be understood in terms of ordinary thinking.

Bion used to speak of 'wandering thoughts' searching for a thinker (or wild thoughts in search of somebody able to tame them, of someone able to contain them, to stand and to understand them). The main problem in counter-transference with psychotic patients is to tolerate madness and at the same time to protect one's self from being seduced or possessed by these very thoughts. It is not just 'Six Characters in Search of an Author', as Bion mentions in reference to Pirandello's play,[1] but multiple characters represented by the fragmentary thoughts trying to find a containing mask, a way of appearing in a meaningful sense, searching for a place where one can become united and whole, rather than a broken actor, a broken person, a fragmentary being suffering from a breakdown. Nevertheless, during a breakdown, though disturbed, a person is alive — living a painful but real experience. In chronic states of madness, inner time is paralysed (*temps vécu*) and the mask is petrified and without hope.

I shall discuss a group of chronic psychotics, some of them with fifteen or twenty years as in-patients, with whom I am going to illustrate some of my views on the individual self, the group self, and the psychotic self.[2]

This group was born on a Friday morning at 11.30 in a very small room, almost a corridor, of the Hôpital Sainte-Anne in Paris, on the first floor of the Henri Rousselle Institute. The birth was very difficult. As usual we were together for one and a half hours. The medical director was present and three observers. The initial idea was to live and to observe a psychotic experience in a dramatic transference or lack of transference which it was difficult to 'stand and understand'.

The members of the group were immobile, bizarre and strange. They looked at me as somebody intruding into their personal world, a world without motion and emotion. A cold world, sometimes animated with unconnected gestures, mechanical and fragmented ones. For them it was I who was bizarre, who came to wake them, interfering with their own space and petrified conception of the world.

At one point one of the group members, Claude, a male patient, said:

'I am a penguin.' That I experienced as an introduction of the group as a faraway animal: not a person, but a bird unable to fly which is very heavy and inarticulate. I looked at the rest of the group which was then being born for me (as I was probably, though not certainly, being born for them).

In the origins of transference, the patient we did not know before is being born for us as we are being born for him (prior to this time we did not exist for each other). The birth of a transference is a double birth in a dyadic context and a multiple birth in a group context.

I saw strange, frozen, 'subhuman beings'. They were inside a narrow uterus or vagina, or a tense vagina which did not allow them to move very much. Besides the penguin was Miss Penguin, a woman dressed as an Eskimo, symmetrically immobile, dressed in furs and wearing a fur hat, and resembling an igloo rather than a person. This pathetic figure, living in the frost and protecting herself, symbolized for me the mental and physical state of the group: immobilization, autistic protection, a state of being and living in a space far removed from ordinary time and space. Claude and Miss Penguin, on introduction to the group, were spontaneous living, metaphorical pictures of what could be experienced by me as the basic personality of the group (Kardiner, 1959) and its basic assumptions; the environment as a social mask, the outer expression of an inner state of petrification of being and hibernation of self.

The basic personality is not synonymous with basic assumption but is related in the sense of personification of a basic, unconscious desire or belief of the group.[3]

Psychotic patients are usually extremist, polar people, in extreme cold or extreme heat; during the acute crisis they are in a burning state. In any case, time – the experience of time – is blocked and reified. Symmetry is an expression of identity without diversity; the mineral is structurally symmetrical; catatonic patients are usually in a state of petrification.

Looking back at the group, which was an agglomeration or a serial world rather than a real group, I could see Dominique, a sort of adolescent troubador of the Middle Ages, neither male nor female nor even both, who says with a mixture of arrogance and pain: 'We cannot get out. We mad people have no place outside. We have a place here – here we can be mad.'

But looking at them almost suffocated in that narrow corridor I said to them: 'But you don't seem very happy here either.'

Dominique, the troubador, was placed topographically at the other extreme from Mr and Miss Penguin and seemed to wake them up. Claude the Penguin started to move his right leg in an insistent rhythmical way and said: 'When are we going to eat?' The newborn child coming in from the frost was impatient and wanted to eat.

From a cold, immobile world, rhythm and motion emerged, but in a context of discontinuity: part of the group self was awakening, part still sleeping or dead (or almost dead), and part silent spectator of the scene.

The atmosphere of the room became warmer and breathable, but feelings of hopeless depression and distrust appeared. Another patient, who was Polish, became frightened; it was too warm for him, too soon to wake up, and although the atmosphere was now more alive, it was upsetting.

A woman in the group, aged about fifty — Mme Robin — looked at the rest as if she were a spectator in a theatre trying to link them with her eyes. She was trying to understand what was going on, and said: 'I am looking for a place. Nobody invites me. All my children are married but there is no place for me.' I understood that she was looking for invitations from the others in order to find a place in somebody else's space. Her own body was not a good house, a living place, but rather a grave (*soma-sema*).[4] This woman personified existence as coming out into the world but she could not stand being in the open. . . . She needed to jump the space in between and find another body where to be and to stay.

After a long silence somebody started to smoke, and then someone else followed and the room began to be inhabited by smoke. This smoke stood for evaporated anguish occupying the whole space. Smoke, an invading language without words, started to take possession of the group space trying to put off the leader — who did not smoke and hated smoking (counter-resistance). I said that we could perhaps try to understand what this smoke-invaded world was signifying.

Our next meeting (we met once a week) was in a bigger room on the ground floor. They did not stop smoking but the space made the atmosphere more tolerable, and besides, for the moment I could not give them anything better than exchanging experience for smoke.[5]

Looking at the smoke rising, Brigitte, a young girl, started to talk about a wonderful cathedral. She said: 'This place is beautiful. It's a wonderful church. I am sure that we are going to be helped.'

Up into the ceiling or heaven idealization substitutes smoke; with the smoke the group was able to build up a clouded divinity. Idealization here is a way of escape, getting away vertically from the unbearable horizontal existence to a new-dimensional or a-dimensional world.

Dominique, the troubador, reacts against idealization and writes on a blackboard: 'Don't listen to the doctor, faith-sellers.'[6]

Levitation, as against gravitation, is a way of reacting against life as a catastrophic fall. Heidegger speaks of falling in the world as constituting a basic ontological experience of life. Existing means being out in the world. In order to exist we need a mother world to receive us (the double of the mother who contains the child before the birth).

A month later, the group was more alive but more upset. We used to look on the group experience, the observers and I, and also the patients, as a sort of Tower of Babel, a confusing 'theological' meeting-place of different languages with so many different things taking place at the same time. The group became lively but also discordant and noisy. Some of the patients wanted to talk, others to sing or dance or to seduce or be seduced. Erotization at all levels started to compete with affection and understanding. Against integration, the psychotic part of the group was trying to impose discontinuity, disintegration and fragmentation. Fragmentation is the result of a psychotic attack on the group's self and the psychotic self is its consequence.

Brigitte, the 'cathedral girl', stopped idealization, became depressed and closed herself into a silent existence. She wanted to get out of the hospital, but was unable to. She lacked both the strength and the agreement of her family. Miss Penguin became more alive, opened her Eskimo house and wanted very much to communicate, but the world was dangerous. People wanted to steal everything from her: her father stole all her money. Perhaps, for her, giving and expressing herself implied a risk, that of ideas and feelings being stolen. The delusional world constitutes capital which patients usually do not want to lose.

Someone mentioned Hitler as being powerful and important. Some of the others reacted against Hitler, and Dominique said: 'Hitler is inside each one of us.' The group was expressing extremes from expansive idealization to destructive narcissism and pleasure in destroying and occupying other people's territory. Brigitte began to sing in a sad, monotonous way. Other people made gestures and movements of a stereotyped kind. One of them, Gérard, introduced the word 'masturbation' and everybody became frenetic and upset, occupying the whole space with impulsive masturbation as in Peter Brook's version of *Marat-Sade*. Then suddenly the group became silent and mechanical like a lifeless marionette, a heavy, melancholic penguin. Someone said: 'It's cold here. We need more heat.'

The group is a multiplicity of things and beings, which changes from extreme cold to a need of warmth, and masturbation is as a burning impulse trying to excite a corpse: a dead body without a future.

'My life', said Claude the Penguin, showing his body with scars from birth (forceps delivery), 'has been marked from the very beginning. Destiny is stronger than chance. Everything is marked and measured.' Brigitte, who used to work in a shoe-shop, said, looking at the medical director: 'You have big feet. Your size is 45.' She needed to know where the medical director stood, if he was strong enough to carry such a heavy load, to handle such a heavy function.

Olivier, a young schizophrenic and also drug addicted, spoke about his breakdown: 'I was in the toilet reading a comic with the door open and people asked the police to take me away.' Each comic strip consists of a series of separate drawings which do not move. Olivier's story became an image of the group at that very moment: different scenes from different strips together making incoherent reality, like a marionette with bizarre gestures.

Another patient spoke about his big body as being the Eiffel Tower. The Eiffel Tower is a vertical metallic shoe, bigger than the horizontal power of the medical director. To be a tower, a metallic one like the Eiffel Tower, is a delusional concept of power without feelings.

Mr Camus, a member of the group who seldom spoke, said: 'I am Camus, not the writer.' 'How do you find this atmosphere,' I asked him, and he answered: 'There are three atmospheres here: one of sex and excitement; one of sadness; and another of trying to find a way out.' This patient looked like a prophet with a long beard who knew the way . . .

The group is a complex self, a neurotic self, a psychotic self, a confused self, a dead self, a living self. Within the self are the objects, the 'others', the self and the others, speaking different languages, and with different ideologies which the psychiatrist calls delusions.

A new patient, Mr Kader, from Madagascar, understood that the group had already been born. Suddenly he began to dance, a frenetic dance which became for some of the group a sort of initiation rite.[7] Olivier was the one who represented the group as a 'Shamanic' figure and went to receive him in the centre. They kissed each other. At that moment Josette, who usually made a couple with Olivier, became upset and jealous and ran away. 'I don't care,' said Olivier of Josette. 'She is too crazy. I believe in God; my God is hashish.' (He was a schizophrenic and was a drug addict.)

Through affinity, confrontation and competition, the group expressed its different views and beliefs. Miss Penguin spoke about the book *Elective Affinities* by Goethe. She meant that empathy and affinity were important. Mr Kader wanted to attach himself to the group and to find affinity through Olivier, but Olivier reacted negatively. Personal beliefs, delusional beliefs, do not agree with affinity. 'I am God,' said Olivier, and another group member, Mr Palenque, replied: 'God is dead.' Olivier spoke of Mitterrand's victory in the elections, about Pol Pot, socialism and dictatorship. He asked: 'Dr Resnik, what does socialist anguish mean?' I answered: 'It's a mixture of opposite feelings, left and right, which is trying to take possession of the whole group. It's a false socialism.'

'I don't believe in my father,' said Olivier, 'I accept him as a brother but my real father is hashish.' Hashish was a god that the group used against the god of medicine, Aesculapius; the god which a child uses against his father and the god which narcissism uses against socialism.

The psychotic experience takes possession of the transference and the counter-transference, and tries to take possession of other people's minds and feelings. But nobody is entirely psychotic; the self is not psychotic; neither is it neurotic. The pscyhotic self is a metaphor we use and need in order to speak about the kaleidoscopic experience of chaos and fragmentation opposing integration.

Two ideologies are in a state of war. The dictatorship of delusion is opposed to medical dictatorship. The danger is always dogmatism, whether delusional or scientific, which is always against understanding and plasticity. The plasticity of the ego and the flexibility of the self are essential conditions (H. Numberg 1961) for relating with the other, in order to tolerate contradiction and ambiguity. Psychotic narcissism hates contradiction; so does dogmatism.

The study of the self in this complex context of a group of chronic psychotics brings us to the myth of origins. The primary structure of the ego, says Edward Glover (1968), might be figured as a kind of skeletal system; in the beginning it is a cluster formation of ego nuclei.

These 'archeological' fragments of a primitive ego come back to life as an unintegrated self who is not prepared for integration. Disintegration stands for the chaotic forces of the primitive ego that cannot bear to be born again, that cannot stand to come out of a frozen world, a drastic solution to a painful catastrophic experience.

Tension between war and peace, Thanatos and Eros, takes a leading part and a ritual function at the beginning and end of almost every session. Between disorder, order and delusional order, the members of group try to speak and to take over the microphone at the same time, as in H. Bosch's *The Ship of Fools* (Plate 11.1): here many people are gathered round a hanging stone which looks like the anticipation of radio; a premonition, the future of an illusion, as Bion said, of something

which has not been invented yet but nevertheless is already there; in fact the hanging stone looks like a microphone and the upper part like an antenna. The space of madness stands in this case for a multiplicity of voices and faces wanting to talk at the same time. A kind of tension comes out before a certain harmony is seen and accepted. Harmony means order of 'sounds', 'colours' and 'forms', agreement as opposed to disagreement, calm as opposed to emotional turbulence. A psychotic breakdown is an upsetting, turbulent experience, something in which birth is inseparable from death, a situation in which the unconscious speaks through the microphone without repression, but at a particular point repression returns as a necessary (needed) law in order to give and create meaning in chaos. In fact, according to Jammer (1954), chaos is the first representation of space. All the forces and possibilities are there, which give rise to 'spatium': extension, distance, space, place and division. Division of the whole is the starting-point of a sense of organization and rhythm in space, therefore time. Anaxagoras or *'nous'*, a latent mind, lives in a latent state, as personification of a primordial experience of life before time, order and space come into existence. In chaos all the forces are there, before any division, before any organization, the basics for all future structure: latent *'nous'*, an original force, is an anaxagoras equivalent.

Bion, in his paper 'Emotional Turbulence', speaks about the expectation of the group being so intense that it can hardly wait to hear what is going to be said. This expectation stimulates a great many feelings which can be so intense that the group becomes resistant to any emotion and falls silent. Silence can be used as a way of creating boundaries to a chaotic and uncontrollable experience.

Brigitte was frightened, and pleased at the same time, that the group had started to think and to exist, but could also break up again and become dismembered and dismantled. It appeared to be a double expectation, one of which was a kind of waiting for a father, for a phallic element, a constructive one who could help in bringing things together, and create a sort of spinal cord that could hold the group intact. (It has been discovered that in prehistoric times people lived in shelters made from the skeletons of the great mammoths.) The other expectation was the defeat of the father, an attack on linking (Bion, 1967: 193). Then the idea of a mother came into the foreground. They spoke about a temple, a house, a hospitable place where they could bring the pieces together, some place to be held within and to be kept warm and protected. The group mother as a matrix is supposed to contain and to appease the war against the father, but children cannot always live together and have the same mother, nor accept the combined parents.

In order that the *logos* can come into the open the group matrix should be organized and prepared to accept its birth. Mr Palenque said that we should be silent in order to allow the first real word to come out. Claude the Penguin suggested that the word should be written rather than spoken. The written word lasts. . . . After a pause the group became tense again and the unconscious forces, envious of the group womb and its fertility, started to attack. Hitler returned and the narcissistic self of the group expressed its admiration for him again.

Dominique spoke and again talked of the danger of Hitler being present and inside each one, the danger of him waking up again.

As in the war between Eros and Thanatos, the members of the group became excited sexually. Life and death, all kinds of opposite feelings, became eroticized. Eroticism, under the form of sadistic phantasies, brings homogeneity occupying the whole field of experience: thinking, feeling and sexual tendencies being equally eroticized.

At a particular point the erotic atmosphere passed and everything got blocked and cold again. Then they started to move, emerging from the frost, trying to understand what was happening. Philippe, another young psychotic, asked me if I understood Chinese, therefore whether I could understand something like Chinese — a mad language, according to another member of the group. Mr Palenque said: 'I am Thanatos whom Freud could not fight against. I personify Hitler.' People started complaining against the Nazis taking possession of the entire place, attacking Harmony and good feelings. Mr Palenque changed his attitude, remembering that he was a Jew as well. He took off his glasses and began to look at them upside-down, saying: 'I am also the other way around, I am anti-Nazi.' He spoke about the *Luftwaffe* (Air Force) and he repeated '*Luft*'. *Luft* means air, being light and able to levitate. Somebody seemed to hear the engine of an aeroplane outside and suddenly the whole group felt light and someone spoke about being transformed into a bird, a crazy bird, losing his head. Someone else spoke about Salomé and Salomon (my name). The group became a wild bestiary (Latin, '*bestiarium*'). Claude the Penguin spoke about a crocodile living in his stomach and after a pause something like a miracle took place. Claude looked through the window towards the sky. Appearing to be in a state of ecstasy, he said: 'The crocodile has gone away and is flying.'

The crocodile became a dragon, a spirit of nature, genesis of the world of madness, an earth monster coming out into the open, a kind of god, something (somebody) to believe in. The dragon became a god of madness, the idealized version of delusional thinking. The ideology of madness competes with the ideology of sanity, but madness and sanity are parts of the same body, the group matrix. Which one is going to cut the head off the other? To cut off madness, to cut off sanity or bring both principles together? One needs a mediator between them. One needs to accept the need of a bridge, the father as a linking figure, with a shamanic function: linking two worlds.

Olivier spoke of a cavalier who jumps with his horse from one side of the river to the other. He does not need a bridge, he does not need a father, his god hashish is a strong horse with great power. Mr Camus, the prophet with the long beard, spoke about risking and not risking, saying: 'In order not to risk we need to play on both sides.' Mr Kader, the boy from Madagascar, said he was struggling very hard in his mind as if something was in danger of blowing up. Mr Palenque said: 'Perhaps we should cut off the head of John the Baptist before he explodes.' At the same time part of the group was playing the role of Salomé, seductively trying to convince someone to be the scapegoat. After the play of seduction and fascination, a great tension appeared and Jean-Paul D., the Polish boy, started to break out in explosive laughter until everybody is laughing.

The explosion had taken place, an explosion of laughter. After this crisis, cathartic crisis, the group became quiet and relaxed. Where had the madness gone? Where was the dragon and delusional beliefs?

At a particular moment Kader looked outside and made a gesture with his hand, dramatizing the group throwing madness out of the window. Then again someone heard the plane engine and Kader said: 'The plane is going to blow up, some strange birds have got into the engine.'

The dragon, omnipotent 'god or evil' stands for the needs of excessive idealization, in order to compensate for the fragile ego and fear of disaster. Being ill, becoming psychotic, has to do with an overwhelming crisis, a catastrophic experience in which everything that was contained and built up internally explodes. The dramatization of the group (through the one eye of the group as a body) of throwing something out of the window is a means of getting rid of a painful memory: the catastrophic experience, the memory of an apocalypse,[8] is still difficult to endure, therefore the need for it to be projected, ejected into the distance in order to avoid pain and destruction again.

Like the mystic, both creative and destructive, the dragon is a personification of a creative phenomenon, the need of a strong super-ego, a strong belief in which faith, in good or bad, can reside and exist.

The problem arises; how does one link these different feelings and opposite beliefs, how can they be brought together to speak to each other and between themselves? War between them can bring about a disaster, while a dialogue can bring peace, constructive feelings and creative thinking.

In the following session, flying (going up into the sky) returned, but this time it came hand in hand with stealing (in French the verb *'voler'* means both 'to fly' and 'to steal'; a phonetic equation where two different words have the same meaning through sounds).

The group woke up and abandoned its lethargic state, but waking up can sometimes be too exciting, too frightening: too much change in too short a period of time within a space where nothing has happened for a long time. The group was more flexible and alive but life can be difficult; everyday life is quite different from delusional truth. Gérard wore a headband, a symbol of his way of thinking, part of his hippy subcultural mask. He took off his band in order to show that the group mind was more flexible and elastic; but one should be careful because it can snap (break) if stretched too fast or too far. Mr Palenque spoke about travelling and communicating over a distance, talking about telepathy and finding out what goes on in the heads of distant people; people living far away in space and time or perhaps those living beyond the usual conception and meaning of the two, but not everyone thinks with his mind or head. Claude the Penguin thinks with his stomach. He looked at his belly, saying 'The crocodile is in here again and knows everything; he says next summer is going to be hot.' To which the group reacted with agitation and sexual excitement. We were already in summer and everybody became warm and hot. As in dreams, the space of madness has a different conception of time. Summer came in only a few seconds. The group could not differentiate between being warm and being hot, between having warm feelings and getting hot (excited sexually). They were equated: delusional erotic transference.

There was a pause and the group became contained again. At this very moment Claude the Penguin said: 'You know, a primitive tribe in the Amazon forest, the Jivaros, are head-shrinkers'.

Mlle Chamerois — a very chronic patient of about sixty — who sometimes thinks she is the queen of France and a descendant of Louis VIII[9] — was frightened about emotional and sexual feelings coming together. She said it was too hot and that we were in danger of losing strength and becoming dehydrated.

Group analysis becomes a dangerous but necessary exploration. To analyse feelings, thoughts and beliefs means also to enter a forest, to go into a primitive and wild environment where primitive tendencies and ancient cultures can be woken up. The group mind is a forest, sometimes a stomach inhabited by strange creatures where the king of the forest is not a lion but rather a crocodile who wishes to become a dragon. Too much was happening: Mr Palenque, wondering if Mlle Chamerois (who stood for the entire group at this moment) 'would not prefer to live in a refrigerator', added: 'perhaps we are going too fast.' 'There is a struggle between different beliefs.' I answered: 'Between going back to the very beginning when the group started as a frozen creature (a penguin) or coming to life again.'

The warm feelings were not controlled yet. Frozen feelings, emerging from a frozen time which has been petrified for a long time, can break out suddenly and uncontrollably, as a fire that can consume the entire existence of a living being who is not balanced yet.

The more the group came to life, the more they were able to transfer feelings and to experience feelings ('normal' and delusional), the more anxious they became at the end of a session at the point where separation takes place. To be together, to put opposite feelings and ways of thinking together is a difficult and painful task. When a group is able to think and feel together, any interruption is experienced as hurting and painful . . . grief is still something difficult to bear but necessary in order to be, to think, to feel: necessary in order to live.

Melanie Klein (1965) speaks about importance of separation and grief as painful but enriching experiences.

There were different fantasies felt and suggested by the group in order to avoid mental pain equated with being alive, coming back to daily life. One fantasy was to freeze feelings and existence again and wait. The other, offered by Gérard (who always looks at his watch), was to change living time to mechanical time; a repetitive and circular time endlessly revolving (out of danger from separation and end). According to the nurse on his ward, Gérard spent most of his time looking at his watch, reducing space and time to the very small and mechanical face of a watch. Gérard, like the Jivaros tribe, wanted to shrink and immobilize experience (being and beings) into a controllable and shrunken space, something he could keep a watch over; an iron, mechanized time as opposed to a flexible and living time.

Catatonic patients tend to petrify space and time. They cannot stand the passing of time; everything animated (Latin, *'animare'*, to fill with breath; *'anima'*, air, soul) must become inanimate.

In this way the world becomes deprived of dangers but also deprived of life which demands movement in order to unfold. The catatonic mask represents a mechanical picture of the world. Paralysis and immobiliz-ation stops memory and history. A sequence in time becomes part of history (social and personal history) and in order to remember we need to travel against the current which can be either strong and fast-moving or slow and dense to the point of coagulation. Starting a session again means to go back in time; to link experience, to build up an idea of sequence and history. The members of the group need to remember and to be remembered to enable them to think. As opposed to memory, a fear of memory (of remembering) provokes a dismembering: time falls apart, disintegrated into pieces. Time is a sequence. In the culture of Western Egypt, time is represented as a snake, in the East as a dragon. In Ancient Egypt the Sun God (lord of time) assumes the shape of a different animal each hour as he traverses the firmament. Time thus acquires changing qualities in an endless circular space. Time brings joy, good fortune and life, but also pain, misfortune and death. In China the play of the opposites is seen as harmonious, not tragic or catastrophic. Heraclitus used war (battle) as a bridge between opposite feelings which tend to come together in excitement. Children often have this image of their parents' sexual relationship and modes of exchange. Curiosity, excitement, envy and jealousy often come into the foreground of all the mating landscapes of opposites. This happens when the subject, though moved by the desire to come together with its opposite, hates at the same time the memory of what mating stands for. This is an attack on linking. Coagulation is a way of stopping the flow, of safeguarding against a dangerous and painful experience; contained time can flow out violently as a kind of haemorrhage.

Mr Kader said we needed a good coagulation at the end of each session so we could wait for the next session. In my countertransference I felt uneasy. How could we coagulate the time of coagulation? How could we stop the haemorrhage of defrosted time?

Language and communication of all kinds (non-verbal modes as well) are part of a changing quality . . . gestures, words and the entire atmos-phere can become solid and dense like iron (catatonic) or liquid and volatile (Latin, '*volatilis*', *volēre*: to fly).[10]

Language has its own nature and can change its nature. It can be rigid, soft or like either; full of meaning or empty. Words at the psychotic level can be empty fragments or meaningful pieces of broken armour . . . words can also be invisible, an entire army with masks. Delusional thinking can become a powerful language, a convincing one if it is delusionally well built up (in paranoid personalities and in paranoiac misunderstandings, non-understanding and delusional thinking can exist within an extremely logical context).

In the next session someone started talking about a fish, someone else about a snake. Then someone added 'smoked fish'. No more a penguin, but now a fish and a smoked fish. The delusional atmosphere of the group, the smoky climate, dried up the group which had become a dehydrated being, not knowing what to do next. Experiencing growing, maturing, moving in time and learning were being interfered with by opposite feelings which lead to blocking, paralysis and coldness. Symmetrical (anti-dialectical) forces had led to immobilization. At that particular moment Claude spoke about the crocodile anticipating a hot summer but not everybody wanted to become mobilized, and Gérard spoke about going to sleep, sending to sleep what might be woken up. At some point Gérard spoke again, about a broken piece of glass from a window: 'This is me, Gérard, when I am a piece of broken glass.' I understood and said to the group that coming back to life can be dangerous when one still feels fragile like a piece of glass and when opening and breaking (breaking up) become equated, one and the same thing.

The psychic texture of a schizophrenic mind is often felt as made of glass. The glass stands for a substance, a particularly fragile self which can break at any moment. Glass also connotes transparency and invisibility: the most powerful way of hiding one's body and mind is to become transparent, allowing everything to come through but nothing is to be found in terms of content. Gérard was frightened of having a crisis and breaking down, therefore wanting to put all possible tension and disturbing impulses to sleep. The piece of glass which he gave his name was his double, his living reflection and shadow already in crisis: his present self was able to look into his future self which was already there in front of his eyes. Visual perspective is already a symbolic form (Cassirer 1964, Panofsky 1927), distance in space a way of anticipating time, a living and frightening time. Uncontrolled tendencies and 'mad thoughts' were impatiently waiting to break out into the open, to break the glass. Gérard was trying to guard against these 'wild thoughts' (Bion), savage thoughts he wanted to calm. The skin of the mind was trying to contain all the opposing forces of an inner group that could not keep reality together; an inner group which was frightening, not getting along with each other, not wanting to think together. Gérard stood for the group as a mad patient who was at the same time sane, trying to control and contain both implosion (inner explosion) and explosion, trying to preserve life (life continuous) of the group as a whole. Claude the Penguin looked at his watch as if miming Gérard and spoke about a mechanical, closed circle which impedes life. Mechanical time is a necessary conception for an institutional time which needs to give points of reference for daily life: eating, sleeping and waking. This repetitive time creates claustrophobic feelings: but being inside is not a protection when living time (*temps vécu*) wakes up. The group wanted to emerge (Latin, '*e*'- out, '*mergere*' to dip: to rise as from a fluid, to come forth into view) from a catatonic body, to become visible, to free itself from a rigid, institutional and personal skin: Gérard said: 'Leave, get the permission to leave' (in French Gérard used the word '*perme*' as an abbreviation for *permission*, which he associated with 'sperm').

Coming out into the world can be risky and dangerous: a catastrophic ejaculation (expression, excretion, ejaculation are equated modes of mental evacuation).

Mme Robin (the old woman who spoke in the first session about not having a house of her own and being neglected by her children) smiled and said in a very detached way: 'My brother died', then added, 'also my nephew, in a car accident.' Jean-Pierre D. responded: 'It is not true, the accident.'

At the very moment that the group wanted to come out into the street of life it was frightening to speak of accidents . . . One had to be detached and able to split feelings from facts; to smile when one is sad. It is difficult to face grief. Entering or jumping into the world is like dying and being born again. To face life, feelings of loss and separation; perhaps it would be better to be far away from one's self when present time and space is difficult and painful to stand. Mme Robin spoke again: 'I am away now, 2,000 kilometres from here. I went to the place where I was born.' Mme Robin had escaped. from the present into a place in space called time, a faraway time − the point of birth, far away from a terrible, painful present and current feelings. To experience the body in the present is to experience commitment. Gérard, looking at his watch, stands for the mechanical ideology of time as opposed to experiencing time (time which moves out and unfolds). Mme Robin stands for linear, mechanical time as opposed to cyclical time.

At the next session the group was very tense, and disturbing feelings were trying to come out through the group skin. Suddenly the tension broke out through Annie Jo, Miss Penguin, who became angry and furious, and broke out in a rage, saying that her mother stole something from her and then abandoned her; she was speaking and looking at the group. She was accusing the group as a mother who has left her alone with tensions and problems for two months. It was our first meeting after the summer holidays. Feelings of anger and resentment were spoiling the good feelings that the group wanted to preserve, but to bear absence when presence is so important is a very difficult task. It is also equally difficult not to know what is happening during the time of separation. The destiny of the internal object in the patient's mind and body and in that of the analyst and staff is unpredictable. The capacity to stand separation depends on one's ability to bear grief, also the ability of one to ingest and assimilate the absent object; the absent object can become a frightening hole, a black hole which can swallow and destroy everything. The mouth of a child who cannot deal with separation can become voracious and uncontrollable; protocannibalistic tendencies can be projected into the empty object or the objectless place where the object used to be, becoming a devouring hole which tries to dissolve and destroy time − an unbearable time of anticipation; a primitive mouth that cannot accept weaning can become very destructive, wanting to destroy (devour) everything, including all that is pure and good. Mr Kader spoke about the danger of impure feelings attacking pure ones: 'The impure is what remains after the pure is volatilized and dissipated, but God has the key to everything, he could solve the problem.' Gérard seemed upset about Kader and represented, at this very moment, the most regressive, infantile part of the group. He could not share with the others, and his aggressive feelings of greed and frustration (impure feelings) were attacking the pure and good desires of the group, making the group atmosphere even more uneasy. The people in the group could not stand the climate, which was becoming more and more unbreathable. If there is not air and freedom to breathe they cannot think or exist. 'I breathe, therefore I exist' wrote Descartes in a letter to Reneri (April–May 1638). The *logos* needs oxygen in order to think, feel and speak. If the *logos* is suffocated it will not be able to articulate, neither verbal nor mental thoughts. When the space of madness becomes unbreathable the few remaining thoughts try to escape through the window or door, in search of a breathable atmosphere, a place where one can breathe and therefore exist. When thoughts and feelings fly away like lost birds, frightened and wild (wild thoughts) the group becomes empty and devoid of good feelings and thoughts. What remains is a frightening hole, a dense and confused climate of emptiness, an unbearable loneliness, a maddening solitude.

How does one go on in this state or how can one change the atmosphere, encourage the lost and wild thoughts to come back? It is like the aftermath of an earthquake. How does one bring back life and a sense of order? Claude the Penguin started to speak about the number three, about twice three being six and six being '*sismique*' (English, 'seismic'). Three stands for original (individual and social) order; one, the other, and the space in between: the bridge (father, mother and child). Twice three means a doubling of the positive and negative picture of triangular relationships. When the three elements, the mother (the group matrix), the father (the formal leader — the analyst or the director of the hospital) and the child (the infantile selves of the group members) cannot bear to be together, tensions between them, everything can blow up and a catastrophic change can take place; a disintegration and a fragmentation, a going back in time where reality becomes again prehistoric, the beginning of life again. Claude spoke about strange and primitive animals. Simians appear, from which man will descend. The explosive impact of the two opposite threes (good and bad triangular relationships) takes humanity back to primitive times; two times three if they are not in harmony with each other produce a seismic and simian reality; six (seismic and simian become part of an exchange of thoughts phonetically equated). Explosive time is a fearful time. Perhaps it would be better to split reality itself and to keep each three on opposite sides of the river: a river with no bridge. Communication between equally symmetrical opposite forces brings immobilization and paralysis but along with these it brings cataclysmic explosions if anything moves.

After a tense fearful silence a stereotypic behaviour returned, repetitive and monotonous, bringing with it circular mechanical time; jiggling legs, metallic and repetitive gestures returned to the ideology of the watch. Claude, jiggling his legs, looked at his watch. Then raising his hands and rubbing them together, he said: 'Two or three, I don't know. I think about god as a grandfather and myself becoming a captain of a sporting club.' Through the waters of purity and impurity, order and disorder, being and not being; Claude the Penguin is a captain, in control, guarding the 'health' of the space of madness, keeping it safe from contamination. The space of madness is a meeting-place, a club where people try to exercise, reinforce, keep the body-mind clean. Madness can be a kind of pollution, a confused pollution which requires hygienic measures or clear-cut rules of etiquette concerning what is pure or impure.

The group became more and more lively; a living metaphor of need, hunger and care, but to ask for help, to express need and experience pain is disturbing. Claude spoke about his mouth having cavities and needing to go to a dentist. Everybody identified with Claude's mouth and the group presented itself as an open mouth, trying to cry out in pain, asking for a good analyst-dentist capable of restoring emptiness, 'holes', capable of relieving mental and physical pain. Kader said that he also had cavities in his mouth and would like to get rid of his holes. He also wanted to get rid of his bad and insufficient fillings. To live in pain is hell. Somebody spoke about paradise. Kader said that the fillings were keeping hell from coming up through the holes. For that reason one must get rid of the cavities and fillings together. The tooth became the symbol of Pandora's box. The analyst-dentist must be careful not to let hell escape into the open. Mme Robin spoke about her feelings having been enclosed in her mind and body for many years. She spoke again about becoming upset. I told her that in her case she wanted me to re-inforce her tooth fillings, in order not to suffer any more. 'It would be better,' she said, 'to see my house by night, so I will not see very much.'

Torn between wanting to get rid of fillings, liberating feelings and not wanting to raise the lid of Pandora's box, the group became insecure and upset, not knowing how to solve the problem, and the dilemma manifested itself as tension. 'There are some tensions,' Kader said, 'between Israel and the Arabs; how do we prevent the danger of destroying one another? I have kept myself away from the world a long time; I am frightened of a relapse.'

Brigitte, the 'cathedral girl', had left the hospital for several months but had returned because of her relapse. At this moment she was tense and enveloped in a heavy silence. She broke the silence, speaking about Christ. After a pause she took off her sweater, rolled it into a kind of rag doll and held it in her arms like a baby; Christ and the Virgin Mary. 'I want to keep Christ safe in Bethlehem,' she said. Mr Kader, very moved, approached Brigitte and tried to keep her calm. He identified with the baby in her arms and wanted some chocolates: 'I am frightened to eat chocolate, it will damage my teeth.' After a pause he added: 'But I am hungry, I feel empty.' Brigitte became quieter and less tense but Kader and the rest of the group became anxious: helplessness and anguish changed place. The tension rose higher and higher until Kader said: 'We are in a state of war, perhaps you could give a chocolate to each one of us.'

In the next session, inner tension equated with war returned, coming down through Annie J., Miss Penguin, who spoke about her parents fighting all the time. 'Perhaps they should get divorced,' she said. Mme Chamerois, turning and showing her bottom to the group on the pretext of looking for an ashtray on the floor, responded with, 'Perhaps we shouldn't care about our parents.' The group was alive but frightened and tense; hell might come out into the open. They looked at each other coldly, trying to freeze their anxiety but they themselves became cold. Jean-Pierre D., the Polish boy, said: 'We should get warmer, we need heating.' Claude the Penguin became anxious and started to jiggle his legs again, at the same time hitting them, trying to make them stop.

He was anxious about going back to the penguin state of existence, returning to frozen, prehistorical time. 'I always run in circles in my club, I get tired and don't know what to do.' Gérard began to look at his watch again and spoke about masturbation. Everyone became frenetic and tried to occupy the space with impulsive masturbation; sexual, mechanical heating as in Peter Brook's version of *Marat-Sade*. Exciting the body and exciting one another made the group hot. Feeling needs warmth, a particular emotional temperature, the right level of understanding. It is difficult to find the right climate, to find equilibrium and not to fall back into a mechanical, stereotypic 'eroticized time', not to get caught in a vision circle. Gérard, for the first time, after looking at his watch again, looked straight into my eyes. He was trying to force himself to overcome circular mechanical time; to change it into linear time, an experienced time, living time (*temps vécu*), which goes in search of the other. Time became a procession of animated feelings, living symbolic forms; a procession of little gods looking for a great belief. He spoke about his mother whom he idealized very much. The group was trying to create a secret space where hope could find an aim and perhaps also a name. This time the group didn't become a cathedral, a closed esoteric space, but rather a ritual place of worship in an open space. Esoteric, mysterious time enclosed in a minimum of metallic space (the watch) became an exoteric reality, an articulated procession of thoughts and beliefs looking for an ideal, the ideal ego, from where the ego-ideal comes to life again in search of its double. 'But life is not linear,' said Mlle Chamerois, 'there are curves.' In fact, the mystical labyrinth, the Christian one, corresponds to a straight belief, looking for god there. Life is an adventurous labyrinth, not a linear one. One doesn't know the who, where and when of what one expects to find. Life is unpredictable. The group was beginning to have a history, a memory and a need for a belief . . . Not just a delusional belief. I was beginning to be able to stand more divergences and ambiguities now. The group had a body and a mind and also a sense of perspective (inner and outer), but life sometimes appears either as a difficult or dreadful space to live in or as an over-idealized space for belief. Different ideologies were confronted, but the main thing is to come back to life and to experience emotion without dread and with a capacity for illusion.

'My heart,' said Jean-Pierre D.; 'L'amour,' said Annie J., Miss Penguin. Love is a way of giving shape to emotions. Love needs a shape in time and to be personalized as a rhythm in synchronization with other rhythms. The space of madness becomes less mad and more harmonious, more creative when opposite forces – love and hate, Eros and Thanatos, war and peace – can live together. The other solution is a depersonalized space and time which works to keep opposites separate; not to listen to each other like two or more deaf people who agree not to hear, not to talk. The right physiological circulation of life, sense and communal feeling within the body-group or the body-mind demands sharing rhythms or to complement them in a way in which the heart can expand and breathe. Systolic and diastolic movements in space are expressive of a living, emotional and harmonious time, as opposed to a mad space-time. In order to bring different rhythms, forces and conceptions together, the group (inner and outer) needs to become a harmonic, expanding, contracting, universe.

A universe means to accept a planetary organization where children, being part of the mother (matrix), accept a father, an illuminating sun which brings warmth, light and energy to each one; the sun, pole of life, as opposed to a frozen pole of death and petrification. To exist means to be somewhere, to have a body, to see and be seen. As in 'ritualized time', not mechanical time, the group was trying to find its way, its place in a world with others; among other 'planets', each life being a synchronous world itself.

Life is a destination, an itinerary, cyclic, linear or labyrinthian. It reveals its meaning in relationship to the man, in relationship to one's self and the one's self to others. The centre of life is perhaps a 'pearl of beginning' from which the germ of the universe evolves: evolves from a basic rhythm of primordial feelings. In the Chinese tradition the 'pearl of beginning' stands for the primal monad – the original oneness which creates the two basic rhythms of the universe: 'yang' – light, heat, hardness, expansion, masculinity – and 'yin' – shade, cold, softness, contraction, femininity – two opposites which come together according to the philosophy of the Tao. The time-bound interaction of these rhythms gives rise to all phenomena in the universe. Symbolically, the group started as a penguin, becoming a bird, then a crocodile that was transformed into a dragon. The dragon symbolizes the dynamic, creative force of the universe in Chinese culture. The male 'yang' and the female 'yin', as basic principles, act upon matter and space. The meaning of time is that in it stages of growth can unfold in clear sequence. Sequence means destination, which means the evolving of life in an unpredictable space of existence.

Conclusion

The term 'group therapy' can have two meanings, according to Bion:[11] it can refer to the treatment of a number of individuals assembled for special therapeutic sessions, or it can refer to a planned endeavour smoothly running co-operative activity.

In another part of the same paper Bion speaks about the 'atmosphere' of a group: he also seems to be concerned, from the very beginning, with the relationship between the individual and the group. Bion believes that the psychoanalytical approach, as seen both through the individual and through the group, was dealing with different facets of the same phenomenon. He speaks about a binocular vision of the same thing.

Kleinian theory provides the idea of an inner space as a multiplicity of 'inhabitants' or objects which behave in a more or less coherent or incoherent way. In the case of the psychotic patients – or 'group-patient' for Bion – coherence is lost. To have a breakdown means to shatter coherence and integrity: to fall to pieces. Those pieces ejected by the 'eyes' of the group, the windows of the room where the group session takes place, can become strange creatures . . . or a mixture of different experiences, strange beings, bizarre objects, which don't 'talk' and 'behave' as 'ordinary' objects and beings.

If the leader present in the group becomes too important – in an idealized or persecuting manner – the group will try to incorporate and to control him into its mask or to expel him, projecting him somewhere far away. 'You seem to be far away', they could say.

An idealized or upsetting super-ego, a delusional object, or part of the Self, can be placed either in Heaven or in Hell; but if so, the excessive projective identification can make the group feel empty or like a big hole. Sometimes this hole can become unbearable and be ejected as well. In that case the body-group becomes a 'no-place', a 'no-time', an 'a-topic' or a 'a-chronic' reality. If they are able to understand and to cope with emptiness, some fragments of experience will come back, but usually changed into something else which the group ego will not always be able to digest. The group space can be a stomach, able or unable to digest experience. In psychotics – Bion said – the mind can work as an alimentary system which cannot always cope with 'mental food' and will try to get rid of or evacuate undigested feelings. Those feelings will sometimes reach the analyst or the observers (in the case of the group) and upset them very much. Here is where the matrix will show or not show its existence and its capacity to bear psychotic experience. Counter-transference is a basic instrument which deals with transference as an expression of diversity, sometimes of an upsetting diversity that 'mother transference' cannot always contain.

Between inner and outer perspectives, which is the 'vertex' that the analyst is going to choose? Which is going to be his expectation or his interpretation? Interpretation can be a way of conveying meaning and order where meaninglessness, disorder and emptiness were before; but it is the quality of experience born from the transference and from countertransference which counts.

Deluded and hallucinated or omnipotent thoughts can try to paralyse time in space, to petrify it: like the Medusa, in order to immobilize an upsetting and 'dangerous' experience of change. Petrification is also a way of avoiding loss: the group will be together for ever. Understanding – a silent or verbal understanding – can protect the members of the group and help them to construct the right boundaries, where madness and sanity can be joined in a coherent and adequate way. Being a psychoanalyst is a very narcissistic and powerful profession; also the patients project power, sovereignty, narcissistic aspects, and sometimes even tyranny into us, making countertransference very difficult.

Interpretation can be a means of conveying understanding and help, but also an expression of power: pathological countertransference can be a way of using interpretation as a mode of action, a mode of occupying other's people space (physical and mental). I must always struggle with myself with this, because sometimes excessive pain and fear of becoming mad can make us omnipotent and unjust, therefore unable to deal with and respect diversity.

What I have learned from Bion, in his seminars, in his personal supervisions and in our personal relationship, is to be able to find my own space, my own way of thinking and developing ideas, but also to be able to cope with different points of view, other living spaces. Life is not a 'supervision', neither a 'super-vision' of things. Nevertheless understanding of an unknown language, the language of the unconscious, can make us feel powerful, and that is the danger.

Excessive narcissism is opposed to socialism, said Bion, but how does one cope with modesty, narcissism and the gratification of understanding and receiving at the same time? On the other hand, the individual and the group is a couple, a pairing reality which is not perfect and it shouldn't be. Children and patients should be able to stand and to understand imperfection and diversity of opinions within the couple. The main point is how much one can tolerate differences with respect. The psychotic and non-psychotic part of the personality behave usually as a divorced couple, as two ways of thinking, two ideological outlooks concerning reality. When time returns to fill a timeless and an empty space, life will come back with it, but also pain and pleasure, which not everybody is able to stand.

The group mask of a psychotic self becomes colourful and alive when fragments of experience come back into the inner world. The mask — which is not only the face, but the entire body of experience — should be able to stand rhythm and change in a continuous state of becoming . . .

When the non-psychotic fragments of the personality and the psychotic ones return, the problem is: Will they be able to talk to each other? To agree or to stand disagreement? What is the 'good spirit' of a group-patient or of a group-person? What is the 'good spirit' of the analyst or of the staff? 'Good spirit' does not mean 'good' in the usual way, but to be able to accept 'the other' within a context where a useful task can evolve.

As opposed to narcissism, a 'socialistic atmosphere' can create the right ground where seeds of different kinds can meet and come together, finding common roots and bearing fruit.

Notes

1 Bion (1980): 49.
2 The term *self* (in old English, *'seolf'* and ancient Celtic *'selva'*) means possession (to possess one's own place). In modern English, 'self' also implies sameness. In French, Voltaire used the term *'mêmeté'*; in Spanish, *'mismidad'* and in Italian, *'ipseità'*. In German, Jung used the term *'Selbst'*.
3 Basic assumption has, for Bion, a restrictive sense for psychotic patients. We can always say the more regressive the group, the more their need for dependency, protection and nourishment (material and spiritual); whereas, in a delusional transference, their *needs* are more specific, different in each case, in each individual and at each instant. Their needs are usually far away from reality and differ from the reality principle. The principle of 'unreality', of delusional ideology of each single patient, creates an eccentric basic assumption which does not necessarily fit into Bion's three categories of basic assumptions.
4 *Soma* means a dead body; *sema* is a grave. Following the Babylonic and Pythagorean conceptions, *dema* = living body. The soul leaves the body after death and looks for another place where it can be alive or dead (*sema*). Transmigration and metempsychosis — where the word *psyche* is implied — correspond to an early belief, a mechanism of the mind which cannot stand the limitations of life.
5 The atmosphere of a group and the 'texture' — solid, liquid or

gaseous — is part of a dramatized language. It is a language which is substantial; different kinds of cement which sometimes become dissolved and the group becomes shapeless.

6 In French, *'foie'* (liver) and *'foi'* (faith) sound alike. Psychotic patients often use phonetic equations: two or more like sounds with different meanings are equated.

7 According to Smith (1956) in all probability ritual was primary and preceded myth or perhaps ritual represents an early dramatization of mythical thinking.

8 Apocalypse, which stands for the end of the world, also means revelation; a double vision of a crucial turning-point. Change in life, sanity and madness, means passing one bank to the other of the same river. The state of becoming in Heraclitus' conception of time is something which constantly changes, therefore never the same. An apocalyptic change is a radical, turbulent transformation where life and death, sanity and madness, come together in a frightening, meaningful experience within space and time. The apocalyptic vision is an intense instant in which different elements unite: seas become floods, mountains tumble into pieces, the earth splits open and the sky becomes fire. In some versions the apocalyptic vision is a bizarre, frightening bestiary inhabited by a seven-headed monster, the Hydra. Some speak about the monster rising from the abyss to occupy the entire world. In the second part of the book of Daniel, both the empires of Greece under Alexander are portrayed as beasts of various kinds, lions, bears, leopards, rams, he-goats, and the final beast is described as a dreadful monster with ten horns, teeth of iron and nails of brass. He speaks 'great' words against the Most High, that is the Jewish people, and attempts to change the times and the law.

   The beginning and the end of all things, in both the natural, supernatural or delusional existence, meet in a circular, global configuration as an upsetting Ouroboros trying desperately to guard his unity.

9 In French *'roi'* (Chame-*rois*) means 'king'.

10 Alvarez de Toledo, in her paper, 'El analisis del "asocian", del "interpretor" y de les "palabres"', *Reviste psicoanalitica argentina*, 12, no. 3, Buenos Aires, 1954, develops an original and interesting view of how words as nature, *logos* or vocal gesture can stand for an experience, be an experience in psychoanalytical setting. Words are not only sounds, formal and informal meaningful expressions, but also matter: a word can also be milk, blood, sand, glass, stones, iron . . . or any other substantial element.

11 See Bion and Rickman, 'Intra-group tensions in therapy', in Bion (1961): 11.

References

Bion, W. R. (1961), *Experiences in Groups and other Papers*, London, Tavistock.

Bion, W. R. (1962), *Learning from Experience*, London, Heinemann.
Bion, W. R. (1963), *Elements of Psycho-analysis*, London, Heinemann.
Bion, W. R. (1967), *Second Thoughts: Selected Papers on Psycho-analysis*, London, Heinemann.
Bion, W. R. (1974), *Brazilian Lectures*, Rio de Janeiro, Imago Editora.
Bion, W. R. (1978), *Four Discussions with W. R. Bion*, Clunie Press.
Bion, W. R. (1980), *Bion in New York and Sao Paulo*, Clunie Press.
Cassirer, E. (1964), *The Philosophy of Symbolic Forms*, Yale University Press.
Glover, E. (1968), *The Birth of the Ego*, New York, Int. University Press.
Jammer, M. (1954), *Concepts of Space*, Harvard University Press.
Kardiner, H. (1957), *The Individual and his Society*, Columbia University Press.
Klein, M. (1965), 'A contribution to the psychogenesis of manic-depressive states' (1955) and 'Mourning and its relation to manic-depressive states' (1940), in *Contributions to Psycho-analysis 1921-1945*, London, Hogarth.
Nunberg, H. (1961), 'Ego strength and ego weakness', in *Practice and Theory of Psychoanalysis*, vol. 1, New York, Int. University Press.
Panowsky, E. (1927), *Die Perspecktive als Symbolische Form*, Leipzig-Berlin, Teuber.
Smith, R. (1956), *The Religion of the Semites*, New York, Meridian.

Chapter 12

The influence of Bion's ideas on my work

Bernardo Blay-Neto

When Bion came to Brazil to lecture, the press referred to him as 'the father of group psychotherapy'. This title resulted from the fact that his contribution to this therapeutic modality received greater attention among us than any other he made to psychoanalysis. His work with groups during World War II had an international repercussion and through it, Bion drew attention to his dynamics.

However, in conducting this research, Bion took a different line from Freud, who also investigated group dynamics. While Bion lived and afterwards described these forces, Freud theorized about them, keeping himself at a distance from the group. Both described their findings in papers that became classics: Freud with *Group Psychology and the Analysis of the Ego* and Bion with 'Intra-group tensions in therapy: their study as a task of the group' and *Experiences in Groups*. The latter became the best known, and in it he explains that groups are subordinated to a basic assumption activity, a function that interferes with the capacity of its members to work in search of a common aim. This search for a common aim was called by the author the 'working group'. Furthermore, he conceives of a cohesive force responsible for the maintenance of group structure, and to it he gave the name of 'valence'. Its purpose was to link this name to the chemical concept of valency. He also investigated and proposed new conceptions related to the leader and leadership. His researches exercised great influence at the time among group therapists, an influence that still prevails, acting as a starting-point for those who write about groups.

In 1957 I presented a report to the first Group Psychotherapy Congress in Argentina, entitled 'Technical Aspects of Group Psychotherapy', pointing out Bion's above-mentioned concepts. On that occasion, I noticed that, like myself, quite a number of colleagues quoted in their papers the two levels of group functions and Bion's concepts of leadership.

247

After almost twenty-five years, Grotstein published a work in Bion's memory, called *A Perspective of His Life and Work*, in which he dedicates one chapter to describe Bion's contributions to groups. In it, the author mentions Bion's investigations in this area, emphasizing his researches described in *Experiences in Groups*. It is interesting to realize that, after so many years, we still consider these to be the only contributions made by Bion to groups. The fact that so many authors quote him and study his ideas explains my difficulties in working on this paper. I started several times and always felt displeased with my attempts. This dissatisfaction, I later on identified, arose out of the feeling that I was writing about a subject that had already been described by someone else. I always felt tempted to talk about the group levels, or the leadership concept, or even the group cohesion, as if these were the only lamps that Bion lit to clarify the complicated group interaction.

At this point I questioned if his experiences in 1943 were really the only contribution he had made to groups. I also questioned the validity of the divorce that used to be made (and which we still do) between Bion's contributions to psychoanalysis and those to groups, as if there could be in Bion two different identities: one, the analyst; the other the group psychotherapist. I found it extremely difficult to separate Bion's group work from his psychoanalytical work: his incursions in both areas constituted an integrated whole because they search for the truth.

Another aspect to be considered is the diversity of opinions about his ideas. Phillips, who was his patient and later his friend, describes the reaction Bion's ideas provoked in Brazilian psychoanalysts: 'Many found them stimulating, some intriguing, some considered them difficult to take in, and the various "old soldiers" simply declared them impossible.' If some praise him and put him on the same level as Freud and Melanie Klein, others classify him as a mere repeater of already known concepts, dressed in new clothes. Some, more exalted, consider his ideas as the fruit of a disintegrated mind.

It is not my intention to analyse these discussions because I, in this paper, shall consider only the influence of his ideas on my understanding of group work. Also, I want to emphasize that my way of understanding Bion's ideas is a personal point of view, without pretending that it represents what he had in mind while elaborating them. Bion himself was often surprised by what he had written some time before.

Many attempts have been made, without success, to limit the scope of his ideas. These reached only a partial vision of their range. I tried to enter into this inventive world by submitting to personal and collective supervisions, attending seminars and reading his articles and books, and noticed that my personal contacts with Bion exercised a great influence over me and, therefore, over my working techniques. My first contact occurred when I read one of his papers called 'Catastrophic change'. His writing style caught my attention as it seemed very different from that of others I had read. He wrote in numbered paragraphs — 'expansions'. While reading, I had the impression I was before a weaver who tied a knot into one already there; this one seemed to function as the supporter of the next. These knots went on and on and it was impossible for me to perceive the weaver's intentions. Similarly, the expansions went on, apparently disconnected. I could not uncover the author's meaning. Thus reading was painful, and many times I thought of giving it up because I felt lost as though in chaos. However, after the introduction of a new expansion, suddenly all the others — that had apparently seemed irrelevant — acquired meaning. I then saw that my lack of understanding of the paper was the consequence of my difficulty in enduring the chaos into which the author induced me to dive and in waiting for something to arise to establish coherence.

While reading his paper I had the possibility of incorporating his concept of the 'selected fact'. This experience became possible when I could endure the tensions to wait during the incoherence till the 'selected fact' emerged, which turned chaos into coherence, thus forming a harmonious whole. Then I could incorporate this concept as something *alive* instead of something *merely intellectual*. On the other hand, his conclusions seemed to me familiar and, in a way, obvious. Obvious and familiar, but to which I had not paid attention until then. The author pointed out the importance of the obvious, while, to me, the obvious did not seem to deserve much attention. It made me recall the story of Columbus' egg. Easy, very easy, after it was all explained.

On one occasion, Bion was asked if he thought he had made an original contribution to psychoanalysis. He answered: 'No, I don't know even one. In reality, I repeated many times that if you read my books, you will only understand them when you realize that you are familiar with my experiences,' and went on, 'from this there is a funny illustration in Sherlock Holmes, by Conan Doyle, in which Holmes makes a deduction to solve a mystery and Watson says: "Oh! yes, it is very simple." Sherlock Holmes says then: "The worst of the situation is that when I make a deduction and solve something very important, everybody thinks that this is nothing, not difficult": and, really, the destiny of the analyst is to make his own existence unnecessary.'

Bion added to the obvious a new dimension, and through it I began to perceive what was in front of my eyes and could not see before. As an example of this dimension, I mention an episode that occurred in one of his conferences. At its outset he picked up a tea-cup so that everybody could see it. Then he asked the audience: 'What is the interpretation of this cup I hold in my hand?' To this question everybody kept silent. Nobody dared say anything. A colleague, seated next to me, whispered: 'Why is Bion worried about the cup?' After some minutes of complete silence, Bion started to talk, to everybody's relief: 'We feel stimulated to imagine why the audience's silence is the answer to this specific problem.' His words made me question why I also kept silent. The answer seemed clear to me – I had disregarded the object presented, worrying only about the possible hidden intentions which I imagined was what the lecturer expected. I didn't see the cup – I tried to guess Bion's intentions. Meanwhile, a colleague started to describe the cup, its form, its utility, as well as its aesthetic vision. After this description, Bion began to make some reflections which I felt represented a series of associations stimulated by the colleague's observations. In my under-standing, Bion was more interested in developing an interaction with the participants than in obtaining answers.

This group experience was very gratifying to me, because it made me an active participant in the lecture; I stopped being a mere receiver of ideas to become a member invited to participate in creative dialogue. Both, lecturer and audience, interacted through free contributions in which a space was opened to be filled by alternatives, a space until then obstructed. Therefore, by raising the cup and asking the question, I understood that Bion was inviting those present to follow him in this experience: that is, the mental adventure he intended to undertake that evening. I also understood that this invitation represented respect for the intelligence of those who proposed to listen to him. There came to my mind a previous occasion, apparently comical, when Bion at the start of one of his lectures said: 'I am anxious to hear what I have to say.' The audience laughed at this, thinking it was a joke. It wasn't so. Bion spoke seriously. This introduction was a demonstration of the line he followed in his lectures. They were never prepared beforehand. They just happened spontaneously. Ideas arose as a result of the inter-action between audience and lecturer, when each contributed momen-tarily to the creative process of his lectures, to Bion's own surprise. These lectures reminded me of the theatre called 'Commedia dell'Arte'. In it, the artists were called to act without rehearsals: they were given only the theme of the play, that could be either a comedy or a drama, and round the theme they had to improvise a performance. The play was structured according to the reaction of the audience, and this provoked scenic dialogues that arose spontaneously, surprising the actors themselves.

After Bion's lectures I asked myself how I behaved in relation to the groups I worked with. Did I conceive them to be participants or mere receivers of interpretation? These questions seemed both fascinating and disturbing to me. I knew that the group stimulates the therapist's narcissism; I even admitted the possibility that I sometimes showed off to the group. This I was able to check, once I made an observation and the group received it with admiration. One of the participants even compared it to a 'goal of Pelé', referring to the very famous football player whose well-co-ordinated moves always ended in a goal. This group reaction pleased me, so both the group and I were happy; the group watching my performance and I seeing myself praised.

Co-participation, in the sense that I understand it today, did not occur then. What really happened was that both the group and the therapist − I, in this case − were connected by a parasitical link; we co-existed without affecting each other. This relationship I attributed to narcissistic reasons, but other causes were involved which I identified when Bion told a legend about the death of the King of Ur. In this tale the king was killed, and buried together with his family and all their treasures; four hundred years later, the tombs were plundered. At this point, Bion said: 'It was a brave thing to do because the tomb had been sanctified by the death and burial of the King. Thus, the robbers were the patrons of the scientific method: the first who dared to break through the ghostly sentinels of the dead and bad spirits.' Bion did not consider the plunder itself, but stressed the thieves' courage in executing it. He used this model to emphasize the analyst's courage when approaching the unconscious, that is, what we *do not* know, not what we *do* know. After a pause, he concluded: 'Anyone who is going to see a patient or a group of patients should, at some point, experience fear. In every consulting room there ought to be two rather frightened people: the group and the therapist. If they are not, one wonders why they are bothering to find out what everyone knows.'

It is tempting to engage upon something familiar. This temptation is greater for psychoanalysts than for others, because it is one of the rare occasions when human beings can feel engaged in a frightening situation without even going outside the door. These observations have been considered by some as already known and that Bion did not add anything new; according to them, everyone knows that the *unknown* brings an attempt to avoid it.

However, Bion's approach to this subject made me suppose that it exceeded the already known. I owe to this proposition the study of my relationship with the group, trying to examine whether my style of work stimulates the approximation of the 'unknown', or separates me from it. To achieve this objective, I considered it necessary to review my capacity to apprehend the group's fantasies. Then, the hypothesis that I might be unable to see them myself arose, but it seemed improbable that it could happen because I felt secure in my work with groups. If at the beginning of my group activity I felt anxiety, it had been replaced afterwards by serenity. Therefore I noticed a discordance between Bion's statement, that both analyst and group should feel some kind of fear, and my calmness when working with the group.

I found that my serenity was the result of my leading the group to function within an area that was familiar to me, by imposing my fantasies on them: the group developed them for me as though they were their own. Thus a comfortable situation was reached: I dealt with my own fantasies, with which I felt at ease, so that I could avoid the anxiety of having to face the unknown that could emerge in the group. Comfortable also for the group, because they did not have to deal with their own anxieties. But this comfortable situation could be maintained only by sacrificing the therapeutic process; so, dressing up the unknown with familiar clothes, the unknown would never have conditions in which to become known.

The adventure of facing the unknown and its anxiety arose when I proposed to deal with a group of deaf-mutes. They were a group of patients who used sign-language (which I had already learned) as a means of communication.

I started the therapy worried by the unusual experience. In spite of my initial difficulties of communication, our relationship was excellent. The patients came regularly to the sessions, pleased and showing a good disposition to carry on this experiment. If at the beginning I felt some difficulty in expressing the words through sign-language, this obstacle disappeared gradually. My quickness increased thanks to their incentive to help me to improve my non-verbal language. Thus a curious situation developed: the group began to take care of me as if I were the pupil and they the teachers; each step in my progress made them very happy. After six months I communicated with them almost as an equal. At that juncture, when everything seemed to be going really well, communication between us broke down and I simply could not understand them any more, even when I asked them to repeat what they wanted to say. As a last resort I asked one of the patients for help. His attempts also were useless. In spite of his assistance I felt confused because I still couldn't understand. Once again I asked him to repeat. Angrily he picked up an ash-tray and threw it in my direction. The situation became even more disturbing now, when the group did not understand my signs. They could not or would not understand what I tried to convey; at the following session, the same thing happened: either I did not understand them or they did not understand me, no matter how much we tried. Chaos. This development made me feel desperate and anguished on account of the violent scenes that began to arise. I felt alone, not knowing what to do and wishing to put an end to this experiment that was becoming a torment to me. Pressed by despair, I suddenly said aloud: 'This therapy cannot go on. Let's stop it!' Nothing happened. I had spoken aloud, forgetting at the moment that I was in front of a group of deaf-mutes.

Why had I spoken aloud? What made me do it, instead of using sign-language? Suddenly I perceived that the group, creating a chaotic situation, wanted me to feel like one bereft of speech. They wanted me, too, to feel dumb. They wanted to make a deaf-mute out of me in order that I might really understand what this physical handicap meant to them. Losing speech and hearing, I was partially losing my identity. In making use of the spoken word I was unconsciously trying to preserve the functions which group chaos meant to take away from me. By talking, I almost put at risk the whole experiment because of the high level of panic I was feeling when I was unable to receive or to transmit communication. When I became capable of assuming for a while the identity the group tried to impose on me, I could once again use the articulate language and through it tell them that I could now share their deaf-muteness. As a result our communication was restored, while I felt affected by the tears I saw in the eyes of some of them.

The emotional reactions that surrounded this experience made me see Bion's contributions as a warning that the group can develop and improve only when the therapist and the group can submerge into a psychosis bearing the pressures of this plunge. To dive into psychosis I conceive of as giving up momentarily one's own identity to assume the one that the group is trying to project. To be able to assume the identity that the group tries to convey, active memory should be abolished as well as desire, according to Bion, as a basic condition for working at psychotic levels.

This is really a threatening situation into which we might go and from which we fear we might not be able to come back. This is why we avoid entering into psychotic levels and consequently losing the opportunity to receive emotion through projections instead of receiving them through description.

The ideas conveyed in this paper led me to identify those contributions of Bion's which seemed to me *the* most significant for group understanding. I admit that even though it is difficult to make this distinction, I point out the one that made the greatest impression on me: his concern about the destiny given to what 'we know'. Knowledge can be utilized as a property: once acquired, it confers on its owner the same sensation that one feels when obtaining the advantages of retirement, that means, no more work to be done, no more thinking, no more progress. On the other hand, knowledge can be used as a stimulus to approach the 'not knowing', allowing us to put up with ignorance as a basic condition for achieving mental development.

To end this report, the following Brazilian tale comes to mind about the relationship between a man and a blue fly. The man became fascinated by the fly's brilliant colour and couldn't stop looking at it. In each flight he discovered new aesthetic perspectives that attracted him. Day by day his discoveries were renewed; there was not a single repetition. Impressed by the fly, the man decided to capture it to make sure that he would be the owner of all that beauty. After he had captured it, to his disappointment, all aesthetic movements disappeared.

I have used this metaphor to transmit the essence of the message I received from what I heard and read from Bion: ideas should not be imprisoned but be free, so that they may, as in the case of the blue fly, enable us to provide progress and mental enrichment.

Chapter 13
Group personality, task and group culture

K. Armelius and B.-Å. Armelius

Although Bion's observations of group phenomena and his theoretical formulations of group processes have received enormous attention from psychotherapists and have had a great influence on the thinking about groups, they have not stimulated empirical research in the field of group psychotherapy or group processes to a comparable degree. Today you can see some associations with Bion's ideas in the research literature, but almost all of them have added something or revised the theory somewhat (see e.g. Babad and Amir 1978; Bennis and Shepard 1956; Tuckman 1966).

Bion's theory may be considered as a very general set of ideas about groups. Much methodological work is needed in order to relate these ideas to empirical phenomena. We shall discuss how we have worked theoretically and methodologically with Bion as a frame of reference for our empirical studies of small group processes. More specifically, we shall describe how *basic assumptions* and *valency* have been operationalized and how we have included the *group task* in a more systematic way into studies of group processes. Finally, we shall propose a theory about group processes based on Bion's theory and a statistical regression model. Much of our methodological developments are based on the empirical work by Herbert Thelen and Dorothy Stock (1954) (see chapter 5). We begin by giving an example of how we have operationalized the concept of basic assumption.

Analysis of group behavior: an example of how intentional behavior may be quantified

We shall describe in detail how we have analyzed the behavior of individuals in groups by means of a Q-sort technique originally developed

255

by Herbert Thelen and Dorothy Stock (1954) to give an example of how intentional behavior may be quantified.

The Q-sort technique has been used extensively in research on psychotherapy. The basic idea in the technique is that single items or proposals about a phenomenon are forced into a frequency distribution that is normal. This makes it possible to interpret the difference in terms of equal steps and the measurements receive interval properties. The subject-matter of items or statements is of no concern as long as the person doing the Q-sort is able to follow the instructions about frequencies. It is important that there is a parallel between the degree of each category of the Q-sort and the numerical system, however. Otherwise, there is no true measurement. The minimum requirement seems to be that it is possible to rank order the items in a rough way. The forced frequency distribution increases the metric properties of the items to an interval scale.

The Q-sort we have used in our research on small groups is based on Bion's theoretical work. It takes the different basic assumptions as a starting-point. A distinction is made between manifest behavior and latent intentions or needs. Both manifest behavior and latent intentions are formulated in terms of Bion's four categories or basic assumptions and work. By using Bion's descriptions of the four basic assumptions and work as a typology, we have been able to construct a set of intentions and behaviors that indicate the different basic assumptions. The number of intentions and behaviors representing the basic assumptions is infinite and our items may be considered as a sample. The construction of the Q-sort is described in Figure 13.1. An example of manifest fight and latent pairing would be: 'Fights to defend people he/she likes in the group'.

Manifest behaviour

		Dependency	Pairing	Fight	Flight	Work
Latent motive	Dependency					
	Pairing					
	Fight					
	Flight					

Figure 13.1 The categories of the Q-sort.

In each of the twenty categories there are five statements. Thus each manifest category is made up of twenty parallel statements and each latent category of twenty-five statements. Each statement receives a score between 1 and 9. Parallel versions of the Q-sort are used for judgment of individual group behavior and the group as a whole. Thus, the Q-sort technique allows us to interpret both individual behavior and the group as a whole in terms of the different basic assumptions and work. In theory we have made a definition of basic assumptions as both latent intentions and manifest behavior. These are concepts closer to data and relatively free from inferences. Of course the judgments of intentions are more inferential than the registration of the actual behaviors. We feel, however, that the concept of basic assumption as described by Bion is a very abstract concept that requires considerable inferential skill by the judge. We think of the basic assumptions as unconscious common wishes in the group. These wishes are mediated by phantasies, feelings, intentions and various forms of behavior. A trained judge may combine all these sources into a relatively certain assessment of the clinical inference is that idiosyncrasies among judges are reduced global inference may, however, be reduced to clinical inferences of intentions, feelings, behaviors, etc. The advantage with such a reduction of the clinical inference is that ideosyncrasies among judges are reduced and interpersonal agreement increased if the complexity of the task is reduced. An interesting research problem concerns the nature of such inferential processes and the importance of various sources for such inferences. In our research we have relied on clinical inferences so far, although we have started to work on the importance of language as a mediator of basic assumptions by means of computer dictionaries.

Bion's view of the relation between individual and group: the concept of valency

One advantage of Bion's theory as a frame of reference for studying small group processes is that he has a concept for relating the individual and the group. Bion's concept of valency describes the individual's tendency to combine with other people in the group to introduce or maintain a certain basic assumption or group culture. Thus, valency is a pattern of relatively stable reactions to various group situations. We may think of them as historically learned reactions that may take the form of transference reactions in relation to other people. These reactions will be released by a variety of situations with a common denominator that can be described as one of the basic assumptions. Further, we assume that there is a reciprocal relation between the group culture and the individual's group behavior. Bion describes how a certain group culture puts pressure on different individuals to take a certain role, e.g. the fight group requires a fighting leader. In this sense, the individual group composition may be considered as the resources that the group has for creating different group cultures. In turn, the group culture that actually develops in the group will influence the behavior of each individual member in the group. Some people are more likely to act in a pairing culture than others, and these people will contribute more to that culture than the others, who may merely support the culture by their passive acceptance. The individual thus influences and is influenced by the group culture.

The translation of Bion's ideas of the relation between the individual and the group into empirical testable hypotheses requires that the concepts of valency and group culture are operationally defined in a way that preserves their theoretical meaning. Thelen *et al.* developed methods for capturing the group personality or valency of an individual by means of a sentence-completion test called the Reaction to Group Situation Test or RGST, which we have adopted for our own purposes.

The RGST is projective in the sense that the situation described by the items are representative of a certain basic assumption and this causes the individual to respond in his typical mood. Therefore, a detailed analysis of the reactions to the different test items gives a picture of the group personality. The analysis of the answers to RGST is made both quantitatively and qualitatively. First, we count the number of reactions related to each basic assumption that the subject gives for each type of situation. Then we classify the reactions according to whether they are cognitive, emotional or activity oriented. This gives us an idea about the form of the reaction and what the typical reaction will be before each basic assumption. The second step is to make a detailed analysis of the typical behavior within each basic assumption. Here we find that a person is more active and comfortable in one basic assumption than in another or that he uses one basic assumption to escape from another that is more loaded with conflict or discomfort. Thus, a person might prefer to operate in a pairing culture in order to avoid feelings of dependency. The last step is to formulate a clinical opinion about the whole person and his probable reaction in different group situations. These predictions about probable behavior are translated into quantitative form by means of the Q-sort technique described earlier (see Armelius 1980 for a detailed description of the procedure).

The validity of these predictions were tested in a small group setting. One group of five members received two different tasks to work with.

The group work was videotaped. Predictions about group behavior based on RGST were made for each member by means of the technique described. Each member's actual group behavior was measured by the same Q-sort technique used to predict individual group behavior (of course different judges were used to do the Q-sorts based on RGST and the Q-sort based on the individual's actual group behavior). The result of this study was that it was possible to capture the individual's valency by means of RGST and to predict individual group behavior from knowledge of his valency. However, it was also clear that the behavior of the individuals differed in the two tasks. That is, actual group behavior of individuals depends not only on their valency but also on what task the group is working with. To illustrate these results two different subjects will be given as examples.

We shall give a brief account of the qualitative analysis of the RGST protocol and a short description of the actual behavior for the two subjects.

Subject 1

Prediction from RGST This is an agreeable person who does not show very much of herself, but who supports whatever the others do. A typical dependency person who waits for others to take the initiative. She has a lot of valency for fight, but it is never shown in the group since it is held at a feeling level of response. Strong conflicts over dependency.

Actual group behavior She is high on dependency and flight in both tasks. She shows very little fight and does not take part in the discussions in task 1.

In task 2 the group chose her as the central person and she got a much more active role when the group started to talk about her silence during the group work. She agreed to this role and assured the group that she had had a good time and that this was her typical behavior (see Figure 13.2).

If we look at Figure 13.2, the RGST results are shown in the X-axis and actual group behavior on the Y-axis. We have one curve for each task. If the predictions were perfectly correct all observations would fall on the diagonal between the two axes. For this person you can see that the highest scores on RGST are dependency and flight, then comes pairing, work and fight last. Her behavior in the first task was mostly flight and dependency and in the second task it was dependency and flight. It is

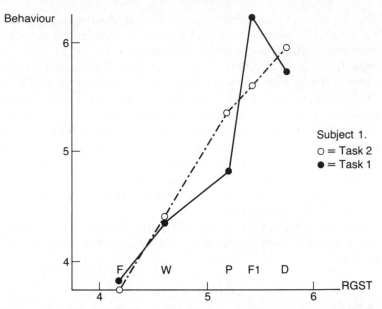

Figure 13.2 Group behavior in two different tasks plotted against RGST for subject 1.

also seen in Figure 13.2 that this person is relatively consistent in her behavior, independent of the task. Her activity may vary, but she always exhibits the same pattern of basic assumptions.

Subject 2

Predictions from RGST   A person who follows others in the group. Fight and work will dominate in task-oriented groups and flight will be the modality if the situation becomes more personally intimate. Pairing is avoided by either fight or flight. The basic conflict is with intimacy and not dependency.

Actual group behavior   This person is high on fight and work in task 1 and shows great interest in the task. She fights for leadership and is a dominant person during this task. However, in task 2, the dependency task, she withdraws and does not take part in the discussion. Typical flight behavior. The degree of intimacy was very high during this task.

In Figure 13.3 it is shown that she is high on fight in task 1 and low on flight, in task 2 the reverse is true. The important thing about this

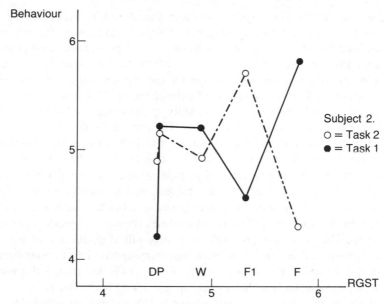

Figure 13.3 Group behavior in two different tasks plotted against RGST for subject 2.

person is that her behavior is dependent on the task. This could be predicted, although not translated into quantitative form unless two separate Q-sorts had been made for her, one for each task.

To summarize, it is possible to capture the individual's valency and to predict how he will behave in a group situation by means of RGST. However, it is also clear that at least some individuals will behave very differently in different group situations. Our hypothesis is that one important factor determining both individual group behavior and the group culture is the task the group is working with. In accordance with Bion, we think that the group should be seen as an entity of its own and treated separately from the sum of the individuals constituting the group. On the group level we are interested in the group culture, which we define as the pattern of basic assumptions and work that exists in the group. Next, we will discuss our ideas about the importance of the task for both group culture and individual group behavior.

The importance of task demands for group processes

Many writers in group psychology make a sharp distinction between task-oriented groups and psychotherapy groups (Tuckman 1966;

Hartman 1979). This implies some idea that there is no task in therapy groups or that the task is unknown. Certainly, in therapy the task is difficult to define in concrete terms since it is dependent on what problems the members of the group contribute to the group. We think, however, that it is necessary to specify the task for any group in order to understand why certain group phenomena occur. This is an application of the interactional view on personality at the group level (Endler and Magnusson 1976; Ekehammar 1974). The problem is that there are no good typologies of tasks and that we still lack theories that explain group phenomena in terms of task or task demands. We consider the task to be a motivating force that puts pressure on the group to do certain things and which evokes feelings and phantasies among the members of the group. These pressures are called 'task demands', and may be described by different probabilities for certain behaviors in the group. Thus, it is more probable that there will be expressions of anger in a group working with a task requiring competition among the members than if the task requires cooperation. Our theory is that group culture is dependent on the task that the group is working with. The group as a whole has to respond to the task demands, but the reactions of individual members are going to vary, dependent on their personalities.

Certain individuals will be stimulated to take certain roles and fulfil the requirements of the task, and others will be inhibited in their behavior because the requirements are experienced as threatening or impossible to them. Our theory about the importance of the task for group phenomena may be described by two separate steps. The first step is that the task puts pressure on the members to do certain things in order to solve the task. This may be called a requirement for a certain group culture, where group culture is defined as a pattern of actions, feelings, phantasies, etc., summarized by the basic assumptions. The second step is that individuals will vary in their behavior dependent on the match between their personalities and the group culture that is required by the task. For certain individuals the group culture will be stimulating and for others it will be an inhibition.

These ideas about the influence of task demands both on group culture and on individual group behavior were tested in the experiment described earlier, where the same group of five individuals worked with two different tasks.

The first task was to rank order a list of items to take along after a crash landing on the moon. This is a group dynamic exercise called 'the astronauts', and it is done first individually and then by the group as a whole. This task was supposed to stimulate fight and inhibit dependency.

The second task was a more human relation kind of task. The group were asked to talk about their feelings and ideas about working together in this group, both at that time and during previous tasks. We also introduced a group leader for the last task. His role was to help the group to keep to the task and intervene at a group level. This task was supposed to stimulate dependency and inhibit fight both due to our introduction of the leader and to the unstructured nature of the task. In addition to these two experimental tasks, a distractor task was given to the group between the two other tasks. The purpose of this task was to minimize interference between the two experimental tasks.

The results of this experiment were those expected. In the first task, fight was high and dependency low, while in the second task, the reverse was true. Dependency was high and fight was low. Further, there was an interaction between individual behavior and the task. To summarize our empirical findings, the group task makes some group cultures or basic assumptions more likely to develop in a group than others, and the individuals' behavior in the group is dependent on the task the group is working with.

The experiment thus confirmed our ideas about the importance of the task for the development of different group cultures as well as for individual group behavior. We also got support for our ideas about stimulating and inhibiting effects of the task on individual behavior in a group. Our problem now was to conceptualize these experimental results and our interpretations in a fruitful way.

For that purpose we turned to a mathematical model proposed by Shiflett (1979).

A regression model for studies of group processes

In order to account for the influence of tasks on individual behavior and group performance, some authors have proposed the use of mathematical models (Shiflett 1979; Steiner 1972). These models have mainly been developed and used in problem-solving tasks and decision-making tasks but may be applied to others as well. In their general form these models may be written as

$$P = R \times T \tag{1}$$

where P = performance or group output
      R = resources or individual characteristics
      T = transformations

In the model group outcome, P, such a group decision is conceived of as the result of the individual resources, R, e.g. intelligence, and some transformation, T, working on the resources, usually task demands. The formal characteristics of the model are given by matrix algebra and behind all parameters of the equations there are matrices; i.e. P is a matrix of performance measures, R is a matrix of resources and T is a matrix of transformations.

For our purposes Bion's theory is used to give psychological meaning to the different terms in the model. When we apply Bion's theory to equation (1), we interpret P = group culture in terms of Bion's basic assumptions and work and R = the individual's valency as measured by the RGST, which may be thought of as expected values for individual group behavior, and T = task demands. When the model is written as in equation (1), the impact of the task is different for different individuals dependent on their valency or their values of R. E.g. individuals with high valency for fight may be influenced more by a task that stimulates fight than other individuals.

However, it is also possible to think of the task as having the same influence on all individuals in the group irrespective of their valency. E.g. a task that stimulates fight will influence all individuals in the group to increase their fighting behavior by the same amount, irrespective of their valency for fight.

It is apparent that these two possible effects of the task may be written as a general model where both additive effects of tasks and interactions between tasks and resources may be studied separately in the same model. Such a model may be written as an ordinary linear equation or

$$P = R \times T + C \tag{2}$$

where C is a constant.

This is the standard form of a regression equation, or

$$Y = bX + a \tag{3}$$

where Y and X are deviations from the average, and b is the regression weight and a the slope.

This obviously is the most general model and all the possibilities we have considered may be expressed in terms of the linear regression model. In the model the constant a will express *general effects* of tasks on the individuals. All individuals in the group may be stimulated or inhibited by the task demands. A positive value of a means that behavior is inhibited by the task. The constant b will express what we call *differential effects* of the task on the individual behavior. This means that the influence of the task depends on the individual resources. One possibility is that people with high values of R show much of their potential in behavior and decrease their behavior as compared to the expected value. This will show up in the model as a value of *b* larger than 1.00. This task effect is called a *polarization effect*, since it means that the individuals will differ in their behavior more than expected from knowledge of their resources. When *b* is less than 1.0 the effect of the task on the group may be described as a *conformity effect*, since people with high values of R will show relatively little of their resources in actual behavior and people with low values of R will show relatively much in actual behavior. Of course, it is necessary to adjust the expected value of *b* after the reliability of the measurements before analyzing empirical data. Otherwise regression effects due to errors of measurement will be interpreted as group processes.

Next, we will apply the regression model to our empirical results in the experiment described earlier.

Application of the regression model to empirical data

In our example we have a set of resources which in our case consists of valencies for the different subjects in the different basic assumptions and work. Table 13.1 shows the resource matrix which is the result of the Q-sort based on the sentence-completion test, RGST, described earlier.

Table 13.1 Personality descriptions, or resources of the group of five subjects

| Basic assumptions | Subject | | | | |
	1	2	3	4	5
Pairing	94	100	105	102	97
Fight	107	81	114	85	109
Dependency	83	118	87	112	94
Flight	112	111	80	*	105
Work	105	90	113	*	96

* These two values are excluded from the example because of a systematic error in the estimation of resources.

The performance of each subject in the group was described by the same Q-sort based on observation of a videotape of the group session. These results are shown in Table 13.2 for task 1 and Table 13.3 for task 2. These constitute the performance matrices of task 1, P1 and task 2, P2 in the model.

Table 13.2 Performance in task 1 for each subject

Basic assumption	Subject				
	1	2	3	4	5
Pairing	97	96	102	109	104
Fight	115	76	105	89	116
Dependency	79	115	100	106	84
Flight	95	126	81	*	93
Work	114	87	112	*	104

* These two values are excluded from the example because of a systematic error in the estimation of resources.

Table 13.3 Performance in task 2 for each subject

Basic assumption	Subject				
	1	2	3	4	5
Pairing	94	107	102	105	103
Fight	95	75	104	90	86
Dependency	113	119	87	110	98
Flight	118	111	90	*	114
Work	80	88	117	*	99

* These two values are excluded from the example because of a systematic error in the estimation of resources.

Now we apply our mathematical equation to the data. This is done by computing the linear regression of R on P1 and P2 for each basic assumption. Since the theoretical mean of the scales is 100 in the Q-sort, the deviations are taken from that and not from the actual mean for both R and P. Naturally, the estimates of the values of *a* and *b* will be imprecise because of the small number of subjects. The purpose is not to estimate exact values of the parameters, however, but rather to exemplify the use of the model on some empirical data. The results of the linear regression analysis are shown in Table 13.4.

Interpretation of a

As can be seen from Table 13.4, the values of *a* are very much in the direction of our hypotheses about the influence of tasks. In task 1 there are positive values for work and fight and negative values for dependency

Table 13.4 Empirical values of *a* and *b* for each basic assumption in the two tasks

Basic assumption	a	b
Task 1		
Pairing	1.80	0.51
Fight	1.03	1.04
Dependency	−1.84	0.80
Flight	−3.22	0.86
Work	3.19	1.06
Task 2		
Pairing	2.48	0.70
Fight	−9.58	0.53
Dependency	5.97	0.48
Flight	6.64	0.80
Work	−4.85	0.85

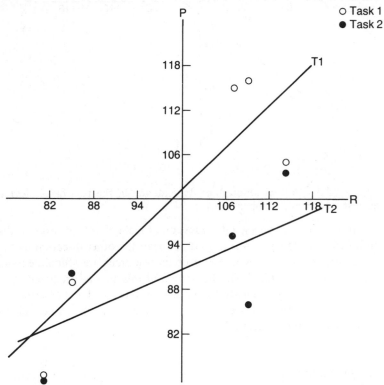

Figure 13.4   Actual amount of fight in the two tasks plotted against resources for fight.

and flight. In task 2 almost the reverse is true. These effects for fight and dependency are also illustrated in Figures 13.4 and 13.5.

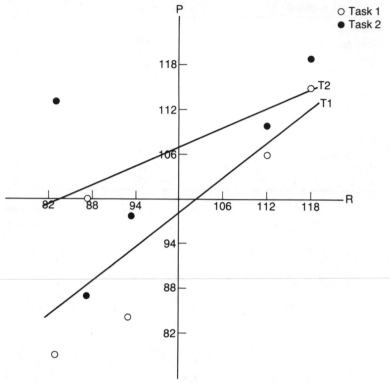

Figure 13.5   Actual amount of dependency in the two tasks plotted against resources for dependency.

Thus, *a* seems to be a good expression of main effects of tasks on the group culture. The group is moved in one or the other direction by the characteristics of the tasks. Some of its resources are stimulated and other resources are inhibited. The pattern of this may be predicted from analysis of the task demands. In mathematical terms this is described as an additive constant to the resources which is the same for all individuals irrespective of their values of R.

Interpretation of b

As already mentioned, it is necessary to estimate the value of *b* that is expected due to error variance in the measurement of R and P. Since the reliability of both R and P was around 0.60, on the average a good estimate of *b* would be 0.60 if there are no group process effects but only statistical regression effects. Values larger than 0.60 are interpreted as conformity effects of tasks. As can be seen from Table 13.4, the values of *b* tend to exceed 0.60, which means that there has been a polarization effect in the group. This is especially true for task 1, but not so much for task 2, where the values are closer to the expected value of 0.60. For e.g. fight, the group was polarized in task 1 in such a way that people with much fight valency were those who were fighting more than expected. People with little valency for fight fought less than expected. This was not the case in task 2. Here the distribution of fight behavior was much more uniform and the effect may be described as a conformity process, where people became more similar than expected from RGST. A polarization may also be traced in work on task 1. All other processes may be described as those expected from knowledge of individual personalities.

The advantages of the regression model

The use of models in group psychology is not new. A common model, originally borrowed from physics by Freud, is the conflict model. As a group theory this model is recognized in Stock-Whitaker and Lieberman's (1964) focal conflict theory of groups. The fruitfulness of the use of a certain model is dependent on characteristics of the model as well as on the psychological theory that is used to interpret the model in psychological terms.

In our case the model is the regression model and the psychological theory is Bion's theory of small groups. The use of the regression model has some advantages that we wish to point out. First, the model contains terms for capturing the relation between the individual and the group which is a requirement for a theory of small groups. The constants *a* and *b* express different kinds of relationships between the individual and the group or *how* the behavior of each individual is related to the group level.

On the individual level the resources of each individual may be stimulated or inhibited, e.g. by task demands. On the group level this shows up as general effects, which are expressed by the size and sign of *a*, or differential effects, which are expressed by the size and sign of *b*. Further, *b* will tell us if the group process may be described as a conformity process or as a polarization process. In this respect the regression model is a development of Bion's concept of valency, which is a more crude description of the relation between the individual and the group.

Further, the use of the regression model makes it possible to test different hypotheses about groups. In our frame of reference the most important hypotheses are about the effects of group composition and group task on both individual group behavior and the group process. For psychotherapy research it is possible to consider e.g. therapist interventions as transformations and to study how these influence individual behavior and group processes.

The fruitfulness of the regression model depends heavily on which theory of group processes is employed to fill the model with psychological content. We feel that Bion's theory serves this function in a satisfactory way. In particular, we think that it provides good concepts for linking the socio-emotional aspects of group life with the task-oriented aspects. So far, the attempts at formalizing group processes by mathematical analogies have focused exclusively on the work aspect or on productivity in task-oriented groups (Steiner 1972; Davis 1973). It is our conviction that this is only half the cake, and the need for precise formulations of the socio-emotional aspects is at least as large as for productivity.

Finally, we shall summarize our empirical findings and the regression model in our own theory of group processes (see Figure 13.6).

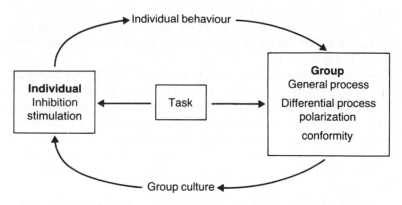

Figure 13.6   The relation between task, individual and group.

The theory assumes a reciprocal relation between individual and group. The individual is a prerequisite for the group and the group is a prerequisite for the individual.

Group composition in terms of each individual's valency pattern sets limits to what group culture the group will develop. At the same time the behavior of the individual is dependent on which group culture that is prevailing in the group. Group culture is, however, not dependent only on the group composition.

One important independent factor that will determine the group culture and which we are able to isolate is the task. Tasks influence both the individual behavior and the group culture that is developing in the group. We think that the task has its effect through an *inhibition* or *stimulation* of individual behavior. To decide if an individual has been inhibited or stimulated we need a base line to compare with. This base level is given for each individual by the sentence-completion test, the RGST. The picture of a person's valency pattern that emerges from RGST is interpreted as the expected value for the behavior over an infinite number of different group situations or tasks. In this way it is possible to compare the behavior of an individual in a given group situation with the expected value of the same individual and decide if his behavior is an expression of inhibition or of stimulation of his resources.

Further, we see the group as an expression of common processes among group members. The processes that we are interested in are if the individual resources have been inhibited or stimulated. The group processes may be of two different kinds; general group processes or differential group processes. A given task may e.g. stimulate the basic assumption dependency in *all* individuals in the group. This will show up as a general increase in dependency behavior compared with what could be expected from the individual valency pattern for dependency. The corresponding general effect may of course also be an inhibition of the individual resources. These are general group processes in the sense that *all* individuals are influenced in the same way by the task.

If the task has a systematic but not equal influence on individual behavior we speak of differential processes. E.g. a given task may stimulate those individuals that have high valency for dependency while those who have low valency for dependency are inhibited in their dependency behavior. If such differential effects are systematically related to the individual resources we interpret them as expressions of differential group processes.

In principle there are many such systematical non-uniform relations between behavior and resources in a group, but the most interesting ones are those we call *polarization* and *conformity*. A polarization in the group means that individuals with high values on the resources show *more* of their resources than expected and individuals with low values on R show *less* than expected. This will show up as an increased variance in the behavior in the group. The individuals are more different in their behavior than what could be expected from their resources. Conformity is an expression of the opposite. That is, individuals with low values on R show a high degree of the actual behavior, while individuals with high R have a small degree of the behavior. That is, the individuals in the group are more *similar* in their behavior than what is expected from their resources.

We shall end with a discussion of in what ways we think that we have developed Bion's theory in our work.

One aspect of Bion's theory that we have worked on concerns the relation between the different basic assumptions. According to Bion, one basic assumption and work may coexist in a group but he says nothing about the relationship among the different basic assumptions. Our empirical research suggests that the different basic assumptions tend to be related to each other in a systematic way. Pairing and fight are positively related both to each other and to work while flight and dependency are positively related to each other and negatively related to work. With some modification this seems to be true for different kinds of tasks and situations (Armelius and Kataja 1980; Fogelstam and Kjellberg 1981; Armelius 1980; Babad and Amir 1978).

As mentioned, a second aspect of Bion's theory that we have elaborated on is his concept of valency. Bion states only that the individual has a tendency to combine with other individuals in the group and act on the basis of the different basic assumptions. He does not say anything about how this relationship between the individual and the group may be conceptualized. Here we have used the regression model to describe how the individual resources are stimulated or inhibited and how these individual processes may be described on the group level as general or differential processes.

Third, a main issue in our work has been to pursue Bion's ideas of the importance of the task for the group process. By means of the regression model we have tried to capture the impact of the task on both individual group behavior in terms of stimulation and inhibition and on the group process in terms of polarization and conformity. In future research we plan to work further with these ideas of the importance of the task for individual group behavior and group phenomena, such as different group processes and group culture. Perhaps it is possible to describe our work with Bion's theory as an example of how knowledge grows in an area. Different stages in the development of an area are characterized by different problems and methods used to attack these problems. The task for the first generation of researchers is mainly to describe and conceptualize the phenomena of interest and to define some broad hypothesis; in other words, to function like an 'inventor' in the area. These hypotheses and conceptualizations are then worked on by later generations of researchers and the hypotheses are refined and tested by more sophisticated methods. In this way the theory is changed and refined but the work is still dependent on the 'detections' made by the 'inventors'.

References

Armelius, B.-Å. (1980), 'Group personality and group behavior: an expansion of Bion's model', *Department of Applied Psychology Reports*, no. 1.
Armelius, B.-Å. and Kataja, P. (1980), 'Developing a questionnaire for measuring work-emotionality on wards', *Applied Psychology*, Umeå.
Armelius, K. (1980), 'The task as a determinant of group culture', *Umeå Psychological Reports*, no. 156.
Babad, E. and Amir, L. (1978), 'Bennis and Shepard's theory of group development: an empirical examination', *Small Group Behavior*, 9: 477-92.
Bennis, W. and Shepard, H. (1956), 'A theory of group development', *Human Relations*, 9: 415-37.
Davis, J. H. (1975), 'Group decision and social interactions: a theory of social decision schemes', *Psychological Review*, 80: 97-125.
Ekehammar, B. (1974), 'Interactions in personality from a historical perspective', *Psychological Bull.*, 81: 1026-48.
Endler, N. and Magnusson, D. (1976), 'Toward an interactional psychology of personality', *Psychological Bull.*, 83: 956-74.
Fogelstam, H. and Kjellberg, B. (1981), 'To measure ward-atmosphere: validation of a questionnaire', *Applied Psychology*, Umeå.
Hartman, J. (1979), 'Small group methods of personal change', *Annual Review of Psychology*, 30: 453-76.
Shiflett, S. (1979), 'Toward a general model of small group productivity', *Psychological Bull.*, 86: 67-79.
Steiner, I. D. (1972), *Group Process and Productivity*, New York, Academic Press.
Stock-Whitaker, D. and Lieberman, M. (1964), *Psychotherapy through the Group Process*, Chicago, Aldine.
Thelen, H. A. and Stock, D. (1954), 'Methods for studying work and emotionality in group operation', compendium, University of Chicago.
Tuckman, B. W. (1966), 'Development sequence in small groups', *Psychological Bull.*, 63: 384-99.

Chapter 14

Ambiguity and paradox in group relations conferences

Barry Palmer

Early in 1948 the Professional Committee of the Tavistock Clinic
asked me to take therapeutic groups, employing my own technique..
Now, I had no means of knowing what the Committee meant by this,
but it was evident that in their view, I had 'taken' therapeutic groups
before . . . However, I agreed; so, in due course, I would find myself
sitting in a room with eight or nine other people — sometimes more,
sometimes less — sometimes patients, sometimes not. When the
members of the group were not patients, I often found myself in a
peculiar quandary. I will describe what happens . . .

So begins Wilfred Bion's first paper on his experiences in groups (1961:
29). From the work he describes, and the prior work with patient groups
which he believed led to the Committee's invitation, there developed
the Study Group, as a means of providing an opportunity for men and
women to learn about group processes and about the personal demands
of seeking to act responsibly in a group setting. Study Groups continue
to be offered to participants by a number of institutions, and it is
difficult to judge the extent to which the original model has changed
and diversified over the years. The Study Group is an essential element
in the working conferences on group relations developed initially by
Trist, Rice and their colleagues at the Tavistock Institute of Human
Relations, and later by a number of other bodies including my own.
These have been described elsewhere (Trist and Sofer 1959; Rice 1965;
Rioch 1970; Gustafson and Cooper 1978b). These conferences may
include Study Groups of different sizes — not only the eight to twelve
members of the usual 'small' group, but groups as small as five or as
large as seventy.

I came on the scene too late to take part in a group led by Bion, and
so cannot distinguish with certainty between Bion's influence on this

method and the subsequent modifications introduced by those who mediated his ideas to the Grubb Institute — in particular Kenneth Rice and Pierre Turquet. It appears that Bion's influence on the conferences was not restricted to the sessions devoted to the study of small groups, but permeated the conference as a whole.

It includes his distinction between the two types of mental activity discernible in social interaction, the work group and the basic assumption group. It also includes the model of the role of the staff member — the 'consultant' — and the manner in which the context in which the participant finds himself is defined, verbally and behaviourally.

As Gustafson and Cooper have pointed out, no detailed analysis of this role has been published since Rice's original account (1965), at least until their own papers. The role is learned through member experience and apprenticeship, and while the sphinx-like figure of the literature is a bit of a myth, it is probable that certain invariants continue to be transmitted, which are a determinative influence on the character of the conference milieu as experienced by participants.

In this paper, I shall seek to characterize the method of the Study Group and of the conferences in such a way that its particular potentialities and stresses can be better understood. I hope to clarify under what circumstances the conference method is appropriate, and what are the relevant criteria for deciding between this and other methods of human relations training.

The uncertainties of the conference context

Most of those who take part in the conferences are in positions of leadership in their own organizations. Their work entails making decisions and taking action without certain knowledge of all the relevant facts or of the outcome to be expected. The conferences similarly require members and staff to act in conditions of uncertainty and to provide an opportunity to learn about some of the problems of doing this. In saying this, however, it is possible to play down the distinctive quality of the uncertainty with which the conference participant is faced. The ways of characterizing this uncertainty which follow are not meant to be wholly distinct, but approach the problem of description from different angles.

The context in which the uninitiated participant finds himself (or herself) is profoundly *ambiguous*. While he is usually sponsored and paid for by his employing organization, he finds himself culturally as well as geographically outside his organization, and it may be very unclear to him how the activities of the conference are related to his organization's goals or his own responsibilities. He cannot take the language or outlook of his own organization or profession as 'given' in conversation with other participants, who are drawn from many different walks of life. He may see all the participants as members of the same society, but it is unclear what this supposition amounts to, especially when some are from overseas.

Rice's description of the conferences, and that of the typical conference prospectus, do not convey this ambiguity. They imply that the participants have unambiguous common ground, in that they are all in positions of leadership and encounter similar problems in exercising authority, influencing others, initiating change, and so on. The role of 'leader' or 'manager' is, however, an elusive one, outside the setting of a particular type of enterprise. Rice himself defines a manager as one who regulates the activities of his department or enterprise in such a way as to promote the performance of its primary task. If a group of managers do not have their primary tasks broadly in common, there is little common ground left.

The tasks of the conference events, as stated verbally and as communicated through the roles of the staff, are *recursive* and *reflexive*. The recursive element is inherent in the usual task statement provided: 'to provide opportunities for members to study the behavior of the group, as it occurs'. Members are thus invited to study themselves studying the behaviour of the group — behaviour which consists, if they stick to the task, of studying themselves studying themselves . . . Members frequently comment on this infinite regress, or propose ways of extricating themselves, for example by discussing an agreed topic for a period and then pausing to consider what happened; or by doing something else and leaving it to the consultant to study them. As consultants, we never show much enthusiasm for these suggestions, yet they are expressions of insight into the nature of the context as the staff have defined it.

One of the difficulties of making a usable statement about the task of the Study Group is that it is reflexive. It is not a matter of observing what is going on in the room and then drawing conclusions about it, though this is what it sounds like. More accurately, it is assumed that at any given moment the individual has already unconsciously invested what is going on, including his own part in the proceedings, with meaning, and that he has access to the meaning it already has for him through his feelings, his fantasies and his impulses to act, whether carried through or simply noted. The focus of the consultant's attention is therefore not so much upon what is happening, as upon his own experience of what is happening. In psychoanalytic terms, he attends to the counter-transference, and seeks to distinguish between his responses to the social system of the group and other feelings he brings into the group from elsewhere.

Bion describes his method in these terms:

> Now the experience of counter-transference appears to me to have quite a distinct quality that should enable the analyst to differentiate the occasion when he is the object of a projective identification from the occasion when he is not. The analyst feels he is being manipulated so as to be playing a part, no matter how difficult to recognise, in somebody else's phantasy − or he would do if it were not for what in recollection I can only call a temporary loss of insight, a sense of experiencing strong feelings and at the same time a belief that their existence is quite adequately justified by the objective situation . . . I believe ability to shake oneself out of the numbing feeling of reality that is the concomitant of this state is the prime requisite of the analyst in the group . . . (1961: 149).

(It is nice to know that the experience of countertransference had such a distinctive quality for Bion. For myself, trying to sort out whether or not my feelings have been engendered by my involvement in the group is the most difficult and sometimes painful aspect of the role. As Meltzer says, the feeling that one does not measure up to the role as described by Bion frequently 'crowds in upon the reader in a daunting way' (1978: 8)).

Some participants have little difficulty in attaining this reflexive mode of consciousness, at least enough to have an idea of what the consultants are doing and how they can work with them. For most first-timers, however, this is a big jump, and no amount of explanation would get them there. The knowledge of group processes which the conference or Study Group offers is thus not accessible without at the same time learning a new way of knowing.

The conference method also *disconfirms* the individualistic epistemology of most participants. The consultant starts from the hypothesis that the contributions and actions of the participants, including himself, may be construed as the responses of a social system, having meaning in relation to the context of the system and the situation it has reached, as well as to the character and personal history of individuals. This is not how Western man habitually thinks: it is a shocking way of looking at the world. In my experience consultants frequently forget this. We fail to create conditions in which participants can adopt the hypothesis provisionally, and perhaps discover that it opens up another dimension of understanding human behaviour. We press our interpretations too dogmatically, and take dissent as denial.

Paradox

We have described how in various ways the context created in the group relations conference can be bewildering and sometimes disturbing to the participant. Whether it can be used for learning depends among other things upon the expectations of the participant, and how he understands his contract with the organization sponsoring him. If he has come expecting a traditional kind of instruction in management skills, or knowledge which is immediately applicable to the current demands of his job, and if he is unable or unwilling to revise those expectations in the light of the conference as he finds it, he may evolve a strategy for surviving the conference without really joining it, or, as occasionally happens, leave.

A similar kind of statement could be made about the position of someone attending any kind of conference who finds it is not what he expected. It is necessary to consider more closely the particular kind of stress engendered in group relations conferences. Rice devotes several pages to psychotic breakdown in conferences, and the attitude of the staff to this possibility and eventuality (1965: 157–61). Members of our own conferences have occasionally become seriously disturbed. Usually they have been adequately 'held' by the conference, and have recovered before the end, often coming to regard the episode as a constructive one for their own lives. Occasionally members have required hospitalization, during or after the conference.

It is not the purpose of this paper to discuss all the questions about selection and psychiatric cover which this fact raises. It does however highlight a question which is central to this paper: under what circumstances does the design of the conference and the way the staff role is interpreted create conditions which may be psychologically untenable for an individual?

Drawing upon the work of Bateson (1973), Palazzoli *et al.* (1978), and Watzlawick *et al.* (1974) on paradox in schizophrenia and in therapy, I have considered whether the conference method creates a context which is inherently paradoxical. This is not merely a question of whether there are *logical* paradoxes in verbal statements made during the conference, but of whether the participant *experiences* the demands upon him as paradoxical — in the extreme case as commands which can be neither obeyed nor disobeyed, constituting, in the strict sense, a double bind.

It seems to me now that, in common with many forms of psychotherapy, with play in general, and with other activities like religious ritual and drama, the Study Group method is inherently paradoxical, and this constitutes its creative possiblity (cf. Bateson 1973: 150 ff. and below, p. 283). The participant is not however necessarily placed in a double bind, though a combination of errors on the part of the staff and factors in his own personality may contrive to create one.

As described by Bateson (1973: 178 f.) and others, the basic conditions for a double bind are as follows:

1 A strong dependence of the subject upon another person, who may be a patient, a captor, or, as here, a consultant or the staff group.
2 An explicit instruction to do something, backed by real or imagined sanctions.
3 Another injunction, which is not explicit, but is conveyed by the tone and gesture, which prohibits the behaviour prescribed under (2); also backed by real or imagined sanctions.
4 A real or imagined prohibition against escaping from the bind imposed by the previous two injunctions, either by identifying and naming the conflicting injunctions, or by leaving the situation.

In a later paper Bateson (1973: 242 ff.) clarifies that the double bind is not constituted simply by *contradictory* injunctions. If a child is given contradictory commands by its two parents, or by one parent at different times, he may be confused and frightened, but he can in principle resolve his predicament by choosing between the alternatives. The subject of the double bind cannot extricate himself in this way, since the requirements upon him are included in the same instruction at different levels. He is in an analogous position to that of the person confronted with a notice saying 'Disregard this message'. To obey is to disobey, and to disobey is to obey.

In the literature, the command 'Be spontaneous!' is often given as an example of a paradoxical injunction. If the subject seeks to obey it, and act spontaneously, he is by so doing obeying a command and not acting spontaneously. The behaviour of the staff towards the members in a group relations conference conveys a similar paradoxical message, perhaps more accurately translated as, 'Be autonomous!' The stated task of the Study Group, although it is of the same form as more ordinary commands such as, say, 'Study this mathematical problem', can be performed as intended only if the member brings to it his own innate

curiosity and spontaneous responses, feelings and judgments. Recognizing this, the staff member seeks to parry moves by members to get him
to take charge, define the situation in the group, or tell people what to
do next, or how to go about studying the group's behaviour. But unless
the member appreciates the nature of the problem, the consultant's
behaviour can only be experienced as a way of unilaterally *insisting* that
he exercise his own authority in studying the group. He cannot freely
choose to study the behaviour of the group, because the consultant
gives him no alternative.

The problem for the member is compounded by the fact that the staff
have been presented to him as those with knowledge or skill relevant to
the work of the conference — which is indeed how they see themselves.
The title 'consultant' invites the member to consult them. The group
lists usually leave a gap between the name of the consultant and the
names of the other members. The staff usually sit in a separate row
facing the members in the introductory session.

In the family the power of the double bind resides in the dependence
of the victim, usually a child, upon the parents, and his inability to contemplate leaving the family. There are also powerful inhibitions against
speaking (that is, meta-communicating) about the conditions creating
the double bind. In the conference, the power of the staff is largely
illusory, projected upon them by the members. When therefore the
member recognizes this, the paradox may remain, but the double bind
has no force. When the member takes authority for the way he relates
to the staff, and for whether he accepts the task definitions as injunctions
to himself, he is in a position to manage his own learning according to
his own needs and capabilities.

We should note, however, that the felt power of the staff is not
always solely a manifestation of transference within the conference. If
the member has been sent on the conference by his employer, if a
member of the staff is also a member of his employing organization, or if
the staff as a whole have been hired by his organization for an in-company
course, he is then not necessarily wholly wrong in supposing that his
job or his promotion may be at risk if he fails to co-operate.

The paradoxical aspect of the conferences may be described in another
way. They are, like psychoanalysis, religious ritual, drama, and many
other human activities, sophisticated forms of play. As such, they
depend upon the recognition that what people say and do to each other,
while expressing real feeling, do not signify what they would signify in
'real life'. While this distinction is frequently in danger of breaking
down, and sometimes does, participants are on the whole capable of

'holding' the anger or attraction they feel for each other from one session to the next, and engaging in ordinary social conversations during meals and breaks.

The careful attention which conference staff give to defining and observing certain boundaries — time-limits of sessions, rooms for different purposes, and the specified tasks of events — may therefore be seen as intended to signal clearly which occasions are 'play' and which are not. If, however, the staff direct attention to these boundaries, they create paradox, since it is impossible to decide whether the act of defining these boundaries is itself 'play'. If, for example, a consultant says or implies that the members of a group are not working at the task of the event, does he imply by this that they have mentally left the event, or that their non-work (as he sees it) is itself to be seen as 'play'?

For some time now, conferences have included events which invite the study of the total inner life of the conference, thus proposing that all the decisions of the staff, for example about the timetable, should be regarded as 'play', or material for learning. The creative potentiality of the conferences is closely related to these possibilities for paradox. The potentiality may, however, not be realized, and the result may be confusion, if the staff fail to understand the signficance of the boundaries they are defining.

This analysis provides a theoretical basis for a judgment that many participants in conferences and Study Groups have reached through their own experience: that these events constitute a profound personal challenge, calling in question the processes by which the individual represents the world and himself to himself. This may be literally more than he bargained for. A manager who attends a conference on the recommendation of his company, and expects to address problems specifically connected with his working role, may feel that he is being asked to involve himself to an extent not made explicit in his contract with his company. He is like someone at a party who accepts an invitation to join in dancing the 'Hokey-Cokey', not realizing that the last movement in the dance is : 'You put your whole self in'. Although this is outside my experience, I imagine that a patient applying for group therapy might have a similar reaction if he found himself in a group conducted in a way which did not confirm the therapeutic 'frame' in which he expected it to be contained.

Some people certainly revise their expectations in the light of the situation in which they find themselves, and value the experience. But it appears that for many the experience leads to confusion, anger, waste of the opportunity, and perhaps rejection of the whole method. This has led my own Institute, while not following this precise train of thought, to seek to devise educational models which incorporate some of the key insights of the conferences without setting up such an ambiguous context. It also appears to us that others, notably Gustafson and Cooper, have made analogous though not identical experiments. We discuss these developments in a later section (p. 296). First, however, we continue the above analysis to consider the responses of the participants, members and staff, to the 'pedigree' conference model.

Member responses

The context created in the Study Group, and in the conference, if experienced as we have described, threatens to throw the member's habitual ways of viewing the world and himself into confusion. Members describe the group or themselves as falling into chaos. Turquet, in an unpublished paper, preferred to refer to the state of the member as one of '*désarroi*' (disarray), seeming to imply a state of being temporarily off balance and mentally dishevelled, requiring time to regain a suitable balance of mind. Bion (1961: 89) wrote of the 'hatred of learning by experience'. He has been criticized by Gustafson for seeming to imply that people never seek and welcome opportunities for development, or enjoy the process of learning. He appears to us to be focusing upon the resistance of the ego to its own disruption or dedifferentiation, and overlooking the possible wish of the self for such a creative reorganization.

Faced with this threat, members extricate themselves in various ways, either to obtain a temporary respite while they size up what is happening, or in such a way as to fend off the threat for the duration of the event.

Some ignore or lose their grip on the question of the task of the group, and submerge themselves in the moment-to-moment flux of the group's excitements and depressions. If this becomes the dominant strategy of the group as a whole, we may expect to find the fantasies associated with one of the basic assumptions emerging. The member becomes what Turquet (1975) called a 'membership individual', the group equivalent of an 'organization man'. Others address the threat as a purely intellectual problem, becoming remote observers or commentators or proposing false solutions to the group's dilemma. In both cases, there is a difficulty of integrating primary and secondary processes: either intuitive rapport or rational investigation is suppressed (cf. Bion's description, 1961: 90).

Alternatively, he may arrive at a false sophistication, no longer troubled by the ambiguities of the context, but having learned to live with them rather than engaging with them. This appears to be the condition of some who return to conferences for a second time, who give the impression of having learned the language without any development in their own consciousness.

Others appear to accept the ambiguities of the situation, and to exercise the 'negative capability' described by Keats (1817) (and quoted by Bion in *Attention and Interpretation* (1970)): 'Negative Capability, that is, when a man is capable of being in uncertainties, mysteries, doubts, without any irritable reaching after fact and reason.' This seems to entail some kind of disclosure about the situation, in which the member trusts and speaks from his own experience of his relatedness to the groups, and view of it, not because he is required to but spontaneously, because he wants to. He 'takes authority' for his own view and his own behaviour. He may then find that the stated definition of the task of the event is a good enough definition of the task he is working to; but the verbal definition is meaningful to him because it puts into words what he is already doing, rather than because it prescribes what he should do. (This account is based on memory rather than specific observation, and is no doubt somewhat idealized. It may be that some participants perceive that the task definition fits only very poorly what they are doing, and wish to do, in which case it becomes for them a dead letter.)

Under these circumstances, the paradoxes inherent in the context no longer trouble the member. The task description no longer appears recursive. He oscillates in his conscious awareness between alert attention to specific contributions and happenings and to his own responses – his feelings, fantasies, and impulses to act. This frame of mind is not easily described, and has not been discussed in the terms we are using here, within the conference context.

Implications for the consultant role

The outcome for the member may be influenced positively or negatively by the interventions of consultants. The dominant image of the consultant, which tends to be reinforced by *Experiences in Groups*, is of one who sits above the water-floods and can distinguish very clearly between feelings projected on to him and feelings proper to himself. This has made it more difficult to discuss the kind of confusions to which the consultant is subject; though in the more satisfactory conferences I have attended, it has been recognized that the consultant contributes more by seeking to understand his own dilemmas and errors with the membership than by maintaining an aura of perfection.

The consultant is inevitably exposed to being caught up in the same confusions as the members: he is no less a participant than they. He may for example become confused as to whether basic assumption behaviour is to be welcomed, because this is what they are there to experience and learn about, or to be opposed, because it obstructs work at the task of the group. Consultants frequently compound the confusion of the members by insisting that they stick to the stated task of the group. The insistence may not be explicit in the interpretations they make, but it is experienced by the members in the tone of voice used, the penumbra of connotations of the words chosen, or facial expression and posture. As we have seen, this can only grind the member into the 'be autonomous' paradox. It is not to be expected that consultants will always be able to tolerate the uncertainties with which they are faced; only that they will know when they have lost their way. This is less likely if they do not understand the paradoxical nature of the method they are using.

Gustafson and Cooper (1978a: 155 ff.) have maintained that consultants, following the model depicted in *Experiences in Groups*, precipitate defensive reactions in their groups, through failing to provide an adequate holding environment. They systematically abandon the members when they require support, and intrude upon them when they require space, replicating 'the cardinal characteristics of very primitive images of the bad mother' (p. 162). I shall return to this criticism in a later section, but suggest that one source of this maladaptive behaviour is a failure to understand the paradoxical position of the member. By not acknowledging and working with comments by members which indicate awareness of their position, consultants abandon members to their confusion, a confusion which is compounded if the member takes their silence as implying a judgment that his insight is invalid. Conversely, by using interpretations to put pressure on members to 'work', the consultant intrudes into the space the member needs to explore his situation.

The analysis offered here implies a different approach on the part of consultant. First, he knows that he does not know in advance the nature of the context in which he and the members will find themselves. He is therefore alert to work with other participants in exploring and exchanging perceptions of this context. This entails listening to the contributions of the 'work group', as well as of the 'basic assumption group'. We should emphasize that this is not a matter of providing support by making encouraging noises when people seem to be on the right lines:

the consultant is not signalling 'hot' and 'cold' as the members search for something he has previously hidden, but is seeking to recognize what they have perceived and he has not.

Second, he allows the members space in which they have the maximum opportunity to recognize that the force of the double binds in which they find themselves is illusory, and so 'take authority' for their own constructions of the task and of the behaviour of the group at any moment. The statement of the primary task of the event is not an instruction, as from a superior to a subordinate, to be obeyed or disobeyed. It is an injunction indicating an activity through which the member will have the opportunity to gain understanding of group processes. It is on the member's own authority whether he chooses to respond to this injunction or not. In order to recognize this, he requires space to reflect upon the assumptions about authority which are shaping the way he relates to the consultant and to the stated task of the group.

Third, the consultant places a positive valuation upon manifestations of primary process, and upon the emergence of basic assumption phenomena, even though he may also experience their impact on himself as a threat to his sense of control or competence. This entails holding onto the recognition that the purpose of the event is to experience and understand the interplay of the work group and the basic assumption group, of secondary and primary processes, not to take sides with the first against the second.

An example of this stance is provided by an analyst, Levenson (1972: 151), who describes his approach to the patient's misperceptions of the therapist:

> One could read the patient's 'distortion' of the therapist not as a misinterpretation or exaggeration but rather as an aesthetically authentic representation of something *really* there and observed. Thus, from the most benign neurotic 'distortions' to the outrageous misinterpretations of the paranoid, one could say that the perception, albeit not literally correct, is a *relevant* perception of the therapist. What makes a poem true? Why does a caricature look right to us, immediately identifiable although literally grotesque? The gestalt is right: it is *aesthetically* true.

In a comparable way, Gustafson and Cooper seek to interpret repetitive and obstructive patterns in the behaviour of the group, not as resistances to learning in the classical psychoanalytic sense of 'resistance', but as healthy defences, through which the group wards off the possibly destructive consequences of pursuing its intended line of exploration. They thus read the group as foregrounding its own unconscious plan for development, and also its fears about the consequences. The demand upon the consultant is not to clobber or insinuate his way through these defences, but to understand and articulate them, so that the members are better placed to judge how and when they will relax them.

Thus the consultant who finds himself being treated as though he were an omniscient leader, surrounded by a passive group of disciples waiting to be filled up with knowledge, might do better to entertain their view as, in Levenson's terms, an aesthetically true perception of the 'here and now' state of affairs, rather than as an obstructive fantasy of which they need to be disabused. The intention conveyed by his words is more important than their precise sense. If the force of his words is: 'Stand on your own feet; don't lean on me', he denies their recognition that he has resources for understanding the situation, and has been presented to them as having these resources by the sponsoring institution and by signals he has himself put out. By this denial, he is more likely to reinforce their defences than to enable them to relax them. The force of his words may alternatively be: 'You are right in supposing that I have more experience of these groups than most or all of you have. I see myself as responsible for working with you towards ways of under-standing what is going on: so use me in that capacity as much as you wish.' In this case he places a positive connotation on their dependence, and leaves open the opportunity for them to discover and explore the limits of his skill and the extent of their own.

This positive valuation of primary process thinking is in contrast to that which is implicit in the theory of primary and secondary processes which Bion carried over from Freud's account of the 'two principles of mental functioning' (1958). While Bion says that work group activity is 'on occasion assisted' by the 'powerful emotional drives' of the basic assumption group, the dominant view in his work, carried over into the group relations conferences, is that the basic assumption group is regressive, anti-reality and anti-work. We are only gradually taking on board the thinking of such writers as Rycroft (1968), Ehrenzweig (1970) and Milner (1950), all of whom propose an alternative view, in which it is the dissociation of the primary and secondary processes which is dysfunctional, and their integration which is necessary for adaptive and creative activity. It is significant that these writers have reached these conclusions through reflection on artistic activity, religion, culture, and healthy human relationships, rather than primarily on neurosis and the affairs of the therapist's consulting room. Rycroft refers to primary and secondary processes as the 'libidinal component' and the 'self-preservative component' of adaptation. Ehrenzweig describes the primary process as being superior to the secondary process in unconsciously scanning and perceiving/creating form in complex structures.

The context of learning

At this point it is relevant to offer an interpretation of the way the activities of my own Institute have developed over the years. In retrospect, it appears that institutional decisions about what educational opportunities we should offer, and what form they should take, have run on ahead of our understanding of why we were doing what we were doing.

The contact of our institution with Rice and his colleagues, in the years from 1963 onwards, was a highly significant one, leading to the setting up of a new company with a new name, and to the establishment of a series of group relations conferences which continue to the present time. These have constituted a core event in our programme, and the main training experience for our own staff. For many years we viewed these conferences as potentially valuable to anyone in a position of authority or leadership, as Rice himself describes them (1965). Our brochures suggested that anyone whose work entailed working with and influencing other people, in groups and institutions, could benefit from greater awareness of group processes and of the problems of leadership and representation. In confirmation of this, we saw some participants' approach to their work radically altered by the conference experience; and we derived continuing illumination from the conferences ourselves as we grappled with the demands of taking consultant, administrator and director roles.

It gradually became apparent, however, that many participants did not seem to gain this insight, or if they did, it did not survive their return to their own organizations. We also observed that those programmes of conferences which were organized on an in-company basis, by ourselves or other bodies, tended to be discontinued by the company's higher authorities, rather in the way the human body rejects foreign tissue which is grafted onto it.

Information about the results of courses is always scanty, and we have adopted Rice's practice of not chasing course members with enqiries about the value of their courses. The 'feed-back' one receives is difficult to interpret with confidence: sometimes the most antagonistic members appear to other people to have gained more insight and benefit than more enthusiastic 'converts'. However, the economics of life in an independent institute mean that in the long term most of the conferences we run, for client organizations or under our sponsorship, have to be paid for through the fees of participants. Economic realities therefore underlined our own wish to offer learning opportunities which were more obviously and immediately useful to clients and conference members, without abandoning the key principles on which the group relations conferences were based.

In 1973 we began to offer one-to-one consultations for individual managers, referred to as Organizational Role Analysis or ORA (see Reed 1976), and soon recognized that this was an effective way into behavioural learning for a wider spectrum of people than would be likely to attend, or benefit from, a group relations conference. Later, in 1978, one of my colleagues, Bruce Reed, had the opportunity to work with a group of staff engaged by an international company to develop an in-company management seminar, drawing upon Bion/Rice principles, whch did not provoke the immunological reaction we have referred to. After experimenting with various models and designs for events, the group developed a seminar very different from the group relations conference, which was widely used in the company. The design included three main events, focusing respectively on the person, his role, and the organizational system in which he took that role, and became known in our Institute as the 'PRS Seminar'. We have used this design with managers and senior staff in other industrial companies and in schools, universities, churches, and the probation service.

In September 1981 we found ourselves writing a brochure for our January 1982 group relations conference which defined the intended membership in very different terms from those employed in the past. This section of the brochure began: 'Experience of running conferences over many years indicates clearly that they are not for everyone'. We went on to say that those who had valued the conferences in the past were 'not looking for solutions to immediate practical problems', but had a 'longer-term, strategic concern for the work of their profession or organization'. They had 'taken part as persons, with a curiosity about human behaviour, rather than merely as employees of an organization'. They had had 'the capacity to tolerate feeling confused, frustrated or de-skilled, and to struggle through this to new insight'. They had 'reached a basic level of competence' and were now 'looking for enrichment of the perspective from which they may view their work'.

It appears to us now that, having established at least two educational models, ORA and the PRS Seminar, which have credibility with clients and with ourselves, we have been enabled to look again at the group relations conference, and define its optimum membership with more discretion. The group relations conference is no longer loaded with expectations of being a universal panacea. There is now a reasonably clear distinction between events for men and women attending in and for the sake of their current roles, within an organizational context which is provisionally taken as 'given', and events for persons who are ready to regard not only their roles but the organizational ideology to which they are committed by taking them, as open to scrutiny in the conference.

In an important discussion prior to the writing of this paper, Bruce Reed and I concluded that there is an important difference in the ambiguities of these two learning contexts. I shall outline the features of the two contexts, which I shall refer to as Type R (in which R may stand for 'role') and Type P (in which P may stand for 'person'). For the sake of analytical completeness, I shall first sketch in a third, more restricted learning context, Type A (A standing for 'activity'). It should be emphasized that these are ideal types: actual events may be expected to conform more or less closely to a particular type, or to be a muddle of several types.

The *Type A event* is offered to participants as a means of increasing their skill in, or knowledge about, certain activities which they perform in the course of their job. The nature of their role is taken for granted, and also the organizational context in which it is performed. In the Type A event, the trainer is an expert, with skill and knowledge to impart to the trainee. Competence in most jobs entails formal or informal training at this level.

My own Institute is occasionally asked to conduct Type A courses, for example to provide the staff of an organization with training in conducting meetings or in interviewing. We usually turn these invitations down, or invite the potential client to re-examine what he is really looking for, on the grounds that we do not feel that we can assume how the staff can most effectively carry out these activities without our having a better understanding of their roles. The group relations conferences are occasionally used as Type A events, by participants who take the Study Group and the consultant role as models which can be replicated when working with groups in other situations. In case the tone of this paragraph conveys the feeling that Type A events are inherently inferior to Types R and P, I should add that in some circumstances the opportunity to master essential skills is of greater value than insight into oneself and one's role. For example, those working with offenders are recognizing that some of their clients require assistance in learning to read and write, rather than insight into their criminal tendencies.

The *Type R event* is offered to participants as a means of examining their organizational role. Wherever it takes place geographically, it is formally, like the Type A event, *within* the participant's organization and culture. As a context it is not therefore ambiguous, in the way the context of the Type P event is ambiguous; or perhaps we should say that its ambiguities are only those with which the participant already has to live by virtue of his job. The values, aims and conventions of the organization can be taken as 'given'. The learning event may stimulate the participant to question and reconstrue them, but if he does so, it is on his own initiative and authority. If such questioning arises during the event, it involves the staff as much as themselves, since the staff have also accepted, at least provisionally, the organization's aims and values, by entering into a contract to run the event on its behalf.

In the Type R event, the participant is the expert, since he is the one with experience of performing his role and knowledge of the organizational context. The staff member is more appropriately referred to as 'consultant' or 'adviser', since his role is essentially one of putting certain specialized skills and knowledge at the disposal of the participant experts. He has no sanction to instruct them what to do. Although I have no direct experience of group therapy, I imagine that this also takes place in a Type R context. The participants attend in the role of patients, within an institution which presents itself as concerned with enabling people to understand and resolve personal problems. The therapist, at least with self-referred participants, has a 'consultant' position, since he cannot dictate how the participants will live their own lives.

The *Type P event* presupposes, as the quotations from the Institute's 1982 brochure show, a participant who, while committed to a role within an organization, is prepared to look critically at the aims and values of the organization which shape his role. The Type R participant takes part as a person *with* a role — with several roles, in fact, through one of which he earns his living.

Wherever the Type P event is located, it takes place *outside* the participants' institution or professional world. The difficulty of specifying *where* it takes place is, as we have seen, an aspect of the essential ambiguity of the context. In principle there are no experts in a Type P event. It is a conversation between autonomous persons, each of whom speaks from his (or her) own awareness of what is happening in his inner and outer worlds. In practice, of course, it does not seem like that to the naive participant, if he does not trust, or is not reflexively aware of, his own experience. For him, the staff member is a highly perplexing kind of expert, whose title of 'consultant', 'trainer' or 'facilitator' signals a Type A or Type R context, and who is felt to be more adequately described by means of mythical titles, like 'God', 'Madonna', 'Buddha', 'sphinx', 'guru'. Under these circumstances, it is necessary for the 'consultant' to hold on to the knowledge that the participants are persons who are speaking from their unique awareness of the 'here and now', even if they are not reflexively aware of this; and to see himself perhaps as a master in the distinctive sense employed by the Tai Chi Master Al Huang, who is reported as saying: 'A master is someone who started before you did' (Zukav 1980: 34).

It is probable that the staff of any event require training at the level above that of the event they are running. If this is so, it means that the Type P event is necessary for the development of staff who are competent to conduct Type R events, for without access to the reflexive awareness fostered by Type P, they will have insufficient capacity to look critically at the values and assumptions which are implicit in, and reinforced by, the Type R event.

Concepts: levels of control and levels of learning

The distinction between these different types of event may be conceptualized in various ways. In an organizational context, Boxer distinguishes between three levels of management control (1979, see also 1980). *Operational control* is the activity which controls the task activities through which the organization produces its product or delivers its services. There is then a higher level of control, which he calls *managerial control*, which is concerned with 'integrating the different task activities into an organizational whole, by controlling the availability and use of resources: money, manpower, machines and materials'. This level of control is exercised within a framework of organizational and ideological assumptions — assumptions about the purpose and values of the enterprise — which are in the short term taken as 'given'. The third level of *strategic control* is concerned with the identification and formulation of these assumptions, and of the nature of the task activities required to implement them. In Rice's terms (1965) managerial control is exercised with reference to an explicit or tacit concept of the 'primary task' of the enterprise: strategic control is concerned with defining this primary task, reviewing the fit between this formulation and what is actually happening and, if necessary, taking steps to change it. It will be seen that strategic control cannot by its very nature be a solely rational or objective activity, since the ethos and goals of any enterprise depend upon the vision, energy, ambition, commitment, hopes, fears and values of those who in practice have the power to determine its course.

It would be tempting to marry off Boxer's three levels of control with the three types of learning context I have described. I doubt whether this is sound. I suggest however that the Type R event is directly relevant to problems of operational and managerial control, and is not closed to the consideration of problems of strategic control. Exploration of strategic questions is however liable to involve members and staff in paradox, since it entails calling in question the very suppositions on which the event itself was commissioned and is being conducted. The Type P event is directly relevant to the problems of strategic control, since it makes no assumptions about the task and values of the enterprises from which the participants come.

The distinction between the three types of learning context may also be conceptualized in terms of Bateson's theory of levels of learning (Bateson 1973; Palmer 1979). The theory of levels of logical typing on which this theory is based is also implicit in the analysis of paradox put forward earlier. Bateson proposes the following distinctions:

Learning I: trial and error proceeses through which the individual adapts to his environments, finding new responses or patterns of response to given situations. Learning practical or communicational skills takes place at this level. Learning at this level has its joys and its miseries, as anyone who has sought to master, say, a musical instrument or a sport will know.

Learning II: processes through which the individual comes to modify the way he views (or construes) the context in which he applies the knowledge and skills he has gained through Learning I. For example, if a doctor comes to see his role as that of helping a person in physical or mental distress, instead of that of repairing a faulty biological mechanism, he may begin to make use of his medical knowledge and skills in different ways. Such a reorientation may be very painful, and/or may be a great release.

Learning III: processes through which the individual learns to attend to, and hence bring within conscious control, the habitual ways of construing situations which are the outcomes of Learning II. Learning

III entails reflexive awareness. Our imaginary doctor might for example learn to monitor the idea of his role which was implicit in the way he was dealing with his patients, with the possibility of continuing Learning II. In so doing, he would find himself reflecting upon his deepest beliefs, about himself and his patients and about human life, suffering and death. Thus Learning III involves the whole man or woman, and is likely to initiate change in other areas of his or her life. Such disturbance is frequently frightening and painful; and once again, it may also be a matter of joy and gratitude.

Learning at all these levels is *possible* in any context, and it would be absurd to suggest that the possibilities for learning are wholly circumscribed in any of the types of event we have described. We may say, however, that the design of a particular learning event 'proposes' a certain level of learning, through the way the context is defined, organizationally, behaviourally, and through the practical arrangements. The Type A event 'proposes' learning at Level I. The Type R event 'proposes' Learning II: that is, it invites the participants to reflect upon the ways in which they habitually construe their dealings with the other people they meet at work, to make these tacit constructions conscious, and perhaps to begin to modify them. The Type P event 'proposes' Learning III. It invites participants to become reflexively aware of the person who is committed to certain ways of construing his role relationships rather than others and who invests them with personal meaning. Having set up a typology of learning contexts, we are now in a position to re-examine a number of educational and therapeutic events. I shall first consider Bion's account of his own groups at the Tavistock Clinic, and then in turn the group relations conferences (briefly, since most of the ground has already been covered), and the conferences described by Gustafson and Cooper.

Bion's groups

We should at the outset acknowledge the inevitable uncertainty which attaches to analyses based on written accounts rather than direct experience. Bion himself points out that his account of occurrences in his groups is necessarily shaped by the theories he believes explain them (1961: 145 f.). There are considerable gaps in our picture of how Bion worked with the groups he describes, and it is quite possible that aspects of his method which he did not think worth mentioning were in fact significant.

The first paragraph of Bion's account of his experiences, quoted at the beginning of this paper, presents us immediately with a difficulty. The groups described consisted of 'sometimes patients, sometimes not'. He goes on to say that in the non-patient groups (which included Rice and some of his later colleagues in the group relations conferences), he often found himself in a peculiar quandary, which he goes on to describe. This concerned the members' expectations of himself, as an eminent 'taker' of groups, which he did not immediately satisfy, and which he pointed out were based on hearsay rather than direct experience.

This early crisis of confidence will be familiar to those who have taken part in Study Groups. But are we to understand that similar crises did not arise at the beginning of his patient groups? In the papers which follow, Bion is careful to distinguish between patients and non-patients, yet I have detected no difference in the kind of incidents reported nor in Bion's manner of working with the different kinds of group. Discussions of Bion's work, such as those of Meltzer (1978) and Brown (chapter 10 in this volume), understandably assume the writer has before him an example of group therapy, rather than interweaving accounts of two different types of enterprise. There is little or nothing in the text to contradict the impression that, in both types of group, Bion treated his own status as designated 'taker', and the sanctioning of the event by the Committee of the Clinic, as fictions, or in Oriental terms as *maya*, illusion. The first pages of the first paper demonstrate that this was so for the non-patient groups. The following passage implies that it was so for the patient groups too:

> When I spoke of the group that wished to see the session as a seminar, I said that one reason for this was an unconscious fear that unless the group were pegged to a mature structure the obtrusion of the kinds of group I have described would be facilitated and the ostensible aims of the individuals in joining the group thwarted . . . This impulse is expressed in the therapeutic group in the very fact of calling it a therapeutic group. It seems so rational that we should think of it as a therapeutic group, that we should assume that the psychiatrist is the leader, and that we should talk only about neurotic ailments, that it may not be observed that by thinking in this way, and behaving appropriately, we are attempting to peg the group to a mode of behaviour that will prevent the obtrusion of the kinds of group that are feared (1961: 75).

It appears to me that Bion constituted both his therapeutic groups and his non-patient groups (Study Groups) as Type P events. In neither type of group did he apparently allow responsibilities to the sponsoring institution to determine his perceptions, and not surprisingly he speculates in at least one group on the possibility of it being stopped (p. 35). He regards his own role as leader or therapist as a fiction from the beginning. In the case of the non-patient groups this was clearly a shock to the participants, but his strategy is intelligible, if he saw the purpose of the group as to learn about intra-group tensions, rather than to ameliorate the personal problems of individuals. In the case of the patient groups, however, Bion's approach seems disingenuous. He does not acknowledge that, whether he likes it or not, he has, by accepting the Committee's invitation, put himself in a position where patients will inevitably expect him to behave like a therapist. He chides them for equating the label on the box with the nature of the contents, but ignores his own responsibility for the labelling of the box. Gustafson and Cooper make a similar point (1978a: 162):

> Bion's wry comment, 'It was disconcerting to find that the Committee seemed to believe that patients could be cured in groups such as these,' refreshing as it may be in candor, still conveys the contradictory situation he allowed his groups to be placed in, namely, of expecting something from someone who made no claim to be offering what they wanted.

(It should be noted, however, that the above writers take the account of Bion's behaviour in the paragraphs which follow this reference as an account of his behaviour with patient groups, which it is not — the difficulty already referred to.)

It is interesting to compare Bion's approach as described in these papers with that described in the Pre-View paper about his project in the rehabilitative wing of a military hospital. This is clearly a Type R enterprise, set up under medical auspices within a larger military organization, with the task of enabling men to return to active service. Bion construes the rehabilitative task in military terms: it is necessary to identify a common enemy, and to provide them with the leadership typical of a certain kind of military officer (1961: 12 ff.). Furthermore, while the method he evolved was obviously disconcerting, and the experiment was discontinued after six weeks (for whatever reason), there is no evidence from the brief account we have that Bion regarded his own status, or the hospital, the army, or the war, as fictions.

Group relations conferences

I have suggested that the model provided by Bion had a determinative influence on the method of the group relations conferences, and continues to do so. (The outcome of inviting Bion to join the staff of a group relations conference in the USA was not however regarded as altogether successful. Hearsay accounts suggest that he regarded the organization of the conference as a fiction, to the discomfort of other staff!)

I have already discussed the conference method in some detail. I believe that these conferences are rightly presented as Type P events, but that various inconsistencies in recruiting policy and staff practice have for members added to the confusion which is inherent in the task of studying group processes as they occur.

This analysis also underlines the conclusions which had been reached on other grounds, about the unsoundness of mounting group relations conferences on an in-company basis.

The conferences of Gustafson and Cooper (see chapter 8)

In a series of papers, Gustafson and Cooper have presented criticisms of the group relations conferences and the theory on which they are based, and have described a number of short conferences and Study Groups conducted on what they regard as sounder principles. They have published this impressive work with the explicit intention of presenting an antithesis to the thesis constituted by previous accounts of conferences, in the hope that this may lead to some new synthesis (1978b: 860).

The writers approach the conferences they describe with the hypothesis, derived from theories of Weiss and Sampson (1971, 1976) about individual psychotherapy, that in the early meetings of groups individuals agree unconsciously upon shared goals for the group, which they subsequently pursue, within the constraints of the resources available, which include the willingness and capacity of the consultant to assist them. The writers thus assume that the activities of the work group may be unconscious, and observable at an early stage.

They construe blockages and defensive patterns of behaviour, not as resistances (in the Freudian sense) to insight, but as means by which the group makes prominent conflicts and obstacles which require resolution if they are to pursue their goals. For example, they regard a series of violent clashes between individuals as a means by which the group displays its concern about how aggression is to be handled (1978b: 854). Through these prominent conflicts the group tests the extent of the consultant's capacity to assist their development; the writers describe the group as tempting the consultant to respond defensively or in a partisan way, hoping against hope that he will resist the temptation.

They present their reasons for believing that this hypothesis of unconscious planning is supported by the results of working with it, while acknowledging the possibility of setting up self-fulfilling prophecies, as other writers in this field have done in the past. I have several comments on these findings. First, in another context, that of Organizational Role Analysis in a business school, I had concluded independently that the way the managers used the ORA sessions made more sense if it was assumed that they had, whether or not this was clear to themselves, arrived at a plan for how they would use their time at the business school, and that they had taken the opportunity provided by the ORA to pursue this plan. The parallel with the Weiss–Sampson hypothesis is close.

Second, irrespective of the validity of the hypothesis, it clearly disposes the consultants to place a positive connotation upon the behaviour, including the defensive behaviour, of the members; whereas the expectation of resistances, and of manifestations of hatred of learning by experience, makes for a conflicted relationship between consultant and members.

Third, the approach of Gustafson and Cooper highlights the nature of theories of this kind, which it is misleading to regard simply as conjectures about the properties of groups 'over there'. They are also, necessarily, announcements about the way the investigator proposes to approach the group he is studying. They are examples of the class of propositions identified by Bateson (Ruesch and Bateson 1968: 225 f.), the validity of which is a function of the extent to which they are believed (and acted upon). The theories of Gustafson and Cooper, like those of Wilfred Bion, are both communications about the behaviour of people in groups, and also 'meta-communications' about the beliefs and values of the theorisers.

Gustafson and Cooper propose that, in the early sessions of the Study Group, the consultant should seek to identify and articulate the shared plans of the group, and then to work with them to resolve the successive blocks to the achievement of these plans. It is not my intention to follow the method through in detail, but to examine this approach in the light of the considerations put forward earlier. It appears that these writers have in principle unwound the paradox which is inherent in regarding as work group activity only that reflexive activity which is directed at interpreting the behaviour of the group. The writers discern constructive intention in a range of contributions other than direct comment on the behaviour of the group, and thereby adopt a stance from which work group activity (as they understand it) as well as basic assumption activity, can be observed and studied. This is in line with their own stated belief, which is that the usual group relations conferences do not enable people to learn how to work constructively in groups, because they do not support work group activity.

It becomes problematical whether, and in what sense, the Study Groups described by Gustafson and Cooper are the 'same' event as those described earlier, based on Bion's model. They employ the same task definition: the task of the group is to study its own behaviour in the 'here and now'; but it is not clear from their accounts to what extent participants engage with each other on such study explicitly. The conference described in the October 1978 paper is introduced in the opening session in a way which would sound odd in one of our own conferences:

> We described the preparations of recruitment, space, and schedule we had made and said that the groups belonged to them for whatever they saw fit to discuss or express, with the understanding that they had come to think about what went on as well as take active part, and that we expected this to be useful because we thought, from past experience, that it would mirror fundamental social processes that they continually had to live with outside (1978b: 853).

Our own conferences do not allow for any such 'as well as' notion.

I am struck by the fact that the writers are able to assume that whatever unconscious plans are agreed by the groups will be consonant with the purposes of the conference. This suggests that the context they have created is significantly less ambiguous than those of our own conferences. It is possible to assume an underlying oneness of purpose, more in the way we have done in our PRS Seminars. In these seminars, the members are regarded as the experts, since the subject matter is their professional experience. The staff come in as behavioural specialists who can help them in examining their own concerns. This is similar to the stance of Gustafson and Cooper, who emphasize to their members (1979: 1048) that, for them, 'the study of authority' means the study of the 'authorship' and 'steering of group events' by *participants*.

These comparisons suggest that the conferences described by Gustafson and Cooper are closer to the Type R than the Type P model. This is

supported by their account of the membership and staff of the conferences as being drawn from one professional base — universities — and
having a predominantly left-wing political commitment (1978b: 859).
Significantly, they see the British conferences, and those in the USA
based on the British model, as similarly reflecting a particular political
bias (in effect, as Type R events for managers):

> The material basis of this tradition in England has been aristocratic
> and managerial interests, upper and middle class; and its ideology . . .
> non-developmental. Authority in this context roughly means mana-
> gerial right over others. Conferences bring out the dynamics of
> relations between groups and their managers (consultants) (p. 859).

The usefulness and limitations of Bion's concepts

In conclusion, I wish to offer and then examine critically an account of
the difference between the Type R and Type P contexts, formulated in
psychoanalytic concepts, and in particular those of Bion and of the
group relations conferences. The account deals with the nature of the
security and insecurity fostered in the two settings. Until recently, I
would have distinguished between the two types of event in terms such
as these. While I believe that some such view has shaped the thinking
of others involved in the conferences, the precise view criticized here is
solely my own. Through this exercise I hope to convey something of the
limitations, as I see them, of the dominant language of the conferences.

It is characteristic of Type R events that they provide the participants
with a safe, or at least a 'safe-enough', environment for learning. The
institution within which the event takes place is a good object, a benign
figure in the group mythology; in Winnicott's phrase, a 'good-enough
mother' (Winnicott 1965). The participants may at some stage wish to
question this mythology, and face uncertainties about the wisdom,
strength or benign intention of this institution towards them, but this
is not required of them or forced upon them; any such examination is
on their own initiative.

In Type P events, attention is also given to creating a dependable environment. The staff invest great importance in the reliable provision of
accommodation, meals and administrative support, and in precise observation of time-limits, and of 'boundaries' of territory and task-definition.
We have found that the dependability of the consultant and administrative staff in this respect is the greatest single factor in containing

disturbance and enabling members to take responsibility for themselves.

How then may we characterize the difference between the two types of event? One way of doing this is in terms of the different basic assumptions which are mobilized by the work group. In the Type P context, it is assumed that people can look after themselves. They are assumed to have a secure dependence upon internal objects (what Reed has called a state of 'intradependence' (1978)), which makes it possible for them to invest a minimally secure environment with 'good-enough' reliability. Winnicott describes how the individual in therapy is able to 'cash-in' on his internalized experience of 'good enough' mothering. By attending to certain essential boundaries, the staff prevent the precipitation of deep confusions about what is inside and what is outside, and so confirm the participants in their own autonomy. This leaves them exposed to considerable stress and uncertainty, but has the kind of safety identified in one of Blake's 'Proverbs of Hell':

No bird soars too high, if he soars with his own wings.

The Type P context is thus one in which the participants can assert themselves in a fight, against the ignorance of members and staff, and against their bondage to restrictive ways of seeing and acting. This is reminiscent of the fight against a common danger mobilized by Bion and his colleagues in the military hospital, a common danger which he identified as 'the existence of neurosis as a disability of the community' (1961: 13). According to this argument, therefore, the Type P event mobilizes *fight and flight*, and restricts the expression of dependence and pairing. In such a context, those who do not have sufficient inner resources are likely to get into difficulty, and it is a necessary element in the 'fight' culture that the possibility of 'casualties' (the military term used by Rice) is accepted.

In the Type R event, the question whether the participant can take care of himself is ideally not raised. The defensive impulses of the participant, to defend his own autonomy and counter threats to his identity, while they inevitably arise, are allayed by a leadership which is consistently attentive to, and valuing of, his feelings and views. The Type R event thus mobilizes *dependence and pairing*, and limits the emergence of fight and flight. As we have seen (p. 296). Gustafson and Cooper criticize consultants working in the traditional group relations conference for, at different times, intruding upon, and abandoning, group members. I have said that I think this criticism is well founded. It can also be seen that fight and flight behaviour are liable to be experienced as intrusion and abandonment in a Type R context.

Each of these models can be seen to have its inherent hazards. The Type R event is liable to foster addiction to the security it offers, so that participants are protected from facing radical questioning of the values taken as normative within the event, and their compatibility with the demands of living in the world outside the event. How does the staff member behave when he believes that the unconscious plans of the participants, which his role as a consultant commits him to supporting, pursue illusory goals, or will lead to ways of behaving in the outside world which will prove disastrous? It is noteworthy that several of the leading practitioners in the traditional conferences have placed a high value upon living without illusions. Rice used to introduce the conferences he directed with the statement that the method of the conference entailed being prepared to question all assumptions, including one's own. Rioch refers to the difficulty of pursuing this goal: 'The formation of a human group seriously and consistently dedicated to a serious task, without fanaticism or illusion, is an extremely difficult process and a relatively rare occurrence' (1970: 347).

The failures of the Type P event are more conspicuous than those of Type R, since its conflict and breakdown are more noisy than self-deception. The Type P event is liable to precipitate a crudely 'basic assumption' level of fight and flight, in which no one can be depended upon, and everyone struggles to secure his own boundaries. Gustafson has described (1976) how an early failure by a consultant to be sensitive to the meaning of a group's behaviour reduced what could have been a collaborative venture to a 'serial grouping of singletons'. He continues: 'A basic assumption fight-flight pattern was then made prominent . . . of "every man for himself"'. We have described earlier how impatient consultant behaviour can very easily make the inherent paradoxes of the method into a double bind, and so provoke an impulsive fight-flight response.

In the terms we are using, we could say that each of these types of event seeks to mobilize a particular culture in a sophisticated way — that is, integrated with the work group — and is prone to mobilizing it in an unsophisticated way — that is, dissociated from the work group and running amok.

My doubts about the adequacy of this analysis, in spite of what it usefully clarifies, have increased as I have worked on this paper. The need to end the paper and maintain its proportions means that these doubts can be discussed only briefly here.

I doubt the adequacy of a model of working institutions which proposes such a sharp opposition between the basic assumption which is mobilized and the basic assumptions which are contained or suppressed. Bion seems to be right in saying that, when they are uncontained by the work group, they exclude each other; but feelings of security, hopefulness, aggression and caution are not mutually exclusive in effective institutions. More specifically, a theory which construes the autonomous human person as in a dominant state of fight and flight with his environment seems to be too close for comfort to the dominant ideology of Western civilization, which has brought itself to the brink of catastrophe through pursuing a dominant relationship of 'fight' between man and the resources of the Earth, the rest of the biosphere, and other men and women. The above analysis implies an opposition between dependence and fight, whereas, in Koestler's words, every human individual, group, institution and larger social unit 'has the dual tendency to preserve and assert its individuality as a quasi-autonomous whole; and to function as an integrated part of an (existing or evolving) larger whole' (1978: 306).

The above analysis also implies that the two types of event are alternatives on the same level, which is reinforced by my selection of the symbols to refer to them from a homogeneous set of alternatives, the alphabet. I have suggested earlier that the Type P event proposes a level of learning which is 'meta-' to that in the Type R event. This is not apparent in the way group relations conferences have typically been offered to participants, and indeed cannot be said in the language of Bion and Rice.

The issue of levels of learning may be illustrated from one of the papers of Gustafson and Cooper:

> Unconscious planning in groups now proceeds best not through overcoming resistances to recognition of unconscious forces but through unconscious planning to control dangerous regressive potentials. Members come to study groups not to have their resistance broken through, but to protect the 'self' and augment their capacities for self-preservation while working in depth with others (1979: 1046 n.).

This may be a valid statement about the frame of mind in which many participants now attend group relations conferences. In this case, it is an argument against offering Type P events, since in these events, as I see it, it is assumed that it is the 'self' that is the problem. It is the individualistic way in which the 'self' is constructed which precludes awareness of our participation in group and social processes, and allows us to disown those aspects of ourselves which we locate and live out in other people. The level of re-organization proposed by the Type P event could be described in the terms used by Laing (1961: 25):

Phantasy can become conscious, insofar as a person can allow his own reflective awareness to be open to it. In becoming thoroughly and radically aware of phantasy, both in terms of content and modality, the person is subject in his whole being to a re-evaluation of himself and others.

At this point the language of primary and secondary process, of basic assumption group and work group, becomes inadequate. It becomes necessary to distinguish between the 'self', or ego, of which the primary and secondary processes are functions, and the person, the 'I', who can lose himself in these processes, or can become reflexively aware of them (see chapter 2). We have quoted above (p. 277) Bion's account of the experience of being momentarily lost in phantasy, and then recovering reflexive awareness. It seems, however, that Bion's theory of group behaviour does not accommodate this experience. By stating as he does (1961: 97) that his interpretations, if accepted, are interpretations *by the sophisticated group* (i.e. the work group), Bion reduces a personal intervention to the operation of a mental mechanism.

I wish to acknowledge the personal support and intellectual stimulation of Bruce Reed, on whose belief in the importance of writing this paper I leaned heavily in the early stages, and with whom a timely conversation generated many of its key ideas; also of Philip Boxer, whose thinking about knowledge, learning and the self is immanent throughout the paper, and has provided me with a foothold outside Bion's theory from which to view it; and of James Gustafson, who wrote to me a year ago sending me one of the papers in which, with Lowell Cooper, he has elaborated a penetrating critique of the group relations conferences, on which I have meditated long and hard.

References

Bateson, G. (1973), *Steps to an Ecology of Mind*, St Albans, Paladin.

Bion, W. R. (1961), *Experiences in Groups*, London, Tavistock.

Bion, W. R. (1970), *Attention and Interpretation*, London, Tavistock.

Boxer, P. J. (1979), 'Managing Metamorphosis', paper prepared for Silver Anniversary of the International Meeting of the Society for General Systems Research, London, London Business School.

Boxer, P. J. (1980), 'Supporting reflective learning: towards a reflexive theory of form', *Human Relations*, 33, 1: 1–22.

Cooper, L. and Gustafson, J. P. (1979a), 'Planning and mastery in group therapy: a contribution to theory and technique', *Human Relations*, 32, 8: 689–704.

Cooper, L. and Gustafson, J. P. (1971b), 'Towards a general theory of group therapy', *Human Relations*, 32, 11: 967–81.

Ehrenzweig, A. (1970), *The Hidden Order of Art*, St Albans, Paladin.

Freud, S. (1958), *Formulations on the Two Principles of Mental Functioning*, Standard Edition, vol. 12, London, Hogarth Press and Institute of Psycho-analysis.

Gustafson, J. P. (1976), 'The passive small group: working concepts', *Human Relations*, 29, 8: 793–803.

Gustafson, J. P. and Cooper, L. (1978a), 'Collaboration in small groups: theory and technique for the study of small group processes', *Human Relations*, 31, 2: 155–72.

Gustafson, J. P. and Cooper, L. (1978b), 'Towards the study of society in microcosm: critical problems of group relations conferences', *Human Relations*, 31, 10: 843–62.

Gustafson, J. P. and Cooper, L. (1979), 'Unconscious planning in small groups', *Human Relations*, 32, 12: 1039–64.

Keats, J. (1817), Letter to G. and T. Keats, 21 December.

Koestler, A. (1978), *Janus: a Summing Up*, London, Hutchinson.

Laing, R. D. (1961), *The Self and Others*, London, Tavistock.

Levenson, E. A. (1972), *The Fallacy of Understanding*, New York, Basic Books.

Meltzer, D. (1978), *The Kleinian Development*, part III: *The Clinical Significance of the Work of Bion*, Perthshire, Clunie Press.

Milner, M. (1950), *On Not Being Able to Paint*, London, Heinemann.

Palazzoli, M. S., Cecchin, G., Prata, G. and Boscolo, L. (1978), *Paradox and Counter-paradox*, New York and London, Aronson.

Palmer, B. W. M. (1979), 'Learning and the group experience', in Lawrence, W. G. (ed.), *Exploring Individual and Organisational Boundaries*, New York, Wiley.

Reed, B. D. (1976), 'Organisational role analysis', in Cooper, C. L. (ed.), *Developing Social Skills in Managers*, London, Macmillan.

Reed, B. D. (1978), *The Dynamics of Religion*, London, Darton, Longman & Todd.

Rice, A. K. (1965), *Learning for Leadership*, London, Tavistock.

Rioch, M. J. (1970), 'Group relations: rationale and technique', *Int. J. Group Psychotherapy*, 20: 340–55.

Ruesch, J. and Bateson, G. (1968), *Communication: the Social Matrix of Psychiatry*, New York, Norton.

Rycroft, C. (1968), 'Beyond the reality principle', in *Imagination and Reality*, London, Hogarth Press and Institute of Psycho-analysis.

Sampson, H. (1976), 'A critique of certain traditional concepts in the psychoanalytic theory of therapy', *Bull. Menninger Clinic*, 40: 255–62.

Trist, E. L. and Sofer, C. (1959), *Exploration in Group Relations*, Leicester University Press.

Turquet, P. M. (1975), 'Threats to identity in the large group', in Kreeger, L. (ed.), *The Large Group: Therapy and Dynamics*, London, Constable.

Watzlawick, P., Weakland, J. and Fisch, R. (1974), *Change: Principles of Problem Formation and Problem Resolution*, New York, Norton.

Weiss, J. (1971), 'The emergence of new themes: a contribution to the psycho-analytic theory of therapy', *Int. J. Psychoanalysis*, 52: 459–67.
Winnicott, D. W. (1965), *The Maturational Process and the Facilitating Environment*, London, Hogarth Press and Institute of Psycho-analysis.
Zukav, G. (1980), *The Dancing Wu Li Masters*, London, Fontana/Collins.

Chapter 15
Beyond the frames

W. Gordon Lawrence

> my way is in the sand flowing
> between the shingle and the dune
> the summer rain rains on my life
> on me my life harrying fleeing
> to its beginning to its end
>
> my peace is there in the receding mist
> when I may cease from treading these long, shifting thresholds
> and live the space of a door
> that opens and shuts (Samuel Beckett 1961)

The idea of frame

There exists a striking fourteenth-century Syrian miniature of the Archangel Gabriel. What disturbs the Western eye, at first, is that the bell of the horn which Gabriel blows bursts through the exquisitely limned frame that the artist has placed around the figure of Gabriel and the text below. Although the figure is flat, and there is no sense of perspective, the visual effect of the horn bursting through the frame is that the picture has a third dimension; the picture jumps out of its frame. It is only on reflection that the observer realizes that Gabriel's horn cannot be contained within a mere frame, for he is the bringer of good news, having been visited by a vision (Daniel 8: 16–26).

In the context of this essay, that is perhaps not quite so important as the simple idea that frames have both an inside and outside; they contain the space inside and leave undefined the space outside. Furthermore, frames are artifacts which can be delineated at will. This is one leitmotiv of this essay.

Within the frame

Wilfred Bion, whom this book commemorates, was able to create hypotheses about the nature of human groups that took us beyond the frames. Compared with his predecessors, Freud and Trotter, Bion was able to make a quantum leap in understanding. In particular he identified the basic assumption states that members of a group can take part in, quite unconsciously, while, at the same time, they are trying to pursue some work task. I believe this to be Bion's major, awesome, contribution to our knowledge about groups.

Isabel Menzies Lyth has made the point well. In her review of Bion's contribution to thinking about groups, she notes that Bion insisted on 'the use of the group per se, the dynamics of the group in the here and now, as the instrument of therapy and learning' (Menzies Lyth 1981: 662). She goes on to write (p. 663):

> My second point concerns his elucidation of the psychotic elements in groups. Previous reference to psychotic group behaviour had almost exclusively described gross phenomena, akin to diagnostically psychotic disorders. The subtlety of Bion's intuition was in pinpointing the less obvious but immensely powerful psychotic phenomena that appear in groups that are apparently behaving sanely, if a little strangely, groups that are working more or less effectively and whose members are clinically normal or neurotic. He describes the clusters of these psychotic phenomena as the three basic assumptions of dependency, fight-flight and pairing. They have in common massive splitting and projective identification, loss of individual distinctiveness or depersonalisation, diminution of effective contact with reality, lack of belief in progress and development through work and suffering.

This is the second leitmotiv of this essay: how to explore psychotic phenomena in groups incuding any personal and social defences against such an exploration because of the anxieties invoked.

The focus of this essay is on groups as an instrument of learning. At one level the essay is about learning within the frames of groups as such, but it is also a record of going beyond these frames to fathom larger issues of institutions and societies. It is also a record of my puzzlement about the unconscious world.

One of the outstanding outcomes of Bion's thinking about groups has been the growth of group relations training conferences. What commonly is known as the Tavistock method, or model, arises from Bion's pioneering work. Since 1957 when the Tavistock Institute of Human Relations, then in conjunction with the University of Leicester, sponsored the first experiential working conference for studying the behaviour of groups, there has been an unbroken tradition till now. Under the leadership of A. K. Rice there was a shift in the direction of these conferences towards learning about leadership (Rice 1965). Later the emphasis moved towards the study of authority and the problems encountered in its exercise within organizations and institutions (Lawrence 1979a: 2). Since then, I think, there has been a push through to the experiential exploration of the politics of relatedness, the theme of destructive differences (gender, age, race, etc.) and the study of social innovation. This last change of focus has been attempted by the current two joint directors of the Group Relations Training Programme of the Tavistock Institute of Human Relations, Eric J. Miller and myself.

Parallel to the Tavistock conferences, other institutions have been founded to pursue the same kind of work. In the USA there is the A. K. Rice Institute and an apparent proliferation of others. In the UK there is the Grubb Institute of Behavioural Studies and the Chelmsford Cathedral Centre for Research and Training. There is also an institution in Sweden (AGSLO) for the study of leadership and organization. There have been other institutions which have risen and died, and others may now exist of which I do not know. My purpose, however, is not to set out a detailed history but to try and identify a social process which I am postulating influences the elaboration, through these institutions, of Bion's original insights about groups.

Through the growth of enterprises to provide group relations training there has been the phenomenon of institutionalization. From my role perspective, as joint director of a Tavistock Institute programme of work, I find myself, at times, in the thick of this experience of institutionalization. Bion, himself, has identified this phenomenon (1970: 82):

> The institutionalizing of words, religions, psycho-analysis — all are special instances of institutionalizing memory so that it may 'contain' the mystic revelation and its creative and destructive force. The function of the group is to produce a genius; the function of the Establishment is to take up and absorb the consequences so that the group is not destroyed.

There can be little doubt that Bion had the qualities of a mystic (cf. Grotstein 1981: 33) if only because of his contribution to our thinking about groups. The paradox is that the disruptive ideas he first presented have resulted in an Establishment(s), i.e., the group relations training institutions to which I already have referred. I am in doubt as to whether 'Establishment' is singular or plural. My postulate is that there is an Establishment 'in the mind'. Each institution (such as the Tavistock Institute, the A. K. Rice Institute, and the others) at times actually becomes the Establishment for the others. The Establishment 'in the mind' is the ideal-typical institution purveying the very best of Bion's thinking and those who were immediately associated with him and who began the various institutions for group relations training. Here, I suggest, a number of individuals have been put into the role of representing the untarnished truth of Bion, Rice *et al*. Each conference sponsored by any one of these Establishments can be seen as the 'group' in Bion's terms. The mystic who could be either a member of the conference or the conference staff will have his or her disruptive ideas dealt with by the group, the members of whom must preserve coherence even at the risk of new understanding. I can write more pertinently from my own experience. A few years ago I used the word 'relatedness' in a conference staff group. Even though Turquet had introduced the concept earlier, I found myself regarded with puzzlement by my then colleagues. Now, 'relatedness', as a term, is part of the language of any conference. At best, the Establishment(s) come, in time, to have a symbiotic relationship with the mystic. But the possibilities of commensal and parasitic relationships are always present.

The other aspect I want to pursue is the postulate that institutions for group relations training come, at times, individually to act as an Establishment for the others. Thus, at best, another institution can take on the role of mystic in the sense that the term is being used in this context.

This, however, is both complicated and enriched by issues of institutional transference and countertransference. Clearly, institutions themselves are not capable of transference but their agents or employees are. Lomas, in his discussion of psychiatric clinics, makes the point that there is transference on the part of agents of clinical institutions towards their clients. He identifies

> a type of institutional countertransference, a transference of attitudes and feelings on the part of employees to the imagos that haunt the halls of the clinic itself. These attitudes and feelings, be they latent or manifest, inevitably cause such employees to become agents of the institution, executing the expressed mission of the organization, often without any regard for the clientele; and, worse, these attitudes

and feelings cause such employees to carry out procedures that are in direct conflict with their own personal feelings (1979: 548).

While a group relations training institution cannot be readily likened to a clinic, with its buildings and permanent personnel, it would be worth while systematically considering the types of transference which occur between conference staffs and members, conference staffs and their Establishment(s) and the imagos of the Establishment 'in the mind'. To avoid the disentangling of this and the testing of the reality or not of particular conference staffs being caught in the impersonalized procedures identified by Lomas, other institutions grow up with the latent task of providing a less painful experience than a Leicester Conference, as has been reported to me more than once.

All I can offer, at this point, is my experience that there are transference and countertransference feelings between agents of Establishments. So, if you will, the relationships and relatednesses of mystic, group and Establishment and the dynamics of commensality, symbiosis and parasitism come to be worked out at both interpersonal and institutional levels.

To put my concern in concrete terms: the felt pressure on the programme of the Tavistock is never to be innovative; it must be saddled with stability, certainty and perseveration. But it must never disappear, as this would leave other comparable institutions with problems of rivalry for succession that would have to be fought out. So the idea of the Tavistock programme as a dead, hollow container or spittoon easily comes to mind, even though individuals as agents may feel differently within themselves. Essentially I am also saying that the memory of group relations training conferences is so powerful because of institutionalization that new transformations which might lead to a deeper ignorance and then a more profound understanding of groups are constrained. As Establishments have grown to perpetuate the work of Bion, the world of groups with their psychotic phenomena is in danger of being defined for ever. The possibility of suggestion that might lead to tentative new insights can be squeezed out. Remember:

> To define is to kill
> To suggest is to create. (Stéphane Mallarmé)

The puzzle is how to generate symbiotic relationships between new ideas and the Establishment(s) and avoid the commensal and parasitic ones, to use Bion's formulation. This is another leitmotiv.

Once in Ireland a motorist stopped his car to ask a pedestrian the way to Ballykinler. His informant said he could certainly tell him the way, but added, 'I wouldn't be starting from here!' I feel much the same about group relations working in conferences at times. I have a sense that with the institutionalization of Establishments a technology has developed. I purposely use the term 'technology' to give the sense that, in the process of institutionalization, the perseverators of the Tavistock method/model become technicians as opposed to being *makars*, which is the old Scottish word for poets.

As, then, with any inheritance, there are puzzlements around what ought to be discarded in order to break through to some new understanding in the context of the times in which we live. What I am quite sure about, from my role perspective, is that to take psychoanalytic and Bion's thinking about groups out of this tradition would be to end it. And there can be a sense of an ending as I experience it occasionally when working with some staffs of group relations training conferences who are preoccupied with pre-conscious material and not struggling to elucidate unconscious phenomena, or, alternatively, when I find myself in a consultant staff which is in a pre-emptive frame of mind, that is interpreting staff and member experiences in such a way that further exploration is truncated. It is in such contexts that mutative[1] interpretations, which are those which engage with puzzling and lead to change, are destroyed.

What I am less sure about, and continually want to question, is the continued acceptance of the 'frames' and 'orders' which have been established and institutionalized to capture and explore the kind of group phenomena that Bion first illuminated.

By 'frames' I mean the 'small study group', the 'large study group', the 'institutional event', and all the other events. In order to explore the phenomenal stuff of the existence of people in groups, we, in our roles of conference designers, draw outlines or contours around selected numbers and frame them. The figure twelve is traditionally a small group; six, a very small group; twenty-five plus, a large group, or is it a median group? To be sure, there can be no identifiable group without such a contour or frame. But, at the very same time, it is known that such frames, outlines or contours impose limits which have to be accepted by the people involved. Those limits become boundaries enabling the differentiation of what is inside the frame from what is outside. Nevertheless, they constrain the exploration of experiences and phenomena that cannot yet be imagined. The paradox is inevitable.

Another paradox arises when the 'orders' associated with these frames and their selection are considered. I use the term 'order' in the same way as Weber. Some years after he had developed the concept of bureaucracy which described the kinds of organization that man had evolved to execute tasks, he said in a debate:

> This passion for bureaucracy . . . is enough to drive one to despair. It is as if in politics . . . we were deliberately to become men who need 'order' and nothing but order, who become nervous and cowardly if for one moment this order wavers, and helplessness if they are torn away from their total incorporation in it. That the world should know no men but these: it is such an evolution that we are already caught up in, and the great question is therefore not how we can promote and hasten it, but what can we oppose to this machinery in order to keep a portion of mankind free from this parcelling-out of the soul . . . (quoted in Bennis 1971: 144).

The theme of 'order' has always been present in the work of the Tavistock conferences with their emphasis on responsibility, leadership, authority, organization and, now, the politics of relatedness. While the fantasy will persist that Tavistock conferences are 'authoritarian', the commitment of staffs of such conferences is to exploring these dimensions of 'order' in order to ensure that they are scrutinized and questioned. One way in which this is done is by holding to the psycho-analytic tradition of trying to make as explicit as possible transference and countertransference feelings between the managerial and consultant staffs of a conference and the membership. The staff, in fantasy, at times will be seen as a privileged sub-group of the conference, at once destructive, persecuting, protective, benign. The collection of these transference feelings and the working through of them is one way that a staff can help the membership find its authority to take responsibility for making the conference a learning institution.

To be sure, there will be ambivalent feelings about authority. There will often occur as a social process a 'rage for order' on the part of some members and staff that is reminiscent of Weber's insight, but there will also be a wish for absolute autonomy and freedom; even a hunger for disorder.

It is around this theme of order that the subjectivity of the individual is most closely engaged because order, while it may appear to be rational and logical, is often supported by unspoken and unconscious wishes for protection against the anxiety of finding authority to take initiative to feel and see beyond the orders.

The connection between the inner world of conferences and the external authority and power structures is easy to see. On the face of it, it looks as if internal and external management structures are matched. In fantasy and because of transference feelings the membership of a conference will tend to see them as exactly the same, even though the management of a conference may be directing its efforts to providing conditions for the membership to manage themselves in relation to their learning. Here I want to emphasize that I see conferences as being an opportunity for members and staff to re-affirm their capacities to inspect and question the social contexts in which they are existing. The hope is always that members will internalize from staff modes of inspecting the unconscious aspects of social arrangements and go on to forge their own perspective for questioning the social meaning of frames and orders.

A central heuristic tool for such questioning is provided through the concept of primary task. Every working conference on group relations is bounded in time, space and activity. The boundaries (frames) of time and space are obvious. What is less obvious, on first inspection, is the boundary between work that is directed at understanding and non-work which is to avoid insight. Here, there is a seeming paradox. The experience of Bion's basic assumption states (crudely, and by some oversimplistically defined as non-work) within the boundaries of a conference and its activities come to be the work of a conference. Work directed at coming close to what may be the truth of a situation can only be attained through the experience of the basic assumption states; the psychotic phenomena.

The ideal work of a conference is differentiated from other subjective experiences through the use of the concept of primary task. It is a heuristic device and not a prescriptive one, though it can be reduced to that by some practitioners. It is based on

> the proposition that every enterprise or part of it, has, at any given moment, one task which is primary. What we (E. J. Miller and A. K. Rice) also say, however, is that, if, through inadequate appraisal of internal resources and external forces, the leaders of an enterprise define the primary task in an inappropriate way, or the members – leaders and followers alike – do not agree on their definition, then the survival of the enterprise will be jeopardised. Moreover, if the organization is regarded primarily as an instrument for task performance, we can add that, without adequate task definition, disorganization must occur (Miller and Rice 1967: 27-8).

In order to elucidate what is taking place both consciously and uncon-sciously among the people who make up the organization of an enter-prise — and here groups of various sizes are to be included — the heuristic concept of primary task has been further elaborated. On inspection, it is possible to differentiate between the normative primary task, the existential primary task and the phenomenal primary task. The first is the task which the people in an enterprise consciously and rationally know has to be performed if the enterprise is to survive as an institution. The existential primary task is the one which people believe they are executing. On occasion there will be agreement between the normative and existential task but not at other times. The existential primary task is the individual's perception of the purpose of his or her activity. If the individual has internalized the normative primary task the chances are that he or she will be able to take up a role in the system of activity. If the individual is concerned more with self-survival than institutional survival, the existential primary task will be salient. These two definitions of the situation of an individual in role in a system of activity are con-scious in the sense that they can be established through a question and answer process, for instance. What is less obvious is the phenomenal primary task. This is the unconscious task which is being pursued. It can be hypothesized that within any system of activity there will be this task sitting alongside the other two. At times all these will coincide to produce high calibre work but there may be tensions between the three. If the phenomenal primary task is salient in a system of activity, it is a mental world of the psychotic, i.e., the basic assumption states of Bion. Although I am not certain about this, I would suggest that the existential primary task enables the neurotic quality of life in systems of activity to be identified. Certainly, the phenomenal primary task is the one of which people are not consciously aware (cf. Lawrence 1977: 24). By holding these three versions of primary task in mind it is possible to generate hypotheses as to the conscious and unconscious behaviour of people within the boundary, or frame, of a group or a larger enterprise with its fantasied and reality orders.

Working conferences have a primary task, but a conference designer only can state a primary task on behalf of the staff who constitute the collective management of the conference. For example, the primary task for the September 1978 working conference, entitled 'Individual and Organization: The Politics of Relatedness', was stated as follows: 'To study and interpret experiences of political relatedness within the conference Institution'. Such a primary task definition differentiates the working conference as a temporary learning enterprise or institution

from its environment. It also enables the people taking part in the conference — both staff (as collective management and consultants) and
the members — to join the conference by taking and making roles in it
in contradistinction to attending it. Without a primary task there can be
no conference.

Working conferences are based on the postulate that they are open
systems interacting with their environment (cf. Rice 1958: 40 of 1970
edn; Rice 1965: 2–27). Essentially a working conference provides
opportunities for members and staff to transform themselves from a
state of not knowing so much about groups into a state of further
understanding groups at first hand through experience, as opposed to
learning about groups from written sources, for example.

Within a conference boundary — itself a frame — there are such
events as: the small study group, the large study group, the inter-group
event, the institutional event, review groups, application groups, and
conference plenaries. These have all been framed by conference designers
in order to pursue the aim of experientally understanding group phenomena. Each of these events has a primary task which enables both
members and staff to differentiate appropriate work from non-work.
From the conference staff group — members of which have the two
sub-roles of collective management and consultants — consultants are
delegated authority to work with a section of the membership, say, in a
small study group. It is unlikely that in the opening stages of a conference
the members will have the political machinery to execute a similar kind
of delegation but in the course of a conference a shared sense of delegation by members of members is likely to increase, particularly within
the inter-group and the institutional events. Indeed, the staff both in
their managerial and consultant roles are working to enable the membership to find their authority.

To these have to be added other events which do not appear on the
programme of the conference. There is 'the-event-of-the-staff-as-a-group'
and, similarly, 'the-event-of-the-membership-as-a-group-and-in-groups-of-
their-own-choice'. I shall simply call these the staff group event and the
membership group(s) event(s). About these very little is known because
they are rarely open to direct study as they are regarded as being private.
Nevertheless they are important because they influence other events in
the conference.

To be sure, in the institutional event and in some versions of the
inter-group event the staff are present as a group and their behaviour is
open to observation and interpretation as they make their roles both as
management and consultants. In these events they are present as a staff

group with work to do, but I am interested in the influence of the private events of the staff as a group and the membership as a group as they relate outside the stated, defined, framed events as sentient groups.

Miller and Rice introduced the concept of 'sentient group'. They wrote:

> We have chosen *sentient* − 'that feels or is capable of feeling; having the power or function of sensation or of perception by the senses, 1632 (*Shorter Oxford English Dictionary*) − as expressing most clearly what we mean without using the specialised vocabulary of psycho-analysis. We shall therefore talk of *sentient system* and *sentient group* to refer to that system or group that demands and recieves loyalty from its members; and we shall talk of *sentient boundary* to refer to the boundary round a sentient group or sentient system. We shall also use *sentience* to mean 'the condition or quality of being sentient' (*Shorter Oxford English Dictionary*) (1967: xiii, italics in original).

Clearly, members can develop sentience only during the course of a conference though it is quite clear that those who are acquainted beforehand might arrive at a conference with that potentiality. The chances are that a staff group will have more sentient qualities at the start of a conference than the members. Within a staff group there may be a tension between sentient sub-groupings and the staff as a work group. In my experience this most commonly takes the form of a pair which I assume, at worst, is a formation that is used by the pair and by the remainder of the staff, whose relations come to be influenced by the pair, as a defensive system against the anxieties of engaging with the psychotic qualities of the framed events. At the same time the pair comes to be used in exactly the same way as Bion identified when he described the basic assumption pairing culture, i.e., a hope for creativity, but doomed to failure.

Sentient groups and groupings will develop and change within the period of a conference both for staff and members. From these groups and groupings individuals can be seen as taking up roles in the framed events and through their work experiences within them making sentient groups and groupings.

There is, then, within a conference and its framed events a substantial richness for learning, not all of which has yet been identified. If we accept the inescapable paradox that to draw a contour, frame or boundary precludes experiencing what is outside the frame, we can have an opportunity, if we give ourselves authority, to explore even more deeply within the frames of conference events. If the basic assumption states which Bion first identified are understood to be, in Conrad's words, 'the heart of darkness' (Broadbent 1979: 193 ff.) there are opportunities within a working conference on group relations to be in touch vividly and vitally with unconscious processes.

One framed event, for example, that ever continues to stir me, whether as a member or a taker of it, is the large group. This event grew out of the experiences which the members of staff in the 1960s were having in conference plenaries. These occur at the beginning and towards the end of a working conference and are designed to offer a frame within which both members and staff can reflect on their experiences of joining, participating in and leaving the conference.

Pierre Turquet, in his paper 'Threats to identity in the large group', points out that it was the inexplicability of social forces which occurred in conference plenaries that brought about the specific study of large groups in their own right. A new frame was created.

From his experiences as a consultant to the large group, Turquet developed a rare phenomenological description of what takes place for the participating individual. His working hypothesis was that the individual member comes to a working conference, and therefore the large group, as a 'singleton'. Turquet introduced this term

for this person entering into a new conference totally on his or her own, not yet part of a group but attempting both to find himself and to make relations with the other singletons who are in a similar state. As yet within the large group situation no relationships with other singletons have been established; nor do previous acquaintanceships seem to operate.

One of the characteristics of a large group is that many of its members remain in the singleton state, unable, possibly unwilling, to join in and so go through the necessary change of state. This conversion process is part of the dislocation every conference member experiences as he takes himself into a world which transcends the usual parameters of his own individuality (1975: 94).

Turquet develops his ideas about the conversion process available to the members of the large group. He or she can become an individual member (I.M.), i.e., convert from the singleton state as he or she struggles to make relationships with other singletons. Once the large group assumes some meaning for the individual and he or she tries to make a

construct of it in the mind the chances of converting to the 'membership individual' (M.I.) are enhanced. To be sure, this conversion process
is not without its risks because the construct may only express the
destructive feelings of the singleton and his fears of being annihilated
by the large group and its members. So singletons can use the large
group as a repository for negative feelings in order to maintain their
own sense of a positive, individual boundary. There are, of course,
other possibilities.

The struggle between the I.M. or M.I., or I.M. back to singleton states
is experienced as flux. It is in these transitional states that the importance
of the personal boundary, or external skin, is paramount. The dilemma
can be stated as: 'This is me; that is not me.' With subtlety, Turquet
goes on to describe the necessity for what he calls the 'second skin', the
internal skin which

> is needed so that the singleton can separate himself out from his back-
> ground, more specifically from the undifferentiated non-singleton
> matrix out of which he has developed and to which he might return
> again, if the I.M. status is not securely established, the various prob-
> lematic processes having failed him and the defensive manoeuvres
> having broken down (1975: 97).

This internal skin includes a history of past and present. Thus the
'here and now' can be separated from the past by the individual that,
for him or her, becomes 'a background called the "past"' (p. 97). Turquet goes on to say that this background boundary skin has another
aspect: 'While the presence of the past gives rise to a sense of continuity
of growth out of all our yesterdays, the singleton's immediate experience
is nevertheless one of discontinuity, of being different, of being other
than he was yesterday' (1975: 97).

This sense of discontinuity and dislocation is very frightening but
brings the singleton up against larger existential issues than just his or
her private troubles. As Turquet says:

> Anxiety surges up with a developing content of annihilation, becoming
> fear of a void in which to be lost. Since internally nothing can be
> found, there is nothing there. The move to try and re-establish a 'here
> and now' contact with the skin-of-my-neighbour can then be very
> quick. Macneice puts these aspects of the singleton's dilemma very
> aptly: 'An historical sense is essential, which means that we must
> know how to be new as contrasted with repetition — psittacosis — on

the one hand, and with escape from tradition — aphasia — on the other.' He adds both graphically and dramatically: 'We must sit in the seats of our ancestors, i.e., we must turn our ancestors out of them.' As far as man in a group is concerned, whether it be large or small, that is easier said than done (1975: 98-9).

From Turquet's unrivalled exploration of the phenomenological experiences of large groups I want to draw out three points.

First, in a footnote, Turquet, using the *Shorter Oxford English Dictionary*, defines a 'matrix' as 'a place or medium in which something is bred, produced or developed and hence in the sense of a place of origin or growth' (1975: 96). As I understand it, at present, there is a distinction to be made between a matrix and a framed event such as a large group. If you will, matrix holds the potential creativity of a large group and indeed the matrix qualities have yet to be explored experientially or, rather, the tension between the matrix in the mind and the group in the mind.

Second, Turquet has set out some of the dimensions of dislocation available for members of a large group. The theme of dislocation is one that I want to hold on to. Later in the same paper Turquet introduces the neologism 'dissaroy' which is 'a state of complete bewilderment'. He writes (1975: 103):

> 'disarroy' becomes the overwhelming experience, including a picture that the world can never be the same again. The word 'disarroy' is used here not only to describe the actual experience of change, with an inherent notion of disintegration and collapse, but also to indicate the presence of a wish to return to *status quo ante*, with further wishes not to know, never to return and would that he had never been there.

The experience of dissaroy (which I take to be derived from the French word *'désarroi'*) is thus essential for learning in that it is a fulcrum experience from which the individual can tilt himself or herself in various directions for knowing and not knowing.

Third, I think that the large group is a framed event that gives us a glimpse of society as refracted through members and consultant staff at a particular point in time. There are larger public issues than the private struggles of the individuals as they engage with the experience of disarroy. To be sure, a large group can mobilize the topic of 'society' as a defence against the problems of disarroy but, at other times, there can be a real sense of seeing how people are reacting to the larger group in the mind, i.e., society. At present, large groups seem to be characterized by members, or more accurately singletons, having no potentiality for experiencing any faith or belief in the dependability of any grouping that is larger than a face to face one. Hence, large groups become repositories for all that is negative and destructive in order that the individual as singleton can preserve himself or herself in a pre-experience, pristine, narcissistic state. Disarroy is to be avoided. This I can see mirrored in institutions outside conferences, particularly as the environment becomes more uncertain and menacing.

Alongside these points, I want to set a personal experience which occurred in a large group and which caused me to think further in terms of the leitmotivs of this essay. Once, as a large-study-group-taker, I felt that beyond the section of the membership I was looking at I could see a 'black hole'. For me, the darkness of bewilderment and chaos seemed unfathomable; the terror was making me feel nauseous. I had visions of the whole membership and the consultants being sucked into that hole never to reappear. In that moment two lines of a poem were born that became:

> Mind holes in blind space are ours of choice,
> questing neoteric echoes of our voice (Lawrence 1979b).

The pun on 'mined' and 'mind' is obvious but 'neoteric' was used to give the sense of a 'fresh' voice. Why 'echoes'? I was aware at that time that any voice echoes a past of other voices (cf. Turquet 1975: 98–9, already quoted).

What was important, at the time, for me was the coming up against the inaccessibility of experience *per se*. Words came to my mind to fit the experience but, finally, took over and made an experience. The astronomical metaphor became what I believed was the reality of the time. Patterns of thought, perception and 'understanding' – 'memory' in Bion's terms – intervened to frame the senses. And then it is an easy matter to associate mentally at a preconscious level. The experience comes to be named as 'blind space', 'nothingness', of being in the 'abyss', of seeing the 'void'. But in naming what is believed to be the experience, the possibility of knowing what the experience might be in itself is lost. To be sure, I could have expressed much of this in terms of Bion's transformations into O. What I want to hold on to, at this juncture, is the overpowering wish for the ordering of experience, in terms of a metaphor, for example, within the frame of an event. I go so far as to say that there is a rage for order to defend against a sense of annihilation and a fear of disappearing into a black hole; psychosis.

At the same time as I was becoming caught up in the astronomical metaphor I started to have more elaborate fantasies as to what would happen (a) if the large group *en masse* went into the black hole or (b) if the participants in this large group were able to rise from their seats and spill all over the room as a crowd, even a mob; disordered and destructive.

Let me stay with the idea of 'order'. There is increasingly in conferences within framed events a rage for order in terms of memory. Bion once wrote somewhere about the hatred of learning from experience. Just because a working conference exists for the purpose of providing opportunities to study, at first hand, experiences in groups, does not mean to say that the participants (both staff and members) will not be free from the hatred of learning. The hatred I see most clearly as being around discovering or tumbling into the psychotic experiences that Bion first identified.

Pressing this further: in my most disillusioned state I begin to have the suspicion that working conferences can be interpreted as well-rehearsed dramas with the title 'Oedipus Vivat!' How far, at times, are both the staff and members orchestrating the fugue of work group versus basic assumption groups, albeit with variations?

To re-state what, in part, I have already said: have the frames (conferences and their events) with all their potentiality for dislocation, disorder and disarroy that could lead to new learning come to be so potent that they have to be defended against mobilizing, for example, the rage for order? To be sure, the interpretation of resistance is a major pivot that can tip both the members and the staff into new learning.

But, at the same time, I want to hold on to much that is rich and positive in working conferences and try to build on what my predecessors in this kind of venture have discovered and illuminated, even though the capacity to speak with the dead is easily eroded. What is enormously exciting about working conferences and their framed event, such as I am puzzling around, is that, at their very best, they provide what Winnicott called a 'cultural space'. His ideas or formulations on the location of culture experiences make sense in relation to working conferences. His quotation from Rabindranath Tagore is apt: 'On the seashore of endless worlds – children play.' In puzzling around frames and orders I see myself as exploring the seashores of endless worlds and wishing to play with the wonderment of a child, discovering for the first time.

Winnicott's main thesis is so succinctly stated that it deserves to be quoted rather than paraphrased. I quote the first three points:

1. The place where cultural experience is located is in the *potential space* between the individual and the environment (originally the object). The same can be said of playing. Cultural experience begins with creative living first manifested in play.

2. For every individual the use of this space is determined by *life experience* that takes place at the early stages of the individual's existence.

3. From the beginning the baby has maximally intense experiences *in the potential space between subjective object and the object objectively perceived*, between the me-extension and the not-me. This potential space is at the interplay between there being nothing but me and there being objects and phenomena outside omnipotent control (1971: 100, italics in original).

I postulate that group relations working conferences offer individuals a unique potential space in which to be playful and creative between themselves and the environment of the conference. In turn, this experience can be transferred to other interfaces with environments. Working conferences can, of course, only provide a potential space which is analogous to Winnicott's cultural space. But given that members have the opportunity, if they take the authority, to regress in the service of the ego — to experience, as adults, disarroy — within framed and contained time, space and task boundaries of a conference and its events, the possibility of a novel cultural space being evoked and experienced is enhanced.

In the same paper, 'The location of cultural experience', Winnicott goes on to describe the *third area* which is the one between 'the inner or personal psychic reality and with the actual world in which the individual lives' (1971:102–3). Within the framed events of a conference the possibility of rediscovering and remarking experiences in the third area is always possible (cf. Turquet's discussion reported above).

The search for the third area has preoccupied me for a number of years in the course of my professional practice as a consultant at the Tavistock Institute. By this I mean that I am trying to make opportunities for my client and myself to clear a third area for play and cultural experience. In relation to the subject of this essay I am aware how easy it is to have that area made into a desert full of memories and desires, rage for order, and a hatred of learning. How I have tried to struggle with a tradition, but avoiding psittacosis and aphasia, in order to develop some something fresh I shall now try and outline.

Outwith the frame

The leap beyond the existing framed events of working conferences to the interstices or gaps between them is what I now want to explicate. And here I am in difficulties in the role of a writer: on the one hand, I am under an obligation to communicate directly but, on the other hand, I know that the thought processes which led me to explore beyond the frames into a fresh area for me were not strictly logical. My dilemma is well stated by McLuhan and Nevitt:

Beyond *Exposition* for *Exploration*

Civilized, rationally educated people expect and prefer to have problems described and analyzed sequentially. They try to *follow* your argument to a conclusion. They expect the conclusion to be your *point of view*, illustrative of your *values*. In contrast to the method of exposition is the method of exploration. This begins by the admission of ignorance and difficulties. Such statements will tend to be a tentative groping. The blind man's cane picks up the *relation* of things in his environment by the quality of resonance. His tapping tells him what objects are adjacent to his stick. If his stick were *connected* to any of these objects, he would be helpless so far as orientation was concerned. This is always the plight of the logical method. It is useless for exploration. Its very strength makes it irrelevant. 'Proof' of sanity is available only to those discharged from mental institutions (1972: 8, italics in original).

I hold to the idea of exploration of the interstices between the framed events about which I have been puzzling. What resonates in the spaces between them? So I cull a number of ideas from the text so far:

frame, contour, space;
order;
psychotic, heart of darkness;
'We penetrated deeper and deeper into the heart of darkness.
      It was very quiet there . . . ' (Joseph Conrad);
memory, desire, the institutionalization of words;
'I wouldn't be starting from here';
makar;
fugue;
singleton, I., I.M., M.I., I. (Pierre Turquet);

dislocation, disarroy;
matrix = a place or medium in which something is born;
'and live the space of a door that opens and shuts' (Samuel Beckett);
the third area (Donald Winnicott).

To these I add other associations:

making it new
in a land heavy with stones
and each stone has a history (Robin Fulton);
interstice, gap, hiatus, lacuna;
ectopia, from the Greek ἐκτοπος = out of place and, in
    New Testament Greek, τοπος = desert but can also mean
    a person's final resting place where destiny brings him;
counterpoint, contrapuntal.

And bear in mind:

in any cultural field *it is not possible to be original except on a basis
of tradition.* Conversely, no one in the line of cultural contributors
repeats except as a deliberate quotation, and the unforgiveable sin in
the cultural field is plagiarism. The interplay between originality and
the acceptance of tradition as the basis for inventiveness seems to be
just one more example, and a very exciting one, of the interplay
between separateness and union (1971: 99, italics in original).

But also think about:

The visionary artist is the artist of the irrational, the obscure, the
monstrous: his values lie not in order and discipline, but in inspiration,
whether sublime or perverse. His subject matter is not the everyday
world, but the ancient and dangerous archetypes which lie hidden in
the deepest regions of the unconscious. If the danger to the psychological artist[2] is barrenness, sterility, a vitality — destroying discipline,
the danger to the visionary artist is incoherence, or even madness. To
reside absolutely at one or the other pole means at the very least
artistic death: either sanity bought at the price of sterility, or immediate experience of the unconscious at the price of psychosis
(Day 1973: 468).

And:

The spaces between the stones is where the survivors live (Robin Fulton).

At Santinikiten, north of Calcutta in India, is the ashram of Rabindranath Tagore. There can be seen a sufficient number of his pictures to understand his development as an artist. His pictures are of an abstract nature. They arose directly out of his writing. As he corrected his poems by heavily scoring out words, lines and whole passages, he found that the deletions made patterns. These he elaborated subsequently into paintings. What was ground became figure. In much the same way the event I am about to describe arose out of the ground that was figure of working conferences.

Because of the kind of puzzlements which I have indicated in the first part of this essay I had been brooding about an event which would be contrapuntal to other recognized events in a working conference. What I was quite sure about was that the event had to be grounded in the tradition of group relations training associated with the Tavistock Institute. At one and the same time the event had to be within the task, time and territorial boundaries of a conference and be ectopic. It had to be an event that provided opportunities for both members and staff to take authority to be out of their framed, ordered places in the conference life so that they could look at the regular, framed events with fresh wonderment.

My anxieties were (and still continue to be) many: would I be betraying the tradition from which I have derived so much? Would I be in danger of creating an event with insufficient boundaries which would result in the anxieties of both staff and members becoming so high that nothing could be learned? Was I in danger of creating an event which would have untold effects on the working-through of transference and countertransference feelings which are critical for the discovery by members of their authority to interpret? Indeed, would the event be an elaborate system to defend against the staff's anxieties about transference feelings? How far was I caught up in destructive feelings about conferences because of my growing disillusionment about the technicians?

The new event – the Praxis Event – was introduced at a working conference at Gif-sur-Yvette in France in 1978. The title of the conference was 'Exercising Authority for Social Innovation', which was sponsored by the Group Relations Training Programme of the Tavistock Institute of Human Relations and La Fondation Internationale de l'Innovation Sociale, Paris.[3] The conference programme included conference plenaries, a large study group, an institutional event, and the equivalent of review and application groups which were called innovation study groups. The primary task of the conference was:

> to provide participants with opportunities to learn about and interpret their experiences of managing personal and social innovation within the organizational boundaries of the conference.

The French conference, because of its primary task, could allow for a new venture in group relations training. In particular, I wanted an event that would allow different opportunities for managing personal and social innovation than were available within the framed events. There had to be an opportunity for action and practice, i.e., praxis.

With the authority of the staff as collective management I, in the role of director, negotiated a primary task for the praxis event in a plenary session. The negotiation of a primary task was seen as being an essential element of the event because it would not be given as in other events but be worked through in plenary sessions. The criterion which was made explicit was that the primary task of the praxis event had to be congruent with the primary task of the conference. What was set were the time and territorial boundaries of the event.

In the opening plenary of the event the point was made that once a primary task had been negotiated and to which participants could give their authority, the director would give up his role for the period of the event as would staff cease to be management and consultants. During the period the administrators would hold the conference management role. This is no different, in fact, from times in any conference when all the staff are deployed in consultant roles to events. Here the punctilious establishment of boundaries was to create the optimum conditions for containment and dependability in order that members and staff could be free to manage their explorations within the praxis event. Roles within the praxis event arose out of the primary task of the event.

I see little point in describing what took place during that first praxis event. I want to avoid premature institutionalization! My experience has been that each one is different. Now that it has been incorporated into other working conferences, I find, in terms of conference design, that it is better to have the praxis event before the institutional event because what is learned from the former gives a new political dimension to the latter.

Rather I want to give three associations. First, a participant[4] in one praxis event subsequently wrote to me enclosing a quotation from *The Selections from the Prison Notebooks of Antonio Gramsci*:

> The philosophy of praxis is consciousness full of contradictions, in
> which the philosopher himself, understood both individually and as
> an entire social group, not merely grasps the contradictions, but
> posits himself as an element of the contradiction and elevates this
> element to a principle of knowledge and therefore of action.

What I take out of this is the notion that an individual is a social group
in the sense that we each carry in our inner worlds a cluster of imagos
of all our previous relationships and also a version of society in the
mind. In addition, each person has the potentiality and possibly the
experience of a range of roles. Some of these may be contradictory,
e.g., a manager who is concerned about productivity, production and
profit is also a citizen who may have different views about the effect of
some work practices on individuals. Such an individual may also be the
parent of a young school-leaver who may not be able to get employment,
and so on. The contradictions are apparent but are often not available
for scrutiny in everyday life. This is because rarely can a way be found
for doing so. So a praxis event can provide a space where societal puzzlements can be engaged with.

Second, it was within a praxis event that I discovered afresh what I
shall call the Moment. I am aware that others have used this term and
given it their meaning. For me, it is the discovery of an internal space
where one has never explored — it may be between the first and second
skins which Turquet described, but I am not sure. The experience is of
being in internal disarroy and then being able to put together feelings
in a new way, for example something of one's personal history and the
present. It is a moment of internal making and is purely of feeling. It is
the nearest I have come to what I understand to be an epiphany, i.e.,
any moment of great or sudden revelation. My guess is that the praxis
event provides a different kind of framed space and time for personal
and social exploration than other events. This is because it has a short
history to date, is ectopic in the sense that roles are different from other
events in a conference, provides a third area and allows opportunities
to experience a matrix rather than a group as such. Perhaps, the strength
of the praxis event rests in its contrapuntal quality, i.e., being in the
interstice of other events. Such conditions are conducive for self and
social revelation.

Third, for a long time I have been disillusioned with the technical
preoccupations of participants in conferences. At worst, this is a schizoid
type of leadership which is very competent about the Tavistock method,
group dynamics etc. Such leadership takes a long time to fathom because

those in that role are very adept and skilled in interpretations. If this kind of leader is in the membership he or she will be supported by others even though they become victims of the desperate processes which are engendered. Group psychosis is manipulated on such occasions. Such leadership is difficult to interpret because the leaders use interpretation in the service of the defence of their own egos. Hence, I am concerned to find complementary ways of understanding group phenomena to break some of the rituals I pointed to earlier in this essay to get through to dissarroy.

It is therefore through experiences in working conferences of the Tavistock, particularly the large study group and the praxis event, that I have been led to explore a different language to express what I feel groups are about. The praxis event, because it is new, results in one not being prey to memories and desires. In other events it is a conscious act to forget. Hence, privately, I find myself using words such as 'soul' and 'epiphany' to give meaning to experiences.

To conclude: I have tried to set out some of the thoughts that led to a new event within working conferences in the Tavistock (Bion) tradition. Despite my misgivings, I still feel committed to the kind of exploration of the unconscious that working conferences offer. Why? They are one of the few locations in time and space where individuals have a chance to reflect on the connections between private troubles and public issues; the nexus between the individual and society. For me, the experiences of working conferences with their framed events, and now having gone beyond the frame into the praxis event, have offered a glimpse of the roots of creativity of the 'visionary artist' which Jung first described (cf. Day 1973) to enter the heart of darkness.

I end with a seeming paradox: in framing the praxis event, by wresting potential experiences from the interstice between other framed events, I have drawn a contour but, as is known, contours can signify arrest because they involve the acceptance of limits and restraint. But, in fact, as George Eliot observes in the Finale to *Middlemarch*: 'Every limit is a beginning as well as an ending'.

Notes

1 I am grateful to Mrs Eleanore Armstrong of the Adult Department in the Tavistock Clinic who first pointed out this distinction to me.
2 The psychological artist is one who derives his material from 'the sphere of conscious human experience — from the psychic foreground of life' (Day 1973: 467).

3 I am glad to acknowledge the encouragement to try new ideas by, first, Georges Gueron who was then director of Les Conseillers de Synthèse, and Angela Curtis (now Norris) who always in her role of conference administrator gave me space to make forays into the unknown; and, third, to the members and staff who engaged with the conference and the event.
4 Derek Raffaelli, Psychologist, Scottish List D Schools, Edinburgh.

References

Beckett, S. (1961), *Poems in English*, London, Calder & Boyars.
Bennis, W. (1971), 'Beyond Bureaucracy', in I. L. Horowitz and M. S. Strong (ed.), *Sociological Realities*, New York, Harper & Row.
Bion, W. R. (1970), *Attention and Interpretation*, London, Tavistock.
Broadbent, J. (1979), 'Darkness', in W. G. Lawrence (ed.), *Exploring Individual and Organizational Boundaries*, Chichester, Wiley, 193–203.
Day, D. (1973), *Malcolm Lowry*, Oxford University Press.
Fulton, R. (1971), *The Spaces between the Stones*, New York, New Rivers Press.
Grotstein, J. (1981) (ed.), *Do I Dare Disturb the Universe?* New York, Aronson.
Lawrence, W. G. (1977), 'Management development . . . ideals, images and realities', *J. European Industrial Training*, 1, 2: 21–5.
Lawrence, W. G. (1979a) (ed.), *Exploring Individual and Organizational Boundaries*, Chichester, Wiley.
Lawrence, W. G. (1979b), 'Exiles', *Aberdeen University Review*, no. 162.
Lomas, H. D. (1979), 'Institutional transference revisited', *Bull. Menninger Clinic*: 547–51.
McLuhan, M. and Nevitt, B. (1972), *Take Today*, New York, Harcourt Brace Jovanovich.
Menzies Lyth, I. E. P. (1981), 'Bion's contribution to thinking about groups', in Grotstein (1981): 662–6.
Miller, E. J. and Rice, A. K. (1967), *Systems of Organization*, London, Tavistock.
Rice, A. K. (1958), *Productivity and Social Organization*, London, Tavistock, 1970 edn.
Rice, A. K. (1965), *Learning for Leadership*, London, Tavistock.
Turquet, P. M. (1975), 'Threats to identity in the large group', in L. Kreeger (ed.), *The Large Group*, London, Constable: 87–144.
Winnicott, D. W. (1971), *Playing and Reality*, London, Tavistock.

Chapter 16

The problem of context in group-analytic psychotherapy: a clinical illustration and a brief theoretical discussion[1]

Earl Hopper

My purpose here is to discuss certain aspects of the 'problem of context', primarily in order to indicate a distinguishing feature of group-analytic psychotherapy as developed by S. H. Foulkes (1948),[2] namely: the clinical application of the axiom that the nature of the 'human' is social, and of the 'social', human, at all stages of life and at all phases of history. After defining the concept of context, I will state the problem in formal terms, and illustrate it with a brief clinical vignette, which includes my interpretation and its effects. I will also mention certain theoretical aspects of the problem, in particular those which suggest a limitation inherent in the approach of W. R. Bion (1961).

I Introduction

The concept of 'context'

'Context' refers to those parts of a text which precede and/or follow a particular passage, and which are sufficient in number to enable a person to determine the meaning or meanings which the author intended. In the first instance, I would like to draw attention to the etymology of the word 'context'.

The prefix *con-* is related to *cum*, meaning 'together', 'together with', 'in combination' and 'in union', and further, 'altogether', 'completely', and 'intensive' or 'in depth'. It is closely related to such words as 'community', 'communion', and 'common', which is reminiscent of the word 'religion', meaning 'to connect', 'to bring together in entirety', 'to make whole', etc., and connoting 'being bound together through oath' or 'being part of an unaltered whole'.

This line of association should not be surprising, because the stem word 'text' has at least two elementary but interdependent roots. The first, *textus*, means 'tissue' and 'style of a literary work'; later, *textus* was used to refer to the Gospel, precisely as it was written in all its authoritative glory. The second root is *texere*, meaning 'to weave'.

These two sets of connotations are infinitely suggestive, but especially intriguing is the implicit idea (or perhaps metaphor) to the effect that a thread and its properties will always be governed by its location within a larger whole, in this instance a fabric or textile. So, too, is the implication that logically the aetiological chain for any dependent variable will always stop with 'God', who will always be the hypothetical author of any definitive text concerning the Beginning, or the hypothetical weaver who has created the textile. In other words, in all schemes of thought the context of the context will always be some form of the Holy.

It follows by definition that properties of both material and non-material pheonomena are characteristic only of wholes that are located within contexts, which are woven together from their constituent elements. Properties of contexts are, therefore, emergent and irreducible to the properties of any of their elements. With respect to persons, the true Oedipus complex could be seen as an emergent phenomenon; and with respect to social formation, structures of authority or group morale would be in this category.

The meaning of the word 'context' is also related to the meaning of the word 'understand'. In order to understand an event it is necessary to locate it within an abstract category of such events, and then to relate this category to at least one other such category, the existence and qualities of which are less puzzling.

The problem of context

One type of event is a communication. Holding aside a variety of problems in the philosophy of science, especially concerning the topic of hermeneutics, let us consider the phenomenon of transference as an event in communication between two or more people. A 'transference' refers to an unconscious repetition or replication in the present, in a more or less crystallized or fossilized way, of impulse, pain, defence, and internal and external object relationships as they have occurred in the personal past, usually in infancy but including those of childhood and even of adolescence. As such, a transference contains a coded account of its own social and psychological aetiology. 'Theory' offers a set of rules according to which the code of a transference can be deciphered or interpreted, usually by one of the parties within the relationship.

It follows that in order to understand a transference, it must be contextualized, that is, related to other categories of events that are thought by certain people to have a particular relationship to it, a relationship that may be delineated in terms of time and social psychological space. The contextualization of the collective transference of a group, for example to its conductor, is especially difficult. After all, the boundaries of a group are not identical with those of its members, and the principle of apperception leads relentlessly back towards the Beginning and into the Womb. Thus, typically, but somewhat curiously, the contextualization of the collective transference is limited to two categories of events: those which are socially near and comparatively recent in the group's history (which means comparatively late in the life cycles of the group members); and those which are socially distant and pre-historical (which means during the early infancies of the group members, when it is assumed that, in so far as biological constraints predominate, idiosyncratic variation in experience will tend to be minimal, and the content of unconscious fantasy, universal). However, this approach is both too narrow and too shallow, which brings us to what is problematic about the phenomenon of context.

A 'problem' is neither more nor less than a question or a set of questions that is hard to answer, and I would like to ask a few of them. In attempting to contextualize a transference is it possible and is it therapeutically useful to explore a full range of events on the dimensions of time and social psychological space? How far from the so-called 'here and now' should we go? The later phases of life? The structure and function of social institutions, not only now but also in a person's past? Should we take account of events which occurred even before a person was born, and located in another country? (Of course, a transference contains information about what people anticipate and what they may strive to make happen, a point which did not go unnoticed by D. M. Thomas, in *The White Hotel*, but I will not discuss here the notion of precognition, and will limit my enquiry to replication.)

My answer to each of these questions is, on balance, yes, but very much on balance. I do not confine my attempts to contextualize a transference only to the infantile unconscious, but try to explore a fuller range of events on the dimensions of time and social psychological space. In this connection, it is worth recalling Bion's cryptic remark that the 'basic assumption group knows no time', and although he did not quite say so, knows no space (1961).[3] Actually, this is much more sociological than his few statements about social insitutions and society, and about the existence of social facts, and may be the basis for a dynamic social psychology of group processes within their societal context. It offers a point of convergence between the sociological and psycho-analytical points of view, and is reminiscent of the basic approach of Foulkes (1948), as refined by de Maré (1972) and Pines (1978).[4] Certainly, it was the starting point for my own thinking about the application of the problem of context to clinical work.

A brief outline of what I think is my clinical technique

Before turning to a clinical illustration of my tentative but affirmative answer to the questions with which I have defined the problem of context, I would like first to describe a few central aspects of how I think I usually conduct groups who meet for psychotherapy. My groups meet for forty weeks per year, and the sessions last for one and one-half hours. On a few occasions per year I allow them to meet without me, but at the usual time and place. The groups consist of from seven to nine patients, usually four men and five women, ranging from around 25 to 65 years of age, representing a cross-section of neurotic and personality disorders, not including more than one really difficult patient or more than one of a really distinctive type, such as an addict, criminal, a depressive, a paranoid, etc. During the last few years, I have tended to see my group patients individually for at least a few months before they enter the group; this is in keeping with the evidence concerning favourable outcomes, but I work this way primarily because I enjoy it. By and large the patients are a cross-section of the urban and suburban middle class, with a slight bias towards the professional upper middle class and the helping professions in general. Jews are not over-represented, as they are in most studies of the patient population in the urban areas of North America. The average length of stay is about four to five years, which seems to surprise people who do not know much about group-analytic therapy, including our most severe critics within psychiatry and psycho-analysis, who assume that patients stay in treatment for a matter of months, if not a few weekends. In any case, I have what we call 'slow-open' groups; they go on as long as I do, but new patients come in when old patients go out.

Ordinarily, I speak after about twenty to thirty minutes, but I have no general rule. Sometimes I start the group, and sometimes I remain silent all the way through. Usually, I try to sense the common group tension (Ezriel 1950 and 1959), which almost always involves basic assumption patterns (Bion 1961), and then to interpret this collective transference from the group to the object or objects in question – usually, but not always, to myself. Afterwards I try to help the group discover what each person has contributed to it as well as how each is affected by it. However, and this is important because it distinguishes the way I work from the approach of those who follow what they take to be the conventional 'Tavi' model, I may talk first to a particular person or to the partners in a sub-group, depending on how they may be dramatizing or personifying the general theme. I often talk to individual members of the group, not only because they have come to me as patients and not as students of group dynamics, but also because I perceive them in terms of their location within the group matrix, so that talking to one person is not necessarily in conflict or at odds with the concern of the group as a whole (Foulkes 1948). I also try to be alert to the recapitulations within the group process of each individual's early family life (Schindler 1951).

Several groups may go by before we (the group and I) have made anything like a comprehensive interpretation, and there are always an indefinite number of loose ends. Although I am obliged to see my patients essentially as patients, I do regard the group, and even use the group, as my co-conductors. I value their capacity collectively to be holding and containing.

I rarely go beyond interpretations and 'interpretative actions'. I assume that this encourages the development of 'psychic muscle', as well as the capacity for reflection. Although I break rules more often than I abide by them, I try to communicate in an intelligent and organized way. I think of myself as a fairly spontaneous and warm type of therapist.

I am not particularly concerned about my own transparency. Patients see what they see, and they make whatever use of it they wish and can. However, I do not favour self-disclosure. At certain times 'judicious self-disclosure' may be necessary and helpful, but usually it is a therapeutic burden.

In my attempts to understand what my patients are asking me to understand, I allow myself to be guided by certain aspects of counter-transference, which can be used as though it were litmus paper in a chemistry experiment. Although one's counter-transference can be a source of difficulty, it may also be a source of information about the transference – an issue to be discussed further below.

II A brief clinical vignette

This session is from a group who were meeting in my consulting room at home one autumn in the early 1980s. In its conscious and unconscious themes, the material is fairly typical, not only of this particular group but also from my other groups.[5] It is necessary to trade the accuracy of a recording for the communication of a mood, and to remember that this passage is taken out of context.

1. I took a seat, the group continued to complain about the weather, it was cold and damp — 'It's not the cold, but the damp' — and the rain beat against the window panes of my consulting room, which is in the attic of my house. Someone said, 'Still, mustn't complain, it could be worse.' The group drew closer together around our centre table. I felt that their sense of solidarity increased — not unlike what happens at the beginning of a 'ghost story' or at the beginning of any ritualized story-telling event. It is not for nothing that so many stories start with storms.

I thought to myself that nothing changes: 'It's not the cold, but the damp', and 'Still, mustn't complain' were the first words I heard when I came to England over twenty years ago. The weather in the late autumn was seldom different — for that matter the summer isn't either — and rarely had I heard a group discuss the weather, although they probably do talk about it while waiting for me to come into the room. So, my antennae went out immediately.

2. The discussion shifted to a critical appreciation of my house and consulting suite. They remarked upon its late Victorian style — 'or is it Edwardian?', the way I had converted it, especially the alterations to the staircase, the general mixture of old and new (brick, pine and glass combined with high ceilings, old mouldings, large architraves, etc.) and, turning to the room itself, the colours ('buttermilk, oatmeal, and earth clay', as one patient put it, 'colours of trendy architects and feminist earth-mothers'), the two austere double-glazed windows set into the eaves, and the 'director's chairs' from Habitat (which members of the group set up for themselves when they come in after the other seats are taken). They neglected to mention those items of furniture which pertain to my work as a psycho-analyst: the two comfortable chairs, for which there is some competition, and the couch, which comes apart into three seats for group work.

I was feeling very uncomfortable, too closely examined, as though they were inspecting my private parts and parts of my private life. After all, they had been coming to my house once a week for eight years. Why suddenly should they have become so preoccupied, ostensibly with my room? Why should they have cut themselves off from our history?

3. They returned to the weather outside, reassuring themselves that it was dry and warm inside. A woman said that the staircase on the side of the house, which they had to use in order to reach the suite, was too exposed — cold, wet, windy, dark, not at all safe, and she wondered why I had not enclosed it, since they had been complaining about it for as long as she had been in the group (over five years). Another said that this was obviously because my family and I didn't have to use it (which was probably correct). The group's Non-Complainer said, 'Still, it's nice inside.'

I was thinking about my house as a symbol of Mother's Body, my own body and of my own mind; about passages into and out of Mother's Body as well as my own; how often one overlooks the importance of the material surroundings of a group — perhaps as one kind of transitional object; how early the Oedipus complex really begins; how ubiquitous and deep are the problems concerning the boundaries between the inside and outside of persons and groups, etc. I was also reminded of a lunch-time discussion I was having a few days previously at the London School of Economics about the history and scope of the literary usage of a ship as a symbol for Society and for the State.

4. The group came back to the consulting room. An older man spoke about the cost of housing and conversion work nowadays, and supposed that the Habitat chairs must have cost about £5 when I bought them, whereas they were now closer to £20. Another man said that everything goes up but his income. This remark was met with silence (partly, I suspected, because he is impotent; and I detected what the author of *Brideshead Revisited* might have called a 'bat-squeak' of anxiety). He then apologized for messing up the carpet with his wet, muddy shoes (which he did all the time anyway, for he really was an archetype of a Mess), and the group echoed that the carpet would be dry by the time the group was over, and the mud could be swept up. Another man asked me what did I expect, for surely this sort of damage was what the estate agents would call 'normal wear and tear', and was probably taken into account in my fees, which was why I put them up every year.

I was feeling annoyed at the mess, and mildly guilty about the fees for 'psychic-conversion work' — but I was also thinking that I was pleased with my house and consulting room. I was tempted to interpret certain aspects of their desires to intrude and to spoil in connection with their envy of me and of my relationships with my family and my 'house', combined with their fear and feelings of guilt, and to show them how this was being manifested in various forms of splitting and projection. However, since I was vaguely aware that I wanted to punish them rather than understand them, I remained silent until I could sort my responses. I have learned that in this frame of mind it is best not to trot out the death rattles of correct interpretations, but to be silent in order to give myself space for reflection — not to defend myself from my patients by putting some theory between us. For example, I did not want to fall back on a 'ritualized' interpretation which involved, for example, feelings of envy, fight-flight patterns, preoccupations with 'Mother's Body', smearing attacks with faeces, etc.

5. The comment about fees prompted a young artist (who had never taken a conventional job in his life, because he had inherited several houses in London and an estate in the country, and of whom in this respect I was myself envious) to offer to paint a mural on my wall (which was in part a continuation of the desire to smear my walls with faeces), but he thought that I was not the kind of person to spend money on art — at least not from an unknown artist. This was followed by a phase of pairing between two young females and him, and between the two females. The communication concerned the problems of careers and marriage nowadays, and their jealousy and envy of his young, anorexic wife who is also from an extremely wealthy family.

Eventually, one of the two women said to me in a flirtatious way that my wife probably worked in the media — but didn't really have to — and that she was undoubtedly a kept woman — which the patient wouldn't mind being herself except that not only did she need a wife rather than a husband, but she also wanted a baby. There is probably at least one such woman in all the groups that we conduct nowadays; she sounded as though she were taken from the notes for Margaret Drabble's next book. In any case, I had to struggle against my desire to become embroiled with her, a type for whom I am an easy mark. I caught myself, remained silent, and realized that I had begun to feel a bit bored, almost a little depressed — although 'depressed' is too strong a term. I sensed that I wanted this flirtatious female to excite me. I was aware that the artist's insult had a grain of truth in it, and that I was hurt by it, but that this alone would not account for my feelings. I continued to monitor my feelings, but I was somewhat perplexed, and a little disturbed. I remained silent, not because I had nothing to say, but because I could not identify the *mood* of the group.

6. My silence was rewarded. The painter commented that Prince Charles and Lady Di were going to live near his house in the country. Someone commented that Lady Di was pregnant, and another said that

her tits would be enormous. The older woman said that Charles was very nice, more like the Queen, whereas Anne was a real cow, more like her father. Several joined in to say how marvellous the wedding was, and one said that she had heard that even the psycho-analysts had watched it on the telly in Helsinki last summer (she was right). The group began to discuss the pros and cons of royalty: the painter felt that although it cost the taxpayers quite a lot, it was one way to maintain these old country houses; others were concerned with snobbery, and felt that the funds for the Royal Family were being 'sucked right out of their pockets'.

Intellectually, I could follow the themes of gender confusion, a preoccupation with my personal and family life, especially during the summer break, my family and the Royal Family and my fees and taxes, not to mention the basic assumption of pairing projected into the aristocracy, sexuality as a manic defence against depression, etc. In fact, I was tempted to call attention to their depression, but I decided to contain their projections for a while longer, mainly because I did not know how to account for their intensity. Also, I had begun to feel somewhat sluggish. I thought to myself that Bion would turn out to be right in all respects, that I had nothing of my own to offer, and that I was out of the group — I was uncertain whether I was being kept out or just felt out of it. I also felt lonely and isolated.

7. After a very brief silence, a girl with the same name as a young female member of the Royal Family, who is usually silent and self-contained, began to cry. (Everyone seemed surprised but me; after all, they had been laughing and pairing in a manic way while I was feeling sad.) Let us call her Elizabeth. She had learned that the house in which she and her husband and daughter of two had their small flat was riddled with wet rot and dry rot and God knows what. The place was virtually diseased. The wet rot was mainly in the basement flats and in the joists below the ground floor flats, and the dry rot ran up one wall all the way to the roof timbers, and her flat had both. The insurance wouldn't cover it. Given the complex pattern of ownership among the freeholder, the leaseholder, several sub-tenants, the banks and the building societies who held long-term mortgages — it was a real mess. She and her husband would have to go further into debt and borrow from her parents, who were retired and whose savings had not kept pace with inflation, and in any case they needed their savings because her mother's cancer was worse, and their expenses were greater. She and her husband agreed to negotiate with the freeholders and insurance company on behalf of all the tenants, *gratis*. When pressed about why, she said that it was because

they didn't trust anyone else to do it, and they couldn't afford to pay anyone. She added that it might even lead to paid work; she didn't want to be a typist, her husband refused to drive a mini-cab, and they didn't want to emigrate.

The group knew that Elizabeth's husband had lost his job a year ago, and had set up a small financial services company that he operated from this flat, which was prohibited by their lease. She worked as a part-time secretary for him, but before she became pregnant she was about to become a stockbroker.

I was aware that I was being asked to provide psychotherapy free of charge, but I was fairly certain that the group were not more than preconscious of this. I was also aware that the group continued to be preoccupied with 'houses', and the problem of gender identity. Elizabeth was caught up in a defensive identification with me. Clearly, she needed some personal attention, but I waited to see if someone in the group would give it to her.

The group were moved by her desperate situation, and through their gestures and other noises of involvement and understanding, they gave the impression that they could empathize with it. She went on to say that the freehold was owned by Chasidic Jews through a maze of interlocking companies, and that they were being distinctly unhelpful. They were prepared to buy back the leases at 'current valuation' (which must have been at about a quarter of their cost). Several flats were owned by rich Arabs who used them to house their servants, and they were hard to contact. One flat was owned by a nice Iranian couple who had got out a few years ago, and who had put all their savings into their flat. The other English couples were also broke, and in one case the husband had just lost his job.

I began to feel drowsy, which usually means that I am defending myself against the experience of being hated by people who are not fully aware of their feelings, and against my desire to confront and attack in response to my own hurt and, I suppose, fear. I was unable to concentrate on the details of how her life seemed to be collapsing around her, and realized that the group seemed more compassionate than I. They began to share similar experiences with Elizabeth. This is an example of how a group can function as a co-therapist, but in retrospect I believe that it was primarily a continuation of their attempts to make me feel excluded while at the same time to make themselves feel that they had something of great, exclusive value, an issue to which I will return.

8. In our field details are everything, but it is necessary now to condense this report. In the ensuing discussion, I noticed three related

themes, the first of which was the malady of the building itself. An entire house could be eaten away by rot. From the inside. You wouldn't even know that it was there until the house fell down. Timber could be turned to fungus. Like a dried-up leaf in which only a few stems held it all together. A debate developed about the origins of rot: whether wet rot comes before dry rot, or vice versa; was it best to keep it under control and live with it? Or would it be better to tear the whole thing down and start again, which would be painful in the short run, but better in the long run. It was necessary first to stop all the leaks (from the roof, from the plumbing, rising damp, penetrating damp, etc.), but 'dry' was not enough, 'well-ventilated' was also important. Be careful about modern building materials — they do not breathe.

I was aware that the group were concerned with the design faults of the female body. They were also deeply affected by what they imagined was the distintegration of the body of Elizabeth's mother. Also apparent were the problems of gender identity and its connection with Elizabeth's marriage to a man who was perceived as 'wet'.

The second theme concerned the type of people involved. Wasn't it ironic about the Arabs and the Jews? The Arabs were all over London. But the Jews had in fact survived. They owned all the property. They always came off best. Typical. Also the architects and lawyers. They always get their fees. Social parasites and prostitutes living off the misery of ordinary people. The group knew that I had been working with survivors of social trauma, and had been involved in bringing the Survivor Syndrome to public attention. It was reasonable to suppose that the group believed that I was a Jew. I had become familar with the apparently universal usage of 'Jew' as a highly condensed symbol of feminity and perversion in men.

The third theme was that things were not what they used to be. It was impossible to trust anyone in London today. Chasidic Jews were frightening in their black clothes and hats, and they ought to try harder to fit in. If they wanted to live in England then they ought to act like English people. Someone remarked on the hairstyle of Chasidic Jews.

I sensed that I was being asked to explain this custom, but I remained impassive. I thought that this last remark might, at the very least, have been a veiled reference to my own change of hairstyle a few months ago from long to very short. The interrelatedness of these last few themes was striking, in a way that ordinarily I find intellectually stimulating.

At this point I intervened. However, before I report what I said, I would like to write more about what I was feeling and about how I used this knowledge in order to formulate a particular interpretation of the group's collective transference to me.

III An interlude: reflections upon technique and theory

The session was almost over. I was still silent. I said to myself that although silence was not always rewarded, it was seldom wrong or destructive, and that on such an occasion self-containment was especially important. This gave me space for reflection.

I had considered various interpretations concerning sexual and aggressive impulses and fantasies, paranoid-schizoid and depressive anxieties, personal and collective defences – including the three basic assumption patterns and combinations of them, etc. I had discarded them, not because they would have been incorrect, but because somehow they would have been restrictive rather than enabling; they might even have been collusive. I decided that the group had been asking me to understand them; I felt the strong pull to reassure them that I did. After all, this was group-*analytic* therapy. It occurred to me that even this was a subtle defence on my part, and that it was probably stopping me from really understanding.

I tried, therefore, to review what I had been feeling rather than thinking. As the collective transference of the group towards me developed, I felt anxious, somewhat de-personalized, excluded, lonely, isolated and a bit drowsy – more-or-less in that order. Specifically, I had come to feel in my counter-transference that the members of the group were full, that I was empty, and that I was being kept out of their lives, relationships, and bountiful stores of all good things. In other words, I had come to be envious of the group, especially of their sense of cohesion and exclusiveness, based partly on their sense of being English and of belonging to England. I had a sense of myself as an American Jew who only *lived* in England, and as a sociologist who had subsequently become a psycho-therapist, group-analyst, and most recently a psycho-analyst, but who had not become a 'Doctor.'[6]

Yet, I was familiar with these feelings of an outsider, a marginal man. They are the product of my early life experiences, and of a mixture of old and new experiences in the sense that I remain influenced by the old and on occasions am prone to provoke the new. In any case, I felt that I had come to terms with these matters, at least more than my personal responses in this session would suggest. Whatever I might think and feel in my personal life, I did not feel this way 'usually' and 'really' towards this group of patients.

I concluded that my counter-transference was not primarily pathological but an important source of data concerning the nature of the collective transference. Whether or not I was feeling envious of the group on my own behalf, I was holding envious feelings that the members of the group had unconsciously denied, split-off, and projected into me. They had succeeded in making me feel towards them what they had been feeling towards me.

I would like now to discuss certain aspects of envy, and to make explicit certain of my beliefs. First of all, feelings of envy are always painful. They involve a sense of emptiness and the loss of all sense of value. They diminish the capacity to hope and be hopeful. However, as in the case for all feelings, the object of envy should be distinguished from its aims, defences, origins and functions:

1. In this instance, I was the *object* of the group's envious feelings, as were my possessions, ranging from the group itself to aspects of my body, personality and situation. Of course, people may not be fully conscious of the objects of their feelings, and their objects may be merely the last in a long series of objects which are associated unconsciously over time and space. For example, the group were not aware that they were feeling envious of me and my possessions, and that they were re-living earlier feelings (which they may have continued to feel) towards the members of their families of orientation (not to mention still earlier part objects).

2. Their *aim* was to spoil the pleasure, power, and security which I was perceived to be deriving from the possessions and qualities that they were attributing to me.[7]

3. Their main *defence* was projective identification, its intensity having been amplified because it had been used collectively. No defence is really efficient, but with respect to envy, projective identification both facilitates its aim, and offers a further degree of relief from the pain involved. The object is spoiled by evoking the same feelings which prompted the defence, thereby making the object less enviable; at the same time, parts of the self are disavowed or disowned, and unwanted feelings are evacuated. An attempt is also made to communicate and to ask for understanding, especially concerning those anxieties which are linked to envy both developmentally and aetiologically.[8]

4. Although envy appears in early infancy, its aetiological *origins* are subject to debate. Is it the purest manifestation of the death instinct, and, in turn, does it evoke the first mental representation? Is it rooted

within the social psychology of the mother–infant relationship which is itself part of a larger social and cultural network? If determined by both instinctual *and* environmental factors, what weight should be assigned to each, and what is the nature of their inter-action? Is it useful to distinguish actual envy from potential envy from so-called predispositions towards envy? Is it important to consider circumstances which characterize later phases of life-trajectories? Do factors which account for the origins of envy differ from those which contribute to its maintenance, and with respect to the latter, might such factors vary over time? It is impossible to answer such questions here, but they indicate the scope and complexity of this issue (Hopper 1981 and 1982a).

5. Preoccupation with the origins of envy detracts from a consideration of its *functions*, especially those which are benign. Since envy involves pain, rage and the desire to spoil, it is difficult to imagine that it might function in the service of maturation and growth. For example, envy might be essential for the development of the capacity for competition, rivalry, self-determination and autonomy, all of which are important for the fulfilment of a variety of achievement orientations, especially with respect to goals associated with a society's system of stratification. Envy might serve as a defence against the anxiety inherent in feelings of personal and social powerlessness or helplessness, aphanisis or annihilation anxiety, confusion and other forms of 'nameless dread'; it helps to shift attention from such feelings themselves to their source, and from their source within physical sensations to one within the external world. As such, it might stimulate the desire to understand, to master and even to change the external world. After all, the desire to 'change the world' may be essential for the survival of the species, and since it may sometimes be necessary to be destructive in order to be constructive, it is wrong to assess envy in terms of the value that particular interest groups assign to its objects.

I would now like to make explicit several aspects of the above considerations, but these are more a matter of personal opinion than of clinical fact or theory. I *believe* that in so far as a therapist is able to understand and to convey that a meaningful communication has in fact occurred between his patient(s) and himself, it is possible to break vicious and malign circles of internal and external relationships of a certain kind, especially those involving envious retaliation, and to establish a sense of safety sufficient to permit self-containment, reflection, and, ultimately, more effective action. However, this is especially difficult when feelings such as envy have been communicated through projective identification, and interpretations of a transference that has been made manifest in this way may easily become persecuting rather than helpful.

Thus, it is reasonable to wonder how I had been able to conclude with confidence that the feelings that I experienced within my counter-transference were not primarily my 'own', but the denied, split-off and projected feelings of my patients? In other words, how could I have been sure that I was not prejudiced, not to say 'paranoid', or at any rate not more so than usual? It is impossible to answer such questions here, but, basically, I had to trust my own *trained* and *experienced* intuition. After all, projective identification is based upon processes which can be used in the service of empathy, without which it would be impossible to do ana-lytical work. It will always be difficult to distinguish certain types of transference from approximately accurate perceptions, and extremely difficult to distinguish certain types of counter-transference which facili-tate communication from those which impede it. Communications of this sort will always involve complex processes of reciprocity and comple-mentarity — of asymmetrical mutuality, and it will always be impossible to know with certainty where projective identification ends and intro-jective identification begins. Psychic reality is always inter-personal, and, thus, the truth of statements about psychic facts is always negotiable. In other words, the 'politics' of knowledge in the human sciences are inevitable, especially at this very basic level of perception, definition and construction of psychic and social facts concerning an interpersonal relationship in which the participants are also the negotiants.[9]

An interpretation, which is one type of explanation or hypothesis, is always part of a larger theory, which will always involve assumptions and various other untestable axioms. Thus, interpretations always have moral and political implications, especially when they concern elemental feelings which occur early on in life, and which raise questions concern-ing the boundaries of physical, social and psychological realms. Interpret-ations of these phenomena will always be controversial, and will always require acts of faith to the tenets of one school of thought rather than another. For example, those which emphasize instinctual origins rather than social facts imply that 'human nature' cannot be changed, and that social institutions cannot be changed because they are based on human nature. Thus, the existing distributions of economic status and political power, whether within a society or a particular organization, are always seen as natural, especially because they are correlated inevitably with age, sex, and other ascribed characteristics, such as 'natural talent'. It follows from this point of view that whereas expressions of discontent are rooted in pathology, attempts to maintain the existing order are based on health.

In contrast, it could be argued that such explanations are nothing more than heuristic devices for the closure of theoretical systems, for the neutralization of recalcitrance. Theories of instincts do not explain phenomena.[10] They merely rename them. They turn us away from wondering about object relations throughout life, and lead us back to the so-called environmental constraints of the intra-uterine world, and, ultimately, to the zygote. Where will this end? Is the density of cilia in the Fallopian Tubes more relevant than the structure of the education system? Why not explore more fully the implications of Freud's ironic truism that out of this world people do not fall? For example, with respect to feelings of envy, surely it is as important to consider the effects of a mother's ability and capacity to provide good-enough-mothering, and the constraints upon her of the stratification system of an industrial society, as it is to cite the effects of the so-called 'death instinct'. Her child may be as helpless in the face of social constraints as biological ones, but social arrangements are not made in heaven.

Clearly, I am making a plea for the development of a more sociologically informed theory of object relations, one which requires an inter-personal model of the mind and a recognition of social facts. Organisms, persons and groups are not the same order of phenomena. Statements about one do not necessarily apply to the others, although they must be consistent. Psychic facts presuppose the prior and simultaneous existence of social facts as well as of organic facts. In other words, organisms, persons and groups must be viewed as open systems. This means that the personalities of the members of a group are elements of the context of a group, while at the same time a group itself is part of the context of the personalities of its members. It also means that the structure and process of a group express hologramatically the configurations of its societal context. Although basic personality pattern and character structure may be established during infancy, important elements of intra-personal and inter-personal functioning continue to emerge and to develop throughout life, which is governed by both the structure of the organism and the structure of the society. It would be impossible to derive this perspective from the Platonist epistemology which Bion acquired on his journey into the Cave, where many of his disciples remain, and thereby risk the entombment of group psychotherapy — not to mention psycho-analysis itself.

To return to my main theme: I wondered whether an attempt to clarify the group's envious hatred and their defensive projective identifications should be followed by a statement that connected their collective transference with those events which are supposed to be the original source of envy and potential envy within us all? Or, that they were using their envy as a defence against other feelings that were even more painful, such as helplessness, and, thus, in the service of passivity and inactivity with regard to their attempts to understand and even to change the sources of these feelings within their contemporary worlds? In other words, I asked myself specific forms of the more general questions with which I defined initially the problem of context. In answer, *on this occasion*, as a matter of judgment and emphasis, I would contextualize the collective transference in terms of the 'far-away-there' and 'now', and in terms of the 'far-away-there' and 'then'. More precisely, I would focus upon the unconscious effects of social facts that operated during the infancies of these patients and during their daily lives as adults.

IV The clinical vignette continued: the interpretation

Finally, I broke my silence. Unfortunately, I made an interpretative speech. However, I would not want this mistake, which was based on my anxiety, to overshadow the essence of the matter, namely, a particular contextualization, not a particular aspect of technique.

I said that to feel helpless when one is helpless is not necessarily a bad thing.[11] In fact, it may be the first step towards finding a good, constructuve and realistic solution. If you can tolerate the anxiety of it all, you may have some time to think, and you may be able to avoid making things worse.

Yet, I went on, I suspect that you may not be fully aware of what is really making you feel so helpless. Most of you know that you will be able to cope with dry rot and wet rot and all the difficulties that go along with it, and I suspect that most of you have been hearing what has been said in terms of disturbing desires and fears about everything that comes to your mind in connection with such words as 'wet' and 'dry', feelings which may have already begun to give us some trouble when you were talking about the rain and the mud, the painting, the Royal Family and the Royal Baby, husbands and wives, males and females, etc., and I guess that you are almost aware of what this has to do with me and us here! But many of you have been denying (the defence) how frightened, helpless, and confused you feel (the feeling of pain against which they were trying to defend themselves) about the state of the nation, and in particular about the battles between the 'wets' and the 'drys' in Mrs Thatcher's cabinet (a source in the 'there' and 'now' of the painful feelings).[12]

I will go even further, I continued. Some of you may be feeling something like what the Germans felt in the 1930s, when — like now — everything was so topsy-turvy, and nobody knew who was who. These conditions make your feelings of fear, helplessness, and confusion even worse, but they may also be leading you to deal with these feelings by looking for scapegoats (in this instance scapegoating is a form of instrumental adjustment to the painful feelings and to the sources of the feelings).[13] You are very ready to blame Jews, professionals, and so on, including me — and maybe even especially me — an American Jewish professional who you think will be safe from all this because you think I have two jobs as well as two countries. In other words, you are scapegoating me because you envy me, and you envy me because you think I am free from the painful feelings of helplessness that many of you are experiencing as a result of social forces which seem to you to be beyond your control, in the same way that you tend to scapegoat Jews and others whom you also envy — outside the group — and for the same reasons. We seem to be recreating before our very eyes the same sort of problems that are going on in our society. And they are not so different from what has happened at other times and at other places.

Following a brief silence, I went on to say that it was curious that although the group knew that I would understand their feelings about this type of thing, they seemed to feel too ashamed to talk about them openly, almost as though they had fallen into a state of 'group disgrace' (Weber 1947). I said that this may have had something to do with their fear that if they lost their jobs they would not be able to afford my fees, and that they would lose their contact with me and the group. Although many had owed me money in the past, it seemed that they had become reluctant to discuss this openly with me now. I suggested that perhaps they felt that I would go back to America soon, and reject them, but also that I was responsible for their economic insecurity (although in fact every one of the patients in this group was better off economically than they were when they started treatment — as I have often observed to be the case).

Finally, by way of concluding my interpretative lecture (I emphasize again that this was very poor technique) I said that precisely because all this is so painful and confusing, you would like to throw me off the scent. You would like me to lose my sense of smell. You want me to direct your attention to the *infantile* origins of your envious feelings, the ones against which most of you are fairly well defended at this very moment. You know so much about psycho-analysis nowadays that you want to explain everything away in terms of your mothers and fathers when you were babies. Tits, willies, bums and pooh-poohs! You don't really want to go where it's hottest and smelliest tonight. But if we allow ourselves to be seduced in this way, we would make a mockery out of what we have learned from psycho-analysis.

V The aftermath of this interpretative intervention

Following my intervention the group was silent. I found myself thinking that they were probably feeling chastised by my overly long and somewhat fervent comments. Yet, I also sensed that their silence was thoughtful. They seemed to be using the psychic space which my boundary-maintaining (both mine and theirs) intervention had helped to create in order to reflect upon the many implications and meanings of what had transpired.

During the silence I found myself thinking about a public lecture that I had attended recently at the Tavistock Clinic. It was one of a series on the application of psycho-analytical ideas to community issues. The speaker suggested that young black men in Brixton were unable to trust older white men in positions of authority because they had failed to work through the anxieties inherent in the paranoid-schizoid position, and that they were poor and unemployed because they were unable to make healthy introjections of the opportunities available, or in other words, that an unemployment rate in excess of 30 per cent over a decade was due to the experience which the males (but apparently not the females) had at '*the* breast' during their first few months of life. In the discussion, I said (or hope that I said) that unless we can acknowledge the reality of the helplessness that confronts people, we will be unable to help them filter out their accurate perceptions of reality from their fantastic distortions of it; unless we can acknowledge our own feelings of guilt, we will be unable to help our patients find the most effective and efficient forms of instrumental adjustment available to them; and that unless we can help them endure the pain inherent in feeling help-less, we may have to accept that paranoid fantasies and their attendant consequences are, inevitably, the only *defensive* solution available to them. To explain poverty and unemployment primarily in terms of the character traits of the poor and the unemployed is insulting and pre-sumptuous. It makes a mockery out of what we have learned from psycho-analysis, and it ignores what we have learned from sociology about how social facts affect psychic processes, and vice versa. One does not have to be a political activist to believe that psychotherapists ought to learn something about the nature of social processes, and to try to understand how our patients are constrained by social events. My remarks were met with silence and hostile embarrassment.

In retrospect, this event may account in part for my having approached my group's communications in the way I did. It may also help to explain why I reacted in the way I have described, and why I spoke for so long – so long that the session had to stop soon after I did. However, the group took up my interpretation in depth and in detail during the next couple of months. The material which followed was characterized by a mixture of themes, but they were preoccupied with issues concerning sexual perversion, the perversion of power, and the social psychology of envy, and, in this connection, with the meaning attributed to 'Jew' and 'Jewishness'. In my experience, this combination is not unusual, but it is often easier for an English group to talk about their sexual perversions and even their most bizarre masturbation fantasies than about the occupations of their fathers or where they went to school. In fact, if a conductor does not consider such matters more or less in the beginning, a group can go on for a very long time without ever knowing what its members do for a living. Why this should be so is a topic in itself, but it offers another example of the unconscious effects of social facts, which are denied.

Later that evening, while I was dictating my notes about the group process and the contributions of the various patients to it, I found myself ruminating that given the impossibility of ever giving a so-called 'complete interpretation', would it have been better to have gone directly to the usual 'there' and 'then' origins of envy, rather than to the aetiology that I had chosen, or, in other words, whether giving emphasis to the infantile origins of their feelings would have been less defensive and more helpful than looking at the social constraints inherent in their adult lives? I am still uncertain about the answers to this question, and I am still without rules concerning interpretative contextualizations of the transference. More importantly, I continue to wonder if I gave Elizabeth enough personal attention. Actually, I know that I did not, and that in a group I could not, and I worry about this feature of all forms of group psychotherapy.

Notes

1 More cryptic, even ambiguous versions of this article have been published previously (Hopper 1982a and 1984).
2 The use of 'analysis' or 'group-analysis' or 'group-analytic psycho-

therapy' or 'group-analytic therapy' is often a matter of the politics
and sociology of the profession, and not a theoretical or technical
problem. Many in the helping professions need to emphasize 'analysis'
in order to assert their power over those who are not psycho-analysts
or to assert some kind of identity for themselves within a jungle of
confusing professional labels. However, when compared to psycho-
analysis proper, group analysis is 'therapy', especially when practised
by those who do not have a psycho-analytic perspective; yet, when
compared to encounter groups and such like, it is much more akin to
'analysis'.

3 This remark is somewhat typical of Bion in that after countless
hours of reflection I am still not certain whether it is banal or an
insight of genius. Many in London have responded to his utterances
as though they are from a Buddha, thereby underestimating their
own creative insights as readers of his text. In this, he is not dissimilar
to Foulkes, whose work on the 'matrix' has had the same effects.
Perhaps this is an aspect of a kind of genius in our profession.

4 Although this is not a theoretical paper, it is worth calling attention
in this connection to the 'collective unconscious' and the 'social
unconscious', both highly ambiguous but perhaps overly neglected
concepts. Modern London Jungians have begun to rework Jung's
weird concept of the 'collective unconscious' with its foundations in
phylogenesis, the inheritance of ascribed characteristics, and such
notions as the 'consciousness of race' (and it is unfortunate that
space does not permit a further discussion of such topics as the
philogenetic aspects of the source and development of the 'super-ego'
according to classical Freudian thought) – all of which were, of
course, entirely consistent with some of Freud's central themes
(Zinkin 1979). In so doing, they have come close to what Fromm
meant by the 'social unconscious' (Fromm 1970 and 1980). Although
Foulkes was interested in the clinical application of these notions,
he was unable to transcend the ambiguities inherent in them. It
would be helpful, therefore, to differentiate at least three aspects of
the social unconscious: that the impulses and attendant fantasies of
which people are likely to be unconscious are governed by cultural
beliefs, values and norms; that as a result, specifically, of their fear
of feelings of isolation, shame and helplessness, people are likely to
become, and to remain, unconscious of those social arrangements
which govern their power to control their own and other people's
life chances; and that societies and their constituent social groupings
have ways of ensuring that people remain unaware of their non-
conscious ones. However, it would be misleading to use the term
'mechanism of defence' to refer to social processes; for example,
although the institution of education is an important agency of
socialization, it should not be regarded as a society's 'mechanism
of defence' any more than as an ego-based creative activity, which is
precisely why it is so misleading to think about groups as though
they were persons.

5 Typicality and topicality are always danger signals, but I am satisfied

that in this instance I was not looking a gift horse in the mouth — except in so far as the group wanted to help me prepare this article. Material which seems typical and topical may alert one to the unconscious constraints of social facts, but it may indicate that one is eliciting the material.

6 I suppose that even a Doctor is not a 'Doctor', and certainly a PhD does not entitle one to be a 'Doctor'. One day I shall ask my mother what a 'Doctor' is, but I suspect that not even by a 'Doctor' would a Doctor be a 'Doctor'.

7 It is worth noting that I was in fact deriving these goods from these possessions and qualities, but not to the extent believed. I was better off than some of them, but worse off than others.

8 'Projective identification' is, of course, one of the cornerstones of modern Kleinian Theory, a judicious review of which can be found in Spillius (1983), who locates Bion within this development.

9 The only justification for the institutionalized arrogance of those psycho-analysts who work only on the basis of projective identification, and who neglect the problem of their own introjective identification, is that if they were not always right they would have to become their patients' patients.

10 Closed ideologies based on simplistic theories of instincts are especially noxious and self-defeating when they characterize forms of psychoanalysis and the therapies derived from them, ultimately because they imply that people cannot really change anyway, at least not very much — a view that must be unacceptable to those who contract to offer help. Of course, adherents to such systems of thought always allow for one degree of freedom, namely, approved actions based on reflective insight which has been acquired in a particular way in association with approved members of the 'school'. This goes far beyond the altogether reasonable view that the untrained must be trained by the fully trained, and that important actions must be based on thought. Instead, it functions as an institutionalized form of protection of persons and their local interests, and may lead to the ossification and demise of what could otherwise be a continuing and vital source of ideas.

11 I realized that I had written this sentence in my last book (Hopper 1981), thus illustrating how one can use thoughts and words as a 'security blanket'.

12 This very pregnant sentence refers to what may well be the essence of a group experience. I have referred, on the one hand, to what is virtually protomental, and, on the other, to social factors which constrain the lives of adults. Thus, it could be left to the group to respond to my interpretation in whatever ways they wished. In this sense, a good interpretation should have the quality of an 'image' in a good play or novel; however, in so far as it comes from the conductor, it should reflect back to the group the image which they have created. In fact, I should have stopped with this sentence, and waited to see how the group responded. Readers from outside the United Kingdom may not know that the slang 'wet' has many and

various connotations, but in this context it refers to those who are 'soft liberals', economically and politically, e.g. who might favour higher and more progressive income taxes combined with greater government expenditures to help the poor and particular industries, whereas 'dry' refers to the 'hard-liners', the pure 'monetarists', etc.

13 It is worth noting that an 'instrumental adjustment' is more than simply a defence. It is a form of action which affects others, and which can also be assessed in terms of its effectiveness and efficiency. Since an action will almost always involve the actions of others, it becomes an interaction, which is a feature of a group process (Hopper 1981).

References

Bion, W. R. (1961), *Experiences in Groups*, Tavistock, London.

Ezriel, H. (1950), 'The role of transference in psycho-analytic and other approaches to group treatment', *Acta Psychotherapeutica*, supplementum of vol. 7.

Ezriel, H. (1959), 'A psycho-analytic approach to group treatment', *British Journal of Medical Psychology*, 23.

Fenchel, G. (1982), 'Counter-transference: its pitfalls and utilization', *Issues in Ego Psychology*, 5, 4–10.

Foulkes, S. H. (1948), *Introduction to Group Analytic Psychotherapy*, Heinemann, London.

Fromm, E. (1970), *The Crisis of Psycho-Analysis*, Penguin, Harmondsworth.

Fromm, E. (1980), *Beyond the Chains of Illusion*, Abacus, London.

Hopper, E. (1975), 'Sociological aspects of large groups', in L. Kreeger (ed.), *The Large Group: Theory and Dynamics*, Constable, London.

Hopper, E. (1981), *Social Mobility: A Study of Social Control and Insatiability*, Basil Blackwell, Oxford.

Hopper, E. (1982a), A comment on Professor Jahoda's 'The Individual and the Group', in Malcolm Pines and L. Rafaelsen (eds), *The Individual and the Group: Boundaries and Interrelations*, Plenum, New York.

Hopper, E. (1982b), 'Group-analysis: the problem of context', *Group Analysis*, XV, 2, August.

Hopper, E. (1984), 'Group-analysis: the problem of context', *International Journal of Group Psychotherapy*, 34 (2).

de Maré, P. (1972), *Perspectives in Group Psychotherapy*, Allen & Unwin, London.

Pines, M. (1978), 'Contributions of S. H. Foulkes to group analytic therapy', in L. R. Wolberg, M. H. Aronson and D. R. Wolberg (eds), *Group Therapy 1978*, Stratton, New York.

Schindler, W. (1951), 'Family patterns in group formations and therapy', *International Journal of Group Psychotherapy*, 1: 100–5.

Spillius, E. (1983), *Bulletin of the British Psycho-analytical Society*, October.
Weber, M. (1947), *The Theory of Social and Economic Organization*, ed. T. Parsons, Oxford University Press, New York.
Zinkin, L. (1979), 'The collective and the personal', *Journal of Analytical Psychology*, 24, 3: 227–50.

Chapter 17
Beyond the small group: society as an intelligible field of study

Olya Khaleelee and Eric Miller

Introduction

In his series of papers, 'Experiences in Groups, I–VII', which appeared in *Human Relations* (Bion 1948–51; reprinted in Bion 1961), Bion put forward certain propositions about unconscious behaviour in small therapy groups, of up to a dozen members, in relation to him as therapist. Applications of psychoanalytic theory and insights to understanding of group processes were not novel, and Bion acknowledged his debt to Freud (1913, 1921); but Bion's own work both made a distinctive contribution to psychoanalytic theory and broke new ground in theories of group behaviour.

In contrast to earlier writers he emphasized the importance in group life of the 'sophisticated group' or 'work group', which corresponds to Freud's picture of the ego in individual functioning. The work group mobilizes internal resources and relates to external realities for performance of a task. Work group activity, however, interacts with, and is sometimes supported but often obstructed by, the unconscious processes of what he called the 'basic assumption group'. Bion offered convincing evidence for the operation in groups of three mutually exclusive basic assumptions: fight/flight (ba F), pairing (ba P), and dependency (ba D). In a further paper (Bion 1952; also reprinted in Bion 1961) he emphasized the primitiveness of the emotional states underlying the basic assumption phenomena: 'The basic assumptions now emerge as formations secondary to an extremely early primal scene worked out on a level of part objects' — for example, the phantasy that mother's breast or body might contain parts of father — and thus 'associated with psychotic anxiety and mechanisms of splitting and projective identification such as Melanie Klein has described as characteristic of the paranoid-schizoid and depressive positions' (Bion 1961: 164; cf. Klein 1928, 1945, 1946, 1959; Heimann

1952). In general, therefore, 'basic assumption phenomena appear . . . to have the characteristics of defensive reactions to psychotic anxiety' (1961: 189), and thus 'the attempt to make rational investigation of the dynamics of the group is . . . perturbed by fears, and mechanisms for dealing with them, that are characteristic of the paranoid-schizoid position' (p. 162).

Bion insisted that the behaviour observed in groups was not a product of groups as such but of the fact that 'the human being is a group animal'. 'No individual, however isolated in time and space, can be regarded as outside a group or lacking in active manifestations of group psychology' (p. 132). The individual's very belief in independent existence of 'a group' was evidence of regression; and at one point Bion defined a group as 'an aggregate of individuals all in the same state of regression' (p. 142). We carry our groupishness with us all the time. Physical assembly of people into a group simply makes 'political' characteristics of human beings more easily demonstrable. Also, as a matter of practicality, 'It is important that the group should come together sufficiently closely for me to give an interpretation without having to shout it' (p. 132).

Bion's argument therefore was that, so far as the *existence* of group phenomena was concerned, the assembly of a group and the size of that assembly were irrelevant. He was concerned, however, about what constituted 'an intelligible field of study' (p. 104). Studies of neurosis had been largely sterile so long as the focus was on the individual alone: Freud's shift to the two-person relationship and examination of the transference produced an intelligible field of study which generated many new understandings about the individual. Our judgment today must be that Bion's further shift to the small group demonstrated new phenomena and produced new insights which justify it as another such intelligible field. He himself was more cautious and also more ambitious. He thought the small therapeutic group deserved further attention; but he wanted also to shift to a wider field, partly because this might shed more light on the small group and partly because he was impatient to uncover wider societal processes: 'The small therapeutic group does not produce evidence . . . fast enough for my purpose and does not produce enough of it' (p. 105).

The evidence Bion was seeking at that moment was about disease. His theory of proto-mental phenomena had led him into what might be called psycho-epidemiology. The operating basic assumption serves to suppress emotions associated with the other two assumptions; these are confined within the proto-mental system; and the proto-mental levels then provide the matrix of 'group diseases'. Drawing on Wittkower (1949), he had evidence that tuberculosis, for example, was 'very sensitive to developments in the psychology of a group', the incidence 'fluctuating in what appears to be some kind of sympathy with changes in the mentality of the group' (Bion 1961: 107). Given that the prolonged nursing, diet etc. of tubercular patients associate to the mental state of ba D, then one might expect a higher incidence of tuberculosis in phases when ba F is the dominant basic assumption and emotions associated with ba D are locked in the proto-mental system. He wanted statistical evidence. Similarly, he wanted data to test another of his speculations at the societal level about the meaning of money: he postulated that money might carry different and fluctuating psychological values depending on the prevailing basic assumption and corresponding proto-mental state.

He recognized that in larger systems phenomena might be more difficult to detect: 'The glaring difficulty is to state what assumption is operating in a large group' (p. 112). He nevertheless offered stimulating suggestions. For example, in discussing his notion of the 'dual of ba D' – that is, the phenomenon in which the leader has failed to sustain and nourish the group, so the group takes on the task of sustaining and nourishing the leader – he cited the phase in ancient Egyptian history when the country was manifestly exhausted by the building of the pyramids for the Pharaohs. He saw this as 'a group movement to allay the anxiety state of the leader of the group. The nature of that anxiety . . . appears to be centred on the death of the leader and the need to deny its reality' (p. 120).

In his 1952 paper, 'Group dynamics: a re-view' – again building on earlier speculations by Freud – he postulated that society hives off specialized work groups to deal on its behalf with basic assumption emotions that would otherwise obstruct the work group activity of the whole. The well-known examples he offered were church (dependency), army (fight/flight) and aristocracy (pairing).

Provocative though these ideas were, Bion did not elaborate on applications of basic assumption theory to wider societal dynamics. In this last instance he seemed almost to back away from the societal level and was at pains to point out that church, army and aristocracy were often identifiable as specialized sub-groups within the small therapy groups about which he could speak with less uncertainty. And after 1952 his interest turned away from groups and he applied his wisdom more specifically to the therapeutic process with individuals.

Both his theory and the role-model he developed have nevertheless continued to have a pervasive influence directly and indirectly. One stream of work stimulated by Bion's ideas is the Group Relations Training Programme (GRTP) at the Tavistock Institute. This began in 1957 with the first of a continuing series of 'Leicester Conferences'. In progressive developments since then, it has become possible to extend and build on the ideas and thus to find ways of studying unconscious processes not only in small groups, but in large groups, in inter-group relations and in a whole conference as an organization. Fed by and feeding into these conference developments have been some conceptual advances, notably by Rice.and Turquet, and also advances in practice, particularly in consultancy to larger institutions.

Between 1974 and 1979, the authors (who had been and continue to be involved in the GRTP) were engaged in one such experimental application in an industrial enterprise, in which the focus of interpretation became the organization as a whole. More recently, in association with other colleagues in OPUS (an Organization for Promoting Understanding in Society), we have been trying to develop one methodology for the study of societal dynamics. Our aim in the present paper is to describe this approach, which is still very much in the experimental stage: its achievements, limitations and difficulties. First, however, we shall try to trace the lineage back to Bion by outlining relevant developments in and around GRTP and by giving a brief account of our 1974-9 experiment.

Group relations training: developments in theory and practice

It is not surprising that Bion should have become something of a guru for the Tavistock Institute during its formative years. Originally set up as a department of the Tavistock Clinic in 1946 and then separately incorporated in 1947, the Institute was essentially dedicated to translating the model of clinical research to group and organizational settings. Anatomical research can learn a lot in the dissecting room, but physiological, and still more psychological, research, if it is to engage with dynamic processes, requires living subjects with real problems in their physiological or psychological functioning. Treatment and research therefore go hand in hand. Data are derived from the experience of treatment. Consequently the research worker has to be a professional, taking clinical responsibility for the patient, and at times this means that treatment must take priority over research objectives; but the compensating research advantage is that the professional role in relation to the patient or client secures access to living problems and dilemmas that would be closed to the 'pure' research worker. In applying this approach to organizations, the Institute had to create a new professional role and a new methodology; and it needed new theory. In this respect the work of Kurt Lewin during the 1930s and early 1940s furnished an important contribution. Particularly relevant was his insistence that groups could and should be considered as wholes: 'In the social as in the physical field the structural properties of a dynamic whole are different from the structural properties of subparts. Both sets of properties have to be investigated' (1947: 8). One further input into the Tavistock Institute's theoretical framework at the beginning of the 1950s was von Bertalanffy's open system theory, which was seen as relevant not simply to biological organisms but to human organizations (Bertalanffy 1950).

Bion's formulations not only shared these gestalt perspectives but had two added attractions: they supplied a bridge between psychoanalytic theory and group behaviour, thus opening unconscious group processes to scientific examination; and they also took full account of the relatedness of therapist/consultant and group as a crucial element in the phenomena to be studied. Transference and countertransference, in other words, were seen as applicable beyond the one-to-one therapeutic relationship. Moreover, by 1948 Bion had already showed that his methodology and propositions held good not only in therapeutic groups of neurotic patients but also in training groups of managers and professionals who met for the understanding of group behaviour rather than for treatment.

An early paper by Rice, entitled 'The use of unrecognized cultural mechanisms in an expanding machine-shop' (1951), shows the influence that Bion was already exerting on the concepts that the Institute was using in its research and consultancy activities; and the value of the Bion-type small group for learning about group dynamics was being recognized; but not until the first of the Leicester Conferences in 1957 was it incorporated systematically into the Institute's training activities (Trist and Sofer 1959; Rice 1965).[1] In that initial two-week conference the small study groups were the only experiential event for the examination of group behaviour in the here and now. In later conferences other events were added with the same existential primary task. First came the inter-group event, introduced by Bridger (Higgin and Bridger 1964; Rice 1965, 1969; Astrachan and Flynn 1976).[2] The next step was the introduction of the 'large group' by Rice and Turquet in 1963 (Rice 1965, 1969; Turquet 1975). Numbers were as high as seventy to eighty in some conferences, and — following the maxim that 'it takes a group to understand a group' – from the beginning of this new event there were almost always from two to four consultants. Variations on the inter-group event were developed in the 1960s, the most complex being the 'institutional event', in which the task was the here-and-now study of the relatedness between members and staff within the framework of the total conference as an institution and the beliefs and fantasies about it (Guereca 1979). Other events were designed in the 1970s to examine phenomena in groups of different sizes: the 'median group' (15–30) and the 'very small group' (5–7) (Gosling 1981). The most recent innovation, by Lawrence in the late 1970s, was the 'praxis event' which stripped away the differentiations – and defences – supplied by structure and role: starting simply with individual and task, it was possible to explore the emerging dynamics.[3]

Group relations training expanded not only at the Tavistock Institute but outside. Other institutions with which the Institute collaborated in extending this work included: Christian Teamwork (now the Grubb Institute), the Chelmsford Cathedral Centre for Research and Training, Bristol University Department of Education, and the Manchester Business School in Britain; the Washington School of Psychiatry (now the A. K. Rice Institute) in the United States;[4] the Rosehill Institute of Human Relations in Canada; the International Foundation for Social Innovation in France; and the Indian Society for Individual and Social Development. This model of training has also been taken into many organizations, in education, the social services, industry and government, and has proved itself as a valuable tool in elucidating organizational cultures. It has influenced the design of therapeutic communities and in at least one hospital has been adopted quite directly as a regime for the rapid reconstitution of psychotic patients (Lofgren 1976).[5] In addition, the conceptual framework that informs the conferences has been applied by consultants and research workers to the understanding of a variety of different organizations.[6]

Arising from this activity, the most direct extensions of Bion's concepts were by Turquet and Rice. Turquet (1974), for example, began to elucidate the characteristic dynamics and myths of groups of different sizes: the pair, the triad, 5–6, 8–12+, 20–30, 50–80. He also proposed a fourth basic assumption to add to Bion's three: the 'basic assumption oneness' group, in which 'members seek to join in a powerful union with an omnipotent force, unobtainably high, to surrender self for passive participation, and thereby to feel existence, well-being and wholeness' (p. 357). In a second paper, which carried the sub-title 'A study in the phenomenology of the individual's experience of changing membership status in the large group', Turquet (1975) pointed out that the consultant to such a group is present in a dual capacity, both in a defined role and as a person, and in the latter capacity shares inescapably in the difficulties and dilemmas of the individual member. In this identification with members, he was expressing the central objective of GTRP, which is to help the individual to understand and grapple with his 'groupishness' and to discover within himself authority for his own interpretations and actions. Turquet went on to argue that whereas in the small group the operant basic assumption makes it relatively easy to establish leader and member roles, 'no similar encompassment seems to be immediately available or discoverable in the large group' (p. 116). Larger numbers allow the individual more opportunities for projections, but correspondingly he finds himself fractionated into multiple parts; moreover,

> the introjected vastness of his external world meets a similar internal experience [i.e., of an internal world that is unencompassable and boundless] and by their mutual reinforcement the level of the anxiety is raised, requiring a further projection into the outer large group of the now reinforced sense of vastness, only to increase the fantasied percept of the large group as now greater than ever before, not only vast but endless (p. 118).

Turquet's paper also explores the large group's potential for violence – errant violence – the fears this evokes, and the defences that are mobilized. The hunt for a victim can feel implacable and – though he does not make this point so explicitly – at times this can test to destruction the consultant's capacity to manage the boundary between interpretation and control.

Rice (1969) applied the system theory of organization (cf. Miller and Rice 1967) to individual and group behaviour. Bion, as we saw earlier, had spoken of the 'glaring difficulty' of determining what basic assumption was operating in a large group (and for Bion 'large' could describe a society, not merely the 50-80 of a conference 'large group'). Rice felt that Bion's concepts described 'special cases which are most easily observable in small groups, because they are large enough to give power to an alternative leadership, and yet not so large as to provide support for more than one kind of powerful alternative leadership at any one time' (1969: 40). He argued that task performance (of the work group) uses only parts of group members. If the members find a commonality in the unused parts and invest sentience in it they may then overtly or covertly be agreeing on a role that is irrelevant, and perhaps antagonistic, to the work task. If conscious, this may lead to revolt; if unconscious, to a shared basic assumption opposed to task performance. The larger the group, the greater the threat that such agreement would pose, but the greater the difficulty in agreeing.

Implicit in the design of the conferences is the proposition that the phenomena — often seemingly psychotic — experienced and observed in the relatively unstructured temporary groups, with their task of studying their own behaviour in the here and now, are likely to be present in all such groups of equivalent size; but in everyday life — say, in work organizations — structures and conventions will overlay these phenomena. Most of the time they are less visible, and when they do obtrude they appear all the more irrational and dangerous. Menzies (1960), building on Jaques (1955), argued that the structures themselves, though ostensibly created for task performance, are a defence against persecutory and depressive anxiety, and she showed how the specific anxieties of hospital nursing can produce defensive structures which actually reduce the effectiveness of task performance. The resultant increase in anxiety erects further defences, and so on in a deteriorating cycle.

This concept has proved fruitful in analysis of various types of organization.[7] Published material, however, is disappointingly scarce. A recent book entitled *The Psychoanalysis of Organizations* (de Board 1978) offers few examples.

Perhaps we should not be surprised by this. Given that western man tends to pride himself on his invention of organization as a rational means of performing large-scale and complex tasks and given too the difficulty of providing scientific proof of the kinds of insights that Jaques and Menzies offered, we can hardly expect such interpretations to be greeted with enthusiasm. And even if clients accept such interpretations of organizational defences — which tend to have a static, structural, 'this-is-the-way-things-are' quality — there is the question of how to help them use the understanding dynamically and effectively. This is a critical problem for members leaving group relations training conferences and returning to their own institutions (Miller 1980). So the applications of Bion's theories and of psychoanalysis generally to organizational consultancy have tended to be unintegrated. Thus we have theoretical contributions on the experience of work (e.g., Pederson-Krag 1951, on mass production) and the defensive use of structures (e.g., Jaques 1955); we have much evidence of consultants using their experience of the transference and countertransference to garner insights into the dynamics of the client system (cf. Rice 1963; Sofer 1961; Miller and Gwynne 1972; Miller 1976, 1977; Lawrence, in press); we have individual members of organizations enlarging their understanding of unconscious processes through attending group relations conferences (and in exceptional cases of a significant number of employees being exposed to this type of training as an instrument of organizational development: cf. Menninger 1972); and where a consultant has worked with a client group in elucidating unrecognized and unconscious organizational processes, it generally turns out that the group is only a small sub-system, usually a management body, within the larger client system — thus leading to ethical and political questions about the consultant's role in reinforcing the status quo. Moreover, in these cases it has been almost unknown for the consultant to preserve in relation to such a client group the austere role of, say, a Freudian analyst. (Writing of his Indian work, for instance, Rice recorded: 'My clients and their families became my close friends' (1963: 9). This may well be appropriate or at least unavoidable in organizational consultancy; but it clearly reduces the consultant's availability as a projective receptacle.) The only case we are aware of in which the action research team consciously tried both to maintain some distance and to collaborate with the total organization as the client system was the early Tavistock Institute study at the Glacier Metal Company (Jaques 1951).

An experimental intervention in a manufacturing company

Between 1976 and 1979 the authors had an opportunity to take this approach further. The earlier stages of this intervention have been described elsewhere (Miller 1977) and we shall merely outline them here.

The client was a manufacturing business with its main factory and head office in the Home Counties and a small plant in the Midlands. It was part of a large international group. When help was sought in 1973, the presenting problems were low output, a high scrap-rate, poor morale and imperviousness to attempts to increase efficiency. It teetered between making a marginal profit and losing money. It transpired that the main factory had belonged to a company that the group acquired a few years previously. The Midlands site was the remains of the group's own former subsidiary producing a similar product: it had been decided to amalgamate the two businesses — previously competitors — and concentrate production mainly at the southern site, where a two-shift operation was introduced. This had led to a damaging loss of female labour and thus of production expertise. Selling had been removed from the acquired company and incorporated in the group's separate sales organization. A questionnaire administered to all employees — approaching 1,000 — revealed responses to these changes. There were notable internal splits cutting across one another — between management and workers, between employees from the two amalgamated enterprises, and between departments. Identification with the organization was notably lacking: the boundaries had been fractured and had to some extent disintegrated; and employees had fallen back onto their individual boundaries in a culture of survival.

The understanding of the consultants[8] was that the fragmented boundaries of the organization needed to be reconstructed at three levels at least — between individuals, between groups and between the organization and the outside world — in order that a more integrated sense of identity could be developed. Based on the diagnosis, the consultants initiated what came to be called the 'People Programme'. Its main feature was an extended, non-residential version of a Leicester Conference, comprising small study groups, inter-group events, and a large group, which fitted precisely the need to work at the three levels: the individual in interpersonal relations; the department and other groupings in their inter-group context; and the organization as a whole in relation to its environment. One hundred and twenty employees took part in the programme which extended over a period of eight months.

Outcomes over the next year were impressive. The People Programme, having been run by the consultants, was taken over by the participants and the training extended to other echelons of employees; weekly meetings of the 'Large Group' continued for three years; spontaneous task groups arose at various levels — including engineers and apprentices — to tackle pressing work issues; internal co-ordination improved; a noticeable new air of purposefulness, competence and self-confidence appeared in transactions across the main boundary with group headquarters; and there was a surge in manufacturing performance and profits.

The next innovation — and this is the one we are concerned with here — was the formation in mid-1976 of a quasi-independent Consulting Resource Group, comprising initially the three consultants though later including seconded employees. Up to that time consultancy had been provided, on request, to various internal groups. This the CRG would continue. But in addition it took on a new task, which was to try to elucidate the underlying dynamics of the organization and to interpret them to the whole organization as client. One analogy was of CRG as a man-made satellite which, from its orbit, would have a perspective on the organization not available from the surface of the planet. To be more specific, our proposition was that in taking a consulting position outside the boundary, we would be better able to help the organization explore the interrelatedness between its internal dynamics and its transactions across the boundary with systems in its environment; the transference to the CRG would reflect significant aspects of these other transactions.

We had to devise a technique to get round the problem posed by Bion of being able 'to give an interpretation without having to shout it'. Each week therefore, members of the CRG held a $1\frac{1}{2}$-hour 'private' meeting, at which we would review our experience of the week, think out loud, and begin to formulate working hypotheses – i.e., interpretations. But this 'private' meeting was held in public: any member of the organization could attend. It was immediately followed by an open meeting, at which those present could question our interpretations, confirm or modify them with evidence from their own experience, and bring forward other preoccupations. In this way we provided participants with a new role – as 'citizens of the organization' perhaps – from which they could examine their experience in their other roles as members of work groups and of trades unions. It was as if the organization as a whole was the analysand; and we always tried to perceive these visitors' inputs as expressing something on behalf of the whole organization in relation to us. Our aim in doing this was to help them to recognize how much they might be caught up in the underlying organizational dynamics.

Attendance at these sessions was variable and never higher than 2 per cent of the total personnel. (It was realistically very difficult for most employees to be released from their jobs, particularly on the production lines.) However, our working hypotheses were also used directly and indirectly in our regular consultations and meetings with sub-groupings, and we had evidence that our voice was being 'heard' – albeit sometimes distorted – by at least a quarter of the organization. That sounds unimpressive until one remembers one's frequent experience as a small group consultant that not more than one or two members out of the dozen are hearing what one has to say.

As in work with small groups and individuals too, it was difficult to be sure of any cause–effect relationship between interpretation and subsequent action. The most overt evidence was in the growing number of individuals able to perceive organizational processes in which they were implicated and able also to act on their understanding by taking greater personal authority in their other roles. Other evidence that we were heard was the strength of the organizational defences that were mobilized to throw the satellite out of orbit. It was either to be brought down to earth — by absorbing the CRG into the organization as just another department — or it was to be despatched into outer space. At times the CRG was internally split, part being drawn right inside, and part extruded so far out as to lose sight of the dynamics. Another device was to mobilize a split between the (usually good, caring, participative, creative) CRG and the (usually bad, neglectful, authoritarian) management group. Or again, the CRG would be converted into prophets and priests of a new religious group: for worshippers it was enough to listen to the evangelists and attend the rituals; the rest of their work-place lives could remain unaffected. Sometimes we were totally ignored; yet there were also indications of considerable concern that the rituals should continue even if there was no congregation. Dependency, fight/flight and — rarely — pairing were therefore observable at the organizational level, and could be used to elucidate both the shifting internal dynamics — for example, splitting and projection between departments, with one department carrying for a time all the negativity — and the changing postures towards the external world, particularly towards group head-quarters.

We should have foreseen that the client's success would be the undoing of the People Programme. Its transition from the bottom of the league-table to the top in terms of profit aroused envy in other companies in the group and put them under pressure to improve per-formance; and at group headquarters pleasure that this sick patient had recovered radiant health began to be overlain by anxiety about the shift from compliance to assertiveness, which seemed tantamount to insub-ordination. Group headquarters therefore applied various sanctions on the client organization's management to get rid of CRG, which was perceived — not inaccurately — as a core of dissidence. Sanctions ranged from withholding managerial promotions to, eventually, installing a new general manager to re-impose compliance. A sharp trade recession and pressure for redundancies gave him added power in re-installing a more familiar authoritarian regime. The belief developed, with some substantiation, that 'friends of CRG' were particularly vulnerable. With official and personal support withdrawn, the intervention came to an end.

In this sense, the intervention failed. Members of the client system did not acquire enough authority to manage their collective future. Their new insights had to be privatized or denied. Technically, however, it showed that methods could be devised to detect and interpret unconscious processes in sizeable systems. (See Lawrence 1980, for a report of another related method.) This provided encouragement for the more ambitious experiment described in the final section.

Society as an intelligible field of study: an experiment

We saw earlier that Bion properly recognized that the small group (10–12) is an 'intelligible field of study'. Experiences with the Leicester Conferences suggested that the large group (from 40–50 up to 80) mobilizes a sufficiently distinctive set of dynamics to be classed, at least provisionally, as another such intelligible field. This applies both to the 'large group event' as such, in which numerous members meet with (say) four consultants to study their own behaviour, and to the 'institutional event', which explores the relatedness of the membership with the total staff group, in their managerial, consultative and administrative roles. In terms of dynamics, the main observable differences between the two arise from the greater structuring of the latter — membership formation into self-chosen sub-groups; differentiation of role among staff — which crystallizes and gives quasi-permanence to the more shifting splitting processes of the large group event. Perhaps because of this, the phenomenon of mirroring is much easier to see in the institutional event. For example, one sub-group of members may precisely mirror the composition of the staff group in overall numbers and in numbers of men, women, ethnic groups etc.; or different phantasied aspects of the staff group may be clearly expressed by the different sub-groups into which the membership divides. These unconscious representations may be potentially present in the small group — and indeed, as we saw earlier, Bion was sometimes able to identify church, army and aristocracy in small groups — but the fact that the larger group of fifty upwards throws them so much more sharply into focus justifies the argument that somewhere around this size a frame-change occurs and another intelligible field of study has been identified.

The question that now arises is whether with our manufacturing company, with nearly 1,000 members, we had advanced to another field. Our provisional answer to this is 'No'. Technically, to be sure, we had to invent new ways of communicating to a group that was beyond shouting distance; but working at this level did not seem to elicit phenomena distinctively different from those we have observed in groups of 50–80. 'Society', therefore, may well be the next higher intelligible field.

However, before discussing our attempts to interpret at the societal level we want to examine the appearance in lower level systems of dynamics belonging to a higher level. Our tentative proposition is that number as such is not the determining factor. In other words, groups that are small in size may express phenomena that do not belong to the small group in itself but are manifestations of the large group, or even of society. Thus, in our work with the manufacturing company, organizational dynamics were readily apparent in the shifting groupings of ten or fewer that we met each week, whilst the dynamics that one would expect to see in the small group were much more elusive. There is other supporting evidence. For example, colleagues conducting therapy groups have reported the occasional experience of working with a group depleted to two members or even one; and there have been similar occurrences in GRTP conferences. In such instances the transaction with the 'group of one' is markedly different from, say, individual therapy. What happens is that the absent group held in the minds of both parties to the transaction has a profound influence on the unconscious dynamics that are mobilized: in Bion's terms it is the 'groupishness' of the individual that comes to the fore. Another way of explaining this is through the concept of 'role'. A psychologist observing the behaviour in a small group of ten people and using the individual as his interpretive focus will not 'see' small group phenomena. Conversely, the consultant to the small group as a system sees the individual's behaviour wholly or primarily as a contribution to group processes (cf. Miller 1976). The perceived role and role relationship tend to determine those aspects of himself that the individual consciously and unconsciously brings forward, while other aspects are suppressed or repressed (Rice 1969). Hence if the consultant addresses a solo individual as a representative of a group whose other members are absent, it is the 'groupish' role that will be mobilized. Our method of working in the manufacturing company used and validated this proposition.

There is, however, one further complication: because the larger group is always potentially present in the smaller, at times the larger group phenomena break through. For example, the individual at times may experience in a very small group of six people the same problems of holding on to his skin as he might experience in a crowd: the six have become a crowd. This can be put to constructive use. For example, the group relations methodology has proved a valuable tool in identifying organizational cultures: a group composed of people from the same organization will display often unrecognized elements of the culture, in particular by mobilizing them as part of their defence against pursuing the primary task of 'here and now' study. At a broader level we have increasingly become aware of the influence of societal phenomena on GRTP conferences, particularly in the large group but also more generally in the defences adopted. Indeed, the conference is often called, not inaccurately, a microcosm of society. As Rioch (1979: 56) puts it, discussing the American scene:

> It is now expected not only that local issues that affect the institu-
> tional applications of members will show up in conferences, but
> often, even more strongly, that the tone or preoccupation of a
> nation will appear. [For example,] in one conference in 1973 the
> dominant theme . . . seemed to stem from concentration camps: not
> to let oneself be noticed. Fascism and terror . . . were casting a dark
> shadow, as if the membership were already responding with a
> concentration camp mentality to such things as the use of the
> Internal Revenue Service as a weapon against political enemies. In
> the first half of 1974 corruption, deception and lack of trust in
> management were important themes.

She notes that after 1968-9 memberships were less prone to violent revolt and less able to mobilize effective leadership of the whole. Parallel changes had been noted in the British conferences. The myth that the group is a creative matrix has been progressively submerged by the countervailing myth that groups and institutions are dangerous and destructive. Correspondingly, there has been a withdrawal of commit-ment to groups, an increasing reluctance (noted also by Rioch) to use the conference setting for experiment and play (in the Winnicott sense), and a tendency for the individual to put up protective boundaries against group influences or to seek security as an isolate or in a pair.

Up to now, identification of such societal dynamics has been a by-product of GRTP conferences. Since mid-1980 the group of staff as-sociated with OPUS (many of whom have been actively involved in the conferences) have been trying more directly to tease out these dynamics. OPUS works on the proposition that if the individual citizen has a fuller understanding of the processes operating in the society of which he is a part then he will learn to manage himself in his own roles with greater maturity: its aim in other words is that of the GTRP writ large. The method used so far has been simple. Every three months the staff of OPUS, who come from all over Britain, meet for a day and attempt to distil, from their experiences in their various roles and institutional settings, current themes and preoccupations in society. A written version of this discussion is offered in a following meeting to the OPUS Forum. This, in contrast to the staff group, which is comprised mainly of middle-class professionals, is a group selected for its diversity of backgrounds — a more genuine microcosm of society perhaps than a staff group. The Forum reviews the staff's distillations and its members offer evidence, confirming or otherwise, from their own experience. As a next step, OPUS is beginning to build up a number of 'listening posts' in different parts of the country. These will be groups of a dozen or so people, also meeting quarterly to share their preoccupations, which will then enlarge the input into staff meetings. So far the only voice, outside Forum meetings, that OPUS has devised to 'shout' its interpretations to society is its quarterly *Bulletin*, which publishes an account of the staff and Forum transactions (OPUS 1980-1).

One way of looking at this approach is that OPUS staff are formulating a role of 'consultant' in relation to society as client and from this position are able, however crudely, to identify and interpret societal dynamics. This would seem to be a natural extension from the analyst/consultant working at the transference in the analytic pair, the small group and the large group, and from the role of the Consulting Resource Group in our manufacturing company. But in these other cases the client gives at least some degree of sanction to the consultant role. And it is the consultant's boundary position, pulled inside and pushed outside, that generates the data for interpretation. However, as we shall argue below, if the putative client is society there is no outside: the Forum is only a representation of society-as-client; and moreover the consultant role is self-defined. This poses a technical difficulty for staff. As we write this paper, we and our colleagues are in the process of examining whether the task boundary and the institutional boundary of OPUS are sufficient to contain the diversity and the chaotic and violent feelings that staff as societal members find they are bringing into it. It seems that each staff member at times is frightened and angry to discover such feelings in himself or herself.

A theoretical difficulty is that OPUS's approach is premised on society being an intelligible field of study; hence there is a risk familiar to physicists that the phenomena observed are a function of the measuring instrument used. This argument could equally be used against Bion's small therapeutic groups but was in fact controverted by the quality of the evidence and the theory that he was able to adduce. We shall return to this point after presenting our own evidence so far.

At the time of writing, the cycle of Associate Staff and Forum meetings has been repeated five times. Here we briefly review the emerging themes and offer some interim comments on the experience to date.

Summer 1980

A pervasive motif of everything falling apart, impending dissolution and disaster. Falling apart linked to fall-out and the bomb. A theme of waiting helplessly, impotently — waiting for the end, the bomb. A tentative hypothesis: — Anxiety about the bomb/doom/destruction is a defence against a deeper fear of anarchy. The bomb is fantasied as an uncontrollable retribution for mankind's hubris; whereas anarchy is a consequence of the individual's greed and irresponsiblity, which he could do something about, but the action is unpalatable. The unemployed and the blacks represent the threat of anarchy and are seen as contaminating. The price paid for trying to avoid contamination is isolation, lack of meaningful intercourse. Perhaps the ultimate terror is the blackness/anarchy/uselessness/nothingness inside.

> The current government is seen to mirror these processes, partly because it represents an ideology of *survival of the fittest* in economic terms . . . and also because it came to power on a platform of *law and order* and therefore was a response to anxiety about anarchy. But the more you provoke a belief in the survival of the fittest — self-seeking, individuation, greed — the greater the fear of a 'Lord of the Flies' situation . . . Greater inequalities . . . increase the anxieties of the winners and survivors about protecting their gains against the attacks of those impoverished by the process. The process is escalating; anxiety is mounting; the demand for law and order is intensified . . . The demand for control from outside is a response to failure in exercising personal authority, which relates to feeling valueless, and therefore powerless. But powerlessness is a myth which leaves the individual exonerated from personal responsibility (OPUS October 1980: 12–13).

One further theme that emerged in the Forum meeting was loss of ideology, which makes freedom frightening, because we cannot imagine what to do with it: in the current environment freedom means survival of the fittest, which does not mean survival of the majority. Loss of ideology was equated with loss of meaning and therefore of anarchy. Linked to this the Forum also noted that the organization had lost credibility.

> The notion that one was actually part of several sub-systems was not felt to be evident in British society at the moment. The tension

between individual and organization which provides dynamism and a force for change seems to be missing. It is either individual or society. Where is Organization? (p. 18).

Autumn 1980

Withdrawal from organization comes up again in both meetings as part of the dominant theme of retreat: retreat as temporary withdrawal to re-engage better with reality, and retreat as flight from reality, flight for survival. Retreat is from feelings of impotence, of being locked into a situation. Holidays were a retreat into sanity; returning to normal life is a return to madness. Television has been offering a crop of period-pieces: when the future is frightening, there is a reassurance and comfort in looking back. There is a demand for teaching, a search for 'the word', as opposed to thinking for oneself, a wish to go back to old knowledge and received thinking (cf. the Conservative government's monetary doctrines), to a fundamentalist position. Tradition may be a defence against finding alternative modes of being, relating and organizing ourself to lead through the future. The retreat is also flight from violence: non-involvement, lack of courage, self-preservation at the expense of others. The redundant – victims of an enforced retreat – are again seen as an embarrassment, a source of contamination.

It seemed that at this time flight was a defence against fight – which is not quite in accord with Bion's view of this basic assumption in the small group context, where he saw flight and fight as readily inter-changeable and as having the function of containing within the proto-mental system emotions associated with the other two basic assumptions. At the time of these meetings, however, fight was unthinkable: there was no external enemy, so it would have to be civil war or – still more likely – anarchic violence. A speculation we made then was that to keep this possibility at bay British society had created the Thatcher/ Foot split – the Conservative right wing and the Labour left wing – so that fight could be projected into the familiar, and therefore 'safe', class war. A second speculation was that the myth of a shared national economic crisis and the myth of the threat of nuclear holocaust were both being invoked so as to preserve the social structure and keep order: they offer a justification for feeling impotent; they restrain impulses to burst out in violent protest.

One proposition put forward in the Forum meeting was that there was almost a wish for a holocaust: 'The problems of the world call for changes that we as a society recognize we are incapable of making: they can be tackled only if most of it is destroyed and the survivors can begin afresh' (OPUS January 1981: 23). But the individual had to see himself as surviving: 'Each one of us is going to be Noah.'

Early 1981

The recurrent theme in meetings of both Associate Staff and Forum was failed dependency. Individuals feel increasingly let down by the institutions to which they look to meet their needs. Institutions seem to be engaged in a search for a 'clean' model of the world: it is becoming more difficult to put the work and the being together. So the person I am and the aspirations I have are not being recognized and met in the way that they were; there is a gap between what I think I am and what I get. Institutions do not make space inside them for people; they are constructs of power, antagonistic to humans, concerned with cleaning things out. Or alternatively, as one staff member experienced when his wife was hospitalized, they may seem too human, ordinary and casual, when 'what you really want is reassurance and tight guidelines and a consultant dressed in a white coat.' But having responded in this human way they do inhuman things to us. (The telling examples given were mastectomy and orchidectomy.) And since they no longer meet our dependent needs, there is a hope and wish to be taken care of, to be rescued, to be saved from one's own feelings and the situations one finds oneself in.

> It is no longer clear what feelings belong to whom. We project our inhumanity into institutions – prisons, hospitals, bureaucracies – in order to remain human ourselves.
>
> The problem is that institutions are the only way society has found to . . . enable people to cope with primitive feelings like dependence, hate and rage. We have developed a pattern of projective receptacles. In the analysis of organizations we have a rational picture of a person in a role in an institution. But implicitly we are describing a process through which we can get rid of bits of ourselves that we want to disown. Those are the bits that the person transmits into the 'containers' of 'role' and 'organization'. So at present institutions are failing us either by becoming more humane and more like us, or they fail us by becoming more extreme and inhumane. If they are too humane, they can't carry things we'd like them to hold for us, but if they're really extreme they become persecutory and frightening.

The reality of unemployment means that, in the absence of alternative mechanisms, we have to come face to face with the feelings that we put into organizations. We have to take them back inside ourselves and put them to creative use. We have to hold on to hope, while giving up childish fantasies of having all our wishes fulfilled (OPUS April 1981: 12).

We are ashamed when we discover the dependency we have invested in institutions and frightened when we have to take it back. External changes rub up against parts of oneself that were not available before. One feels exposed, vulnerable, uncertain. People still employed feel increasingly unsure about the worthwhileness of the work they do — hence the demands for reassurance and rescue. They envy the freedom of self-employment — breaking through the employment barrier, risking the abyss of no structure — but not its risks and anxieties. ('You have to create it: you don't know what it will be till you get there. You just have to hope it will work out OK'.)

The question of where to put one's hopes was taken up by the Forum. Religion, education and political parties have failed us in turn. Perhaps the attraction of the new Social Democratic Party lies not in its policies but in the offer of an alternative hope. (And the prospective royal wedding suggested that aristocracy was living up to the role that Bion assigned to it.) Union solidarity is crumbling; the role of shop steward is unenviable and hard to fill; different levels in the union hierarchy state contradictory opinions. It was also suggested in the Forum that

People are no longer sure of what is the optimum number of people to join forces with. There's a contradiction between the needs for survival and the needs for achieving something. To survive, I'm forced back on myself and my family. If I'm not employed, I'm safe in the sense that I can't be made redundant; but I can only do so much as a loner: to achieve I have to be connected into the society. And if I've previously accepted the dependent position — that the state should provide employment — when that dependency fails me I can survive only by being angry, against the Government, against the unions (ibid.: 18).

The government is increasingly perceived as being highly insensitive, uninterested in the people it purports to represent and pursuing an obsessional preoccupation of its own. Staff suggested that as our other institutions, especially employing institutions, decline and crumble, some of the negative feelings normally carried by them are displaced into government instead. The final question that summed up both meetings was: 'Where can we put our trust?'

Spring 1981

The Forum meeting was characterized by two sharply different interpretations of what is happening in society: that there is no real change and what we are experiencing are slightly different manifestations of the same patterns; and that there is actually a massive change in society which is leading to an experience of disillusion and disconnectedness for the individual. A third perspective was that the onus is now on the individual, whether inside or outside institutions, to produce solutions for himself and others.

Interestingly, this had followed a meeting of staff in which a dominant theme had been splitting — the emergence of a strong sense of differentiation and clear splits in individual, group and organizational life.

Rules are increasingly being invoked in organizations. Role and status differentiations are also expressed more sharply — for example, in psychiatric hospitals between patients and staff, sick and well, and among professional groups; and in schools between teachers and pupils, between acceptable and unacceptable children. Splitting comes from a sense of being beleagured. Amidst turbulence, rules give certainty and professional role boundaries are defended to confer a sense of identity; but it means that people are much less able to act with personal authority. They huddle in smaller and smaller groups, with mounting anxiety about what is going on outside, fearful of power and ruthlessness. Society is preoccupied with structure, not content. If you lose your role, you are nothing. Redundant people disappear into an unknown underworld. Your mates deny the pain by expunging the memory that you were ever there: open mourning is impermissible. In this way the rest of us stay on top, but insecurely.

This is linked to another major theme: deception, betrayal, treason. To quote from the record of the Forum meeting.

> Once you're out of a job, as well as coping with the feeling of being hopeless, you've got to hold inside envy and jealousy of colleagues who are doing the work you'd like to do. Holding these feelings inside yourself corrodes you — you feel betrayed (OPUS July 1981: 10).

You deal with your aggressive feelings not by attacking the manager who has told you that you are redundant but by displacing all the anger into a faceless management, a non-caring institution. But if you protect yourself by splitting in this way, your feelings never get worked through. The Forum persisted with the theme of being locked in, locking yourself in, locking things inside yourself, and its connection with splitting. For example, people who know their job is the only thing they can do — those who work to live rather than live to work — cope with being locked in by splitting themselves: they do their work automatically and meanwhile travel elsewhere in their fantasy life. But the staff meeting was more preoccupied with betrayal. Where there are redundancies, as an employee you either get rid of yourself or you collude with the process that gets rid of other people. You may feel betrayed by your institution; but not supporting and not speaking up are also betrayals. In that sense we all betray part of ourselves. Yet by acting on what you believe in and being true to yourself you can still be seen by others as betrayers — for example, the MPs who transferred to the Social Democratic Party. Treason in the Establishment is in the news, following publication of Chapman Pincher's book. Although the allegèd betrayals occurred thirty years ago, they strike a contemporary chord. In one sense,

> the individual's sense of betrayal is based on fantasy . . . In childhood you believed in all the rules . . . absolutely and were appalled when people broke them . . . But around us is real betrayal. So . . . we feel that perhaps it is the version [of history] we've been using that has betrayed us. We are at present in a situation which history does not explain, so there's an urgent need to rewrite history. It's as if 30 years ago there was a fall or betrayal and we search for a myth to explain how we have got to where we are now (ibid.: 16–17).

Politicians, for example, are betraying us today by treating us like dependent children, so we are prevented from coming to terms with the reality that, say, full employment is a myth. We are being betrayed by failures of institutions: trade unions, religious institutions.

In turn we as adults are betraying and sacrificing the youth of today. But this was only one side of an ambivalance about the young: on the one hand, the older generation feels that it has failed them, so we deserve to be punished by them for our sins of omission and commission; and on the other hand, we expunge them and push them out, into unemployment, into detention centres. Parents are not providing secure boundaries any more against which the young can find out who they are; and we refuse to accept our responsiblity for their plight. No wonder we are frightened of their violence. Maybe they are going to act out *my* destructive impulses, do the things *I* do not have the guts to do.

Summer 1981

Fear of violence and experience of actual violence provided the dominant theme for this next staff meeting, which took place just a few days before the new round of inter-city rioting in Toxteth, Moss Side, etc. Splitting was still around, but the sense was that it would no longer hold as a defence. Forum members — meeting after the riots had subsided and also after the royal wedding — advocated action by OPUS; but it was difficult to design actions based on thought and reason that might effectively combat mindless, violent action.

It is convenient to apportion thought and action between old and young. A staff member saw a youth trying to break into a flat and expected him to run off. 'He didn't; he came at me [with a knife] : "What is it to you?" he said. Shook me rigid. I had a real sense of this not being fair. All I was doing was to warn him that he'd been seen. Then he'd run away: those are the rules. I didn't expect him to threaten to cut me up.' Yet the older also see the need to break through conventions that no longer work. They envy the young. Perhaps there is a demand for psychopathic leadership. A quotation from Norman Mailer: 'Only psychopaths can save us.' Disturbing echoes of Germany in the 1930s. An older man has been terrified to recognize his own violent fantasies: a suicidal impulse to play Russian roulette; a murderous impulse towards a baby grand-daughter. He finds he is transferring commitment from society to his family; but perhaps the cost of doing this is that you have to bring back into the family violent feelings that have been projected outside. Anti-Thatcher feelings are an important social phenomenon. People have to look elsewhere for humanity, for ideas about the future. Anger and rebelliousness are becoming much more overt. Felt hopelessness of the future is the kind of vacuum that psychopathic leadership is sucked in to fill. Desperation creates ready-made victims for exploitation and fraud. You have only to offer hope. For example, a new factory in a new town is opened with much fanfare and the fact that the same company has closed a much larger factory elsewhere, making many people redundant, is irrelevant. People cope by splitting: at one level they know it is a fraud; at another level they deny it and cling to the hope.

As the staff saw it, on the one hand there was violence, real or close to the surface, coming out of feelings of being defrauded and exploited, and on the other hand a wish for a way through. One positive model, put forward in the Forum, was simply of performing one's own roles more effectively and more responsibly. But is that enough asked the staff. How do you engage at the societal level? If society is split and psychotic, how do you communicate? People have to believe in linear progress and not hear scepticism; so they are ripe for totalitarianism.

Into this climate came the royal wedding, offering hope, renewal, involvement — at least for the day. For most it was a unifying experience: one felt a greater belonging to family and country. Besides being comforting and uplifting, re-evocation of the hierarchies of church and state also brought out the negative: 'Lord of the Manor' feelings are still around — the envy and anger alongside respect and submission — but ceremony and ritual were important in sustaining a sense of belonging and keeping negative feelings at bay. Rituals have been destroyed in our society. (Whatever happened to the harvest festival? A Forum member's daughter brought home a message from school: teachers do not want vegetables or fruit for this year's festival — they go off — so bring something like a packet of tea instead.) We allow contemporary institutions to impose their values on us; so perhaps instead of rituals that have meaning we have observance of bureaucratic rules and conventions. Can we manage without them? One encouraging snippet: During a recent power-cut which shut off the traffic lights in Winchester the traffic moved more freely. So at least motorists could manage themselves. But is that expandable?

> Our educational institutions are engaged in disseminating 'acceptable meanings' — established ways of understanding the world — which are becoming discredited; whereas it is OPUS's job to disseminate 'unacceptable meanings'. But the question then is: How can we pursue that role in a divided split society? (OPUS October 1981: 24).

* * *

What we have offered above are summaries of summaries — over twenty hours of meetings condensed into a few pages. Moreover it is an account of the earliest stages of an experiment. However, it allows us to offer some tentative conclusions, first about society as an intelligible field and second about the role of consultant.

To begin with we can state with confidence that 'society' has been a significant construct in all these meetings. We mean by this that the individual apparently needs to have a picture of something beyond

institutions or organizations in order to explain his experience of relatedness (or non-relatedness). 'Society' as used in these discussions is clearly
not synonymous with 'nation' or 'state'. It is a more formless notion,
though occasionally given a boundary by being equated with 'country'.
The stronger evidence that it is an intelligible field is the way in which
society is used as a projective container. Bits of the self are projected
into bits of society; yet at the same time the individual acknowledges
that he is part of society. It seems to us that it is the inexorableness of
societal membership that gives rise to distinctive dynamics. One can opt
out of a role in an organization – for example, a particular job, membership of a union, a marital relationship – and, with perhaps greater difficulty, one can opt out of participation in a whole institution – for
example, the institution of employment or the institution of marriage.
But, as Bion so correctly observed, not even the hermit can escape an
ultimate relatedness to a group; and the inescapable group is society. If
I become a disenchanted émigré, my use of projective containers may
change, but I am still only shifting my relatedness from one society to
another.

   It further seems to us that the nature and quality of the projections
is different. Splitting and projection manifestly occur in the 'conference-
sized' large group and in the larger manufacturing business described
earlier, and they serve to provide the individual with some confirmation
of role and identity; but the projection in these cases is into identifiable
sub-groups. Even though the large group at times feels boundless and
even though the boundaries of the sub-groups may in some instances be
blurred – for instance, 'workers' or 'management' – there is in every
case a nucleus of perceived sub-group members who are known to the
individual by direct contact and many more who are known by sight.
So there is a sense that when the individual employee in a factory is
projecting on to 'management' or on to 'workers' he can feel that he
knows whom he is talking about; and reciprocally at least some of the
people in his mind will accept his label, even though they may regard
the projections as unjustified. At least potentially, therefore, projections
in groups up to this size are discussable, examinable, negotiable and
even capable of resolution. More often there is a collusive interplay of
projections between these groupings and this in itself confers on the
organization some structure of predictability and therefore stability –
which gets sustained even though overtly no one is comfortable with it.

   In society, the combination of size and physical dispersion permits
projection into whole categories of people – the young, blacks, Jews,
the disabled – or whole institutions – the church, big business, the

unions – and their common characteristic for the individual is that he is personally acquainted with only a minuscule sample from them. Paradoxically he may regard these as exceptions; but the paradox disappears if we realize that a satisfactory societal container for negative projections has to be distant and anonymous. In this way a potentially problematic personal relationship that crosses these projective categories can be kept positive, often through an extension into, say, inter-ethnic relationships, of the joking relationships that anthropologists have identified in kinship systems. Thus 'nigger' and 'whitey', which used publicly are taken as insults, become the accepted expression of affection and intimacy in a black-white friendship. We can suggest further that the use of societal containers for negative projections may have a function in enabling organizations to hold together despite deep internal conflicts. Splits can be limited by projection into an ultimate societal 'them' – head office, left-wing agitators, the government, the Japanese, or even an abstraction such as 'the recession' or 'changing society'.[9]

Without attempting to state this in psychoanalytic terms, which is beyond our competence, we would surmise that the need to use 'society' in this way for a different order of projections, beyond the known environment into the unknown, is itself a product of increased societal size and complexity. Starting from what seems to be the universal infantile experience of a polarized world, we can identify some primitive societies, such as the Nuer, whose social structure neatly reproduces a set of nesting good/bad, us/them relationships in an ascending order of sub-systems, systems and supra-systems (Evans-Pritchard 1940); and in relatively modern societies, infinitely larger and more diversified, there have been long periods of relative institutional stability, in which status and values have been unambiguous; but even the very young child today has to manage his way through multiple cross-cutting us/them relationships, with uncertain values that can flick friend to enemy and back again. (How can Mummy be good and Daddy be good if they're divorced and each tells me the other is bad?) We tentatively postulate that what gets projected into the various anonymous categories that comprise 'society' for us is our rage at the contradictions we have to manage closer to home. Our extreme destructive feelings have to be projected as far away as possible to make our day-to-day relationships tolerable: that is the advantage of the common enemy; but Britain has been deprived of that outlet for thirty-six years.

To continue for a moment with one possible interpretation of British society over the last forty to fifty years, we can see Chamberlain's flight leadership of 1938-9 succeeded by Churchill's fight leadership, and then in 1945 an abrupt transition to a dependency culture. This was foreshadowed by Beveridge, implemented by the first Labour government and continued into the 1970s by governments of both complexions. In addition to the welfare state as such, with its provisions for education, health care, pensions, unemployment benefit, supplementary benefit and so on, there has been an experience of economic prosperity based on Keynesian growth and high employment and of political stability in the two-party system. Moreover, the dependency culture has been reinforced by the formation of very large employing organizations, public and private (the ratio of large to small businesses being significantly higher in Britain than in other European countries), with large trades unions ostensibly engaging in fight but essentially also fulfilling dependency needs. In this process welfare functions have increasingly been removed from the family to the state and there has been an effective reduction in familial and individual autonomy and self-reliance. This has been disguised by the pseudo-autonomy of the consumer role, within which, during a period of a steady rise in real incomes, the individual could experience himself as exercising greater choice and therefore having greater autonomy. In a very short period of time, all this has been turned on its head: zero or negative growth, the collapse of manufacturing industry, an unabated escalation of unemployment, reductions in real income, political polarization and instability, and a welfare state that is a diminishingly reliable breast. Moreover, thirty years of an economically oriented dependency culture have effectively eroded alternative institutions, such as the church and the family, that might have provided the fall-back for dependency needs.

There is no doubt, therefore, that what we are picking up in our OPUS meetings during 1980–81 are the dynamics of the relatedness of the individual to society during a phase of failed dependency. Hitherto safe institutional structures have become unreliable: not only are they no longer to be relied upon as sources of employment and prosperity, but they are also too fragile to cope with the force of our negative projections. These have to be taken back by the individual, whose props to identity are already undermined either by unemployment or uncertainty of employment, and re-projected on to 'society'. The force of projection required to defend the individual against the experience of internal chaos aggravates the fear of retribution from the projective receptacles, or, in more ordinary langauge, the fear of anarchy and violence.

Comparing this with Bion's and Turquet's observations of small group behaviour, we can liken this phase of failed dependency to a typical interregnum, when one basic assumption culture and leadership has become discredited and another has yet to be installed. But whereas in small group life such an interregnum usually lasts only for minutes or at most for a session or two, here at the societal level we have a phase that has already continued for at least two years and shows no sign of early resolution.

If it is granted that the phenomena are part of a societal dynamic and do confirm society as an intelligible field of study, then we have to ask whether our observations merely reflect random or idiosyncratic aspects of a *state* of failed dependency, displaying itself in different guises, or whether the observed differences which emerged in the succesive meetings reflect actual short-term changes and developments in the societal dynamic (leaving aside the issue of whether such changes may turn out to be cyclical or linear). If the latter, then one could contemplate development of a method of analysis and forecasting of societal processes analogous to those attempted by several schools of economists. Our tentative view is that we have been observing such changes, albeit perhaps crudely. The reader may or may not agree with us that a significant progression can be traced from the experience of disintegration in summer 1980 to retreat (flight) in autumn 1980, followed by the mixture of anger and impotence at failed dependency in early 1981. Then came splitting, and the mounting sense of betrayal, in spring 1981, and the powerful foreboding of violence in the summer 1981 staff meeting, immediately before the major inner-city riots. After the brief interlude of basic assumption pairing, we were thrown back on the need to act individually — but how? — with the threat of psychopathic leadership hanging over us as the only apparent alternative.

Earlier in this paper we suggested that OPUS staff are developing a role of consultant in relation to society as client in order to identify and interpret societal dynamics. We also discussed Turquet's picture of the large group consultant as being present in a dual capacity, in a defined role and as a person, in the latter capacity sharing inevitably in the difficulties and dilemmas of the individual member. It follows that OPUS staff in their roles of trying to understand what is happening in society are even more inescapably present as persons — as members of society. Indeed, that is their defined role. What distinguishes us from other persons perhaps is simply that we offer a model of trying to understand and communicate our experience as members of a 'psychotic' society as well as enacting our societal roles.

Thus our evidence suggests that, by defining a task boundary, it is possible to evoke, experience and observe societal dynamics in a group of ten to twelve. Society is present in the group; society and the group are present in the individual.

Notes

1 The early conferences were sponsored jointly by the Tavistock Institute and the University of Leicester.

2 In fact, the first inter-group exercise was a two-task event: participants were to agree on the use of a vacant period in the programme and to study the inter-group processes emerging in the negotiation. Bridger has continued with the two-task method; but the stream of work described here – the Group Relations Training Programme (led by Rice 1962-9, by Miller and Turquet 1969-75, and since then by Lawrence and Miller) – has adhered to the single 'here and now' task and has thus remained closer to the psychoanalytical model (cf. Lawrence 1979).

3 He described this innovation in another contribution to the present volume.

4 One of Bion's rare returns to the study of group behaviour was as a staff member of a one-week conference run by the Washington School of Psychiatry at Amherst, Mass., in 1969.

5 This links to our experience within the Leicester Conferences themselves, where in the larger group settings of up to 80 the boundaries are harder to maintain and episodes of bizarre and seemingly psychotic behaviour sometimes occur. But so long as staff adhere strictly to their task (which is educational not therapeutic), resist the powerful pressures to define deviant behaviour as illness requiring treatment, and insistently interpret it as a product of the group, then reconstitution is the normal outcome. Conversely, it can be said that participants will not have progressed very far in their understanding of unconscious processes in groups unless they have at least glimpsed their own psychotic propensities, which may include powerful wishes to find someone in whom to project madness.

6 These include: schools (e.g., Richardson 1967a, 1973, 1975) and other educational institutions (e.g., Richardson 1967b; Gosling *et al.* 1967; Musto and Astrachan 1968; Bexton 1975); hospitals (e.g., Menzies 1960; Astrachan *et al.* 1970; Levinson and Astrachan 1976); residential institutions (e.g., Miller and Gwynne 1972); religious institutions (e.g., Reed and Palmer 1976; Reed 1978); and industry and commerce (e.g., Miller and Rice 1967).

7 Examples include dry-cleaning (Miller and Rice 1967, chapters 7-8), airline operations (chapters 15-28), residential institutions (Miller and Gwynne 1972) and manufacturing companies (Miller, J. C. 1979; Lawrence 1980; Lawrence and Miller 1982; and this present paper).

8 The architect of this programme was our colleague, Andrew Szmidla, who provided many original ideas and who was associated with the project from 1973 to 1977. The authors' involvement was as follows:

Olya Khaleelee as research officer 1973-4 and internal consultant 1975-9; Eric Miller as external consultant 1975-9.

9 In wage-bargaining in Britain during the 1960s and early 1970s, the shared paranoia of union officials and employers' negotiators about the possible influence of left-wing extremists on the labour force led to many agreements on wage-levels and manning that managements, at least, have since had cause to regret.

References

Astrachan, B. M. and Flynn, H. R. (1976), 'The intergroup exercise: a paradigm for learning about the development of organizational structure', in E. J. Miller (ed.), *Task and Organization*, London, Wiley: 47-68.

Astrachan, B., Flynn, H., Geller, J. and Harvey, H. (1970), 'Systems approach to day hospitalization', *Arch. General Psychiatry*, 22: 550-9.

Bertalanffy, L. von (1950), 'The theory of open systems in physics and biology', *Science*, 3: 23-9.

Bexton, W. H. (1975), 'Group processes in environmental design: exposing architects and planners to the study of group relations', in A. D. Colman and W. H. Bexton (eds.), *Group Relations Reader*, Sausalito, Cal., GREX: 251-64.

Bion, W. R. (1948-51), 'Experiences in groups: I-VII', *Human Relations*, vols. 1-4.

Bion, W. R. (1952), 'Group dynamics: a re-view', *Int. J. Psychoanalysis*, 33, part 2.

Bion, W. R. (1961), *Experiences in Groups, and other papers*, London, Tavistock.

de Board, R. (1978), *The Psychoanalysis of Organizations*, London, Tavistock.

Evans-Pritchard, E. E. (1940), *The Nuer*, Oxford University Press.

Freud, S. (1913), *Totem and Taboo*, London, Hogarth Press, 1950 (Complete Works, vol. 13).

Freud, S. (1921), *Group Psychology and the Analysis of the Ego*, London, Hogarth Press, 1955 (Complete Works, vol. 18).

Gosling, R., Miller, D., Turquet, P. M. and Woodhouse, D. L. (1967), *The Use of Small Groups in Training*, Hitchin, Herts, Codicote Press.

Gosling, R. H. (1981), 'A study of very small groups', in J. Grotstein (ed.), *Do I Dare Disturb the Unverse?* New York, Aronson: 634-45.

Guereca, D. (1979), 'A manager's view of the institutional event', in W. G. Lawrence (ed.), *Exploring Individual and Organizational Boundaries*, London, Wiley: 103-10.

Heimann, P. (1952), 'A contribution to the re-evaluation of the Oedipus Complex – the early stages', *Int. J. Psycho-analysis*, 23, 2; reprinted in Klein *et al.* (eds), *New Directions in Psycho-analysis*, London, Tavistock, 1955.

Higgin, G. and Bridger, H. (1964), 'The psychodynamics of an intergroup exercise', *Human Relations*, 17: 391-446.

Jaques, E. (1951), *The Changing Culture of a Factory*, London, Tavistock.

Jaques, E. (1955), 'Social systems as a defence against persecutory and depressive anxiety', in M. Klein, P. Heimann and R. E. Money-Kyrle (eds), *New Directions in Psycho-analysis*, London, Tavistock.

Klein, M. (1928), 'Early steps of the Oedipus complex', in *Contributions to Psycho-analysis, 1921–1945*, London, Hogarth Press, 1948.

Klein, M. (1946), 'Notes on some schizoid mechanisms', in Klein *et al.* (eds), *Developments in Psychoanalysis*, London, Hogarth Press, 1952.

Klein, M. (1959), 'Our adult world and its roots in infancy', *Human Relations*, 12: 291–303; reprinted in M. Klein, *Our Adult World and other Essays*, London, Heinemann, 1963.

Lawrence, W. G. (ed.) (1979), *Exploring Individual and Organizational Boundaries*, London, Wiley.

Lawrence, W. G. (1980), 'Citizenship and the work place: a current case study', in B. Sievers and W. Slesina (eds), *Arbeits Papiere des Fachbereich Wirtschaftswissenschaft die Gesamthochschule Wuppertal*, 44.

Lawrence, W. G. (in press), 'A psycho-analytic perspective for understanding organizational life', in R. N. Ottaway (ed.), *O D Practices in Europe*, London, Wiley.

Lawrence, W. G. and Miller, E. J. (1982), 'Psychic and political constraints on the growth of industrial democracies', in M. Pines and L. Rafaelsen (eds), *The Individual and the Group*, New York, Plenum, vol. 1: 399–403.

Levinson, D. and Astrachan, B. (1976), 'Entry into the mental health centre: a problem in organizational boundary regulation', in E. J. Miller (ed.), *Task and Organization*, London, Wiley: 217–34.

Lewin, K. (1947), 'Frontiers in group dynamics: I. Concept, method and reality in social sciences; social equilibria and social change', *Human Relations*, 1: 5–41.

Lofgren, L. B. (1976), 'Organizational design and therapeutic effect', in E. J. Miller (ed.), *Task and Organization*, London, Wiley: 235–42.

Menninger, R. (1972), 'The impact of group relations conferences on organizational growth', *Int. J. Group Psychotherapy*, 22: 415–32.

Menzies, I. E. P. (1960), 'A case-study in the functioning of social systems as a defence against anxiety', *Human Relations*, 13: 95–121.

Miller, E. J. and Gwynne, G. V. (1972), *A Life Apart: a Pilot Study of Residential Institutions for the Physically Handicapped and the Young Chronic Sick*, London, Tavistock.

Miller, E. J. and Rice, A. K. (1967), *Systems of Organization*, London, Tavistock.

Miller, E. J. (1976), 'Introductory essay: role perspective and the understanding of organizational behaviour', in E. J. Miller (ed.), *Task and Organization*, London, Wiley: 1–16.

Miller, E. J. (1980), 'The politics of involvement', *J. Personality and Social Systems*, 2: 37–50.

Miller, J. C. (1979), 'The psychology of innovation in an industrial setting', in W. G. Lawrence (ed.), *Exploring Individual and Organizational Boundaries*, London, Wiley, 205–16.

Musto, D. and Astrachan, B. (1968), 'Strange encounter: the use of study groups with graduate students in history', *Psychiatry*, 31: 264–76.

OPUS (1980–1), *Bulletin*, nos 1–5, London, OPUS.

Pederson-Krag, G. (1951), 'A psychoanalytic approach to mass production', *Psychoanalytic Quarterly*, 20: 434–51.

Reed, B. D. (1978), *The Dynamics of Religion*, London, Darton Longman & Todd.

Reed, B. and Palmer, B. (1976), 'The local church and its environment', in E. J. Miller (ed.), *Task and Organization*, London, Wiley: 261–84.

Rice, A. K. (1951), 'The use of unrecognized cultural mechanisms in an expanding machine-shop (Glacier Project – III)', *Human Relations*, 4: 143–60.

Rice, A. K. (1963), *The Enterprise and its Environment*, London, Tavistock.

Rice, A. K. (1965), *Learning for Leadership*, London, Tavistock.

Rice, A. K. (1969), 'Individual, group and intergroup processes', *Human Relations*, 22: 565–84; reprinted in E. J. Miller (ed.), *Task and Organization*, London, Wiley 1976: 25–46.

Richardson, E. (1967a), *Group Study for Teachers*, London, Routledge & Kegan Paul.

Richardson, E. (1967b), *The Environment of Learning*, London, Heinemann.

Richardson, E. (1973), *The Teacher, the School and the Task of Management*, London, Heinemann.

Richardson, E. (1975), *Authority and Organization in the Secondary School*, London, Macmillan.

Rioch, M. (1979), 'The A. K. Rice group relations conferences as a reflection of society', in W. G. Lawrence (ed.), *Exploring Individual and Organizational Boundaries*, London, Wiley: 53–68.

Sofer, C. (1961), *The Organization from Within*, London, Tavistock.

Trist, E. L. and Sofer, C. (1959), *Explorations in Group Relations*, Leicester University Press.

Turquet, P. M. (1974), 'Leadership: the individual and the group', in G. S. Gibbard, J. J. Hartman and R. D. Mann (eds), *Analysis of Groups*, San Francisco, Jossey-Bass: 337–71.

Turquet, P. M. (1975), 'Threats to identity in the large group', in L. Kreeger (ed.), *The Large Group: Dynamics and Therapy*. London, Constable: 87–144.

Wittkower, E. (1949), *A Psychiatrist Looks at Tuberculosis*, London, National Association for the Prevention of Tuberculosis.

Article submitted December, 1981.

Bion: an appreciation

Dr Wilfred R. Bion (1906–15) confessed many years later that his first experiences of the Preparatory School were highly traumatic. As a shy and namby-pamby eight-year-old, straight from India, he had held strong views that the only civlized way to spend a cold wet winter's afternoon was to sit reading a book by the fireside, and not to play muddy games outdoors. He conformed with this barbarity, he added, because it did not pay to do otherwise. Within no time his toughness became more than a facade: it became proverbial. Among his peers he was revered as the toughest of the tough: they were blind to his latent sensitivity. By the time I arrived at BSC in the summer term of 1912 he had moved to SHB, was already an established player in the School's 1st VII at the age of fourteen and the following term he gained his 1st XV colours.

Black-haired, swart, deep-chested and muscular, he commanded respect in the School House common-room, where his laconic and gloomy-voiced pronouncements, so often counterpointed by a mischievous grin and a sardonic chuckle, were unchallengeable.

Classroom subjects, apart from history and literature, did not inspire him, and he lodged comfortably about halfway down the end-of-term form order. Indeed in his autobiographical last book – *A Memoir of the Future* he wrote: [on rediscovering 'Paradise Lost' and Virgil's Aeneid] ... 'it involved much painful regret for the way in which I had wasted and hated the privilege of being taught by certain schoolmasters whose devotion had but a sorry response from me. Let me now praise men who ought to have been famous. For my own pleasure I write their names: E. A. Knight, F. S. Sutton, Charles Mellows.'

But he was no Schoolboy Philistine. In his spare time (and often during 'prep') he read, widely and deeply, history, philosophy, essays and poetry. He remembered what he had read and could always quote aptly on occasion. He sketched and painted, studied architecture, and sang among the basses in the choir. Already he possessed that intellectual curiosity which was to render him an outstanding polymath. But it was with rugger and water polo that his name at that time was associated. He was a formidable Captain and leader of the scrum, and in the swimming bath his powerful 'sling shot' would thunder on the wall behind the goal.

World War I came, and he probably harboured doubts as to whether he would survive, for on the afternoon he joined up in 1915 he summoned Reg Newcombe and me to his study and bade us split up all his precious books and personal effects between us: he would never need them again. In the event such a premonition might very well have proved valid. His disabled tank became lodged down under intensive machine-gun fire. He emerged with hand-grenades, charged the enemy's post and demolished it singlehanded. For this heroic act he was awarded the DSO: which he found very disturbing, for thereafter everyone expected him to be brave, and much braver than he could ever hope or pretend to be. Nevertheless in 1918 he was also awarded the Legion of Honour, and was again mentioned in dispatches.

After the war, at Oxford where he took his degree in history, he became Captain of Swimming and Water Polo, but his rugger career was met with disaster. He was playing regularly for the Oxford XV all the 1919 season and had been selected to play in the 'Varsity match against Cambridge but a last-minute cartilage trouble during a practice game prevented his playing; so he did not get the Blue he expected and deserved.

In the early 1920s each Boxing Day he, Nokes, Tid and I would converge on Church Farm, Happisburgh for a 'reading party' (where it was one of our traditions to bathe in the North Sea on New Year's Day). It was at one of these parties that Bion seized and devoured one of Freud's works I had brought with me, and which may possibly have sown the seed for his eventual life-interest. Be that as it may, his immediate problem after Oxford was to make a living, so he decided to try his hand at schoolmastering, and let an eye witness now take up the tale:

Wilfred Bion's arrival as Master in the Christmas Term of 1922 caused a considerable sensation. Here came a young OS, just turned 25, built like an ox, with a distinguished athletic background and a fine war record: what would he be like as a Master? At first, frankly, he frightened us to death with his impassive face and brusque speech —

and maybe in truth he was just as frightened of us. But fear didn't last long: it drained away, to be replaced by the greatest respect and in the end, for many of us, by adulation this side of idolatory.

He led rather than drove. He decorated his classroom with Medici prints and was able and willing to discourse on them — when asked. It was as if he wanted to share with us the cultural riches he had acquired. In English classes he quoted from his voluminous well-stocked mind, and might suddenly read Hardy's account of Gabriel Oak's telling the time from the stars in the midnight sky. History to him was not about deadly events but about real live people with colourful personalities. His casual reference to England's king-maker as 'Uncle Warwick', earned him the nickname by which he was there-after known. Lastly, no one in 'Warwick's' classes will forget his invariable imposition — so many copies of Hebrews XII: 6–11, nor his huge oaken sword, used not for blows but for insertion down the neck of a miscreant and levering the collar until gurgles were the only possible reply to his remonstrative question.

Naturally he took an active interest in school sport, and used to train the 1st XV scrum, having roared up to Upper Field on his motor-bike. It was spectacular to see him instructing them, the whole scrum in working position supported solely by Bion's shoulders against the front row. In the Baths he helped Chas. Mellows with the coaching. When the news of BSCSC's first victory in the Bath Club Cup arrived at the school, he was in the baths, and with a roar of 'Waves!' he proceeded to lead everyone in the forbidden sport of flooding the changing-room.

Invitations to Sunday afternoon tea at his digs in Rye Street were much prized as opportunities for wide-ranging talk and discussion on any subject under the sun, presided over by this polymath — who was also a good listener. We were indeed lucky to have known Warwick before he passed out of Stortford life to qualify as a doctor and begin his celebrated life as an adventurous psychoanalyst.

Adventurous is the right adjective for his subsequent career. After two years of schoolmastering he enrolled as a medical student at UCH in order to acquire the medical degree for his chosen profession. He played for the Harlequins, attended concerts, became a bit of a balleto-mane, and attempted (without much success) to master the harpsichord; in passing, so to speak, he collected the gold medal for Surgery (of all things!). Once qualified he set about undergoing his own personal psycho-analysis before tackling those of patients.

When World War II broke out, he joined the RAMC as a psychiatrist, and his unorthodox experiments with Leaderless Group Therapy led him to becoming Senior Psychiatrist to Officer Selection Boards where, by introducing his Group techniques, it was said (by Brig. Bidwell in *The Fighting Spirit*) his contribution to the war effort was probably as important as the 25 lb. gun or the Bailey Bridge.

Towards the end of the war he lost Betty, his first wife, in most tragic circumstances after the birth of their daughter, Parthenope. In 1951 he married Francesca, who bore him a son and a daughter. Latterly, when he needed relaxation, he and his family would pile into the car and rush up to his Norfolk country cottage in Trimingham, a few miles from his beloved Happisburgh (where by his request his ashes were laid to rest). On arrival it was 'rugger vest and shorts', tireless rambles around the countryside, painting excursions, much sea-bathing, and lots of fun.

After the war in 1945 he became Chairman of the Tavistock Clinic Medical Committee, and over the years honours followed: Director of the Clinic, 1955-62, and President of the British Psychoanalytical Society, 1962-5. There can be no doubt that in this Society he was outstanding: head and shoulders above all comers. He led, others followed. Against his exploration of new areas in the field he of course met with chilly opposition from the 'establishment', but he pressed on regardless and extended the boundaries of current thought and knowledge. During the 1960s he showed immense literary productivity. Periodically his papers and lectures were republished in book form. His writings were deceptively lucid, but to follow the philosophical trend of his later work one would need to be an intellectual gynmast, already habituated by his previous relations.

By 1968 he badly needed relief from the distracting work he had been doing for the British Society; so he cut loose, migrated to California and continued his work there for twelve years. Earlier in 1981 he came home hoping to enjoy retirement in the English countryside, but it was not to be: within weeks he fell ill with a rapid and mercifully painless disease. When he had been told it was terminal, he could say to some colleagues, 'Life is full of surprises', adding with his characteristic smile, 'most of them unpleasant.'

Anon

Reproduced, by permission, from the *Old Stortfordian Newsletter*, January 1981.

Bibliography of W. R. Bion

1943 'Intra-group tensions in therapy: their study as a task of the group', *Lancet* 2, 27 Nov. 1943: 678–81.
1946 'Leaderless Group project', *Bull. Menninger Clinic*, 10: 77–81.
1948 'Psychiatry in a time of crisis', *Brit. J. Med. Psychology*, vol. XXI.
1948 'Experiences in groups', *Human Relations*, vols I–IV, 1948–51.
1950 'The Imaginary Twin', paper read to the British Psycho-analytic Society, Nov. 1950. *Int. J. P.A.*, 1955; Published in *Second Thoughts* (1967).
1952 'Group dynamics: a re-view', *Int. J. of P.A.*, vol. 33 (also in *New Directions in Psycho-analysis*, 1955).
1954 'Notes on the theory of schizophrenia', *Int. J. Psycho-analysis*, vol. 35.
1955 'Development of schizophrenic thought', *Int. J. Psycho-analysis*, vol. 37.
1957 'Differentiation of the psychotic from the non-psychotic personalities', *Int. J. Psycho-analysis*, vol. 38.
1958 'On hallucination', *Int. J. Psycho-analysis*, vol. 39.
1959 'On arrogance', *Int. J. Psycho-analysis*, vol. 39.
1959 'Attacks on linking', *Int. J. Psycho-analysis*, vol. 40.
1961 *Experiences in Groups*, London, Tavistock.
1962 'A theory of thinking', *Int. J. Psycho-analysis*, vol. 43.
1962 *Learning from Experience*, London, Heinemann.
1963 *Elements of Psycho-analysis*, London, Heinemann.
1965 *Transformations*, London, Heinemann.
1966 'Catastrophic change', *Bulletin, British Psycho-analytic Society*, no. 5.
1967 *Second Thoughts*, London, Heinemann.
1967 'Notes on memory and desire', *Psycho-analytic forum*, vol. II, no. 3.
1970 *Attention and Interpretation*, London, Tavistock.
1973 *Bion's Brazilian Lectures*, 1. Rio de Janeiro, Brazil, Imago Editora.
1974 *Bion's Brazilian Lectures*, 2. Rio de Janeiro, Imago Editora.
1975 *A Memoir of the Future*, Book I: *The Dream*, Rio de Janeiro, Imago Editora.

1976 'Evidence', *Bulletin, British Psycho-analytic Society*, no. 8.

1977 *A Memoir of the Future*, Book II: *The Past Presented*, Rio de Janeiro, Imago Editora.

1977 *Two Papers: The Grid and Caesura*, Rio de Janeiro, Imago Editora.

1977 'Emotional turbulence' and 'On a quotation from Freud (the Caesura)', in *Boarderline Personality Disorders*, ed. Hartocollis, P., New York, International University Press.

1978 *Four Discussions with W. R. Bion*, Clunie Press.

1979 *A Memoir of the Future*, Book III: *The Dawn of Oblivion*, Clunie Press.

1979 'Making the best of a bad job', *Bulletin, British Psycho-analytic Society*, February.

1980 *Bion in New York and Sao Paulo*, Clunie Press.

1981 *A Key to 'A Memoir of the Future'*, Clunie Press.

1982 *The Long Week-end, 1897–1919*, Abingdon, Fleetwood Press.

Index

393